The Association of Southeast Asian Nations (ASEAN)

Conflict and Development

The Association of Southeast Asian Nations (ASEAN)

Conflict and Development

By

Otto F. von Feigenblatt

Adjunct Professor of Political Science,
Millenia Atlantic University (Florida, USA)
and
Fellow of the Royal Asiatic Society of Great Britain and Ireland.

New Century Publications
New Delhi, India

NEW CENTURY PUBLICATIONS
4800/24, Bharat Ram Road,
Ansari Road, Daryaganj,
New Delhi – 110 002 (India)

Tel.: 011-2324 7798, 4358 7398, 6539 6605
Fax: 011-4101 7798
E-mail: indiatax@vsnl.com • info@newcenturypublications.com
www.newcenturypublications.com

Editorial office:
LG–7, Aakarshan Bhawan,
4754-57/23, Ansari Road, Daryaganj,
New Delhi – 110 002

Tel.: 011-4356 0919

First Published: **2012**

ISBN: **978-81-7708-291-3**

Published by New Century Publications and printed at Salasar Imaging Systems, New Delhi.

Designs: Patch Creative Unit, New Delhi.

PRINTED IN INDIA

About the Book

This study provides a structural analysis of ASEAN's role in Southeast Asia's regional development and conflict. Part I of the book concentrates on ASEAN's dispute management mechanism and applies Robert Fritz's theory of structural dynamics. It introduces the main structural factors influencing the organization's dispute management system and identifies avoidance and consensus building as the two central procedures. ASEAN's oscillation between success and failure is also discussed by identifying the root causes underlying the structural instability. How to overcome ASEAN's internal organization conflicts leading to oscillation through structural dynamics is also discussed. It concludes by presenting a general overview of ASEAN's role in dealing with regional conflict through preventive diplomacy and possibly peace-building.

Part II concentrates on socio-economic development and trade. It provides an overview of socio-economic development in the region as well as some important intra-regional trade barriers. It applies structural dynamics to the problem of economic and trade oscillation in ASEAN.

Based on ASEAN's official goal of creating a socio-cultural community, Part III of the book tackles the structural conflicts present due to the region's diverse socio-cultural makeup. The complementary processes of avoidance and consensus building are presented as the central mechanisms through which ASEAN can construct shared norms and thus overcome inherent organizational conflicts. It also presents an overview of ASEAN's path towards a socio-cultural community through a structural lens.

Part IV of the book presents general conclusions and proposes possible future directions for further research. It ties together the three parts by providing an overview of ASEAN's future in the region's development and conflict.

Author's Profile

Professor Otto F. von Feigenblatt is an elected Fellow of the Royal Asiatic Society of Great Britain and Ireland, an Academician of the Constantinian Academy of Arts, Letters, and Sciences (Palermo, Italy) and a member of the United States Committee of the Council for Security and Cooperation in the Asia Pacific (CSCAP). He is an Adjunct Professor of Political Science at Millenia Atlantic University (Doral, Florida).

Professor von Feigenblatt is the author of *Human Security in the Asia Pacific Region: Security Challenges, Regional Integration, and Representative Case Studies*. His research has appeared in more than twenty peer reviewed academic journals and he is a member of the editorial boards of the *Journal of Contemporary Literature* and *Entelequia.*

Professor von Feigenblatt is serving as the editor in chief of the *Journal of Alternative Perspectives in the Social Sciences, Journal of Asia Pacific Studies,* and as one of the chief editors of the *Journal of Postcolonial Cultures and Societies*. In terms of education, he holds a Bachelor of Social Science degree from Ritsumeikan Asia Pacific University (Beppu, Japan), a Master of Arts degree in International Development Studies from Chulalongkorn University (Bangkok, Thailand), and he is completing the final year of a Doctorate of Philosophy in Conflict Analysis and Resolution with a concentration in International Peace and Conflict at Nova Southeastern University (Fort Lauderdale, Florida).

Acknowledgements

Countless people have helped me in bringing this project to completion. While the writing of this book took less than seven months, the research leading up to it started more than five years ago. During that long period of time I acquired plenty of debts of gratitude. Even though space prevents me from listing all of the people who have helped in this project there are some whose influence is too important to omit. First of all I would like to thank the Faculty of Political Science of Chulalongkorn University for the institutional base it provided for my early research in Southeast Asia. Thanks are also due to the faculty of the Master of Arts Program in International Development Studies for serving as a bridge between the *etic* understanding of Southeast Asia provided by traditional social science theories and the *emic* perspective of the thriving regional epistemic community of scholars and practitioners. Thanks are also due to the Suttichujit family for providing a home away from home in Thailand. Their support and guidance during the early stages of my stay in Thailand were of utmost importance.

Thanks are also due to Professor A. Mani of Ritsumeikan Asia Pacific University for his support of my early research dealing with the Association of Southeast Asian Nations (ASEAN). His valuable comments about some of my early work on the subject proved to be a great asset for this longer project. Professor M. Cooper, also of Ritsumeikan Asia Pacific University, provided considerable support through the International Association for Asia Pacific Studies. Some of the ideas about conflict management included in the present volume were first presented in the flagship journal of the association, Asia Pacific World. Valuable comments of anonymous peer reviewers also helped me develop some of the ideas introduced in that early article. While that article was not included in the present volume some of the conclusions that were reached provided a valuable starting point for more in depth discussions of regional conflict management. I will always be grateful for the international intellectual environment of my *alma mater*, Ritsumeikan Asia Pacific University, which introduced me early in my academic career to a global worldview.

I would also like to thank my present institutional home, Millenia Atlantic University, for the open intellectual environment it provides characterized by academic freedom and a thriving student body. Thanks are also due to my undergraduate students for their valuable insights.

My family has been very supportive during the entire project. Thanks are due to my parents, the Baron and Baroness of Feigenblatt-Miller, for respecting my long periods of seclusion. I would also like to thank Vannapond Suttichujit for her loyalty, support, and great meals. The sections dealing with education policy and human capital formation greatly benefitted from our conversations. Last but not least thanks are due to the faculty of the Graduate School of Humanities and Social Sciences, Nova Southeastern University. Their support throughout my doctoral studies has helped me grow as a scholar and has undoubtedly influenced my work on conflict analysis and resolution.

Contents

Part II: Socio-economic Development and Regional Trade in ASEAN

Part IV: Conclusions and for Further Research

List of Figures

Part I
Structural Analysis of ASEAN: Conflict Avoidance and Consensus

1

Conflict Management in ASEAN: Avoidance and Consensus Building

---

The present chapter analyzes the structure of the Association of Southeast Asian Nations (ASEAN), an important intergovernmental organization in the Pacific Region which has been at the core of regional integration projects. As a theoretical framework, Ury, Brett, and Goldberg's method of structural diagnosis for systems' design is used and critical content analysis is applied as the main research methodology. The chapter concludes that both conflict avoidance and consensus are the most common results of disputes brought to the attention of the organization with the emphasis being on conflict management rather than on conflict resolution.

Introduction

The Association of Southeast Asian States (ASEAN) is an influential intergovernmental organization in the Asia Pacific Region (Komori, 2009; Nair, 2008). It was established in 1967 as a way to manage conflict in Southeast Asia and to promote economic cooperation (Narine, 1998; Suharto, 2009). The original members were Thailand, Singapore, Malaysia, Indonesia, and the Philippines (Komori, 2009). After the end of the Cold War, the organization gradually expanded to include Vietnam, Cambodia, Laos, Myanmar, and Brunei. ASEAN deals with social, economic, and political issues affecting the region and is known for its emphasis on non-interference in the internal affairs of member countries and on its procedural use of consensus building and preventive diplomacy (Narine, 1998; Yzawa, 2006). The previously mentioned characteristics of the organization dealing with its decision making process are known as the "ASEAN way" and due to the organization's pivotal role in the promotion of regional integration in the Pacific, the "ASEAN way" has spread to other forums such as the East Asian Summit (EAS), the ASEAN Region Forum (ARF), and ASEAN + 3 (Komori, 2009).

Ever since the organization rose to fame through its role during the Cambodian crisis and its successful integration of Laos, Vietnam, and Cambodia after the end of the Cold War, the "ASEAN Way" has been the target of much praise and criticism from both policymakers and academics (Collins, 2008; Jones & Smith, 2007; Katanyuu, 2006; Komori, 2009; Nair, 2008; Narine, 1997, 1998; Suharto, 2009; Yzawa, 2006). This chapters aims to analyze ASEAN's conflict management structure by applying a simple generic diagnostic model designed by Ury, Brett, and Goldberg for the relatively recent field of systems' design (Ury, Brett, & Coldberg, 1993, pp. 20-40).

Theoretical Framework

This chapter adopts a structural view of organizations based on Ury et al.'s model of a dispute resolution system (Ury et al., 1993, p. 22). An organization is a structure which in turn is defined as "an entity made up of individual elements or parts that impact each other by the relationships they form" (Fritz, 1996, p. 4). Ury et al.'s model posits that the procedures in use are influenced by factors/structural parts such as the kinds of issues in dispute, the procedures available, motivations, skills, resources, and the costs and benefits (Ury et al., 1993, pp. 22-23). Those factors in addition to the procedures in use are influenced and influence the social, economic, and cultural environment of the organization (Ury et al., 1993, pp. 37-39). The following sections concentrate on the previously identified structural factors/parts as well as on their relationship to the organization's environment in order to provide a holistic analysis of ASEAN's conflict management system.

Methodology

The present chapter is a case study of a single organization, ASEAN. Treaties, the ASEAN Charter, and other policy papers produced by ASEAN are used as primary sources for this chapter (ASEAN, 2008a, 2008b). Primary sources are complemented by an extensive review of the literature dealing with regionalism in the Asia Pacific Region, preventive diplomacy in ASEAN, and regional security in Southeast Asia. The previously mentioned sources are submitted to critical content analysis in order to identify the main structural factors present in the organization. So as to ascertain the validity of the data, triangulation of important concepts and events is undertaken by comparing official statements with reports of regional non-governmental organizations and independent researchers (Creswell, 2007; Stake, 1995).

Analysis of ASEAN's Dispute Resolution System

Ury et al.'s model emphasizes the importance of the kind of disputes submitted to a dispute resolution system. The kinds of disputes influence the procedures in use and in addition to the procedures available, motivations, skills, and resources, are all influenced by the environment of the organization (Ury et al., 1993, p. 22). In the case of ASEAN, a vast array of disputes are submitted to the organization including but not limited to border disputes, trade disputes, and disputes dealing with refugees and population movement.

Some examples include the border dispute between Cambodia and Thailand over the historic Preah Vihear temple, Lao political refugees in the Northeast of Thailand, abuses to human rights in Myanmar, and currency exchange during the Asian Financial Crisis of 1998 (Jones & Smith, 2007; Katanyuu, 2006; Rerksirisuk, 2009; Severino, 2007; Suharto, 2009). Some disputes include the use of force such as the one between Cambodia and Thailand, other disputes include individuals and governments such as the ones related to refugees, and others deal mainly with interstate issues. It is important to note that the disputes submitted to ASEAN's dispute resolution system include intra, inter, and transnational issues. Disputes deal with conflict over resources, territory, the economy, and human rights.

Procedures Available

ASEAN's dispute resolution system can be divided into track 1, track 2, and track three processes (Collins, 2008). The most important bodies of the organization, such as the ASEAN Heads of State Summits and the Ministerial meetings are strictly intergovernmental and thus only representatives of member states can introduce an issue directly (ASEAN, 2008b; Narine, 1998). ASEAN has several bodies dealing with a vast array of issues and the ministers with that issue's portfolio represent their country. Track 2 processes include bodies which are mixed in composition. Government officials may be represented in addition to prominent regional academics and former bureaucrats.

One example of one such body is the yearly meeting between ASEAN and the Institutes of Strategic and International Studies (ASEAN-ISIS) (Simon, 2008). Finally track 3 processes include some officials in their private capacities as well as representatives of approved civil society organizations. The ASEAN Civil Society Conference (ACSC) is one well known example and it includes representatives of regional nongovernmental organizations and other civil society organizations as well as some activists and academics (Collins, 2008, p. 320).

In terms of procedures all meetings and conferences are guided by the "ASEAN Way" which emphasizes consensus building, non-interference in the internal affairs of member states, and preventive diplomacy based on non-binding decisions (von Feigenblatt, 2009a; Heller, 2005; Komori, 2009; Nair, 2008; Narine, 1997, 1998; Simon, 2008). Track 1 meetings allow participants to present their concerns and all types of disputes can be allowed in theory. If a dispute is not resolved during the meeting and consensus is not achieved then the issue is either avoided or an ad hoc committee is set up to continue discussing the issue. Since the lowest common denominator is usually agreed upon, most decisions tend to be very ambiguous, abstract, and non-binding (Jones & Smith, 2007). Track 2 meetings are held at the sidelines of the ministerial meetings and their reports have advisory power. Thus, the report of an ASEAN-ISIS meeting is then passed on formally and informally to the secretariat and members of the pertinent ministerial meetings for their discussion (Collins, 2008). It should be noted that the "ASEAN Way" also applies in this forum and that track 1 forums are not required to heed the recommendations of track 2 meetings nor are they required to include the issues in their agendas.

Finally, track 3 processes are very informal and depend on the good will or interest of government officials in ASEAN. Track 3 meetings lack even an official advisory role and their recommendations usually have to influence track two processes before they can reach track 1 forums. In terms of interaction, track 3 forums do not usually follow the ASEAN way and more closely resemble Western humanitarian NGOs in that they are guided by majority rule and do not respect the principle of non-interference (Collins, 2008).

Finally, in terms of procedures, it should be noted that the secretary general of the organization has very limited powers in terms of dealing with disputes. The secretariat based in Jakarta is in charge of organizing the many meetings held during the year but is not allowed to issue independent statements or to serve as a mediator between disputing parties (Narine, 1998; Severino, 2007). Thus, the secretariat deals with the logistics of the meetings while avoiding the content.

Motivations

It is always difficult to assess the motivations of the members of an intergovernmental organization but several researchers have traced back the actions and statements of the different members of ASEAN and they have identified some underlying motivations for participating in the organization (Komori, 2009; Narine, 1998). Thailand, as one of the original founders of ASEAN saw the organization as a useful way to bring stability and peace to the region as well as to promote trade among the members. Nevertheless, Thailand consistently opted to pursue its national interest over other considerations through much of the organization's history.

In recent years, since 2000, Thailand has promoted the norm of constructive engagement so as to replace the norm of non-interference in ASEAN which would allow the organization to deal with transnational issues and thus circumvent some of the limitations of the "ASEAN way" (Katanyuu, 2006). This shows that Thailand has a motivation to deal with transnational issues such as terrorism, narcotics, and trade through ASEAN. Indonesia and Malaysia are also founding members and both saw ASEAN as a good way to put behind the period of *konfrontasi* in which Indonesia threatened the survival of Singapore and Malaysia and to pursue their policies of non-alignment. Thus, they saw ASEAN as a way to pursue security without the interference of the great powers (Narine, 1998; Rolfe, 2008; Singh, 2008-2009).

Singapore and Brunei both see ASEAN as a way to increase their diplomatic clout as well as a good forum to promote regional trade (Neher, 2002). More recent members such as Cambodia, Vietnam, Myanmar, and Laos view the organization as a way to defend their national sovereignty while at the same time reaping the benefits of diplomatic recognition and regional trade (Katanyuu, 2006; Vu-Tung, 2007; Yu-tzung Chang, 2007). This very brief review of the motivations of the different countries show that the members joined and continue to support the organization for different reasons. It should also be noted that other important stakeholders such as business organizations including the ASEAN Chambers of Commerce and regional professional organizations support community building and want to use the organization as a way to increase their influence internationally (Collins, 2008). Finally, regional non-governmental organizations want to use the organization as a way to deal with human security issues and human rights (Akaha, 2009; Neher, 2002).

Skills

ASEAN members and related stakeholders have continually been improving their skills for dealing with conflict since the founding of the organization in 1967 (ASEAN, 2008b; Severino, 2007). Originally ASEAN concentrated on improving communication between the members. Later on members learned to cooperate on issues such as trade and on tackling the Cambodian crisis. Over the years, ASEAN members mastered the art of consensus building which is a conflict management process common to the cultures of most members (Simon, 2008). Thus, they institutionalized a widespread method of interpersonal conflict management. Indirect negotiation, concern over "face work", a long term time frame, and an emphasis on prevention became the trademark characteristics of the skills developed under the general label of the "ASEAN way" (Jones & Smith, 2007). Members learned to avoid certain topics, to table others, and to word declarations in a very ambiguous and general way.

Therefore, process was favoured over the actual results. In summary, ASEAN members have learned to communicate constructively with each other, their ability to reach consensus on general principles has also improved over the years, and the avoidance of certain difficult issues in favour of reaching general agreement has also become a favourite skill. In conclusion, ASEAN members understand each other's culture and have considerable skill in avoiding insulting their counterparts and in circumventing difficult topics in favour of group cohesion and consensus.

Resources

ASEAN is a very lean organization in terms of resources (Komori, 2009; Severino, 2007). The secretariat is understaffed and has very limited resources. Funds are usually allocated on an ad hoc basis for certain projects or special meetings. This means that most resources stay in the hands of the member states rather than on the organization itself. Nevertheless, ASEAN possesses vast intangible resources in terms of the organization's legitimacy and relatively good reputation in the eyes of the international community (ASEAN, 2008a; Heller, 2005; Yzawa, 2006). Its successful intervention during the Cambodian crisis as well as its perceived role in managing the transition of Vietnam, Laos, and Myanmar into regional membership helped the organization accrue considerable legitimacy (Neher, 2002). The organization also exerts considerable influence over other regional initiatives which include East Asia as well as the Asia Pacific Region (Limaye, 2007; Simon, 2008). ASEAN is at the core of the East Asian Summit, the ASEAN Regional Forum, and many other forums and organizations involving extra regional members (Komori, 2009; Limaye, 2007). Thus, ASEAN's main resources are its legitimacy as well as its strategic role in regional integration efforts.

Environment: Social, Economic and Cultural

Organizations do not operate in a vacuum and thus are influenced by their environment. ASEAN is located in a very heterogeneous region characterized by economic and socio-political diversity (Neher, 2002). Southeast Asia is home to several democracies, one military dictatorship, two communist countries, and several mixed authoritarian governments (Emmers, 2001; Neher, 2002). Economically, Singapore and Brunei are relatively wealthy and developed countries while Myanmar, Laos, and Cambodia are among the poorest countries in the world (Heidhues, 2000).

As a region, Southeast Asia is home to several major

religions including Islam, Buddhism, Christianity, and many forms of animism (Heidhues, 2000; Ishii, 1994; Liow, 2006; McCargo, 2009; Means, 2009; Mulder, 1996). Therefore, it is difficult to generalize about the environment in which ASEAN operates. However, Southeast Asian countries share a history of colonialism (with the exception of Thailand) and great power interference (Wyatt, 2003). This shared "trauma" makes the people and the governments of the region highly sensitive to external interference (Kim, Fidler, & Ganguly, 2009).

The wider environment also includes East Asia and the Pacific Powers. American military power and China's rise are also shared concerns. It should be noted that ASEAN has operated under an uncertain and dangerous environment due to the lack of any effective wider regional organization and the great number of territorial disputes left over from World War II and the end of the Cold War (von Feigenblatt, 2010; Nair, 2008). The region also shares optimism about the common future of the region and the possibility of a Pacific Century (Callahan, 2008; Hwang, 2006; Togo, 2005; Yew, 2000). Finally, culturally most countries in Southeast and East Asia are collectivist cultures with high power distance (Pieterse, 2007). This means that rank and status are very important in determining the appropriate way to communicate with a person as well as the primacy given to the needs of the group over those of the individual. Form is as important as essence in the region and its direct environs and thus ritual and process are of great significance (Heidhues, 2000).

Globalization, the rise of transnational threats, and the subsequent compression of time and space can be seen as the macro environment in which the world currently operates (Battersby & Siracusa, 2009; Friedman, 2000; HSIN-HUANG, HSIAO, & WAN, 2007; Lal, 2004). Economies are more interdependent than ever, threats ranging from haze to international terrorism affect people living in distinct territories and administrations (Garcia, 2009; Glassman, 2005; Storey, 2008; Wongboonsin, Pongsapich, Pongsapich, &

Sookkhee, 2006). Financial flows move faster than ever before and tracking them outstrips the supervisory capacity of most governments and institutions (Hwang, 2006). All of the presently described changes in the global context affect and influence the perceptions of ASEAN members by giving rise to a mixed feeling of uncertainty and opportunity.

Procedures in Use

Now that the kinds of disputes submitted to ASEAN, the procedures available, the motivations, the skills of the main stakeholders, the resources of the organization, and the socioeconomic and cultural environment have been discussed and assessed, it is possible to provide an overview of the procedures presently in use to deal with disputes. Following the Ury et al. model presented in early sections of this chapter it is clear that the present procedures are not equivalent to the rules and norms in the organization's constituting documents but rather they are influenced by a vast a array of factors including the kinds of disputes brought to the attention of the organization, the motivations of the organization and its members, the skills possessed by them, the resources available, and finally the interaction of them with the environment of the organization (Ury et al., 1993).

ASEAN's purview has broadened in the last few decades to include social, economic, security, and cultural issues (ASEAN, 2008a). On the other hand, the official procedures available have remained relatively constant as depicted in the recent ASEAN Charter (ASEAN, 2008b). The motivations of the organization's member have also changed due to transformations in the geopolitical situation and their own national interest (Emmers, 2001). While the funds and resources allocated to the general secretariat have increased in the last decade, they still remain very limited taking into consideration the growing role of the organization in the development and stability of the region. Needless to say there has been a marked improvement in the skills of the members of the organization.

Thus the procedures have continued to embody the "ASEAN Way" but what has changed is the learning experience brought about by the many years of interaction between the states of the region (Narine, 1998). The different players learned more about each other's needs and concerns while mastering two conflict management techniques, consensus building and avoidance (Yzawa, 2006).

Consensus building can be seen in the way ASEAN tackled the Asia Financial Crisis of 1998 by presenting a united front and facilitating regional agreement on currency swaps and levels of control over financial flows. At the time the dispute was over how to deal with the risks associated with unfettered financial flows and currency speculation while at the same time protecting the economies dependent on those same financial flows and foreign direct investment (Tow, Thakur, & Hyun, 2000). Malaysian needs for greater protection had to be balanced with Singaporean fears about financial flight and a slowdown in foreign investment (Shuib, Saludin, von Feigenblatt, Keling, & Ajis, 2010; Yew, 2000). In this occasion, ASEAN's dispute resolution system functioned remarkably well by reaching consensus and thus presenting a united front to a threatening and sceptical international community (Hwang, 2006; Komori, 2009).

One clear case of avoidance was the way the Thai military coup of 2006 was handled by the organization. In this case an internal dispute was brought to the attention of the organization through track 1, track 2, and track 3 processes but the dispute was avoided at all levels due to the principle of non intervention (von Feigenblatt, 2009b). Human rights organizations, democratic governments such as the Philippines, and academics attempted to get ASEAN involved in the dispute over the unconstitutional change of government in Thailand but their attempts were blocked by the primacy of the "ASEAN Way" and the veto power accorded to state representatives by the conflict management process of consensus building (Chang, Chu, & Park, 2007; Hamlin, 2009; Ungpakorn, 2007). Thus, rather than fail in dealing with the dispute, ASEAN chose to avoid the issue completely.

In summary, as the brief examples previously described show, ASEAN's dispute resolution system's procedures in use rely on consensus building which can result in either a strong unified statement based on clearly shared goals or lead to complete avoidance. One other mixed result is the process by which the meeting of Ministers sends an issue to be discussed in a secondary and powerless ad hoc committee to be discarded after a few months. This is just one subtype of avoidance. The next and final section assesses the benefits and the costs of the procedures currently in use and discusses some of the reasons why reform attempts have failed.

Costs and Benefits of the "ASEAN Way"

The previous section identified avoidance and searching for consensus as the two prevalent conflict management procedures in ASEAN. This section explores the costs and benefits of the "ASEAN Way" by identifying some of the possible outcomes of the previously mentioned procedures. Some of the outcomes lead to benefits while others lead to costs however it is important to note that the vast purview of the organizations makes it difficult to quantitatively calculate the net benefits or costs of the "ASEAN Way".

Avoidance

Avoidance refers to conflict management procedures leading to the filtering out of certain kinds of disputes (J.P. Folger, 2005; Kriesberg, 2003; Pruitt & Kim, 2004; Schellenberg, 1996). This procedure can involve the immediate avoidance of a certain issue from discussion in ASEAN to other more subtle methods of avoidance such as the channelling of certain issues to powerless secondary committees and the subsequent delay and final ignorance of its findings. It should be noted that avoidance leads to both benefits and costs for ASEAN. Among the benefits of avoidance are the maintenance of group cohesion and the projection of a unified front in the face of the external environment.

Thus, avoidance has served the purpose of avoiding certain difficult internal conflicts such as those over territory and political persecution of opponents in favour of maintaining the unity of ASEAN and permitting the discussion of other issues while disagreeing on many important ones. This leads to improved communication between parties which may be in conflict over one issue while cooperating on many others. Cooperation on regional concerns such as terrorism and development can take place between members with serious disputes partly because of ASEAN's avoidance defence mechanism. Moreover, avoidance serves the purpose of filtering out disagreement so as to present a united front to the international community (Yzawa, 2006). Since most disagreements are avoided most official statements present agreement over principles and thus give the appearance of policy coherence and unity (ASEAN, 2008a).

Avoidance can also lead to important costs for ASEAN. Conflicts such as border disputes and serious abuses of human rights cannot be tackled by the organization in a timely manner due to the opposition of some member states favouring the principle of non-interference (Heller, 2005; Katanyuu, 2006; Narine, 1997). This leads to serious short and midterm costs during crises such as the military coup in Thailand in 2006 and the recurrent anti-democracy crackdowns in Myanmar (Chang et al., 2007; Keling, Saludin, von Feigenblatt, Ajis, & Shuib, 2010). Avoidance may hamper the possible role of the secretary general as a mediator or third party neutral in intraregional disputes (Jones & Smith, 2007; Severino, 2007). Even intergovernmental issues such as the border dispute between Thailand and Cambodia cannot be dealt with speedily enough to prevent deadly border skirmishes (Simon, 2008). Thus avoidance hampers the taking of decisive action by

ASEAN to deal with short and midterm crises and threats.

Consensus

Consensus building is one of the oldest and most widespread conflict management methods in Asia and involves a long process of communication, indirect negotiation, face work, and subsequent reaching of an agreement based on the least common denominator (Augsburger, 1992; Ishida, 1984; LeBaron, 1998; Ting-Toomey, 1988). Principles are considered to be more important than details and agreements are never final but subject to revision due to changes in the environment and the individual circumstances of the parties (Nisbett, 2003).

ASEAN's method of consensus building is surprisingly informal and protracted. Consensus building requires that all the parties be able to accept the general agreement. In order for this to happen it is often necessary to raise the level of abstraction and lower the specificity of the resulting agreement. The result is that very general agreements based on broad abstract principles are reached. It is important to note that the agreements reached have the legitimacy that every single member accepts it since all have a potential veto power.

It should be clear from the previous paragraph that one of the costs of consensus building is that it is very time consuming. This is one reason why ASEAN is not able to deal with crises in a timely fashion. Finding the lowest common denominator requires constant communication and indirect negotiation. Thus, consensus strengthens preventive diplomacy while it weakens ASEAN's ability to deal with sudden threats. Another cost created by consensus building is that agreements are difficult to implement due to their abstract and general nature. Specific details are avoided so as to reach consensus based on the lowest common denominator.

This leads to problems in operationalizing the policy guidelines adopted by ASEAN. One example of this is the policy goals of building an ASEAN Socio-cultural community by 2020 found in the ASEAN Charter (ASEAN, 2008a, 2008b). Finally one other cost of consensus building is the veto power it affords some members. Since the agreement of every member is necessary to reach consensus, a single member can obstruct the process. This tactic has been used several times by Myanmar and Vietnam to force the avoidance of certain sensitive issues such as human rights and democratization (Simon, 2008).

Consensus building also leads to some benefits for ASEAN. Decisions reached by consensus have greater legitimacy than those reached by other methods such as majority voting since all members agree with the final agreement. Furthermore, consensus building encourages members to communicate more often with each other and to try to understand the needs and interests of their counterparts. Finally, consensus building allows ASEAN to issue official statements representing the agreement of all members and thus presenting a unified front to the outside world. By presenting a unified front ASEAN can increase the diplomatic clout and influence of Southeast Asian nations in the international community (Komori, 2009; Severino, 2007).

In summary, consensus building presents both benefits and costs to ASEAN. Consensus building is compatible with preventive diplomacy and long term development while being problematic for dealing with crises and short and midterm threats (ASEAN, 2008a; Heller, 2005; Nair, 2008; Tow et al., 2000; Yzawa, 2006). It is difficult to ascertain whether the net results of consensus building in ASEAN's dispute resolution system has been positive or negative. Consensus building can strengthen certain important goals of the organization such as the role of engaging all countries in the region in an open process of regional integration. Preventive diplomacy is also strengthened by consensus building while ASEAN's capacity to deal with crises and short term threats is clearly diminished by it. Thus, it is important to deal with the costs of consensus building without giving up the benefits.

Conclusions

ASEAN's present dispute management system is dominated by two main techniques, namely consensus building and avoidance. Both consensus building and avoidance provide benefits and costs. Costs are mostly accrued due to lack of decisive action in tackling short and midterm threats and also in the operationalization of agreed on policy goals. On the other hand benefits cluster around the long term stability of the organization, cohesiveness, and greatly strengthen preventive diplomacy. It is clear from the previous discussion that ASEAN's performance oscillates from periods of success, such as its role during the Asian Financial Crisis of 1997, and periods of inactivity and failure such as during the Thai military coup of 2006. The next chapter provides an analysis of ASEAN based on Robert Fritz's structural dynamics so as to identify the causes of the previously mentioned oscillation and their relation to ASEAN's two main dispute resolution techniques, consensus building and avoidance (Fritz, 1996).

References

Akaha, T. (2009). Human Security in East Asia. *Journal of Human Security, 5*(3), 11-34.

ASEAN. (2008a). *2007-2008 Annual Report: One Vision, One Identity, One Community*. Retrieved November 30, 2008. from http://www.aseansec.org/AR-08.pdf.

ASEAN. (2008b). *ASEAN Charter*. Retrieved November 30, 2008. from http://www.aseansec.org/ASEAN-Charter.pdf.

Augsburger, D. W. (1992). *Conflict Mediation Across Cultures: Pathways and Patterns* (First ed.). Louisville: Westmister/John Knox Press.

Battersby, P., & Siracusa, J. M. (2009). *Globalization & Human Security* (Hardcover ed.). Lanham: Rowman & Littlefield Publishers, Inc.

Callahan, W. A. (2008). Chinese Visions of World Order: Post-hegemonic or a New Hegemony? *International Studies Review, 10*(4), 749-761.

Chang, Y.-t., Chu, Y.-h., & Park, C.-M. (2007). Authoritarian

Nostalgia in Asia. *Journal of Democracy, 18*(3), 71-80.

Collins, A. (2008). A People-Oriented ASEAN: A Door Ajar or Closed for Civil Society Organizations? *Contemporary Southeast Asia, 30*(2), 313-332.

Creswell, J. W. (2007). *Qualitative Inquiry & Research Design: Choosing Among Five Approaches* (Second ed.). London: SAGE Publications.

Emmers, R. (2001). The Influence of the Balance of Power Factor within the ASEAN Regional Forum. *Contemporary Southeast Asia, 23*(2), 275-291.

von Feigenblatt, Otto F. (2009a). ASEAN and Human Security: Challenges and Opportunities. *Ritsumeikan Centre for Asia Pacific Studies Working Paper, No. 09-5*(July), 1-22.

von Feigenblatt, Otto F. (2009b). Comparing the 2006 Military Coup in Thailand and the 2009 Coup in Honduras: Internal Socio-political Similarities and External Normative Differences. *Infinity Journal, 1*(4), 3-9.

von Feigenblatt, Otto F. (2010). *Human Security in the Asia Pacific Region: Security Challenges, Regional Integration, and Representative Case Studies* (Hardcover ed.). Jaipur: YKING BOOKS.

Friedman, T. L. (2000). *The Lexus and the Olive Tree: Understanding Globalization* (Revised ed.). New York: Farrar Straus Giroux.

Fritz, R. (1996). *Corporate Tides: The Inescapable Laws of Organizational Structure* San Francisco: Berrett-Koehler Publishers

Garcia, D. (2009). Arms Transfers beyond the State-to-State Realm. *International Studies Perspectives, 10*(1), 151-168.

Glassman, J. (2005). The "War On Terrorism" Comes To Southeast Asia. *Journal of Contemporary Asia, 35*(1), 3-28.

Hamlin, T. (2009). Bangkok's 2008 Stumble: Time for Reform [Electronic Version]. Retrieved Feb 15, 2009, from http://www.stimson.org/pub.cfm?ID=744

Heidhues, M. S. (2000). *Southeast Asia: A Concise History*. London: Thames & Hudson.

Heller, D. (2005). The Relevance of the ASEAN Regional Forum (ARF) for Regional Security in the Asia-Pacific. *Contemporary Southeast Asia, 27*(1), 123-145.

HSIN-HUANG, HSIAO, M., & WAN, P.-S. (2007). The

Experiences of Cultural Globalizations in Asia-Pacific. *Japanese Journal of Political Science, 8*(3), 361-376.

Hwang, H.-d. (2006). APEC and emerging regionalism in North East Asia. *Asia Europe Journal, 4*(4), 499-510.

Ishida, T. (1984). Conflict and Its Accomodation: Omote-Ura and Uchi-Soto Relations. In E. S. Krauss, T. P. Rohlen & P. G. Steinhoff (Eds.), *Conflict in Japan* (pp. 16-38). Honolulu: University of Hawaii Press.

Ishii, Y. (1994). Thai Muslims and the Royal Patronage of Religion. *Law & Society Review, 28*(3), 453-460

J.P. Folger, M. S. P., R. K. Stutman. (2005). *Working Through Conflict: Strategies for Relationships, Groups, and Organizations* (5th ed.). New York: Pearson.

Jones, D. M., & Smith, M. L. R. (2007). Making Process, Not Progress ASEAN and the Evolving East Asian Regional Order. *International Security, 32*(1), 148-184.

Katanyuu, R. (2006). Beyond Non-Interference in ASEAN: The Association's Role in Myanmar's National Reconciliation and Democratization. *Asian Survey, 46*(6), 825-845.

Keling, M. F., Saludin, M. N., von Feigenblatt, Otto F., Ajis, M. N. e., & Shuib, M. S. (2010). A Historical Approach to Myanmar's Democratic Process. *Journal of Asia Pacific Studies, 1*(2), 132-148.

Kim, S. W., Fidler, D. P., & Ganguly, S. (2009). Eastphalia Rising? Asian Influence and the Fate of Human Security. *World Policy Journal, 26*(2), 53-64.

Komori, Y. (2009). Asia's Institutional Creation and Evolution. *Asian Perspective, 33*(3), 151-182.

Kriesberg, L. (2003). *Constructive Conflicts: From Escalation to Resolution* (Second ed.). New York: Rowman & Littlefield.

Lal, D. (2004). *IN PRAISE OF EMPIRES: Globalization and Order* (1st ed.). New York: Palgrave Macmillan.

LeBaron, M. (1998). Mediation and Multicultural Reality [Electronic Version]. *Peace and Conflict Studies, 5*. Retrieved September 15, 2009, from http://www.gmu.edu/academic/pcs/lebaron.htm

Limaye, S. P. (2007). United States-ASEAN Relations on ASEAN's Fortieth Anniversary: A Glass Half Full. *Contemporary Southeast Asia, 29*(3), 447-464.

Liow, J. C. (2006). *Muslim Resistance in Southern Thailand and the Southern Philippines: Religion, Ideology, and Politics.*

Washington, D.C.: East-West Centre.
McCargo, D. (2009). The Politics of Buddhist identity in Thailand's deep south: The Demise of civil religion? *Journal of Southeast Asian Studies, 40*(1), 11-32.
Means, G. P. (2009). *Political Islam in Southeast Asia* (Paperback ed.). London: Lynne Rienner Publishers.
Mulder, N. (1996). *Inside Southeast Asia: Religion, Everyday Life, and Cultural Change*. Chiang Mai: Silkworm Books.
Nair, D. (2008). Regionalism in the Asia Pacific/East Asia: A Frustrated Regionalism? *Contemporary Southeast Asia, 31*(1), 110–142.
Narine, S. (1997). ASEAN and the ARF: The Limits of the "ASEAN Way". *Asian Survey, 37*(10), 961-978.
Narine, S. (1998). ASEAN and the Management of Regional Security. *Pacific Affairs, 71*(2), 195-214.
Neher, C. D. (2002). *Southeast Asia in the New International Era*. Boulder: Westview Press.
Nisbett, R. E. (2003). *The Geography of Thought: How Asians and Westerners Thing Differently...and Why* (1st Paperback ed.). New York: Free Press.
Pieterse, J. N. (2007). *Ethnicities and Global Multiculture: Pants for an Octopus* (Hardcover ed.). Plymouth: Rowman & LIttlefield Publishers, Inc.
Pruitt, D., & Kim, S. H. (2004). *Social Conflict: Escalation, Stalemate and Settlement* (3rd ed.). New York: McGraw Hill.
Rerksirisuk, C. (2009). Preah Vihear as the last struggle, how history will remember you [Electronic Version]. *Prachatai.* Retrieved September 23, from http://www.prachatai.com/english/node/686
Rolfe, J. (2008). Regional Security for the Asia-Pacific: Ends and Means. *Contemporary Southeast Asia, 30*(1), 99-117.
Schellenberg, J. A. (1996). *Conflict Resolution: Theory, Research, and Practice*. New York: State University of New York Press.
Severino, R. C. (2007). ASEAN Beyond Forty: Towards Political and Economic Integration. *Contemporary Southeast Asia, 23*(3), 406-423.
Shuib, M. S., Saludin, M. N., Feigenblatt, O. F. v., Keling, M. F., & Ajis, M. N. e. (2010). The Role of Malaysian Leaders in Nation Building Process (1957-2003). *Arts and Social Sciences Journal, 2010*, 1-17.
Simon, S. (2008). ASEAN and Multilateralism: The Long, Bumpy

Road to Community. *Contemporary Southeast Asia, 30*(2), 264-292.

Singh, D. (2008-2009). Southeast Asian Security: An Overview. In D. Nair & L. P. Onn (Eds.), *Regional Outlook: Southeast Asia 2008-2009* (pp. 3-7). Singapore: Institute of Southeast Asian Studies.

Stake, R. E. (1995). *The Art of Case Study Research*. Thousand Oaks: SAGE Publications.

Storey, I. (2008). Securing Southeast Asia's Sea Lanes: A Work in Progress. *Asia Policy*(6), 95–127.

Suharto, E. (2009). Social Protection Systems in ASEAN: Social Policy in a Comparative Analysis. *Social Development Issues, 31*(1), 1.

Ting-Toomey, S. (1988). Intercultural Conflict Styles: A Face-Negotiation Theory. In Y. Kim & W. Gudykunst (Eds.), *Theories in Intercultural Communication* (pp. 214-234). Beverly Hills, CA: Sage Publications.

Togo, K. (2005). *Japan's Foreign Policy 1945-2003: The Quest for a Proactive Policy* (Second Edition ed.). Leiden: Brill.

Tow, W. T., Thakur, R., & Hyun, I.-T. (Eds.). (2000). *Asia's emerging regional order: Reconciling traditional and human security*. Tokyo: United Nations University Press.

Ungpakorn, G. J. (2007). *A Coup for the Rich: Thailand's Political Crisis*. Bangkok: Workers Democracy Publishing.

Ury, W. L., Brett, J. M., & Coldberg, S. B. (1993). *Getting Disputes Resolved: Designing Systems to Cut the Costs of Conflict*. Cambridge: The Program on Negotiation at Harvard Law School.

Vu-Tung, N. (2007). Vietnam's Membership of ASEAN: A Constructivist Interpretation. *Contemporary Southeast Asia, 29*(3), 483-505.

Wongboonsin, P., Pongsapich, A., Pongsapich, S., & Sookkhee, C. (Eds.). (2006). *Promoting Human Security in APEC Countries*. Bangkok: Chulalongkorn University Press.

Wyatt, D. K. (2003). *Thailand: A Short History* (Thailand ed.). Chiang Mai: Silkworm Books.

Yew, L. K. (2000). *From Third World to First: The Singapore Story: 1965-2000* (First ed.). New York: HarperCollins Publishers.

Yu-tzung Chang, Y.-h. C., Chong-Min Park. (2007). Authoritarian Nostalgia in Asia. *Journal of Democracy, 18*(3), 71-80.

Yzawa, T. (2006). The Evolution of Preventive Diplomacy in the ASEAN Regional Forum: Problems and Prospects. *Asian Survey, 46*(5), 785-804.

2

ASEAN's Oscillation between Success and Failure: Root Causes

Chapter one provided an assessment of the conflict management system currently in use in the Association of Southeast Asian Nations (ASEAN) and discussed some of the organization's successes and failures. This chapter concentrates on the macro level view of the organization so as to find some of the roots causes behind the organization's oscillation between success and failure. How do we explain the sudden shift from success to failure and then back again to success? While there are many ways to go about answering the previous question this study applies an important theory developed in the field of conflict systems design by Robert Fritz, structural dynamics, rather than follow the traditional approach in political science of concentrating either on the leadership or the agency of the followers (Fritz, 1996).

The main purpose of this chapter is to explain the apparent tension between ASEAN's attempts to grow and then the subsequent lack of capacity for the new functions brought about by that expansion. Centralization and decentralization are also important in explaining ASEAN's oscillation between success and failure since it appears like the organization is attempting to move towards a more centralized structure while then moving back towards its original decentralized structure. Other important instances of oscillation can be found in the functional breath of the organization. ASEAN has attempted to expand its functions beyond regional security to encompass aspects such as cultural integration, economic integration, and regional integration (ASEAN, 2008b; Collins, 2008). The subsequent expansion of the organization's functions has caused severe strains on its resources and on the rest of the structure (Jones & Smith, 2007; Simon, 2008).

Before delving deeper into the structural conflicts hinted at in the previous paragraph it is important to introduce the reader to the theory of structural dynamics which will serve as the most important theoretical framework for the rest of the book. The following section will introduce the main elements of the theory as well as provide a few simple examples of how it can be applied to all kinds of organizational conflicts.

Structural Dynamics

Structural dynamics is a theory that aims to explain structural conflict. Structural conflict in this case refers to both intra and extra organizational conflict. The theory was originally developed by Robert Fritz mostly for the field of systems design in the private sector (Fritz, 1996). Nevertheless structural dynamics is a very flexible theory that explains the role of the individual parts of the structure without losing a holistic point of view. As can be guessed from the name of the theory, the core concept in the theory is structure and the word "dynamics" reflects its resemblance to the field of dynamics in physics. In other words, structural dynamics explains the laws governing the functioning of an organization's structure. Movement and change is implied by the name as well as a certain underlying order.

The holistic nature of structural dynamics can be discerned from its definition of a structural relationship. "A Structural relationship is one in which the various parts act upon each other, and consequently generate particular types of behaviour" (Fritz, 1996, p. 4). Thus, the emphasis of structural dynamics is on the interaction between the parts of a structure and its greatest strength is its ability to predict the result of certain changes in the structure on the behaviour of entire entity. The behaviour of the entire entity can lead to two broad outcomes, advancement or oscillation.

Advancement can be broadly understood as organizational success in the long term while oscillation refers to swings from periods of apparent success to others of failure. Fritz provides a simple example to understand the difference between success and oscillation by comparing the two to the movement of a rocking chair and of a toy car. When the toy car is pushed in one direction or another it will continue to move in that directly and most likely stop after a while. On the other hand a rocking chair will initially move forward but will then move backwards. Thus the first law of structural dynamics is that "organizations either oscillate or advance" (Fritz, 1996, p. 5).

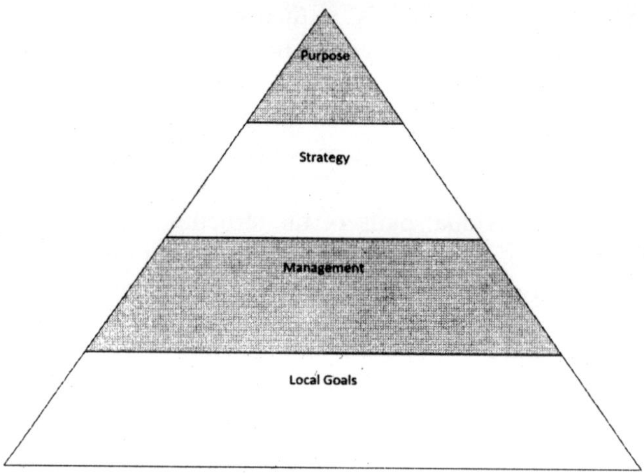

Figure 1. Hierarchy of Goals: Adapted from (Fritz, 1996, p. 27)

Based on the first law of structural dynamics a second law is derived, that "in organizations that oscillate, success is neutralized while in organizations that advance success succeeds" (Fritz, 1996, p. 7). While is seems like a very simply conclusion it is a profoundly important lesson taught by structural dynamics. Oscillation in the long term leads to failure in one way or another regardless of the presence of short term successes. Therefore, the second law of structural dynamics helps us focus on the midterm view as well as on the functioning of the entire organization rather than just some of its parts.

The driving "force" behind structural dynamics is called *tension* and it is "formed by discrepancy, or the difference between one thing and another" (Fritz, 1996, p. 19). Tension leads to a tendency to eliminate the discrepancy by the structure. When the difference between the present state and the desired state disappears then the tension can be said to be resolved. The mechanism composed of tension and its subsequent resolution is the driving force behind structural dynamics. Therefore the basic unit in structural dynamics is the tension-resolution system.

In order to understand how the tension-resolution system works it is useful to look at some simple examples. A man sitting in a waiting room starts to feel cold due to the low temperature of the air conditioning system. After a few minutes the tension builds due to the discrepancy between the actual temperature in the room and the desired temperature preferred in order to be comfortable. The tension created by the discrepancy makes the man lower the temperature of the AC or put on a warm jacket. After the man lowers the temperature or puts on a jacket the actual temperature will be the same as the desired temperature which means that the tension will have been resolved. Another simple example is the one of a person who wants to cross the street to meet a friend. The actual state is one of separation; each person is on one side of the street, while the desired state is one of togetherness. Tension builds due to the discrepancy until that tension moves the person to cross the street to meet his or her friend, at which point the system is resolved.

Understanding the tension-resolution system in an organization context leads to the simple interpretation that the actual state is the current organizational reality while the desired state is the desired result or organizational vision. Thus in an organization the goal could be to provide great customer service. The present state may be that the organization is receiving hundreds of customer complaints per week and losing market share due to it. Structural tension builds between the present state and the desired vision which moves the organization to take action in order to resolve the discrepancy. While it is easy to understand how this applies to an organization it is important to take into consideration the way in which goals are related to each other. There is a clear hierarchy of goals that must be followed in an organization. Purpose, strategy, management, and local goals should be connected by following the principle of subsidiarity. In other words, local goals should serve management goals, which in turn should help strategic ones, and which must all finally move the organization towards fulfilling its purpose (Fritz, 1996, p. 27).

Before moving on to explaining the causes of structural oscillation and of subsequent organizational failure it is important to note that understanding reality is pivotal in order to apply structural dynamics. Accurate organizational assessment is necessary in order to understand the first part of the tension-resolution system. It is important to know where you are before you can start trying to get where you want to be. Due to the importance of understanding reality, the first chapter of this book was devoted to the assessment of the Association of Southeast Asian Nations (ASEAN). Chapters exploring other more specific aspects of the organization will also provide an assessment of the current state of the organization before applying structural dynamics.

Now that the basic principles of structural dynamics have been explained it is possible to move on to explaining the root cause of oscillation, namely structural conflict. A simple example provided by Fritz is made up of the two tension resolution systems of feeling hungry and overweight. The first tension-resolution system starts with a state of hunger which is resolved by eating. Thus the resolution of the system is eating more. The second tension-resolution system starts with a feeling of being overweight and it is resolved by dieting. It is important to note how the resolutions of the two systems are mutually exclusive or incompatible in one way or another. It is virtually impossible to eat a lot and diet at the same time.

This leads to a competition between the two systems. At one point hunger may be the strongest force/tension which will lead the person to eat more in order to resolve the discrepancy. After eating the person may gain weight and feel a discrepancy between their actual weight and their desired weight. In order to resolve the second system, the person will eat less and subsequently lose weight. Nevertheless, eating less will lead to a feeling of hunger which will lead to eating more. As this example shows the person will oscillate from eating a lot to dieting and will feel overweight and hungry alternatively. This phenomenon is called structural conflict and leads to oscillation and neutralizes success. After years of switching from dieting to eating a person does not succeed in having a healthy lifestyle and an appropriate weight.

Structural conflicts also take place in organizations and have similar results. Thus it is important to keep in mind axiom 6 of structural dynamics which states that "structural conflict exists when two tension-resolution systems within the same structure have points of resolution that are mutually exclusive" (Fritz, 1996, p. 36). Axiom 8 predicts the behaviour of an organization when structural conflict is present by stating that "movement in one direction of a structural conflict will precipitate compensating movement in the other direction" (Fritz, 1996, p. 37). Thus the presence of structural conflicts leads to oscillation which hampers the attainment of long term success and advancement. The following section will apply structural dynamics to some important structural conflicts in ASEAN found at the macro level.

Some Important Structural Conflicts in ASEAN

One of the core structural conflicts at the macro level involves the desire to expand both the size and the mandate of the organization running parallel to the desire to bring stability and cohesion to ASEAN. A second core structural conflict is the one involving the desire to achieve long term development and peace in the region and the parallel one aiming to deal with short and midterm crises. A third structural conflict is the one involving the desire to decentralize decision making so as to make the organization more participatory on the one hand and the desire to protect the principle of non-interference and the power of the nation-state on the other. Therefore the three major structural conflicts in ASEAN revolve around six tension-resolution systems which can then be paired into three pairs of systems with mutually exclusive outcomes/goals.

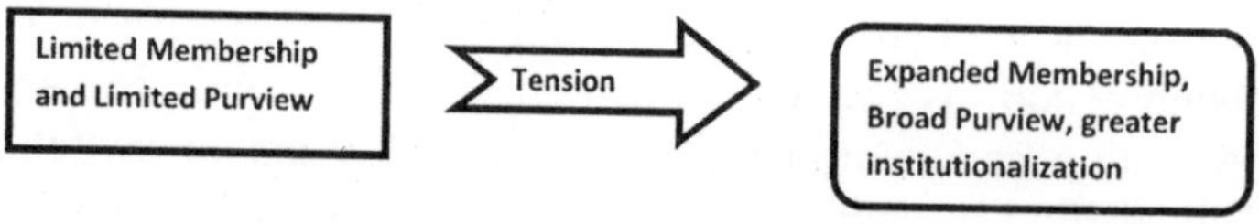

Figure 2. Tension-Resolution System A: Membership and Purview

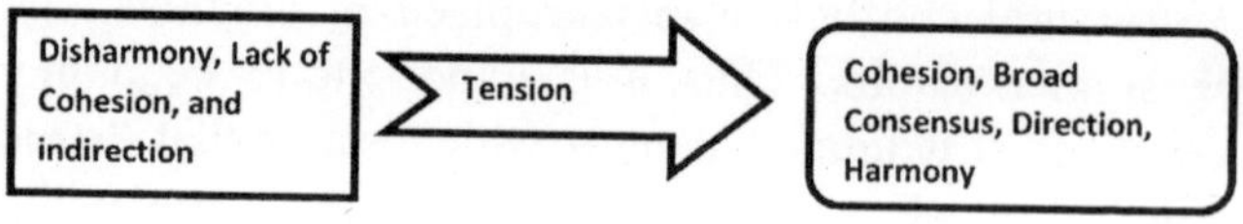

Figure 3. Tension- Resolution System B: Cohesion and Consensus

The first tension-resolution system to be discussed is the one dealing with the desire to expand both the membership of the organization as well as increase the breath of its purview. ASEAN started as a loosely knit intergovernmental organization with five members, namely Thailand, Malaysia, Indonesia, the Philippines, and Singapore (Komori, 2009; Nair, 2008). The original purview of the organization was relatively limited in that its goal was to deal with security issues in the region through informal meetings and consultation (Severino, 2007).

In terms of programs and activities, ASEAN was not very active during the first decades of its existence and most of its efforts went to organizing yearly summits and issuing general statements (Jones & Smith, 2007; Rolfe, 2008). Nevertheless, the small size of the organization and the norms shared by the original members gave rise to high levels of cohesion and stability in the organization (Narine, 1998; Nem-Singh, 2008). This was the origin of the famous "ASEAN way" which favours harmony over overt conflict and enshrines informal communication and consensus building as core principles of ASEAN (Jones & Smith, 2007; Yzawa, 2006).

Nevertheless the small size of the organization and the incomplete membership in terms of geographical reach led to a desire to increase both the size and scope of the organization. In order to increase the influence of ASEAN it was necessary to make it a truly representative organization for the Southeast Asian region which required that at least a majority of the nation-states in the region become members (Neher, 2002; Simon, 2008). Furthermore, the vast array of threats that came to the fore after the end of the Cold War brought about a desire to expand the mandate of the organization in order for it to truly be a factor in the development and security of the region.

It is clear that during its early decades, ASEAN's reality was that it was a very small and limited organization which led to a desire to increase its size and scope. The discrepancy between the reality and the desire goal created structural tension which led to movement towards the desired goal. Membership was expanded to include every single country in Southeast Asia, starting with Brunei, then Vietnam, and finally Cambodia, Myanmar, and Laos (ASEAN, 2008b; von Feigenblatt, 2009a; Rolfe, 2008; Vu-Tung, 2007). The limited mandate of the organization in its early decades led to a need to expand its mandate.

Therefore, the discrepancy between the original mandate and the desired scope of the organization created structural tension which moved the organization towards greater institutionalization as seen in the slow yet clear differentiation of its functional organs (Nem-Singh, 2008; Severino, 2007). The secretariat in Jakarta was formalized and given greater authority, ministerial meetings dealing with a vast array of issues were established as well as a plethora of relationships with extra regional actors (Emmers, 2001; Narine, 1998; Simon, 2008).

Now that the two tension-resolution systems have been described separately it is important to look at their outcomes for the structure of ASEAN. Tension- resolution system A led to a widely expanded membership, to a broader purview, and to greater institutionalization. On the other hand tension-resolution system B resulted in a greater emphasis on cohesion, general consensus, external harmony, and direction. In other words ASEAN expanded its membership and increased the number of its functional bodies (Pitsuwan, 2010; Severino, 2007; Yzawa, 2006). ASEAN also started to emphasize greater cohesion and external harmony among its members by issuing general statements expressing only agreed upon goals and principles (Jones & Smith, 2007). The result was that ASEAN started to act a single block vis-à-vis the international community with the aim of increasing the diplomatic clout of the organization (Limaye, 2007; Pitsuwan, 2010; Severino, 2007). Consensus building was both a product and the process of tension-resolution system B in that it resolved the tension caused by a lack of direction and of harmony among the members.

Independently the results of resolution-systems A and B are both desirable for the organization. ASEAN clearly benefits from have a broader membership in that it is viewed as more representative of the geographical region as well as benefiting from having a more institutionalized structure which can deal with a greater array of issues in a more efficient way. It is also beneficial for ASEAN in terms of its international image and legitimacy to present a common front through consensus building and to agree on a common direction for the organization (Limaye, 2007; Simon, 2008). Nevertheless the two outcomes can be incompatible. Expanding membership brought in a diverse group of nation-states with different levels of development, different political systems, and divergent historical experiences (von Feigenblatt, 2009a; Heidhues, 2000; Mulder, 1996; Neher, 2002). Broadening the mandate as well as increasing the number of functional organs added complexity to the system and increased the number of issues that had to be tackled by the organization.

Structural conflict takes place when the outcomes of two tension-resolution systems are incompatible or incongruent and leads to structural oscillation (Fritz, 1996). The expansion brought about by tension-resolution system A eventually increased the tension in the tension-resolution system B due to the increase in the number of organs as well as in the number of members with different interests and perspectives. Once the tension in system B becomes stronger than the tension in system A, the system will move towards greater cohesion, more active direction, and a greater emphasis on harmony. After a while members will start to feel like the new emphasis on a more active direction and cohesion limits the purview of the organization and then the pressure will build up for movement towards resolution in system A. Thus, since the structure of the organization seeks balance there is movement towards resolution in both systems. Nevertheless at any given point in time there is greater tension in one system than in the other and due to the relative incompatibility of the two resolutions, the structure will oscillate from periods of expansion and broadening to periods of contraction and more active direction.

Oscillation in ASEAN can be observed in the cycles of expansion followed by periods of retrenchment. While expansion in terms of membership is certainly not rolled back, informal methods are used by member states in order to limit the purview of the organization. This was seen in the rise and fall of the concept of active engagement during the 1990s in which several members such as Thailand and the Philippines took tentative steps in the direction of dealing with human rights as well as other internal issues (Chachavalpongpun, 2009; Simon, 2008; Tow, Thakur, & Hyun, 2000). The Asian financial crisis of 1997 as well as the active opposition of Myanmar and Vietnam during the late 1990s and early years of the millennium re-imposed the primacy of the concept of non-interference and the central role of economic issues in ASEAN (Chachavalpongpun, 2009; Vu-Tung, 2007). Nevertheless this was followed by a revival of the concept in 2007 as well as greater efforts to get the organization involved in socio-cultural issues (ASEAN, 2008a).

Thus the purview of the organization expanded during the early to mid 1990s, contracted during the late 1990s and early years of the 21st century, and then expanded again starting in 2007 (ASEAN, 2008b; von Feigenblatt, 2009a; Neher, 2002). The oscillation is clear and it is partly caused by the incongruence between the outcomes of the two previously mentioned tension-resolution systems, namely A and B. Oscillation neutralizes success because for every step that is taken in one direction another one is taken in the opposite direction (Fritz, 1996).

Thus active engagement was followed by a period in which the norm of non-interference was strengthened and then followed by a revival of active engagement; however the starting point during the second cycle was not where discussions left off during the height of the debate over active engagement but rather somewhere in between absolute non-interference and active engagement. In other words, progress was not linear and success did not lead to greater success but rather to movement similar to that of a rocking chair without serving any greater organizational purpose. The failure of ASEAN to intervene during the unconstitutional Thai military coup in 2006 attests to the lack of progress in terms of the norm of active engagement (von Feigenblatt, 2009b; Ungpakorn, 2007).

A second core structural conflict in ASEAN is related to time orientation. Organizations have short, mid, and long term goals. It is very important to have a balanced time orientation in order for an organization to be able to tackle short, mid, and long term challenges. At this point it is important to remind the reader of the optimum hierarchy of goals discussed in an earlier section of this chapter. The purpose of the organization should be a top priority, followed by strategic goals, then managerial goals, and finally local goals (Constantino & Merchant, 1996; Goldsmith, Greenberg, Robertson, & Hu-Chan, 2003).

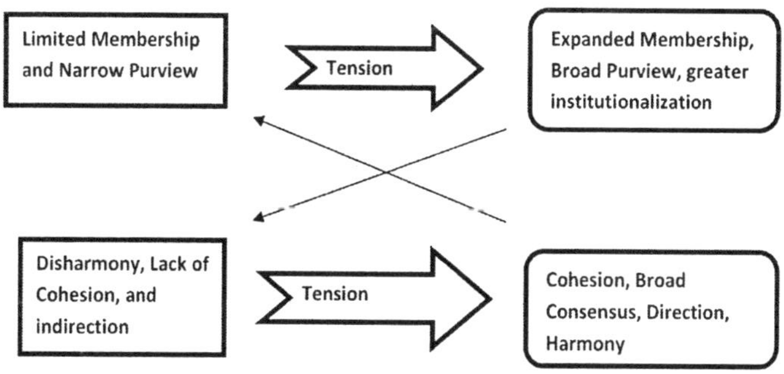

Figure 4. Structural Oscillation in ASEAN due to Incompatibility of outputs of tension-resolution systems A and B (Expansion and Contraction)

Local goals should help the organization achieve managerial goals which in turn should help attain strategic ones, and which should help the organization fulfil its purpose. This principle also applies to time orientation. Long terms goals, should be followed by mid term strategic goals, and supported by short term localized action. In order for an organization to advance, every action should serve a purpose at a higher level of the hierarchy. In other words a short term goal should build up to a midterm strategy which in turn should lead to fulfilling a long term purpose.

Tension should move the organization smoothly from one goal to another up the ladder in the time horizon. Nevertheless

ASEAN faces two competing tension-resolution systems in terms of time orientation. Some important stakeholders such as NGOs and marginalized populations face serious short term threats which create a desire for faster and more decisive action on the part of ASEAN (Akaha, 2009; Collins, 2008). The tension between the realities faced by NGOs and marginalized populations due to human insecurity and the desired goal of amelioration and protection of those affected communities leads to movement towards an emphasis on short term threats by ASEAN (JICA, 2008; Katanyuu, 2006). Emergencies caused by natural disasters such as a tsunami, a cyclone, or a sudden economic collapse give rise to a desire for short term amelioration and protection. This tension then leads to short term emergency responses which have as their goal the amelioration of the symptoms of human insecurity but which do not serve any higher level strategic goals nor lead to the fulfilment of the organization's long term purpose.

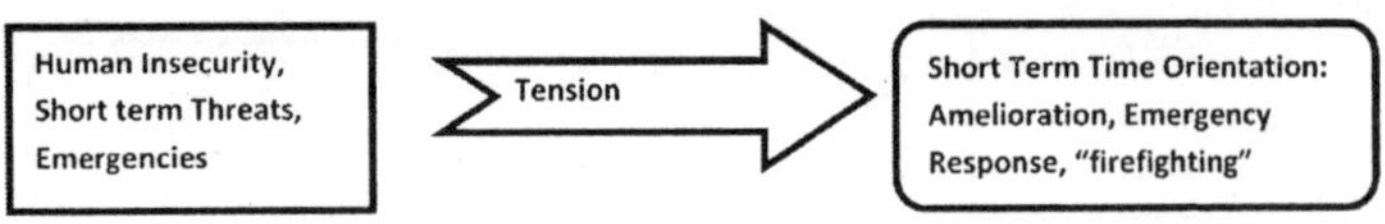

Figure 5. Tension-Resolution System C: Short term Threats and Short Term Time Orientation

On the other hand there is another tension-resolution system caused by the dynamics of consensus building as well as the by the common regional interests of the member states. Common regional challenges such as a dangerous and polarized security environment, economic globalization and greater competition for export markets and foreign direct investment, as well as a common historical experience of extra regional intervention in the region, give rise to the desire to have greater regional integration, peace and freedom from great power intervention, and sustainable development (von Feigenblatt, 2009a; Glassman, 2005; Heidhues, 2000).

The previously mentioned common challenges are present

in the region as evidenced by the increased competition for foreign direct investment (FDI) in regions such as Latin America, Africa, and especially China, as well as by the growing military presence of China in the region (Bitzinger, 2010; Heller, 2005; Rolfe, 2008). Due to the clear discrepancy between the challenges faced in reality with the desired common goals, tension is created which leads to movement toward a resolution. ASEAN's historical reliance on consensus building favours a long term time orientation for moving toward the desired goals due to the method's proclivity to lead to declarations based on the lowest common denominator and on general principles.

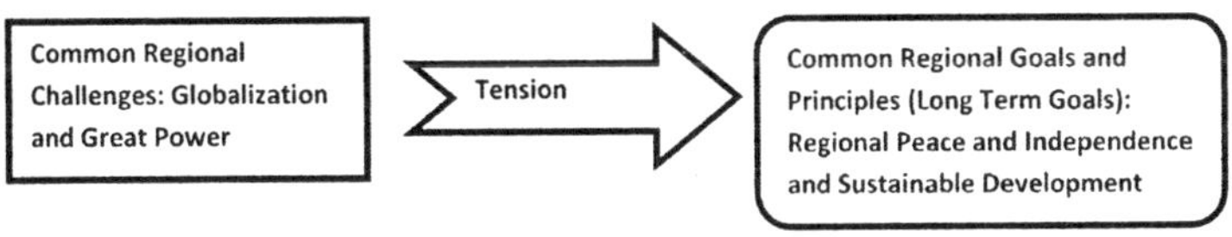

Figure 6. Tension-Resolution System D: Common Regional Challenges and Long Term Time Orientation

Tension-resolution system C leads to a short term time orientation when dealing with short term threats. That short term orientation leads to disjointed national efforts to ameliorate the negative externalities of the aforementioned threats. Thus, the actions taken by ASEAN's members are not part of an integrated strategy aiming to fulfil mid and long term organizational goals. The result of tension-resolution system D is a long term orientation based on common regional challenges such as globalization and the fear of great power intervention. Common regional goals and principles are arrived at through the tedious and protracted process of consensus building resulting in very ambiguous agreements enunciating shared principles and goals such as a regional desire for regional peace and for sustainable development (Jones & Smith, 2007). Therefore, the outcome of tension-resolution system D is very broad and long term, almost at the level of the original purpose and vision of the organization.

ASEAN tends to fluctuate between periods of piecemeal attempts to deal with short term negative externalities to periods of concentration on long term principles and goals. Examples of the two periods include the flurry of activity during the Asian financial crisis of 1997 and the recent period starting in 2007 and leading to the drafting of the very broad and ambiguous ASEAN Charter respectively (ASEAN, 2008b; Suharto, 2009). Thus, ASEAN is characterized by having most of its activities falling into either an extremely short term time orientation or a very long term one.

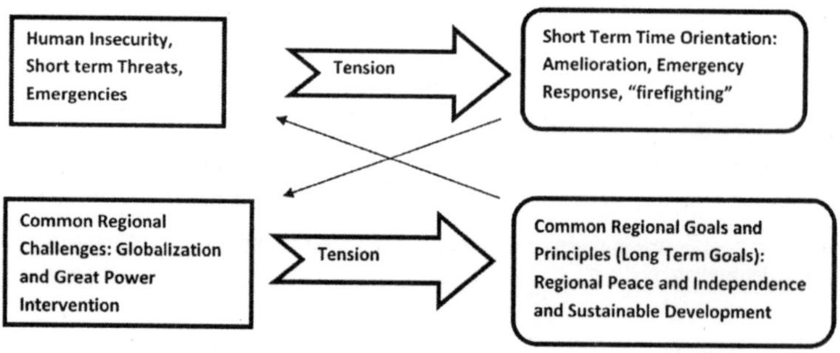

Figure 7. Structural Oscillation in ASEAN due to Incompatibility of tension-resolution systems C and D: (Fluctuation between Myopic Short Term Orientation and Long Term Broad Principles)

The discrepancy between the outcomes of the two tension-resolutions systems, C and D, gives rise to an important core structural conflict in ASEAN. Tension-resolution system C is resolved through a short term time orientation cantered on amelioration and emergency response. On the other hand tension-resolution system D is resolved through a very long term approach leading to the identification of common regional goals and broad principles such as regional peace and sustainable development. It is clear that the outcomes of the two systems are incompatible, at least without the presence of the mediating role of a midterm organizational strategy.

The effect of the subsequent structural conflict is that

ASEAN oscillates between periods of extremely myopic local actions to periods of idealistic concentration on long term principles and goals. There is no organizational advancement due to the oscillation created by this core structural conflict. Small localized successes do not serve any midterm strategy to achieve long term goals and because of this those small successes are reversed during periods of concentration on long term principles and macro level goals. Periods of concentration on long term goals and broad principles lose sight of the need to operationalize those goals in order to agree on how and when to achieve them (Jones & Smith, 2007). The fluctuation between short and long term actions makes it difficult for ASEAN to integrate its many activities into a clear strategy to pursue its core purpose and vision.

Why does oscillation between an emphasis on short term needs and very broad long term goals take place if the outcome is undesirable for organizational stakeholders? The answer is that since the oscillation is due to structural dynamics until the structure itself is redesigned to eliminate the structural conflict in discussion, the organization will continue to oscillate regardless of the actions or wishes of its stakeholders (Fritz, 1996). More concretely, stakeholders are faced with short term emergencies and threats which build tension to deal with them as soon as possible at the local level. These threats and emergencies result in myopic short term responses to ameliorate the negative externalities of the threats be they floods, terrorism, or an economic downturn.

After a while stakeholders, particularly the member states, feel a need to discuss common regional challenges which creates a tension that becomes more pressing than the one for short term threats and causes them to work on very broad and long term agreements reached through consensus building. When grassroots and local stakeholders start to clamour again for action to deal with short term threats and emergencies the tension to deal with short term issues becomes stronger than the one to deal with common regional challenges and the organization oscillates again to a myopic short term view. A midterm strategy to integrate short and long term efforts is clearly lacking in ASEAN which is partly why success in one realm does not lead to success in another. Dealing with a few refugees in the Thai border with Burma does not deal with the roots causes of the displacement but simply deals with the short term effects of the negative externalities of socio-political oppression.

ASEAN's structural conflict of time orientation parallels a final one dealing with centralization and decentralization of decision making. Historically, decision making in ASEAN has been highly centralized with power firmly in the hand of governmental representatives in the Ministerial Meetings and Summits (Collins, 2008; von Feigenblatt, 2009a). Nevertheless, the growing number and nature of challenges faced by the organization gave rise to a desire for a more flexible structure to deal with them. Thus, a centralized decision making structure differed from the desire to have a more flexible decentralized structure.

Tension grew and several attempts were made in order to decentralize decision making in ASEAN and to bring decision making closer to the ground. Examples of attempts at decentralization include the proliferation of first track to second track dialogues such as the one between the Ministerial Meetings and national Strategic Institutes in member countries (Collins, 2008). Efforts at decentralization also include an increased role for subject area experts serving in their private capacities in panels of eminent persons. Those panels were given consultative status when dealing with certain issues but their powers stopped short of decision making prerogatives. A third wave of decentralization is related to the third pillar of the ASEAN communities, namely the socio-cultural community. This is one of the areas in which nongovernmental organizations and other civil society organizations have played a relatively prominent role (Collins, 2008).

From the point of view of structural dynamics the previous

phenomena can be described as a tension-resolution system starting with an unwanted state with a high level of centralization and ossification and a desired outcome of greater flexibility and dynamism through a certain degree of decentralization. The discrepancy between the starting point and the desired goal gives rise to structural tension which moves the organization towards the desired goal.

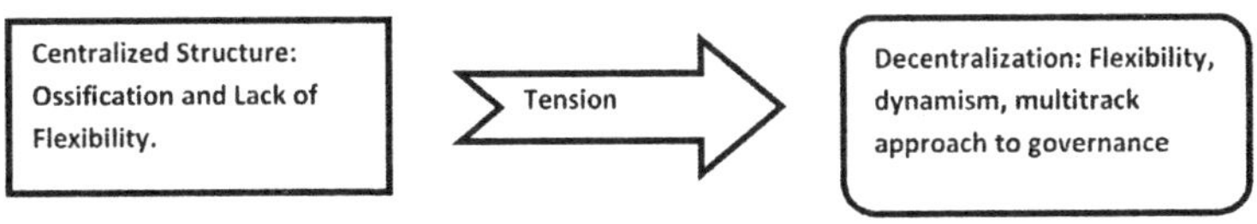

Figure 8. Tension-Resolution System E: Centralization and Decentralization

Tension-resolution system E shows how ASEAN moved towards decentralization due to the structural tension created by the discrepancy between the original highly centralized and ossified decision making structure and the desired goal of achieving a dynamic and flexible organization capable of dealing with a vast array of issues at several levels. A countervailing tension was brought about by the challenges of a more diffuse structure and the subsequent partial loss of control by the member countries. In other words the attempts at decentralization had the effect of including more stakeholders in the activities of the organization which in turn took away a certain degree of control from the original power brokers. Since governments want to avoid uncertainty as much as possible as well showing a marked preference for controlling the flow of information, a desire to centralize decision making and to bring under control the flow of information also grew in the organization.

Using the concepts of structural dynamics, a new organizational reality, a more diffuse decision making structure and a greater flow of information gave rise to the desire to bring the organization back into centralized control. The discrepancy between the organization's reality and the new desired state created structural tension moving the organization in that direction. Some of the ways in which ASEAN has attempted to control the flow of information as well as centralizing the decision making process is by the recurrent emphasis placed on the principle of non-intervention and public statements regarding the intergovernmental nature of the organization (Collins, 2008; Vu-Tung, 2007).

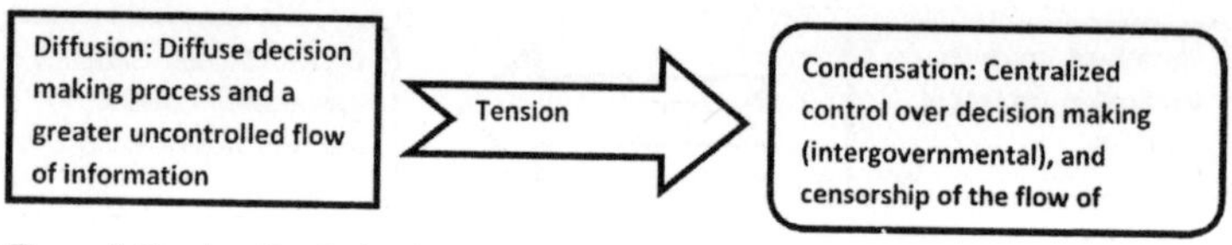

Figure 9. Tension-Resolution System F: Diffusion and Condensation

The outcomes of tension-resolution systems E and F are clearly incompatible in that the former leads to decentralization and diffusion while the later results in condensation (centralization). Structural oscillation results from the incompatibility of the outputs of the two tension-resolution systems giving rise to cycles of attempts to decentralize both decision making and the flow of information and periods marked by efforts to recentralize both decision making and the flow of information in what can be called organizational condensation.

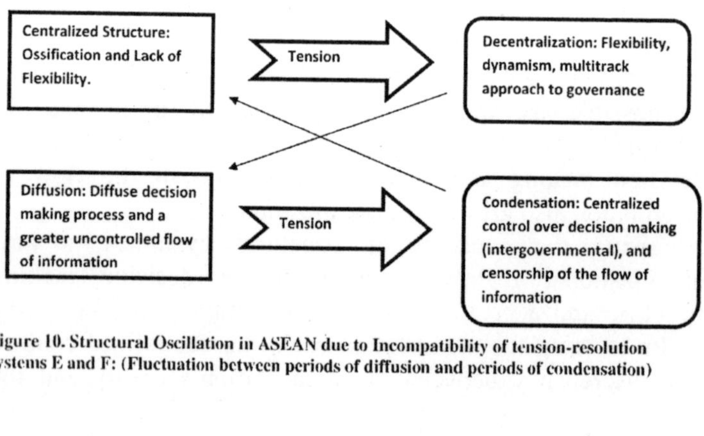

Figure 10. Structural Oscillation in ASEAN due to Incompatibility of tension-resolution systems E and F: (Fluctuation between periods of diffusion and periods of condensation)

Conclusions about Structural Oscillation in ASEAN

This chapter has shown three core structural conflicts present in ASEAN's structure. As explained in earlier sections of this chapter, structural conflicts are created by the incompatibility of outputs of two tension-resolution systems in an organization. The incompatibility of the outputs leads to competition between the two systems and to oscillation between the two. Resolution in one system decreases tension in that system and increases the tension in the competing one with the result of a change in emphasis. Structural oscillation has the mid and long term effect of neutralizing success.

Localized successes are reversed or cancelled out by movement in the opposite direction. A prominent example of reversing early success in ASEAN is the rise and fall of the norm of constructive engagement as a possible substitute for the traditional norm of absolute non-interference. Early progress did not lead to long term success but was rather reversed by a movement in the opposite direction in the period following the Asian Financial crisis.

The three core structural conflicts discussed in this chapter represent the major macro-level conflicts present in the organization. Meta-process issues such as decentralization versus centralization, time orientation, and expansion versus contraction affect all levels of decision making and implementation in an organization. Returning to figure 1 explaining the ideal hierarchy of goals, it can be discerned that oscillation at the higher levels has an effect on the lower ones. This means that structural oscillation at the level of organizational purpose or of strategy will have an exponential effect on management and local goals. Therefore, dealing with the core structural conflicts in ASEAN is imperative if the negative externalities of structural oscillation are to be avoided. Chapter 3 tackles both the core structural conflicts identified in this chapter as well as the various deficiencies in ASEAN's dispute resolution system identified in chapter 1.

References

Akaha, T. (2009). Human Security in East Asia. *Journal of Human Security, 5*(3), 11-34.

ASEAN. (2008a). *2007-2008 Annual Report: One Vision, One Identity, One Community*. Retrieved November 30, 2008. from http://www.aseansec.org/AR-08.pdf.

ASEAN. (2008b). *ASEAN Charter*. Retrieved November 30, 2008. from http://www.aseansec.org/ASEAN-Charter.pdf.

Bitzinger, R.A. (2010). A New Arms Race? Explaining Recent Southeast Asian Military Acquisitions. *Contemporary Southeast Asia, 32*(1), 50-69.

Chachavalpongpun, P. (2009). Diplomacy under Siege: Thailand's Political Crisis and the Impact on Foreign Policy. *Contemporary Southeast Asia, 31*(3), 447-467.

Collins, A. (2008). A People-Oriented ASEAN: A Door Ajar or Closed for Civil Society Organizations? *Contemporary Southeast Asia, 30*(2), 313-332.

Constantino, C.A., & Merchant, C. S. (1996). *Designing Conflict Management Systems: A Guide to Creating Productive and Healthy Organizations* (First ed.). San Francisco: Jossey-Bass Publishers.

Emmers, R. (2001). The Influence of the Balance of Power Factor within the ASEAN Regional Forum. *Contemporary Southeast Asia, 23*(2), 275-291.

von Feigenblatt, Otto F. (2009a). ASEAN and Human Security: Challenges and Opportunities. *Ritsumeikan Centre for Asia Pacific Studies Working Paper, No. 09-5*(July), 1-22.

von Feigenblatt, Otto F. (2009b). Comparing the 2006 Military Coup in Thailand and the 2009 Coup in Honduras: Internal Socio-political Similarities and External Normative Differences. *Infinity Journal, 1*(4), 3-9.

Fritz, R. (1996). *Corporate Tides: The Inescapable Laws of Organizational Structure* San Francisco: Berrett-Koehler Publishers.

Glassman, J. (2005). The "War On Terrorism" Comes To Southeast Asia. *Journal of Contemporary Asia, 35*(1), 3-28.

Goldsmith, M., Greenberg, C., Robertson, A., & Hu-Chan, M. (2003). *Global Leadership: The Next Generation* (Paperback ed.): FT Press.

Heidhues, M. S. (2000). *Southeast Asia: A Concise History*. London:

Thames & Hudson.

Heller, D. (2005). The Relevance of the ASEAN Regional Forum (ARF) for Regional Security in the Asia-Pacific. *Contemporary Southeast Asia, 27*(1), 123-145.

JICA. (2008, October 2008). Cleaning Up After Cyclone Nargis. *JICA News*. Retrieved December 17, 2008, from http://www.jica.go.jp/english/news/focus_on/myanmar/my_3.html.

Jones, D.M., & Smith, M.L.R. (2007). Making Process, Not Progress ASEAN and the Evolving East Asian Regional Order. *International Security, 32*(1), 148-184.

Katanyuu, R. (2006). Beyond Non-Interference in ASEAN: The Association's Role in Myanmar's National Reconciliation and Democratization. *Asian Survey, 46*(6), 825-845.

Komori, Y. (2009). Asia's Institutional Creation and Evolution. *Asian Perspective, 33*(3), 151-182.

Limaye, S.P. (2007). United States-ASEAN Relations on ASEAN's Fortieth Anniversary: A Glass Half Full. *Contemporary Southeast Asia, 29*(3), 447-464.

Mulder, N. (1996). *Inside Southeast Asia: Religion, Everyday Life, and Cultural Change*. Chiang Mai: Silkworm Books.

Nair, D. (2008). Regionalism in the Asia Pacific/East Asia: A Frustrated Regionalism? *Contemporary Southeast Asia, 31*(1), 110–142.

Narine, S. (1998). ASEAN and the Management of Regional Security. *Pacific Affairs, 71*(2), 195-214.

Neher, C.D. (2002). *Southeast Asia in the New International Era*. Boulder: Westview Press.

Nem-Singh, J.T. (2008). Process of Institutionalisation and Democratisation in ASEAN: Features, Challenges and Prospects of Regionalism in Southeast Asia. *UNISCI Discussion Papers, 16* (January 2008), 141-168.

Pitsuwan, S. (2010). ASEAN central to the region's future. *East Asia Forum Quarterly, 2*(2), 4-5.

Rolfe, J. (2008). Regional Security for the Asia-Pacific: Ends and Means. *Contemporary Southeast Asia, 30*(1), 99-117.

Severino, R.C. (2007). ASEAN Beyond Forty: Towards Political and Economic Integration. *Contemporary Southeast Asia, 23*(3), 406-423.

Simon, S. (2008). ASEAN and Multilateralism: The Long, Bumpy

Road to Community. *Contemporary Southeast Asia, 30*(2), 264-292.

Suharto, E. (2009). Social Protection Systems in ASEAN: Social Policy in a Comparative Analysis. *Social Development Issues, 31*(1), 1.

Tow, W.T., Thakur, R., & Hyun, I.-T. (Eds.). (2000). *Asia's emerging regional order: Reconciling traditional and human security*. Tokyo: United Nations University Press.

Ungpakorn, G.J. (2007). *A Coup for the Rich: Thailand's Political Crisis*. Bangkok: Workers Democracy Publishing.

Vu-Tung, N. (2007). Vietnam's Membership of ASEAN: A Constructivist Interpretation. *Contemporary Southeast Asia, 29*(3), 483-505.

Yzawa, T. (2006). The Evolution of Preventive Diplomacy in the ASEAN Regional Forum: Problems and Prospects. *Asian Survey, 46*(5), 785-804.

3

Overcoming Organizational Conflicts in ASEAN through Structural Dynamics

Overcoming organizational conflict is a very complex endeavour and cannot be achieved piecemeal. According to structural dynamics, organizational conflict can only be overcome through redesigning the organization's structure in a way in which the original structural conflict is eliminated or redirected (Fritz, 1996). Nevertheless it is always important to keep in mind the limitations involved in any large scale effort such as redesigning an entire organization. Taking into consideration ASEAN's resources, motivations, present practices and norms, as well as its environment, as identified in chapter 1; it is important to take a two track approach to dealing with the three core structural conflicts presented in chapter 2 as well as the deficiencies of ASEAN's dispute resolution system.

The first section of this chapter discusses some possible ideal ways in which the core structural conflicts could be overcome. Nevertheless, it is clear that overcoming the core structural conflicts present in ASEAN would require considerable political capital, resources, as well as a long period of time. Thus, the second section of the chapter attempts to operationalize the lessons and ideal solutions presented in the first section. Therefore, the last section of this chapter presents a fusion of the lessons learned from structural dynamics with the dispute resolution systems design approach developed by Ury, Brett, and Goldberg through an interdisciplinary proposed model for ASEAN's possible adoption (W. L. Ury, Brett, & Goldberg, 1993).

This chapter is exploratory in nature in that the solutions put forth are tentative rather than definitive. International relations and international studies lack the benefit of a controlled experimental environment to test the validity of possible interventions. Nevertheless, the solutions provided in the first section of the chapter are based on the laws of structural dynamics and are supported by considerable evidence from successful examples in both the private and the public realms (Fritz, 1996; Goldsmith, Greenberg, Robertson, & Hu-Chan, 2003). The proposal put forth in the second section is based on both the dispute resolution systems design approach as well as on some of the best practices developed in the field of alternative dispute resolution (L. Kriesberg, 1997; W. L. Ury et al., 1993).

Overcoming Core Structural Conflicts in ASEAN

Overcoming structural conflict requires a holistic and integrated approach to dealing with the core processes of an organization. In terms of the level of analysis required, a middle level approach is the best option (Fritz, 1996). A very narrow view would only concentrate on local goals and management while a very broad view would only tackle the organization's purpose and vision. Thus a middle level view starting with strategy allows the analyst to link strategy with the organization's purpose and vision as well as with lower level management and local goals. The same applies in terms of time orientation.

A short term orientation will emphasize local goals and short term threats while ignoring other important goals such as midterm strategy and long term development goals. On the other hand, a long term time orientation can become so diffuse that operationalization and implementation becomes impossible. Therefore, in order to be able to tackle core structural conflicts through structural dynamics it is necessary to take into consideration both the level of analysis as well as the time orientation. It is also important to keep in mind that structural analysis takes a holistic view of the organization. Parts are part of an integrated whole. A change in one part affects the others as well as the entire organization. Thus, a core structural conflict can only be tackled through an integrated approach that takes into consideration the importance of organizational strategy as well as the interrelation between short, mid, and long term goals.

Redesigning the structure of the organization is the only way to deal with the actual "forces" causing the organization to oscillate and thus neutralizing success. The goal is to change the relationship of the tension-resolution systems with incompatible outputs in a way in which they either become complementary or at least do not work against each other. If the relationship between the two competing systems becomes complementary, synergy takes place which leads to organizational advancement. The tension leading to resolution in one system creates movement which complements the tension in another system and thus moving both systems and the organization as a whole in a desirable direction. This results in a virtuous cycle in which success leads to more success.

Returning to the core organizational conflicts identified in chapter 2, the first one leads to oscillation between periods of contraction and periods of expansion. As shown in figure 4 the outputs of two tension-resolution systems, namely A and B, result in incompatible outputs leading to competition between the two systems. The first tension-resolution system arises out of a state in which membership is limited and the purview of the organization is very narrow, which in turn creates a desire to expand both the membership of the organization as well as its purview.

Structural tension moves the system towards a resolution involving greater complexity for the organization represented by an expanded membership and a greater number and variety of issues in discussion. That greater complexity gives rise to some negative externalities such as lack of harmony, indirection, and lack of cohesion which gives rise to structural tension to change this new reality. Tension moves the system towards a resolution involving greater cohesion, clearer direction, and harmony. Nevertheless, the previously mentioned resolution to tension-resolution system B also leads to negative externalities such as enforced harmony and conformity as well as a reduced purview for the organization. It is clear that the outcomes of both systems are incompatible and since they cannot take place concurrently they compete for primacy. This leads to periods of contraction and to periods of expansion without any connection neither to the organization's purpose or vision nor to its strategy.

In order to deal with the first core organizational conflict in ASEAN it is necessary to remember the importance of a systemic view of the organization. ASEAN's mission should be supported by its strategy which should in turn be strengthened by management, and so forth. The first core organizational conflict takes place at a very high level of the organizational hierarchy. ASEAN's mission and purpose fluctuate and with them the entire organizational structure.

Since both direction and flexibility are important for an organization it is not possible to favour one or the other but rather both have to be integrated properly so as to lead to organizational advancement in the long run. One way to deal with this organizational conflict is by starting with the nature of each level of the organizational hierarchy of goals. ASEAN's purpose and mission should remain relatively constant so as to provide some stability at the macro level; nevertheless its strategy can show a higher level of flexibility and complexity, while its management goals can support its strategy in diverse ways. Therefore, stability, cohesion, and direction can be maintained at the higher level of ASEAN's goals such as its purpose and mission while lower levels can incorporate greater complexity without destabilizing the entire structure. More concretely ASEAN's long term goals and purpose can remain stable and broad including aspects such as promoting development in the region as well as peace.

Its strategy can be more specific and can involve

presenting a joint regional strategy in terms of development and security in order to increase the influence of the region in the international community. Thus ASEAN's strategy provides the necessary continuity and stability necessary to achieve its purpose which is to bring development and peace to the region. Going down the ladder, ASEAN's management goals can incorporate greater flexibility and complexity by including an expanded membership, a greater array of issues under discussion such as non-traditional security issues and cultural integration, inter alia. The previously mentioned management goals can then be implemented through flexible and concrete local goals which are tied to ASEAN's management goals. Therefore, the top of the pyramid would provide the necessary stability for the lower levels of the pyramid to be flexible enough to deal with the complexity of the real world. Since tension-resolutions systems A and B would have primacy over different levels of the organizational structure they would not compete against each other but rather support the overall advancement of the organization.

One example of how the previously mentioned approach to dealing with the first core organizational conflict can be solved in practice is official development assistance. ASEAN's purpose is to promote the development of the region, broadly defined. Its strategy is to coordinate macro regional policy in intergovernmental meetings which are then presented as unanimous decisions to the international community. Thus official development assistance supports ASEAN's purpose of promoting development.

ASEAN's strategy may have identified certain areas of priority such as the development of certain sub regions or industrial sectors. The development of those sub regions or industrial sectors is then undertaken through more specific management goals in which foreign donors are necessarily involved. At this stage flexibility and expansion are present in that more actors are involved and the range of issues is also expanded. A development project may be originally about industrial expansion but may also involve issues of environmental conservation and socio-cultural issues.

Finally at the level of local goals, official development assistance is used in an even more flexible and nuanced way so as to make the project fit the real needs of the intended beneficiaries while at the same time helping achieve management goals. Thus, as explained by way of the hypothetical example of official development assistance, the structural tension leading to expansion at the lower levels does not compete with the one leading to contraction at the higher levels. Advancement at the lower levels leads to greater advancement at the higher levels. Thus, organizational conflict and oscillation is averted by diverting and channelling

Figure 11. Scaffolding and Transition of Dominance between tension-resolution system A and tension-resolution system B.

structural tension to different organizational levels where it can be used to move the organization towards success.

A similar approach can be applied to dealing with the second core structural conflict in ASEAN. Time orientation in ASEAN was found to be either extremely long term or very short term. The incompatibility between tension-resolution systems C and D gives rise to oscillation between periods of myopic short term orientation to periods of concentration on utopian long term goals based on broad principles. Going back to chapter 2, tension-resolution system C arises from the tension created by the discrepancy between the great number of emergencies, short term threats, and human insecurity, and the desire the amelioration of their negative externalities.

The difference between the actual state of human insecurity and the desired state gives rise to a short term orientation concentration on "fire fighting", amelioration of suffering, and emergency response. On the other hand macro level challenges and environmental factors such as the common regional challenges of globalization and great power intervention create tension for a long term time frame dealing with the long term goals of sustainable development and peace. Thus the output of tension-resolution system D is a very long term orientation based on broad principles and broad macro level goals.

In order to deal with the oscillation created by the competition of tension-resolution systems C and D a holistic systems approach is necessary. Short term local goals affect midterm management goals, which then influence organizational strategy, and ultimately help the organization attain its long term goals and fulfil its purpose. The main challenge in ASEAN's structural dynamics is the disconnect between long term goals and short term emergency responses. ASEAN deals with short term threats in a disjointed and uncoordinated manner (Ichihara, 2009; Peou, 2009).

The process is very similar to "fire fighting" in that the organization responds to the negative externalities created by human insecurity rather than attempting to tackle their root causes. On the other hand the organization attempts to achieve long term stability and development through the discussion of very long term broad projects which remain highly ambiguous and lack clear implementation guideline (ASEAN, 2009). There is a clear disconnect between how the organization deals with short term threats and how it tackles long term goals.

Returning to the principle of subsidiarity stating that local goals should support management goals, which turn should support strategy, and finally help achieve the organization's purpose, one can modify it to reflect time orientation rather than just organizational level. Short term goals should not only help ameliorate the immediate negative externalities of human insecurity but should also tackle some of its causes by supporting broader managerial goals. A realistic midterm strategy should integrate the previously mentioned managerial goals with the organization's long term purpose. Thus, since ASEAN's purpose is to promote stability and sustainable development in the region, the question should be "what midterm strategies can be used to promote stability and development?" Midterm strategies should tackle some of the root causes of human insecurity through a well integrated set of managerial goals. Those managerial goals should be supported by local goals and projects. In this way each short term action that is taken builds up to the long term goals and purpose of the organization.

For example when dealing with the negative externalities of Cyclone Nargis in Myanmar ASEAN could have not only tackled the immediate needs of the population for things such as food and shelter but also used the opportunity to establish effective emergency response centre in villages as well as prepared villages for self-sufficiency in order to survive the inevitable donor withdrawal after the immediate emergency was over (ASEAN, 2008a; JICA, 2008). In other words, the short term goal of dealing with the human insecurity brought about by a natural disaster such as cyclone Nargis could have been integrated in a midterm strategy of strengthening local civil society organizations to deal more effectively with emergency as well as support regional long term development and stability (Sen, 1999). The previous example shows that an effective midterm strategy, as well as the principle of subsidiarity, are the missing links necessary to overcome the structural oscillation brought about by the incompatibility of outcomes from tension-resolutions systems C and D.

Thus a long term time orientation is compatible with a

short and midterm time orientation as long as the different time orientations dominate different levels of the organization's goals and they are integrated properly through an effective midterm strategy. The importance of the interrelation between local goals and the organization's long term purpose and mission is emphasized by the principles of both structural dynamics and of a systems approach in general. Each local action can have an effect in the rest of the organization with the outcome of neutralizing success or of leading to greater success and ultimately to organizational advancement (Fritz, 1996). In order for ASEAN to overcome its second core structural conflict it must integrate short term emergency response with long term goals through the adoption of a realistic and concrete midterm strategy focusing on the main categories of human security, namely "freedom from want" and "freedom from fear". [1]

ASEAN's third core structural conflict can be broadly described as one characterized by fluctuation between periods of diffusion and periods of condensation. The terms diffusion and condensation were chosen instead of the more traditional ones of decentralization and centralization in order to include a broader range of phenomena. Diffusion in this case refers to decentralization in governance while condensation implies both centralization in terms of decision making as well as greater control over the flow of information. In the case of ASEAN waves of diffusion are followed by periods of retrenchment in the form of condensation.

Tension-resolution systems E and F in chapter 2 shows how the negative externalities of a highly centralized structure such as ossification and lack of flexibility gave rise to the desire for greater flexibility in order to foster greater grassroots participation as well as to take advantage of a broader range of resources in both the private and public sectors. The discrepancy between a reality marked by ASEAN's highly centralized structure in terms of the limited number of legitimate actors, mainly government officials, and limited flow of information (mostly official government reports), and a desire to increase the reach and effectiveness of the organization through the involvement of a wider array of actors and information led to the creation of several track II and some limited track III processes. Track II and track three processes involve a greater array of actors in the governance, broadly defined, of ASEAN.

Examples of this period of diffusion involve the creation of several panels made up of eminent persons (prominent academics and government officials serving in their private capacity), as well as more permanent consultative relationships with non-governmental forums such as the Council for Security in the Asia Pacific (CSCAP) which is co-chaired by an ASEAN member and a non-member and presents recommendations directly to the ASEAN Ministerial Meetings and Summits. CSCAP members are prominent academics and government officials serving in their private capacities (CSCAP, 2008). The inclusion of track II processes such as CSCAP increases the number of issues, information, and perspectives in ASEAN. Some attempts have also been made in order to include grassroots non-governmental organizations but with limited success. Very few non-governmental organizations have been given consultative status in ASEAN and their role and influence remains limited (Collins, 2008). Nevertheless, the step of acknowledging their existence is a sign of movement towards diffusion in terms of both decision-making and the flow of information.

After a while greater diffusion in terms of governance leads to some negative externalities such as a loss over control of information as well as towards an increased number of issues in discussion. Thus, diffusion increases not only the resources of the organization but also leads to some loss of control as well as towards greater complexity. Powerful stakeholders such as member governments then feel a desire for greater control over both decision making and the flow of information which leads to structural tension moving the organization towards condensation. Signs of this are the attempts of Vietnam and Myanmar to limit the input of non-governmental organizations dealing with human rights (Katanyuu, 2006; Vu-Tung, 2007). By reducing the number of actors who can legitimately introduce information into the organization, members can control the issues to be discussed and avoid those they do not want the organization to deal with.

It is very difficult to deal with the third core organizational conflict with limited political capital and a very diverse set of preferences among the member states of ASEAN. One ideal way to do it would be to institutionalize the input of track II and track III processes while at the same time allowing member states to keep some form of veto power over official resolutions. Furthermore, track III processes could be given consultative status in track II processes which would the present their recommendations and findings to both the general secretariat as well as to the pertinent ministerial meetings. This would control the flow of information without closing the gate to civil society organizations.

In addition to that, track II processes would add a reality check to popular recommendations and concerns and thus make them more palatable to government officials with very tight schedules and limited budgets. Thus, the information gathering capacity of ASEAN would be greatly enhanced if it were delegated to affiliated track II processes such as ASEAN-ISIS and CSCAP, inter alia. On the other hand, a more explicit veto capacity for member states combined with greater pressure from democratic member states may allow the organization to receive some information regarding sensitive issues such as security and human rights. Thus political capital and greater institutionalization would have to come hand in hand in order to redesign ASEAN in such as way as to overcome the structural conflict brought about by the discrepancy between a need for diffusion and condensation.

From the point of view of structural dynamics, the proposed solution would channel diffusion from the borders of the organization to its centre with the added value of the transformation of raw data gathered by track II processes by objective and highly trained experts in track II processes. This would eliminate the competition between the two tendencies of condensation and diffusion by relegating them to different levels of the organization and channelling the information and input in an efficient and constructive way.

Diffusion could continue flowing down from track II and track II processes by granting consultative status in track II processes to certain representative civil society organizations with a good track record and data gathering capabilities, small non-governmental organizations can then cooperate with those officially recognized NGOs in order to gather data and present recommendations. Thus, small organizations provide input for larger ones until the information reaches track II processes at which time the information is interpreted and packaged in a way that is useful for policy makers at official Ministerial Meetings and the Councils of the three Communities.

Needless to say this solution is not ideal in that there will be a certain degree of filtering undertaken at each stage and the input of certain groups could be drowned in the larger package, but taking into consideration the limited data gathering capability of ASEAN in addition to the fears of most member states regarding the inclusion of non-governmental organizations in ASEAN, this solution would solve the structural conflict and at the same time have a good chance of being implemented with a realistic amount of political capital.

ASEAN's Dispute Resolution System

Closely related to structural conflict is an organization's dispute resolution system. Chapter 1 provided an initial diagnosis of ASEAN's dispute resolution system and identified "consensus building" and avoidance as the two main methods used. This section of chapter 4 picks up where chapter 1 left in order to analyze some of the costs and benefits of ASEAN's present dispute resolution system as well as some ways in which the system can be improved without giving up its advantages.

Costs and Benefits of the "ASEAN Way"

This section explores the costs and benefits of the "ASEAN Way" by identifying some of the possible outcomes of consensus building and avoidance. Some of the outcomes lead to benefits while others lead to costs however it is important to note that the vast purview of the organizations makes it difficult to quantitatively calculate the net benefits or costs of the "ASEAN Way".

Avoidance

Avoidance refers to conflict management procedures leading to the filtering out of certain kinds of disputes (J.P. Folger, 2005; Louis Kriesberg, 2003; Pruitt & Kim, 2004; Schellenberg, 1996). This procedure can involve the immediate avoidance of a certain issue from discussion in ASEAN to other more subtle methods of avoidance such as the channelling of certain issues to powerless secondary committees and the subsequent delay and final ignorance of its findings. It should be noted that avoidance leads to both benefits and costs for ASEAN.

Among the benefits of avoidance are the maintenance of group cohesion and the projection of a unified front in the face of the external environment (ASEAN, 2009). Thus, avoidance has served the purpose of avoiding certain difficult internal conflicts such as those over territory and political persecution of opponents in favour of maintaining the unity of ASEAN and permitting the discussion of other issues while disagreeing on many important ones. This leads to improved communication between parties which may be in conflict over one issue while cooperating on many others. Cooperation on regional concerns such as terrorism and development can take place between members with serious disputes partly because of ASEAN's avoidance defence mechanism. Moreover, avoidance serves the purpose of filtering out disagreement so as to present a united front to the international community (Yzawa, 2006). Since most disagreements are avoided most official statements present agreement over principles and thus give the appearance of policy coherence and unity (ASEAN, 2008a, 2009).

Avoidance can also lead to important costs for ASEAN. Conflicts such as border disputes and serious abuses of human rights cannot be tackled by the organization in a timely manner due to the opposition of some member states favouring the principle of non-interference (Heller, 2005; Ichihara, 2009; Katanyuu, 2006; Narine, 1997). This leads to serious short and midterm costs during crises such as the military coup in Thailand in 2006 and the recurrent anti-democracy crackdowns in Myanmar (Chang, Chu, & Park, 2007; Keling, Saludin, von Feigenblatt, Ajis, & Shuib, 2010). Avoidance may hamper the possible role of the secretary general as a mediator or third party neutral in intraregional disputes (Jones & Smith, 2007; Severino, 2007). Even intergovernmental issues such as the border dispute between Thailand and Cambodia cannot be dealt with speedily enough to prevent deadly border skirmishes (Simon, 2008). Thus avoidance hampers the taking of decisive action by ASEAN to deal with short and midterm crises and threats.

Consensus

Consensus building is one of the oldest and most widespread conflict management methods in Asia and involves a long process of communication, indirect negotiation, face work, and subsequent reaching of an agreement based on the least common denominator (Augsburger, 1992; Ishida, 1984; LeBaron, 1998; Ting-Toomey, 1988). Principles are considered to be more important than details and agreements are never final but subject to revision due to changes in the environment and the individual circumstances of the parties (Nisbett, 2003). ASEAN's method of consensus building is surprisingly informal and protracted. Consensus building requires that all the parties be able to accept the general agreement. In order for this to happen it is often necessary to raise the level of abstraction and lower the specificity of the resulting agreement. The result is that very general agreements based on broad abstract principles are reached. It is important to note that the agreements reached have the legitimacy that every single member accepts it since all have a potential veto power.

It should be clear from the previous paragraph that one of the costs of consensus building is that it is very time consuming. This is one reason why ASEAN is not able to deal with crises in a timely fashion. Finding the lowest common denominator requires constant communication and indirect negotiation. Thus, consensus strengthens preventive diplomacy while it weakens ASEAN's ability to deal with sudden threats. Another cost created by consensus building is that agreements are difficult to implement due to their abstract and general nature. Specific details are avoided so as to reach consensus based on the lowest common denominator. This leads to problems in operationalizing the policy guidelines adopted by ASEAN. One example of this is the policy goals of building an ASEAN Socio-cultural community by 2020 found in the ASEAN Charter (ASEAN, 2008a, 2008b). Finally one other cost of consensus building is the veto power it affords some members. Since the agreement of every member is necessary to reach consensus, a single member can obstruct the process. This tactic has been used several times by Myanmar and Vietnam to force the avoidance of certain sensitive issues such as human rights and democratization (Peou, 2009; Simon, 2008).

Consensus building also leads to some benefits for ASEAN. Decisions reached by consensus have greater legitimacy than those reached by other methods such as majority voting since all members agree with the final agreement. Furthermore, consensus building encourages members to communicate more often with each other and to try to understand the needs and interests of their counterparts. Finally, consensus building allows ASEAN to issue official statements representing the agreement of all members and thus presenting a unified front to the outside world. By presenting a unified front ASEAN can increase the diplomatic clout and influence of Southeast Asian nations in the international community (Komori, 2009; Severino, 2007).

In summary, consensus building presents both benefits and costs to ASEAN. Consensus building is compatible with preventive diplomacy and long term development while being problematic for dealing with crises and short and midterm threats (ASEAN, 2008a; Heller, 2005; Nair, 2008; Tow, Thakur, & Hyun, 2000; Yzawa, 2006). It is difficult to ascertain whether the net results of consensus building in ASEAN's dispute resolution system has been positive or negative. Consensus building can strengthen certain important goals of the organization such as the role of engaging all countries in the region in an open process of regional integration. Preventive diplomacy is also strengthened by consensus building while ASEAN's capacity to deal with crises and short term threats is clearly diminished by it. Thus, it is important to deal with the costs of consensus building without giving up the benefits.

A New "ASEAN Way"

The present system involves a two step process in which informal negotiations based on a mix between rights and interests are immediately followed by rights based approaches (Collins, 2008). Thus, a dispute between two member countries is first discussed informally between the two members and if they fail to reach an agreement the issue is then brought to one of the Ministerial Meetings (ASEAN, 2009; Katanyuu, 2006; Narine, 1997, 1998). At that point the dispute is usually discussed through a rights based approach and due to the primacy of the non-interference principle, the dispute is either "lumped" by the aggrieved party or it is pursued through power based methods (von Feigenblatt, 2009b; Narine, 1997). The result is that the dispute is not resolved and that there are few steps involving the discussion of interests. Following the first principle of dispute resolution systems design it is important to focus on interests (W. L. Ury et al., 1993).

In order to emphasize interests over rights and power it is important to increase the opportunities of member and other stakeholders to use interest based procedures to deal with their disputes. At this point the only interest based procedure includes the brief informal negotiations before the Ministerial Meetings. Respecting the ethos of the "ASEAN Way" which requires the image of general consensus the interest procedures to be included should be low-key, confidential, and non-binding (ASEAN, 2008b; von Feigenblatt, 2009a; Jones & Smith, 2007). One procedure that satisfies all of the previous criteria is mediation by a respected third party after informal negotiations take place and before the issue is taken up to the organization's official forums such as the Ministerial Meetings. Low key mediation before the issue has been brought up in public will encourage the parties to focus on interests rather than on rights (von Feigenblatt, 2009c; LeBaron, 1998).

What kind of mediation and who will serve as a mediator? Due to the traditional emphasis of the "ASEAN Way" on communication and informal exchanges of views two different stages of mediation could be included in the process. After the initial informal negotiation between the two parties, one informal stage of mediation could take place with a member of the ASEAN Secretariat serving as the mediator (ASEAN, 2009). This first mediation effort would focus on reaching agreement on general principles in a confidential and low key manner with the help of the good offices of an insider. If no agreement is reached in this first stage of mediation, then the parties will be required to have another informal session of negotiations before the second more formal mediation stage. After this brief negotiation session the parties will be consulted by the secretariat regarding their dispute and their experience with the process up to that time and the parties will provide feedback.

Then a three member mediation team will be prepared including one high ranking member of the secretariat in Jakarta, one member of a pertinent Ministerial Meeting from a country of origin different from that of the two parties will be suggested by each party and both have to be accepted by the two parties before the actual mediation. The mediating team will then meet with each party separately to hear their views and would then undertake a more formal mediation session in the premises of the secretariat in Jakarta. Confidentiality would be assured and the two ministerial members will be allowed to introduce external resources to deal with the dispute if necessary. This means that they will be serving in their personal capacities, possibly as members of track II organizations such as CSCAP, but will be able to use their connections in order to secure resources or third party concessions that may ease the way to an agreement.

If agreement is reached then the mediating team will provide assistance to the parties to implement the agreement and only the final agreement and results of the implementation will be reported publicly in one of the official forums of ASEAN so as to maintain an image of internal consensus. Nevertheless, if agreement was not reached at this point, a third round of informal negotiations will take place between the parties and another internal report about the details of the dispute will be prepared. Then a final more formal session of med-arb will take place. This mediation-arbitration will make use of all of the information collected during the process and will issue a non-binding decision if no agreement is reached by the parties.

If an agreement is reached then it will be announced in an official forum as it if was reached by the parties themselves through consensus building, however if no agreement is reached then the parties will be given the choice to either issue a public statement and continue with the traditional process of submitting the dispute to one of the Ministerial Meetings or to pursue the dispute through a different venue. If the dispute is not resolved six months after either the conclusion of the med-arb process or its discussion in the Ministerial Meetings, then the secretariat in Jakarta will issue a public statement encouraging the parties to re-enter the dispute resolution process.

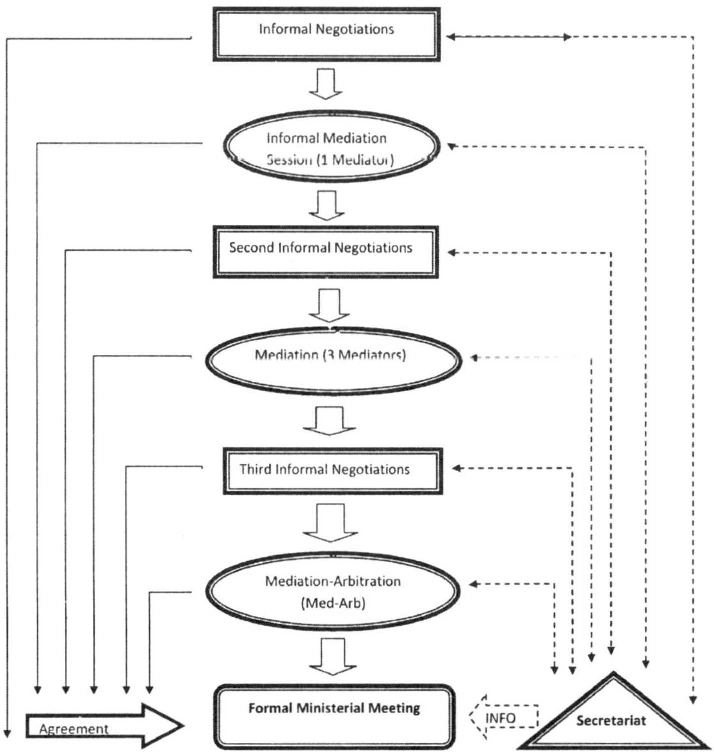

Figure 12. A New "ASEAN Way": Dotted lines represent information while bold lines stand for official statements and agreements.

New "ASEAN Way" and the Six Principles of Dispute Resolution Systems Design

The proposed system favours interest based processes over rights and power based ones. By emphasizing the use of mediation and negotiation at several stages of the process, the system encourages the parties to focus on interests (W. Ury, 1993; W. L. Ury et al., 1993). Moreover, the proposed new "ASEAN Way" includes a return to negotiations at several stages of the process. The dispute resolution process starts with negotiation, returns to it after the first attempt at mediation, and does so again after the second more formal mediation.

Thus, the system satisfies the second principle of dispute resolution systems design (W. L. Ury et al., 1993). In terms of providing the parties low cost power and rights based approaches, the new "ASEAN Way" introduces med-arb as the final stage of the process before formal proceedings at the Ministerial Level. Med-arb includes a rights based approach in that if no agreement is reached by the parties, the arbitrator issues a non-binding decision (Moore, 2003; Phillips, 2001). Med-arb tends to be more rights based than traditional mediation but since it is non-binding it is a low cost process for the parties. Its low key nature is also an advantage since the proceedings remain confidential.

In terms of consultations and feedback, the new "ASEAN Way" encourages the sharing of information and constant consultations with the secretariat since the early stages of the process. The parties are supposed to provide feedback to the secretariat after each substantive step and mediators/ASEAN officials are also supposed to engage in consultations with the parties both before and after each stage of the process. It is also clear from figure one that the process proceeds progressively from lowest cost processes to higher cost approaches. Thus informal negotiations present lower costs than a more formal med-arb session.

Finally, in terms of motivations, resources, and skills, the new "ASEAN Way" makes efficient use of the available resources. In terms of motivations, the parties are provided with the incentive to solve their disputes without staining their reputations and at a very low cost. The process makes good use of the skills of highly qualified members of the secretariat as well as other prominent members of the Ministerial Meetings in their private capacities (Pitsuwan, 2010; Severino, 2007). In terms of resources, the use of the premises of the secretariat in Jakarta lowers the possible costs involved in finding a suitable location for the proceedings. Thus, in summary the proposed dispute resolution system is very efficient in terms of use of resources and skills, and provides the necessary motivation for parties to use the system. Needless to say, some training in mediation and negotiation could be provided for members of the secretariat as well as for members of the Ministerial Meetings. This could be done at a very low cost through ASEAN's partnership with regional Universities and Strategic Studies Institutes.

Conclusions on the Proposed New "ASEAN Way"

The proposed new "ASEAN Way" respects the core aspects of the original "ASEAN Way" by emphasizing consensus building, confidentiality, and non-binding approaches (ASEAN, 2008b; Yzawa, 2006). Moreover, the new "ASEAN Way" strengthens the advantages of the traditional "ASEAN Way" while also dealing with some of its main drawbacks such as a lack of intermediate low cost methods of dealing with disputes. The present proposal is preliminary in that the timeframe for each stage of the process remains to be decided as well as the way in which the new system would be introduced to the members of the organization. It is recommended that the new procedures be tested in one functional area before being introduced on an organization wide scale.

Conclusions on Structural Conflicts in ASEAN

This chapter has taken a twin track approach to overcoming structural conflicts in ASEAN at a macro level. The three core structural conflicts identified in chapter 2 were explained and possible solutions were presented. A dispute resolution systems approach was also applied in order to complement structural dynamics and offer an alternative perspective on the way in which the main organizational conflicts handled by ASEAN can be solved constructively. It should be noted that the solutions provided in this chapter are tentative and deal with very broad issues at the macro structural level.

A few generalizations can be made from the solutions for the three core structural conflicts. The first is that the only way to overcome a structural conflict is through a redesign of the structural factors causing the discrepancy behind the conflict. In order words any attempt to eliminate structural oscillation involves a careful look at the tension-resolution systems giving rise to structural conflict and ultimately facilitating the flow of tension in a direction leading the organization towards advancement.

The flow of structural tension can be facilitated in a variety of ways ranging from diverting the tension in one tension-resolution system to a higher or lower hierarchical level or to adding an intermediate tension-resolution system linking two other systems. Synergy and organizational advancement is the goal and in order to achieve that, the parts have to work together to move the system towards achieving its purpose and mission. The next chapter summarizes the lessons learned from chapters 1, 2, and 3 by providing concrete examples from ASEAN. Structural dynamics' relationship to dispute systems design is also discussed in greater detail so as to show how one serves as the framework for the other.

End Note

1. Note that ASEAN does not use the term "human security" but rather the more traditional one of comprehensive security and non-traditional threats (ASEAN, 2009).

References

ASEAN. (2008a). *2007-2008 Annual Report: One Vision, One Identity, One Community*. Retrieved November 30, 2008. from http://www.aseansec.org/AR-08.pdf.

ASEAN. (2008b). *ASEAN Charter*. Retrieved November 30, 2008.

from http://www.aseansec.org/ASEAN-Charter.pdf.

ASEAN. (2009). *ASEAN POLITICAL-SECURITY COMMUNITY BLUEPRINT.* Retrieved July 28, 2010. from http://www.aseansec.org/5187-18.pdf.

Augsburger, D. W. (1992). *Conflict Mediation Across Cultures: Pathways and Patterns* (First ed.). Louisville: Westmister/John Knox Press.

Chang, Y.-t., Chu, Y.-h., & Park, C.-M. (2007). Authoritarian Nostalgia in Asia. *Journal of Democracy, 18*(3), 71-80.

Collins, A. (2008). A People-Oriented ASEAN: A Door Ajar or Closed for Civil Society Organizations? *Contemporary Southeast Asia, 30*(2), 313-332.

CSCAP. (2008). About Us. Retrieved July 29, 2010, from http://www.cscap.org/index.php?page=about-us.

von Feigenblatt, Otto F. (2009a). ASEAN and Human Security: Challenges and Opportunities. *Ritsumeikan Centre for Asia Pacific Studies Working Paper, No. 09-5*(July), 1-22.

von Feigenblatt, Otto F. (2009b). Comparing the 2006 Military Coup in Thailand and the 2009 Coup in Honduras: Internal Socio-political Similarities and External Normative Differences. *Infinity Journal, 1*(4), 3-9.

von Feigenblatt, Otto F. (2009c). Human Security and the Responsibility to Protect: A Holistic Approach to Dealing with Violent Conflict in Southeast Asia. In A.K. Pandey, S. Verma, R.P. Pathak, B. Paranjape, N. K. Mishra, Gangatharan, D. Pande & B.K. Choudhary (Eds.), *Repositioning 'Subalternity' in Globalized India: The Dynamics of Social Inclusion* (pp. 130). Delhi: Macmillan.

Fritz, R. (1996). *Corporate Tides: The Inescapable Laws of Organizational Structure* San Francisco: Berrett-Koehler Publishers

Goldsmith, M., Greenberg, C., Robertson, A., & Hu-Chan, M. (2003). *Global Leadership: The Next Generation* (Paperback ed.): FT Press.

Heller, D. (2005). The Relevance of the ASEAN Regional Forum (ARF) for Regional Security in the Asia-Pacific. *Contemporary Southeast Asia, 27* (1), 123-145.

Ichihara, M. (2009). East Asia's Challenges to and Changes in the Peace Operations in East Timor. In S. Peou (Ed.), *Human Security in East Asia: Challenges for Collaborative Action* (pp.

94-107). New York: Routledge.

Ishida, T. (1984). Conflict and Its Accomodation: Omote-Ura and Uchi-Soto Relations. In E. S. Krauss, T. P. Rohlen & P. G. Steinhoff (Eds.), *Conflict in Japan* (pp. 16-38). Honolulu: University of Hawaii Press.

J.P. Folger, M.S.P., R.K. Stutman. (2005). *Working Through Conflict: Strategies for Relationships, Groups, and Organizations* (5th ed.). New York: Pearson.

JICA. (2008, October 2008). Cleaning Up After Cyclone Nargis. *JICA News*. Retrieved December 17, 2008, from http://www.jica.go.jp/english/news/focus_on/myanmar/my_3.html

Jones, D.M., & Smith, M.L.R. (2007). Making Process, Not Progress ASEAN and the Evolving East Asian Regional Order. *International Security, 32*(1), 148-184.

Katanyuu, R. (2006). Beyond Non-Interference in ASEAN: The Association's Role in Myanmar's National Reconciliation and Democratization. *Asian Survey, 46*(6), 825-845.

Keling, M.F., Saludin, M.N., Feigenblatt, O.F. v., Ajis, M.N. e., & Shuib, M.S. (2010). A Historical Approach to Myanmar's Democratic Process. *Journal of Asia Pacific Studies, 1*(2), 132-148.

Komori, Y. (2009). Asia's Institutional Creation and Evolution. *Asian Perspective, 33*(3), 151-182.

Kriesberg, L. (1997). The Development of the Conflict Resolution Field. In *Peacemaking, in International Conflict: Methods & Techniques* (pp. 51-77). Washington, D.C.: U.S. Institute of Pece Press.

Kriesberg, L. (2003). *Constructive Conflicts: From Escalation to Resolution* (Second ed.). New York: Rowman & Littlefield.

LeBaron, M. (1998). Mediation and Multicultural Reality [Electronic Version]. *Peace and Conflict Studies*, *5*. Retrieved September 15, 2009, from http://www.gmu.edu/academic/pcs/lebaron.htm

Moore, C. W. (2003). *The Mediation Process: Practical Strategies for Resolving Conflict* (3rd ed.). San Francisco: Jossey-Bass.

Nair, D. (2008). Regionalism in the Asia Pacific/East Asia: A Frustrated Regionalism? *Contemporary Southeast Asia, 31*(1), 110–142.

Narine, S. (1997). ASEAN and the ARF: The Limits of the "ASEAN Way". *Asian Survey, 37*(10), 961-978.

Narine, S. (1998). ASEAN and the Management of Regional Security. *Pacific Affairs, 71*(2), 195-214.

Nisbett, R.E. (2003). *The Geography of Thought: How Asians and Westerners Thing Differently...and Why* (1st Paperback ed.). New York: Free Press.

Peou, S. (Ed.). (2009). *Human Security in East Asia: Challenges for Collaborative Action*. New York: Routledge.

Phillips, B.A. (2001). *The Mediation Field Guide: Transcending Litigation and Resolving Conflicts in Your Business or Organization* (First ed.). San Francisco: Jossey-Bass.

Pitsuwan, S. (2010). ASEAN central to the region's future. *East Asia Forum Quarterly, 2*(2), 4-5.

Pruitt, D., & Kim, S.H. (2004). *Social Conflict: Escalation, Stalemate and Settlement* (3rd ed.). New York: McGraw Hill.

Schellenberg, J.A. (1996). *Conflict Resolution: Theory, Research, and Practice*. New York: State University of New York Press.

Sen, A. (1999). *Development as Freedom*. New York: Anchor Books.

Severino, R.C. (2007). ASEAN Beyond Forty: Towards Political and Economic Integration. *Contemporary Southeast Asia, 23*(3), 406-423.

Simon, S. (2008). ASEAN and Multilateralism: The Long, Bumpy Road to Community. *Contemporary Southeast Asia, 30*(2), 264-292.

Ting-Toomey, S. (1988). Intercultural Conflict Styles: A Face-Negotiation Theory. In Y. Kim & W. Gudykunst (Eds.), *Theories in Intercultural Communication* (pp. 214-234). Beverly Hills, CA: Sage Publications.

Tow, W.T., Thakur, R., & Hyun, I.-T. (Eds.). (2000). *Asia's emerging regional order: Reconciling traditional and human security*. Tokyo: United Nations University Press.

Ury, W. (1993). *Getting Past No: Negotiating Your Way From Confrontation to Cooperation* (Paperback ed.). New York: Bantam Books.

Vu-Tung, N. (2007). Vietnam's Membership of ASEAN: A Constructivist Interpretation. *Contemporary Southeast Asia, 29*(3), 483-505.

Yzawa, T. (2006). The Evolution of Preventive Diplomacy in the ASEAN Regional Forum: Problems and Prospects. *Asian Survey, 46*(5), 785-804.

4

ASEAN and Conflicts: Conclusions

Dealing with conflict is at the heart of ASEAN's original mission and purpose. The challenges of the Cold War and the bumpy process of decolonization gave rise to a desire for peace and stability in the region (Neher, 2002). Most of the early treaties and agreements deal with issues of international security and conflict such as the South East Asian Nuclear Weapon-Free Zone (SEANWFZ) Treaty and the Treaty of Amity and Cooperation (TAC) (ASEAN, 2009; Narine, 1997). Both treaties deal with international security and have the broad goals of security and stability in the region. ASEAN's early successes were also in the field of international security such as its role in the Cambodian crisis and the subsequent Vietnamese invasion (Narine, 1998). The organization was also active in fostering greater cooperation between the formerly antagonistic states of Indonesia, Singapore, and Malaysia (Yzawa, 2006). Thus regional security and dispute resolution were at the core of ASEAN's mission since its formative decades.

This chapter provides a closer look at ASEAN's role in the fields of security and conflict resolution in the Asia Pacific region. Rather than concentrate only on instances of direct action taken by ASEAN, this chapter takes a broader approach which includes its role in regional integration and in fostering regional dialogue. At the same time some of the challenges ASEAN faces in terms of bringing about its goal of building a Political-Security Community in the near future are also discussed. Finally, the chapter discusses ASEAN's regional role in security and some possible directions it might take in the near future.

ASEAN's Political-Security Community

Southeast Asia has experienced some of the bloodiest conflicts in the 20th century and continues to host several ethnic separatist insurgencies. In addition to that traditional security issues such as border disputes continue to play an important part in the region's diplomatic environment (Akaha, 2009; Neher, 2002). Southeast Asia was also an important battleground during the Cold War and due to this, regional governments attempted to turn the region into a neutral zone (Mulder, 1996; Rolfe, 2008). Several attempts at doing so, include the original Treaty of Amity and Cooperation which served as one of the founding documents of ASEAN and declares the neutrality of the region and marks the establishment of the organization itself (Severino, 2007).

The establishment of the South East Asian Nuclear Weapon-Free Zone (SEANWFZ) Treaty was a concrete step toward the twin goals of stability and peace in the region. Other attempts include the promotion of extra-regional dialogue with Pacific and East Asian powers through mechanisms such as ASEAN + 3 and the East Asian Summit (Simon, 2008). The ASEAN Regional Forum (ARF) is another ambitious attempt to tackle security in the Asia Pacific in a first track venue (Narine, 1997).

Nevertheless, the most ambitious plan in the field of security is the planned Political-Security Community. As one of the three pillars of the future ASEAN Community included in the Declaration of ASEAN Concord II approved in 2003, it attempts to tackle some of the main weaknesses of the original organization (ASEAN, 2009). ASEAN's track record in dealing with traditional security issues and political ones such as the promotion of the rule of law and human rights is not very impressive (Ichihara, 2009; Katanyuu, 2006). The respect of sovereignty and the principle of non-interference enshrined in the "ASEAN way" in addition to the expansion of membership to authoritarian states such as Laos, Myanmar, and Vietnam make progress in these issues difficult and slow

(Jones & Smith, 2007; Katanyuu, 2006; Keling, Saludin, Feigenblatt, Ajis, & Shuib, 2010; Vu-Tung, 2007).

Notwithstanding the possible difficulties, ASEAN members realized that tackling traditional security issues and some related issues of governance would not only be advantageous in the path towards peace and development but also increasingly important in terms of attracting foreign direct investment and promoting economic growth. Thus, ASEAN was forced to deal with security and politics through the gradual steps described in the Blueprint for an ASEAN Political-Security Community (ASEAN, 2009).

It should be noted that the ASEAN Political-Security Community is meant to deal mostly with "freedom from fear" and that the concept of comprehensive security is favoured over others such as human security and the responsibility to protect (Ichihara, 2009; Yzawa, 2006). This reflects the fears of some members regarding the possible weakening of the norm of non-interference (Jones & Smith, 2007; Narine, 1997). Thus the proposed ASEAN Political-Security Community is a very ambitious project including governance, traditional security, and human rights.

The Blueprint claims that "the APSC will ensure that the peoples and Member States of ASEAN live in peace with one another and with the world at large in a just, democratic and harmonious environment" and on the political front that it "shall promote political development in adherence to the principles of democracy, the rule of law and good governance, respect for and promotion and protection of human rights" (ASEAN, 2009, p. 5). ASEAN's tendency of concentrating on broad principles and goals is clearly present in its description of the twin goals of the proposed Political-Security Community (Feigenblatt, 2009a, 2009b, 2010).

ASEAN's blueprint for the Political-Security Community places considerable emphasis on the strengthening of international norms as well as on the improvement of basic governance at the national level. One example of this is section

A which deals with the goal of building a "Rules-based Community of Shared Values and Norms" (ASEAN, 2009, p. 6). The implied process is one in which member states are socialized into the norms of the "ASEAN Way" and thus renounce aggression voluntarily rather than through more interventionist means.

It should be noted that the Blueprint is a very ambitious document with broad goals ranging from establishing a Human Rights organism to improving governance through human capital development. Nevertheless most goals reflect ideal principles and the sub-goals and implementation plans remain murky. One example of this is the proposed human rights organism for which the points of reference defining human rights are to be agreed on a later date (ASEAN, 2009; Suharto, 2009). Without even a basic standard the proposed organism is nothing more than an empty shell useful simply as a rhetorical device. As explained in previous chapters, goals such as the promotion of democracy and the protection of human rights in the region are not properly operationalized by ASEAN which leads to a disjointed purpose in relation to actual actions at the local level (Ichihara, 2009).

Section A.1.1 is a good example of the lofty goals with very weak implementation plans. This section presents the goal of promoting "understanding and appreciation of political systems, culture, and history" (ASEAN, 2009, p. 7). The sub-goals of section A.1.1. include such diverse issues as holding track two academic conferences, seminars on democratic experience, the promotion of gender equity, and the compilation of best practices in terms of elections. It is very interesting that the previously mentioned goals are coupled together with an emphasis on greater tolerance and understanding for cultural and historical differences. It is clear that a certain degree of cultural relativism was included so as to weaken and dampen the effort to promote democratic norms based on international best practices.

Probably one of the few sections with a clear

implementation plan is section A.1.7 which deals with fighting corruption. Rather than attempting to reach agreement on a particular ASEAN code containing unique terms of reference, the Blueprint recommends member states to sign and ratify the United Nations Convention against Corruption (ASEAN, 2009, p.10). Having an existing convention saves the organization a lot of time and provides a clear way to implement the goal of eliminating corruption in the region. This is an example of a middle level strategy provided by the United Nations which help bridge the lofty goals of the Blueprint and the local action that is needed in order to bring the desired changes about.

Norms are prominent in section A.1.9 dealing with the promotion of peace and stability in the region (ASEAN, 2009, p. 10). Curricular design at the university level is deemed important in imparting values of peace and tolerance. Interethnic dialogue is also recommended through peace education in schools throughout the region. This section concludes that narrowing the development gap not only within but also between member states is necessary for long term peace and stability. Thus, section A.1.9 shows considerable constructivist influence in the emphasis placed on norms and values.

In the area of traditional security, the Blueprint favours confidence building efforts and preventive diplomacy (ASEAN, 2009, p. 12). Both types of conflict management measures are considered to be some of the weakest forms of conflict management (Feigenblatt, 2009c). Nevertheless, ASEAN plans to move slowly toward more active forms of conflict management such as mediation and peacemaking. The lack of political will to tackle actual conflicts even after the negative international reaction to ASEAN's incapacity to deal with the East Timor crisis, shows that some member states favour regime survival over regional stability (Ichihara, 2009). Confidence building measures are very broad and ambiguous including greater communication between governments, cooperation in other areas such as protecting the sea lanes. Preventive diplomacy implies greater dialogue about real security issues at the diplomatic level. It is still a weak form of conflict management but it is still more forceful than confidence building measures (Yzawa, 2006).

Section B.2.2 provides some possible actions to be taken in order to promote the pacific settlements of disputes and includes the exploration of mechanisms such as conciliation, mediation, and arbitration. Therefore, the flexible proposal presented in chapter 3 is compatible with the framework agreed on in the Blueprint. Point vii of section B.2.2. is particularly promising and recommends developing a "pool of experts from ASEAN Member States as resource persons to assist in conflict management and conflict resolution activities" (ASEAN, 2009, p. 14).

The proposed pool of experts could help fill in the gaps left at the political level with concrete projects aimed at operationalizing the goals of peace and stability in the region. This could be done in cooperation with a track two forum such as the Council for Security and Cooperation in the Asia Pacific (CSCAP) (CSCAP, 2008; Heller, 2005). Moreover, having a group of highly qualified experts in the field of conflict resolution available at all times could help defuse tensions at an early stage rather than having to deal with the dispute after open conflict is present.

Post-conflict Peace-building is the topic of section B.3. which includes humanitarian assistance and long term development after conflict (ASEAN, 2009, p. 15). ASEAN is very weak in this area and the blueprint provides few concrete steps on how to strengthen the organization's present capacity to undertake humanitarian assistance.

The few concrete steps and recommendations such as the repatriation of refugees is qualified by the need to consult the host country at all times and to request its permission for humanitarian activities. Furthermore, the responsibility to provide humanitarian assistance is shifted to the United

Nations by recommending the intensification of cooperation with the United Nations and other organizations (ASEAN, 2009, p.15).

In the area of non-traditional threats two broad categories are emphasized; namely terrorism and organized crime (ASEAN, 2009, p.17). Fighting drug trafficking, crime syndicates, and smuggling are identified as possible areas of cooperation through an increased exchange of information as well as through building capacity through training. Cooperation on border management is a local goal that helps tackle both organized crime and terrorism. The blueprint also recommends member states to accede to and ratify the ASEAN Convention on Counter-Terrorism (ACCT) and other related international treaties (ASEAN, 2009, p. 17).

Overall, the blueprint for the Political-Security Community is a very ambitious document. A wide range of issues are discussed and broad principles regarding their implementation are presented. It should be noted that the structural conflicts identified in previous chapters of this book are clearly present in the blueprint. A desire to deal with human rights and political development is balanced with a strong insistence on the continued primacy of the norm of non-intervention and sovereignty. Moreover, the desire for integration is also opposed by the undercurrent favouring the protection of individual "national" interests to the detriment of the interests of the region as a block. The result is a very contradictory document with strong protection for sovereignty while at the same time a strong undercurrent of humanitarian values.

ASEAN's Regional Role in Security

Notwithstanding ASEAN's contradictory statements regarding its Political-Security Community, the organization has an important role to play in regional security. First of all, ASEAN's central role in the promotion of regionalism in the Asia Pacific makes the organization a central node in the complex web of bilateral and multilateral regional arrangements (Komori, 2009; Narine, 1998). Other than APEC, most other regional multilateral organizations have an ASEAN core. Examples include the ASEAN Regional Forum (ARF), the East Asian Summit, ASEAN Plus Three, as well as second track processes such as the Council for Security and Cooperation in the Asia Pacific (CSCAP). All of the previous organizations have a common ASEAN core which includes not only the physical organization of meetings but more importantly includes the normative framework behind the many complementary processes (Narine, 1998; Pitsuwan, 2010).

A good example of this is the nature of the ARF. The ARF is a first track forum that operates in between traditional intergovernmental forums such as the Ministerial Meetings of ASEAN and cooperates with second track processes such as CSCAP (Collins, 2008; CSCAP, 2008; Narine, 1997). With a broad membership and a wide mandate, the ARF finds a balance between the ASEAN Way's emphasis on non-interference and respect for sovereignty by allowing governmental representation on an individual rather than on an officially representative basis. In other words, representatives to the ARF are government officials who participate in their private capacities. This allows the ARF to discuss issues that would never be discussed in more traditional first track meetings such as the Ministerial Meetings of ASEAN. At the same time, having governmental officials eases the flow of information back to the participating countries. The process also socializes regional officials into a culture of cooperation and openness.

While the ARF does allow for a greater array of issues to be discussed it shows even fewer concrete results than other related organizations such as the Ministerial Meetings, thus opening it to allegations that it is just a "talk shop" (Jones & Smith, 2007). Nevertheless the role it plays in terms of socialization of government officials, the improvement of communication, and the easing in the sharing of information, should not be overlooked. Therefore, the ARF is an important node in the flow of security information in the Asia Pacific region.

ASEAN's broad mandate can also prove to be an advantage in dealing with regional security in that it allows log rolling and tradeoffs rather than presenting problems as zero sum issues. For example two countries may have a boundary dispute but also conduct considerable trade with each other. Discussing the border dispute in ASEAN may be useful in that the organization deals with both security and trade and thus helps put the individual particular dispute in a wider context. This simple mechanism prevents disputes from becoming intractable and allows government officials to use log rolling as a way to avoid difficult issues. For example an important trade deal may convince a neighbouring country to put off dealing with a historical border dispute. Thus, ASEAN's broad mandate emphasizes the interdependence of the region and of its many challenges.

ASEAN's regional role will also include crisis prevention and humanitarian assistance. Only ASEAN has the regional knowledge and connections in order to overcome some of the possible challenges to crisis prevention and humanitarian assistance in Southeast Asia. It is easier for regional government to accept some kind of temporary intervention from a trusted regional organization than from outside actors such as the great powers or even the United Nations. Thus it is imperative for ASEAN to strengthen this aspect of its role through greater cooperation with the private sector and local non-governmental organizations (Collins, 2008).

Conclusions

Part I of this study has dealt with the major structural conflicts present in ASEAN as well as with the organization's role in securing the peace and stability of the region. Conflict is an integral part of any organization and should not be considered as something negative which is to be avoided but rather as energy waiting to be constructively harnessed in the desired direction. Important challenges remain in order to deal with ASEAN's many structural conflicts. Opportunities are also present to take advantage of the organization's pivotal role in regional integration in order to strengthen its role in regional security and peace.

ASEAN is central to the region's peace and stability but important reforms are needed in order for the organization to achieve its potential. The "ASEAN Way" has to be modified in order to enable it to deal with non-traditional security threats as well as human rights issues. In addition to that, the internal conflict management system of the organization has to be revamped so as to emphasize negotiation and cooperation while at the same time avoiding breaking down ASEAN's external coherence and consensus.

In terms of the future role of the ASEAN Political-Security Community, mid-term goals and plans should be properly operationalized so as to avoid some of the pitfalls identified in previous chapters of this study in relation to a disconnection between principles and local actions. Relatively straight forward issues such as agreeing on the terms of reference for a human rights body have reached an impasse and left plans in the drawing board. Two possible approaches can be followed, a minimalist one, or a maximalist one. At a minimum unrealistically ambitious plans, which clearly lack the political capital to be implemented should be eliminated for the time being; so that the resources of the organization can be channelled to those projects with a chance of succeeding.

On the other hand, a maximalist approach, would concentrate on permeating the entire organization with the nascent norms favouring a broadening of the activities of the organization and thus foster greater political capital in favour of controversial measures such as the human rights body. Both possible approaches have advantages and disadvantages and are not necessarily incompatible. A layering approach such as the one presented in previous chapters in relation to a hierarchy of goals can be applied while at the same time fostering normative change in the organization as a whole.

References

Akaha, T. (2009). Human Security in East Asia. *Journal of Human Security, 5*(3), 11-34.

ASEAN. (2009). *ASEAN POLITICAL-SECURITY COMMUNITY BLUEPRINT.* Retrieved July 28, 2010. from http://www.aseansec.org/5187-18.pdf.

Collins, A. (2008). A People-Oriented ASEAN: A Door Ajar or Closed for Civil Society Organizations? *Contemporary Southeast Asia, 30*(2), 313-332.

CSCAP. (2008). About Us. Retrieved July 29, 2010, from http://www.cscap.org/index.php?page=about-us

von Feigenblatt, Otto F. (2009a). ASEAN and Human Security: Challenges and Opportunities. *Ritsumeikan Centre for Asia Pacific Studies Working Paper, No. 09-5*(July), 1-22.

von Feigenblatt, Otto F. (2009b). Human Security and the Responsibility to Protect: A Holistic Approach to Dealing with Violent Conflict in Southeast Asia. In A. K. Pandey, S. Verma, R.P. Pathak, B. Paranjape, N.K. Mishra, Gangatharan, D. Pande & B.K. Choudhary (Eds.), *Repositioning 'Subalternity' in Globalized India: The Dynamics of Social Inclusion* (pp. 130). Delhi: Macmillan.

von Feigenblatt, Otto F. (2009c). International Policymaking: The Case of the Norm of the Responsibility to Protect. *Ritsumeikan Centre for Asia Pacific Studies Working Paper, No. 09-6*(July), 1-11.

von Feigenblatt, Otto F. (2010). *Human Security in the Asia Pacific Region: Security Challenges, Regional Integration, and Representative Case Studies* (Hardcover ed.). Jaipur: YKING BOOKS.

Heller, D. (2005). The Relevance of the ASEAN Regional Forum (ARF) for Regional Security in the Asia-Pacific. *Contemporary Southeast Asia, 27*(1), 123-145.

Ichihara, M. (2009). East Asia's Challenges to and Changes in the Peace Operations in East Timor. In S. Peou (Ed.), *Human Security in East Asia: Challenges for Collaborative Action* (pp. 94-107). New York: Routledge.

Jones, D.M., & Smith, M.L.R. (2007). Making Process, Not Progress ASEAN and the Evolving East Asian Regional Order. *International Security, 32*(1), 148-184.

Katanyuu, R. (2006). Beyond Non-Interference in ASEAN: The Association's Role in Myanmar's National Reconciliation and Democratization. *Asian Survey, 46*(6), 825-845.

Keling, M.F., Saludin, M.N., von Feigenblatt, Otto F. , Ajis, M. N. e., & Shuib, M.S. (2010). A Historical Approach to Myanmar's Democratic Process. *Journal of Asia Pacific Studies, 1*(2), 132-148.

Komori, Y. (2009). Asia's Institutional Creation and Evolution. *Asian Perspective, 33*(3), 151-182.

Mulder, N. (1996). *Inside Southeast Asia: Religion, Everyday Life, and Cultural Change.* Chiang Mai: Silkworm Books.

Narine, S. (1997). ASEAN and the ARF: The Limits of the "ASEAN Way". *Asian Survey, 37*(10), 961-978.

Narine, S. (1998). ASEAN and the Management of Regional Security. *Pacific Affairs, 71*(2), 195-214.

Neher, C.D. (2002). *Southeast Asia in the New International Era.* Boulder: Westview Press.

Pitsuwan, S. (2010). ASEAN central to the region's future. *East Asia Forum Quarterly, 2*(2), 4-5.

Rolfe, J. (2008). Regional Security for the Asia-Pacific: Ends and Means. *Contemporary Southeast Asia, 30*(1), 99-117.

Severino, R.C. (2007). ASEAN Beyond Forty: Towards Political and Economic Integration. *Contemporary Southeast Asia, 23*(3), 406-423.

Simon, S. (2008). ASEAN and Multilateralism: The Long, Bumpy Road to Community. *Contemporary Southeast Asia, 30*(2), 264-292.

Suharto, E. (2009). Social Protection Systems in ASEAN: Social Policy in a Comparative Analysis. *Social Development Issues, 31*(1), 1.

Vu-Tung, N. (2007). Vietnam's Membership of ASEAN: A Constructivist Interpretation. *Contemporary Southeast Asia, 29*(3), 483-505.

Yzawa, T. (2006). The Evolution of Preventive Diplomacy in the ASEAN Regional Forum: Problems and Prospects. *Asian Survey, 46*(5), 785-804.

Part II
Socio-economic Development and Regional Trade in ASEAN

Part II deals with trade and development in ASEAN. The first chapter of the second section of the book, chapter 5, provides a broad introduction to socio-economic development in Southeast Asia. Chapter 6 concentrates on some of the barriers to economic integration such as trade barriers. Structural dynamics is applied to trade and to the regional economy in chapter 7 of section two. Finally, chapter 8 delineates some broad trends as well as explaining the conclusions reached in terms of ASEAN's development and regional trade.

Taking into consideration that economic development and integration has been and continues to be one of the most important goals of ASEAN, section two of this book explores some of the major obstacles towards attaining the goals delineated in the association's Blue Book for the ASEAN Economic Community.

5

Socio-economic Development in Southeast Asia: An Overview

This chapter provides a broad overview of socio-economic development in Southeast Asia. The first section of the chapter introduces the theoretical framework used in this book to analyze and explain development. Amatya Sen's definition of "development as freedom" is complemented by the broad paradigm of human development espoused by the United Nations Development Project (UNDP) (MacFarlane & Khong, 2006; Sen, 1999). Member countries' level of socio-economic development is then explained and discussed in order to identify important challenges to be overcome. Finally, the socio-economic development of the region is discussed in a wider context so as to describe the wider economic environment in which ASEAN has to operate.

Introduction

One of ASEAN's most important pillars has always been economic integration and development (ASEAN, 2008). Needless to say, development was originally viewed narrowly as simply economic growth, however that definition was later expanded to the development of human capital as well as to other aspects of social development (Neher, 2002). Today ASEAN has an impressive aggregate GDP of US$ 3,431 billion and a total population of approximately 577 million (Pitsuwan, 2010).

ASEAN includes some of the most dynamic economies in the world such as Singapore and Malaysia, as well as some of the poorest countries such as Laos and Cambodia. In terms of production, ASEAN produces a wide range of products ranging from staple agricultural products such as jasmine rice and fruits to cars and textiles (Heidhues, 2000; Neher, 2002). Parts of Southeast Asia are highly developed and characterized by considerable population density and urbanization such as Bangkok, Jakarta, and other big cities. On the other hand the countryside in most of Southeast Asia remains underdeveloped.

Differences cannot only be found between countries but they are present within the countries themselves. This aspect of uneven development is called asynchronous development and refers to the difference rates of development between the different regions of a country.

Theoretical Framework

Development is a very broad concept that has been given hundreds of different definitions by scholars and practitioners (Sen, 1999). The classical definition of development defined it as economic growth. Modernization theory then complemented the classical emphasis on economic growth with other socio-political aspects such as education, urbanization, and greater democracy. This book adopts a broader and more people cantered view of development based on the work of the Nobel Prize winning economics, Prof. Amartya Sen and the UNDP's concept of human development (MacFarlane & Khong, 2006; Sen, 1999).

Sen redefined development as "freedom" and emphasized the importance of capabilities rather than just resources (Sen, 1999). Modernization theory concentrated on resources and growth, thus ignoring the growing gap between the rich and the poor (von Feigenblatt, 2010a). Sen's view of development stresses the importance of people in the development process. According to this view the most important thing in development is for people to have the ability to do what they want to do. It is about potential.

In order for people to have the "freedom to" do something there are certain factors that are necessary. First of all basic needs must be covered which include health, adequate food, and a minimum level of education. Without those basic needs a person is not able to fulfil their full potential and development cannot take place. In other words, without those things a person is not truly free to do something that is important to them. This concept is very similar to Johann Galtung's concept of positive peace and greatly differs from the free market approach emphasized by modernization theory (Galtung, 1969).

Human development is a concept that was developed and promoted inside the United Nations by the UNDP (Battersby & Siracusa, 2009). The concept reframes development as cantered on the individual rather than the state and also widens the number of factors required to measure development. Education, gender equity, income distribution, and health are just some of the many factors that are included in the concept of human development (UNDP, 2009b). As a way to operationalize and measure human development, the UNDP developed an index. The Human Development Index is calculated for each country on a yearly basis and serves as a very useful guide for policymakers and scholar for measuring development broadly defined and for identifying areas that need work.

This chapter combines the two concepts in order to deal with both quantitative and qualitative aspects of development in the member states of ASEAN. The concept of development as freedom is very useful in understanding some of the challenges faced by ASEAN and provides a good diagnostic framework for possible interventions. On the other hand the human development index serves as a handy measuring stick to compare the member countries with each other as well as the region as a whole with the rest of the world.

The following section provides a brief overview of the socio-economic development of the member states of ASEAN.

Country	GDP	GDP per capita	Life Expectancy	Total Literacy rate	Human Development Index
Indonesia	$539.4 billion	$4,000	71.05	90.4%	0.600
Malaysia	$193 billion	$13,800	73.55	88.7%	0.744
The Philippines	$161.2 billion	$3,300	71.38	92.6%	0.638
Singapore	$182.2 billion	$53,900	82.06	92.5%	0.846
Thailand	$264 billion	$8,100	75.02	92.6%	0.654
Brunei	$10.41 billion	$49,900	75.96	92.7%	0.805
Burma	$34.26 billion	$1,100	64.52	89.9%	0.451
Laos	$5.598 billion	$2,300	62.00	73.0%	0.497
Vietnam	$93.16 billion	$2,900	71.94	90.3%	0.572
Cambodia	$10.87 billion	$2,000	62.28	73.6%	

Figure 13. Basic Development Indicators for ASEAN Member States

Republic of Indonesia

With a population of about two hundred and twenty million, Indonesia is the third largest democracy in the world, is home to the largest Muslim population, and is the most populous country in ASEAN (CIA, 2010e). Indonesia was a Dutch colony since the 16th century, was briefly occupied by the Japanese during World War II, and later on joined the non-aligned movement after independence (Heidhues, 2000). After a brief attempt at socialism, the post Sukarno leadership adopted the development strategy of import substitution with heavy emphasis on industrialization (Neher, 2002). President Suharto followed a centralized development model with a heavy reliance on government intervention in the economy through ownership of strategic industries and through planning. The strategy was successful in displacing agriculture with industry as the number one source of GDP. Currently Indonesia is considered to be a middle ranked country in terms of human development (UNDP, 2009b). Indonesia's economy represents a large proportion of that of ASEAN and its natural resources fuel the economic growth of major East Asian economies such as Japan and South Korea.

In terms of the general structure of the economy, 15.3 percent of the GDP derives from agriculture, 47.6 percent from industry, and 37.1 percent from services (CIA, 2010e). It is clear that the Indonesian economy is slowly moving from an emphasis on heavy industry to services such as tourism. Nevertheless as look at the distribution of labour by sector gives a better picture of this trend. 42.6 percent of the population is employed in agriculture, 39.3 percent in services, and only 18.6 percent in industry (CIA, 2010e). This shows that while industry is a major contributor to GDP, it is capital intensive and thus contributes relatively little to alleviating the country's unemployment (7.7 percent) and underemployment problem. Poverty is also related to the distribution of labour and about 17 percent of the population lives under the poverty line (CIA, 2010e; UNDP, 2009b).

The years of import substitution and the crony capitalism of the Suharto period gave rise to sharp economic inequality in Indonesia which was further aggravated by the 1997 Asian Financial Crisis (Trinidad, 2010). The instability brought about by the economic crisis in addition to internal pressures for democratization led to the fall of the Suharto regime. During the Suharto regime the military was involved in almost all sectors of the economy and this intervention was justified with the theory of "double function" (Glassman, 2005). This means that the Indonesian army had a double function, security and promoting national development. The transition to democracy brought about some changes in this respect but no widespread redistribution of wealth took place.

Indonesia's economy has reoriented itself towards the free market and export led growth (Trinidad, 2010). Most exports, however, continue to be primary commodities such as wood and other natural resources. The problem with this is that primary commodities have very little value added and their prices fluctuate in the global market. On the other hand, the gradual opening of the Indonesian market to foreign competition has put a lot of pressure on national industries to perform at an international level. Globalization and greater competition has also exacerbated unemployment in the rural and industrial sectors while creating most jobs in the service sector. This socio-economic shift has put considerable strain on traditional Indonesian culture and formed a highly volatile mix when combined with high population growth and unemployment (von Feigenblatt, 2009b; Glassman, 2005).

In terms of foreign direct investment and tourism, Indonesia is plagued by several insurgencies as well as several fundamentalist groups such as Jeemah Islamiyah (von Feigenblatt, 2009b). The previously mentioned threats have created a pervasive feeling of insecurity and thus deprived the country of considerable business opportunities. The Bali Bombing episode in which a suicide bomber blew himself up in a hotel is just on dramatic example of this insecurity. Finally, the increasing power of Islamic political parties and associations in the Indonesian political scene further exacerbate the situation (Singh, 2008-2009).

In terms of other social development indicators Indonesia is ranked much better than in terms of overall macroeconomic performance. Its population has a relatively high education level as attested by a literacy rate of about 90 percent of the adult population (CIA, 2010e). In terms of life expectancy, Indonesia ranks 137 with a life expectancy at birth of almost 71 years.

Nevertheless the government spends only 3.6 percent of its GDP in education reflecting a skewed priority towards military spending which accounts for 3 percent of the GDP (CIA, 2010e). An easier way to understand the spending priorities of Indonesia is by noting that it ranks 47th in terms of military spending and 127th in terms of education (CIA, 2010e).

The Human Development Index for Indonesia is of 0.734 placing it in the 111th place just below the Occupied Palestinian Territories (UNDP, 2009b). In terms of GDP per capita, Indonesia ranks 121th with US$ 3,712. The difference in the ranking shows that Indonesia's main development concern has been economic growth rather than human development. Support for the previous claim is that the Philippines has a higher human development index while having a considerably lower GDP per capita (UNDP, 2009b).

Thus, Indonesia faces considerable challenges in terms of poverty and other important factors of human development such as gender inequality.

Overall, Indonesia represents one of the largest but relatively least successful economies in ASEAN. Its reliance on the export of low value added products in addition to a weak local industrial sector make it a dangerous market for foreign investors. Nevertheless the social policies of the Sukarno and Suharto period did bring considerable benefits to the population in terms of education and healthcare. Some of those benefits are now coming under attack due to neo-liberalism and budget constraints. A final development challenge faced by Indonesia is the disparity between the developments of its regions. Marginal areas such as Aceh lag behind in terms of both social and economic development (Bitzinger, 2010; Heidhues, 2000).

Federation of Malaysia

Malaysia is considered to be one of the economic power houses of the Southeast Asian region. In terms of history, Malaysia is a collection of former British colonies (CIA, 2010f; Heidhues, 2000). The individual Malaysian states were formerly independent and have rich histories before becoming part of the British Empire. Sarawak was ruled by the White Rajas, a British dynasty that ruled the land independently of the British Empire until the end of World War II (von Feigenblatt, 2009c; Payne, 1995).

Many states had hereditary rulers and other regions were formed from the internal migration of workers in the former British Empire. The result of this is that Malaysia is a multicultural country with a majority Malay population but with considerable Indian and Chinese minorities. In the post-war period of decolonization the present states of Malaysia in addition to Singapore formed the Federation of Malaya (Lee, 2000). Due to cultural differences Singapore opted out of the federation and became independent while the rest of Malaya changed its name to the Federation of Malaysia. As the name implies the system is federal in that each state has considerable power in terms of culture and local language. Since several of the hereditary rulers of the original states remained in power, Malaysia is actually a constitutional monarchy (Roger Kershaw, 2001).

Malaysia's history is very important in order to understand its economy since ethnic origin looms large as an important criterion for allocating resources and raising tax revenue. At the time of independence, 1957, the Malaysian economy was deeply integrated into the imperial commercial network which included Hong Kong, British India, and the dominions of Australia and New Zealand (Lee, 2000; Neher, 2002).

Movement of people and goods was easy between the different regions and traders of Indian and Chinese origin dominated the economy. Malays on the other hand were usually employed to assist the colonial bureaucracy and those not employed in government were mostly employed in the agricultural sector. This division of labour along ethnic lines was carried over to the post independence period causing social tension and complicating the development process. Native tribal inhabitants and Malays, also known as *bumiputra* (people of the land), were afflicted by a widespread feeling of relative deprivation vis-à-vis the wealthier Indians and Chinese communities (Millard, 2004). Due to the vast numeral majority of the *bumiputra,* the United Malays National Organization (UMNO) was able to gain control of the government ever since the first elections (Lee, 2000).

UMNO developed a policy of affirmative action and redistribution to the *bumiputra* which has guided its developing policy up to the present day. The previously mentioned historical background partly explains Malaysia's statism and considerable government involvement in the economy. Malaysia's basic development program took off during the 22 years of rule by Prime Minister Mahathir bin Mohamad (1981-2003) who took advantage of high oil prices and reinvested the revenues on the diversification of the economy away from the export of raw materials to the export of electronics and tourism. The period was characterized by mega projects such as the Petronas Towers and several hydropower plants (Keong, 2006).

In terms of basic economic indicators, Malaysia has a GDP per capita of US$ 14,900, is classified as a middle income country, and has a low unemployment rate of 3.7 percent (CIA, 2010f). With a population of almost 27 million Malaysia is ranked as the thirtieth largest economy in the world. Other indicators attesting to Malaysians considerable level of development are an urbanization rate of 70 percent and most importantly the GDP composition by sector.

Only 9.4 percent of the GDP derives from agriculture while industry accounts for 40.9 percent and services for 49.7 percent (CIA, 2010f). Nevertheless in terms of human development Malaysia "punches under its weight" in that indicators such as literacy, gender equity, and civil liberties fare worse than countries with a similar level of economic development (UNDP, 2009c). One example of the previous assertion is that the literacy rate for men is 92 percent while that of women is just 85.4 percent.

Moreover with approximately 60 percent of the population adhering to the Muslim faith and a large Buddhist Minority, the prominent role that Islam plays in terms of legal system also hints at important challenges in terms of minority rights and negative freedoms such as free speech and freedom of religion (Millard, 2004).

A more complete picture of Malaysia's overall development can be obtained from its human development index. According to the HDI, Malaysia ranks 66 in the world near countries such as Montenegro and Thailand (UNDP, 2009c). Nevertheless it is interesting to note that Thailand has a GDP per capita of about US$ 7000 while Malaysia's GDP per capita is much higher. In addition to that, Malaysia ranks 102nd in term of combined school enrolment ratio together with very low income countries such as Fiji and the Maldives (UNDP, 2009c). Other challenges include illegal immigration from Thailand, Indonesia, and the Philippines, as well as inequality between development in the urban centres and the countryside (Millard, 2004; Neher, 2002).

Malaysia's development policy cannot be divided from politics as attested by the early explanation of UMNO's affirmative action programs. As several scholars attest, Malaysia followed Japan's developmental state model adapting it to fit the needs for redistribution of the *bumiputra* and with a much higher government owned share of the economy (Hew, 2008; Keong, 2006; Neher, 2002). Another way to view the government's involvement in the economy and the subsequent system is the concept of embedded mercantilism (Andriesse & Westen, 2008).

This model concentrates on the control of resources by the central government in a similar way as it was done during the colonial period, however this mercantilism is embedded in the broader capitalist system and interacts with the private sector. Thus, the government becomes the central economic player both in terms of size and ownership but most importantly in terms of priority setting and coordination (Andriesse & Westen, 2008).

In summary, Malaysia is one of the most developed and highly industrialized countries in Southeast Asia, however the emphasis placed by the government on economic development and redistribution have created several negative externalities such as a gap between civil and political development, gender equity, and basic indicators of economic growth such as GDP per capita.

The Philippines

The Philippines are a conglomerate of former independent sultanates (Heidhues, 2000). After the Spanish conquest of the region in the 16th century, the centre of the country converted to Catholicism while the border areas remained Muslim or animistic. This early cleavage in the Philippines gave rise to several Muslim insurgencies as well as to a considerable development gap between the Catholic majority and the sizeable Muslim minority (von Feigenblatt, 2009b; Neher, 2002). The Spanish-American War of 1898 resulted in Spain ceding the archipelago to the United States.

This period was marked by considerable development efforts in the fields of basic infrastructure and healthcare (Shatkin, 2006). During World War II the Philippines were occupied by the Japanese and were granted independence after their liberation. Currently the Philippines have a population of almost 100 million spread throughout hundreds of islands. Economically, the Philippines has a respectable total GDP of about 161 billion USD, placing it in 28th place in the world, however its GDP per capita is one of the lowest, US$ 3,300 (CIA, 2010h).

The economy of the Philippines is heavily dependent on services, with an important agricultural sector, and a weak industrial base. Only 15 percent of the population is employed in industry while 51 percent participates in the service sector (CIA, 2010h). Furthermore, the existing industrial base is mostly heavy industry and textiles, sectors considered to be low in the value chain. The picture becomes even bleaker when one considers the makeup of the service sector. Unskilled labour makes up the majority of the people employed in the service sector at home, while skilled workers tend to emigrate to higher income countries in order to send remittances back to their relatives at home (Neher, 2002). It is estimated that about one million Filipinos work abroad.

In terms of development, poverty remains a serious problem in the Philippines with more than 32.9 percent of the population living under the poverty line. Inequality is also a problem with one of the highest gini coefficients in the world, 45.8 (CIA, 2010h). Thus, the Philippines faces considerable development challenges in terms of raising the living standards of its population as well as reducing some of the considerable inequalities left over from both the Spanish and American colonial periods. One of the roots causes of this problem has been the impossibility to undertake land reform due to the considerable influence exerted by landholding families (Mulder, 1996).

The Filipino government has historically avoided the developmental state model in favour of a more liberal approach modelled after the American system. Nevertheless this approach opened its weak industrial sector to international competition and forced the economy to concentrate on the export of natural resources and very low value added products. Due to the failed attempt at industrialization the next step was a move towards the service sector. Language skills (English) and an educated elite, convinced the government since the Marcos administration that the Philippines had to jump on the globalization bandwagon in order to attract foreign direct investment (FDI) and to compete in the global service trade (Shatkin, 2006). Thus, the economy of the Philippines is one of the most investor friendly ones in all of Southeast Asia with very weak laws in terms of national ownership requirements.

In terms of socio-political indicators of development, 92.5 percent of Filipinos are literate, there is an unemployment rate of about 7.5 percent, and an emigration rate of 4 percent (CIA, 2010h). Its human development index score is of 12.4, placing it 54th in the world while the country is ranked 108th in terms of GDP per capita (UNDP, 2009f). This means that the Philippines is doing a good job with its resources in terms of striving for human development rather than just economic development.

In terms of gender equity, the Philippines fares quite well on most indicators such as the ratio of women to men enrolled in primary and secondary education, 104.8 percent, and rational of female life expectancy at birth to that of males, 106.4 percent (UNDP, 2009f). Probably the Philippines' greatest development challenge is inequality between the rich and the poor as well as the Muslim insurgency and its related terrorism (Means, 2009; Millard, 2004). Another important challenge is emigration due to poverty at home.

From a macro perspective, the Philippines have followed a mostly uncharted path in the free market tradition of liberal democracy. Positive results have accrued in terms of democracy and the development of an active civil society (Mulder, 1996). Nevertheless economic growth lagged behind that of the Asian Tigers which followed the developmental state modelled pioneered by Japan. It is very difficult to identify a single casual factor for the slow economic development of the Philippines since government policy operated in a complex socio-cultural context. Difficulties in terms of land reform as well as considerable government expenditures in fighting both an Islamic and a communist insurgency certainly exerted some influence in the countries development.

Overall, the Philippines face considerable challenges in its path towards human development. Considerable poverty, inequality, and important socio-cultural cleavages stand on the way of achieving sustainable growth and a smooth integration into the world economy. Notwithstanding the many challenges, the Philippines is commendable in that its human development index is much higher than expected based on its very low per capita GDP. In other words, Filipinos are healthier and more educated than citizens of other countries with similar per capita GDPs.

Republic of Singapore

Singapore is Southeast Asia's success story. A former British colony located in the strategically important Straits of Malacca, Singapore has become the most highly developed country in the region. In terms of ethnic composition, Singapore has a very diverse population due to the internal migration of the British Empire (Heidhues, 2000; Lee, 2000). There are large Indian, Malay, Eurasian, and Chinese communities (Millard, 2004). It gained independence from the

United Kingdom in 1963 as part of the Malayan Federation but it later left the federation due to the ethnic domination of the rest of the federation by Malays (Neher, 2002).

As a trading port since the time of the British Empire, Singapore concentrated on strengthening its position in the global economy. Considerable improvements to the city-state's infrastructure and large investments in its human capital allowed the country to position itself as a trading and technological hub in Southeast Asia (Lee, 2000). With a nonexistent agricultural base and a service sector employing more than 76 percent of the population, the country adopted an export oriented model with a strong preference for free trade (CIA, 2009a; Neher, 2002). Government policies friendly to foreign investment and a very stable and technologically advance infrastructure attracted considerable foreign direct investment in electronics and pharmaceutical companies. Thus Singapore was able to attract high value added products rather than the traditional Southeast Asian reliance on heavy industry and raw materials (Lee, 2000).

Lee Kuan Yew was the architect of Singapore's rise to economic pre-eminence is Southeast Asia. A Chinese lawyer educated in the United Kingdom, Lee has shaped Singapore's development since its independence to this day (Lee, 2000; Neher, 2002). His party, the People's Action Party (PAP) has ruled Singapore since its creation and Lee Kuan Yew has served in several ministerial posts up to this day (CIA, 2009a). In terms of democratic development, Lee Kuan Yew established very strict censorship laws as well as a very harsh criminal code. It is clear that he was emulating the Japanese developmental state model but wanted to avoid the policy discontinuities of a liberal democracy. The current Prime Minister is his son, Lee Hsien Loong (CIA, 2009a).

In terms of economic indicators Singapore has one of the highest per capita GDPs in the world, US$ 52,300 (CIA, 2009a). This is a considerable achievement taking into consideration that most other states with such high GDPs per capita are petrostates which are highly dependent on natural resources and international prices. Unemployment is virtually nonexistent, 3 percent, and 0 percent of the population lives under the poverty line (CIA, 2009a; UNDP, 2009d). In terms of the proportional composition of GDP, industry accounts for 27. 6 percent, agriculture 0 percent, and services 72.4 percent (CIA, 2009a).

The distribution of labour parallels the one for GDP with 0 percent of the population employed in agriculture, 23.8 percent in industry, and 76.2 percent in services (CIA, 2009a). It should be noted that Singapore's industries are high tech electronic facilities, medical equipment, and pharmaceuticals. On the other hand its service sector is mostly in financial services, trade, and increasingly in education. 100 percent of Singaporeans live in an urban environment and enjoy safe and comfortable living conditions. In terms of education and literacy, Singapore boasts some of the best Universities in the region and the world, the National University of Singapore is consistently ranked among the top 100 global universities. Literacy lags behind in comparison to other indicators, with a total literacy rate of 92.5 percent (UNDP, 2009d).

This can partly be explained by looking at the countries high life expectancy at birth of 81.98 (CIA, 2009a). The older generation is not as well educated as the younger ones which brings down the overall literacy rate. Other important indicators show that the country has a very low fertility rate of 1.1 hinting at future challenges in terms of an aging population (CIA, 2009a). A similar story is told by Singapore's human development index, 0.944 placing it 23rd in the world (UNDP, 2009d). Singapore ranks consistently high in most factors covered by the human development index with the notable exception of literacy which was previously explained. Another important indicator is that it has one of the highest percentages of immigrants in the world, 35 percent (UNDP, 2009d).

Overall, Singapore is a success story in terms of economic development. Nevertheless a holistic view of development must include civil and political rights such as freedom of speech and the right to participate in the country's governance. Singapore's one party system prevents any meaningful opposition from growing and contesting elections. Moreover, strict censorship and the use of civil suits to attack all those who criticize the government and its officials makes political participation difficult to say the least (Akaha, 2009). In this respect Singapore has a long way to go in term of political freedoms and the development of a vibrant civil society. Future developments will depend on whether the present government can maintain its legitimacy through economic growth and whether younger members of the government will move towards reform as the old guard starts to retire or die.

Kingdom of Thailand

Thailand is one of the major economies in the Southeast Asian region. As one of the former Newly Industrializing Nations in the Asia Pacific, its economy boomed during the early 1990s and then again during the middle of the first decade of the 21st century (Neher, 2002; Wyatt, 2003). With a population of almost 66 million and strategic location at the core of the Southeast Asian subcontinent, Thailand is a country that punches below its weight in economic terms.

Historically, Thailand's development has cantered on the capital with the bulk of the government's investment in infrastructure devoted to a few urban centres such as Chiang Mai in the North and metropolitan Bangkok (Ungpakorn, 2007; Wyatt, 2003). The theory behind this emphasis was that development would spread out to the periphery from the developed core. A similar approach was pursued in terms of the development of human capital. The central government emphasized the improvement of higher education in a few elite centres as well as the establishment of a few showcase public schools in the capital to the detriment of the quality of universal elementary education in the interior of the country (von Feigenblatt, Suttichujit, Shuib, Keling, & Ajis, 2010).

After World War II, Thailand followed the path of import substitution industrialization for a few years, complementing it with the export of raw materials (Neher, 2002). This approach to development was unsuccessful and the country remained a backwater exporter of raw materials until the late 1970s and 1980s. The Vietnam War and the increasing tensions of the Cold War increased the country's importance to the United States which stationed thousands of troops in Thai territory (Ungpakorn, 2010; Wyatt, 2003).

Massive amounts of materiel, was procured by the American military from Thailand during this period, boosting the inchoate economy. The subsequent period saw an exponential increase in the amount of foreign direct investment by Japanese and American companies for outsourcing operations. Assembly plants for automobiles and textile mills started to become ubiquitous in the Thai countryside. The service sector also grew in financial services and tourism. This was the golden period for the urban Thai middle class which saw its living standards rise exponentially during the late 1990s (Wyatt, 2003).

The economic crisis of 1997 exposed Thailand's crony capitalism which was based on irresponsible lending by banks due to family and political connections rather than sound financial principles. As a result of the previously mentioned economic crisis, Thailand entered a brief period of economic retrenchment in which the free market was slightly rolled back through capital controls and a more virulent nationalism.

Nevertheless, the rise of Dr. Thaksin Shinawatra, a criminal justice expert educated in the United States, brought new life and dynamism to the economy (Ungpakorn, 2007, 2010). Dr. Shinawatra left, for the first time in Thai history, the centralized development approach by attempting to spread the gains of economic growth to the provinces. Several projects such as the "one product on district" policy drastically increased the economic development of peripheral regions. Policies to stimulate the economy were also complemented by social safety nets such as the 30 Bhatt medical care policy, which made basic medical care affordable to an unprecedented number of people.

The rise of a new entrepreneurial class, represented by Dr. Shinawatra's fortune in communications, threatened the interests of the traditional elites. Landed interests, the Royal Family, and the disgruntled military felt that their power was decreasing vis-à-vis the rising entrepreneurial class (von Feigenblatt, 2009d). They allied themselves with conservative members of the middle class who deplored the minor decentralization of power that had taken place as well as the growing influence of the considerable rural population.

The result of this was the military coup of 2006 which was supported by the palace as the Bangkok middle class (Dressel, 2009; von Feigenblatt, 2009a; Lintner, 2009). One of the main goals of the military coup was to roll back or dismantle the reforms brought about by the Shinawatra administration as well as to re-centre the eco-political interests of the Palace and the military elite (Ungpakorn, 2007, 2010).

The Thai military is actively involved in the Thai economy through the direct ownership of several industries as well as some of the major banks (McCargo, 2008). It is also known that through its influence in the deep South of Thailand, the military has been historically involved in the lucrative timber and rubber trades (Liow, 2006a, 2006b; McCargo, 2008, 2009; Means, 2009). [1] The Palace is another major player in the economy owning large corporations such as Siam Cement and Siam Commercial Bank (Handley, 2006; Ungpakorn, 2007, 2010). Considerable real estate is under the control of the crown bureau.

After considerable military pressure and some support behind the scenes from the Palace, the pro Shinawatra coalition ruling parliament broke down and a Democrat Party led government was installed. The new government adopted the King's pseudo theory of Self-sufficiency Economy which basically encouraged people to be satisfied with what they had in life and to live according to their means. In other words, for the rich to be happy being rich, and for the poor to be satisfied being poor (Ungpakorn, 2010).

Considerable opposition from both popular and industrial sectors is building up against the elitist Democrat government and the economy is suffering from the political instability as well as the misguided policies of self sufficiency economy (von Feigenblatt, 2009d, 2010b, 2010c). The tourism and construction sectors have suffered dearly from the recent downturn in foreign direct investment as well as from tourism. Moreover country's per capita GDP remains low, US$ 8,200 (CIA, 2009b). In terms of economic growth, 2009 saw a 2.2 percent contraction and the prospects for next year remain grim. Structurally, the composition of Thailand's GDP in comparison to the composition of its labour is unbalanced. While agriculture accounts for only 11.6 percent of the GDP, it accounts for 42.4 percent of the labour force.

On the other hand, industry represents 43.3 percent of GDP while only accounting for 19.7 percent of the labour force. In terms of services the picture is more balanced, with 45.1 percent of GDP deriving from services, and 37.9 percent of the labour force employed in this sector. Another significant indicator is the percentage of the population living in cities, 33 percent (CIA, 2009b). This piece of information shows how GDP per capita can be misleading in that the differences in terms of employment and type of labour between urban and rural areas is abysmal. Another misleading statistic is the country's low official unemployment rate of 1.5 percent. With more than nine percent of the population living under the absolute poverty line an official unemployment rate of 1.5 percent shows that a considerable percentage of the population is either underemployed or extremely underpaid (CIA, 2009b). Adding to this a GDP per capital of US$ 8200 shows that poverty and inequality are considerable problems in Thailand.

As previously mentioned in the introductory background to Thailand's development, human capital development has only being a priority in the urban centres and that education in the rest of the country is cursory and superficial (von Feigenblatt et al., 2010). The country's literacy rate of 92.6 percent sounds impressive but barely represents the ability to read very basic Thai and is based on official government reports which can be self-servingly misleading. Expenditure in education, while relatively high at 4.2 percent of GDP, is mostly devoted to higher education and to elite centres in the capital (CIA, 2009b).

With a human development index of 0.783, Thailand ranks 87th in terms of overall development (UNDP, 2009e). Its human development rank is similar to its GDP per capita rank of 82. Nevertheless this does not mean that Thailand's government is doing everything it can to improve the general human development of the country as attested by the fact that China with a GDP per capita of less than US$ 5600 has almost the same human development index (UNDP, 2009e). This shows that much more can be done in Thailand in order to transform economic development into human development. Other important remaining challenges are political development in terms of the strengthening of civil and political rights as well as the promotion of the rule of law.

Brunei Darussalam

Brunei Darussalam is the smallest nation in Southeast Asia with a population of approximately 388,000 and a territory of 5,765 square kilometres (CIA, 2010c). During the 15th to the 17th century Brunei enjoyed its highest peak in terms of influence and power in the region (Heidhues, 2000; Neher, 2002; Payne, 1995). At one point Brunei controlled most of Borneo, part of the Philippines, and Sarawak (von Feigenblatt, 2009c; Payne, 1995). As a trading kingdom, access to the sea was very important in order to connect the many islands of the vicinity into a single trading market.

Nevertheless European colonialism in the 18th and 19th centuries brought a sudden end to the prosperity of the

Sultanate (Chottmann, 2006; Payne, 1995). Several losses of territory such as the loss of considerable territory to the White Rajas of Sarawak further weakened the sultanate. By the beginning of the 19th century Brunei was a backwater protectorate of the British Empire (Stockwell, 2004). Nevertheless, the British respected and protected the six hundred year old ruling dynasty and guaranteed the continued existence of the remnants of the once great Brunei Sultanate (Kershaw, 2003; Ku, 2010).

The discovery of considerable reserves of oil and natural gas in the 1920s near the coast of Brunei suddenly changed the economic prospects of the protectorate (Stockwell, 2004). Imperial decay after the two World Wars also forced Britain to devolve considerable powers to the Sultan until complete independence was granted in 1984 (Heidhues, 2000; Kershaw, 2003). The period between the 1920s and independence saw the strengthening of the monarchy due to the British policy of returning the powers of the British resident to the Sultan even though many of that power had never been in the hands of the Sultan before that time (Chottmann, 2006).

A brief period of democratization resulted in a constitution with limited elections and a weak legislature however an uprising by a pro-democracy leader named Azahari led to a crackdown by British forces stationed in Brunei and to a permanent suspension of the constitution (Stockwell, 2004). The failed uprising and the confrontational diplomacy of Indonesia during the 1970s and 1980s convinced the Sultan, Sir Hassanal Bokiah, of the need to maintain at least one British Gurkha battalion permanently stationed in the country (Kershaw, 2003).

As a multiethnic society composed of 66.3 percent Malays, 11.2 percent Chinese, 3.4 percent indigenous, and 19.1 percent other, Brunei needs a national ideology to keep it together (CIA, 2010c). Melayu Islam Beraja serves that purpose by combining an imagined historical past with Islam (Chottmann, 2006). MIB stands for Malay Islamic Monarchy and serves as a national ideology revolving around the Sultan and his role as the representative of the nation and religion. As an ideology, MIB is relatively new, having its origins in the final period of the protectorate and incorporating many aspects of the absolutist monarchies of the Middle East (Stockwell, 2004). The result of the use of this ideology is that political participation by the majority of the population is discouraged while respect for the status quo is promoted (Kershaw, 2003).

Brunei has a very high GDP per capita, US$ 50,200, the sixth highest in the world (CIA, 2010c). The main reason behind the very high GDP is the income generated by gas and oil exports (Ku, 2010). Therefore, about half of the GDP comes from the export of natural resources while most of the rest depends on the service sector. A more detailed division of GDP per sector shows that less than 1 percent of GDP comes from agriculture, approximately 74 percent comes from industry, and 25 percent derives from services (CIA, 2010c).

A closer look reveals that most of the industrial sector depends on the extraction and export of oil and gas while a considerable portion of the service sector is concentrated in tourism (Ku, 2010). From a macroeconomic perspective, the economy of Brunei is highly dependent on the wealth brought by the export of oil and natural gas making its continued economic success highly questionable (Ku, 2010). Several scholars have classified Brunei as a rentier state with a similar structure to Saudi Arabia. A rentier state distributes the income derived from the export of natural resources to the population in the form of social services, low or nonexistent taxes, healthcare, and government employment (Kershaw, 2003; Ku, 2010). In exchange of sharing the country's wealth, the rentier state expects obedience and hopes that the population will remain apolitical (Chottmann, 2006).

One important challenge faced by Brunei is that in contrast to Saudi Arabia and other well known rentier states, Brunei faces the grim prospect of running out of oil and gas in less than two decades (Kershaw, 2003; Ku, 2010). This means that the government will have to make up for a loss of almost 50 percent of its GDP in less than twenty years. More than 62 percent of the labour force is employed in industry, less than one percent in agriculture, and about 33 percent in the service sector, which means that a decline in industry would bring unprecedented unemployment and strain the government's ability to continue to provide the high quality of life that citizens of Brunei currently enjoy (CIA, 2010c). This is a challenge not only in terms of economic stability but also in terms of political stability since the monarchy's legitimacy partly rests on its ability to provide its subjects a high living standard (Chottmann, 2006).

The government is aware of the challenge that it faces in terms of its disappearing oil and gas reserves and it is attempting to restructure its economy in favour of the service sector. At this point the most favoured sector is tourism followed closely by financial services. There is a chance that Brunei will be able to weather the storm relatively unscathed by positioning itself as a service centre similar to Singapore or Dubai. Courting foreign direct investment is a parallel strategy that is being undertaken by the government in an effort to de-centre its economy and to start attracting capital from alternative sources (Kershaw, 2003).

In terms of other important indicators of development, Brunei still faces important challenges. With a total literacy rate of 92.7 percent, 95.2 percent for men and 90.2 percent for women, Brunei fares worse than many countries with a lower GDP per capita (CIA, 2010c). In addition to that, the difference between the literacy rate for men and for women in considerable and significant and shows the important gender gap in terms of socio-economic status present in Brunei (CIA, 2010c). The country also has a relatively low combined enrolment ratio of 77.7, placing it in seventy-first place in the world (UNDP, 2009a). The enrolment ratio refers to the percentage of people in school age enrolled in schools.

A challenge that will only be discussed briefly in this

section of the book is the multiethnic nature of the population and the exclusionary policies of the dominant Malay group. Only 66.3 percent of the population is Malay while the rest of the population includes Chinese as well as other indigenous inhabitants who do not share the Muslim faith with the dominant majority (Chottmann, 2006; CIA, 2010c). Citizenship is usually tied to ethnicity and it is very difficult for minority groups to receive it. Moreover the little political participation available is restricted to Malays.

From an economic point of view the problem with this policy is that once the oil and the gas run out, the government will depend on the entrepreneurial skills of the Chinese and the labour of the indigenous population. Government allocations and the distribution of revenue from the export of natural resources will decrease in importance while the service sector and commerce will increase. The previous trend could result in considerable racial tensions and an unstable investment environment for foreign ventures.

Finally, in terms of the human development index, Brunei ranks 30th with an HDI of 0.920 (UNDP, 2009a). Nevertheless Brunei could be doing much better in terms of overall human development based on its per capita GDP. Countries like Slovenia and the Republic of Korea rank higher in terms of HDI while having almost half the GDP per capita as Brunei (UNDP, 2009a). This shows that Brunei should attempt to balance the benefits of the wealth brought about by the export of oil and natural gas with basic development needs such as education and healthcare. The previously mentioned needed transition will determine whether Brunei will permanently join the select club of newly developed countries or slide back into underdevelopment.

Burma (Union of Myanmar)

Myanmar also known as Burma was an important kingdom during the 16th to the early 19th century (Heidhues, 2000). Located between Thailand and the Indian subcontinent,

Burma's culture serves as a bridge between West Asia and Southeast Asia both culturally and strategically (Neher, 2002). Burma's decline started with the ascendancy of Siam in the late 18th century which saw considerable centralization and development in the central Southeast Asian kingdom (Heidhues, 2000; Neher, 2002).

Burma on the other hand, suffered from the territorial depredations of both the British from the Indian side and Siam. The result of 60 years of British and Siamese pressure was considerable loss of territory, the transformation of the once powerful country into a British protectorate, and the subsequent abolition of one of the oldest monarchies in Southeast Asia (Roger Kershaw, 2001). By 1886 Burma was under complete British control and was first administered as a province of India and then as a self-governing crown colony (Winfield, 2010).

After World War II, Burma was granted independence and General Ne Win controlled the country up to 1988 when he was deposed by a military junta (Keling, Saludin, von Feigenblatt, Ajis, & Shuib, 2010). Ne Win attempted to lead the country towards socialism and because of that strengthened the role of the state in the economy, something that remains a problem to this day (Than & Thein, 2007). In 1988 the coup leaders decided to hold legislative elections in 1990 which were won by the National League for Democracy, headed by Aung San Suu Kyi. Nevertheless the military junta refused to hand power to the elected government and instead put Aung San Suu Kyi in house arrest and increased its repression of political dissidents (Keling et al., 2010; Thawnghmung, 2009).

The military junta was able to sign armistices with several ethnic guerrillas during the late 1990s but fighting continues in some parts of the country (Falise, 2010). Violence is endemic and the army continues to be the most important institution in the country (Katanyuu, 2006). The country's many ethnic groups such as the Karen and the Shans continue to suffer under the yoke of the military junta's attempts at forced assimilation (Falise, 2010; Neher, 2002). Entire villages are burned by the army under the smallest suspicion of harbouring members of the guerrilla movements. In addition to that, the army practices forced recruitment of young men in order to replenish its numbers (Falise, 2010).

With a population of about fifty three million and a half, Burma has historically dependent on the mass mobilization of labour for agriculture. Obedience and national cohesion was historically attained with the help of the monarchy's control over the Buddhist monks (Winfield, 2010). The legitimacy accrued from this connection proved to be a very effective way to mobilize labour to produce rice. Nowadays, the military junta accomplishes what the monks used to do through persuasion and respect by using the military in massive campaigns of violence (Keling et al., 2010). Rice is still at the core of the Burmese economy and politics due to its central position as the country's basic foodstuff. The government forcefully collects a percentage of the rice harvest each year and spends considerable resources in efforts to increase production (Thawnghmung, 2009).

In terms of natural resources, Burma is a rich land. Emeralds, teak wood, and natural gas are just some of the many riches of the country (Than & Thein, 2007). Nevertheless the military junta has failed to take advantage of the country's natural wealth and has instead chosen to sell them a raw materials rather than as finished goods (Keling et al., 2010). The result of this has been considerable damage to the environment and the loss of valuable economic opportunities due to the myopic vision of the regime. The export of natural gas to Thailand has helped the regime deal with its serious energy shortages but has proved to be insufficient to create sustainable growth (Than & Thein, 2007). Thus, the military junta has failed in its effort to become a rentier state in the mild of Brunei or Saudi Arabia.

Starting in the late 1990s, Myanmar has embarked in an effort to attract tourism and to privatize some of the state owned enterprises (Than & Thein, 2007). The effort has not been very successful due to the government's requirement of maintaining a fifty one percent controlling stake in the corporation, the double exchange rate, and a very inefficient financial sector (Thawnghmung, 2009). Those are just some of the obstacles to increasing foreign direct investment. Added to that is an embargo by the United States as well as deficient infrastructure in terms of transportation and telecommunications.

Myanmar has a very interesting but very inefficient system of having a double exchange rate for foreign currency. There is an official exchange rate which remains at 8 kyat per dollar while the market exchange rate hovers at around 1,300 kyat per dollar (Than & Thein, 2007). The problem with this system is that it makes it very difficult to undertake financial transactions such as paying local employees who work for foreign companies. As a result a very high unofficial tax is charged due to the discrepancy between the two rates. Inflation is also rampant, at about twenty percent per year (Than & Thein, 2007). While the government tolerates the black market for currency exchange it is more difficult for large enterprises to take advantage of the market mechanism than for tourists exchanging a few dollars.

The banking sector is also very weak and loans are approved due to political connections rather than due to proper banking practices. This leads to high levels of corruption and to slow growth in the sector of small businesses. The regime has identified the banking sector as an important sector needed reform and has established the Myanmar Investment and Commercial Bank (MICB) in order to serve as the centre of the country's financial activity (Than & Thein, 2007; Thawnghmung, 2009). Considerable challenges remain on the legal front, since the legal system has seen few reforms since the late 1970s and the complex web of regulations borrowed from common and civil law make the system convoluted and slow (Keling et al., 2010).

While Myanmar experienced double digit growth during the late 1990s, the country remains one of the poorest and most underdeveloped in the world. With a GDP per capita of US$ 1,100 it ranks 210th in the world (CIA, 2010a). About 70 percent of the population is employed in agriculture, 7 percent in industry, and 23 percent in services (CIA, 2010a). This shows that the majority of the population is involved in the agricultural sector while most of the service sector depends on government employment (Thawnghmung, 2009). A third of the population lives under the poverty line while the richest ten percent controls more than a third of the resources (CIA, 2010a).

In terms of other important development indicators such as literacy rate and urbanization, Myanmar has room for improvement, about 90 percent of the population can read and write and one third of the population lives in an urban environment (CIA, 2010a). It should be noted that higher education in Myanmar is virtually nonexistent. Universities have been closed for years by the military junta causing a major shortage of skilled labour (Keling et al., 2010). Academic freedom is nonexistent and the budget devoted to its upkeep is minuscule. The average years of schooling of adults is less than four, further evidence of the weakness of the education sector (UNDP, 2009g).

With a human development index (HDI) of 0.451, Burma ranks 132nd in the world (UNDP, 2009g). Burma continues to suffer from pervasive poverty, lack of proper governance, violence, and a general mismanagement of the economy. A clear sign of the misdirection of the military junta was the decision to build a new capital at Naypyidaw at considerable expense (Thawnghmung, 2009). The move was clearly unnecessary and motivated by regime survival needs and paranoia rather than objective strategic ones.

In summary, the Union of Myanmar (Burma), has the resources and the population to join the more developed countries of Southeast Asia but the main obstacle in the way of development is the military junta ruling the country. With proper governance and a guided transition to a market economy Burma could fulfil its potential as one of the historical powerhouses of the East. Needless to say there is also an argument that Burma could develop economically without democratization in the mould of South Korea in the 1980s and China in the 1990s, however for that to happen the military junta would need a strategy that involves more than just short term window dressing in order to stay in power. It remains to be seen whether Burma will follow the path of China and Vietnam or continue to languish as the pariah of Southeast Asia.

Lao People's Democratic Republic

The present Lao People's Democratic Republic traces its lineage to the former Kingdom of Lan Xan founded in the 14th century (Kershaw, 2001). Lan Xan later on divided into two smaller kingdoms and only the Kingdom of Luang Prabang survived Siamese expansionism during the 19th century (Neher, 2002; Wyatt, 2003). Laos came under French rule during the 19th century but managed to retain its own identity and administration separately from the other Indochinese colonies of Cambodia and Vietnam (Kershaw, 2001).

The current borders of the country were defined by the French and the Siamese in 1907, subsequently the borders moved again for a brief period during the Japanese occupation, after the end of the war they moved back to where they were in 1907 (Heidhues, 2000). Laos is a small landlocked country with few natural resources other than an abundance of fresh water. Its small population of about 6.3 million is composed of Tai peoples in the plains of the country and several minority ethnic groups in the mountainous regions such as the Hmong (Neher, 2002).

In order to understand present day Laos it is important to provide a brief overview of the recent historical experience of the country in relation to the wider region. After World War II the French renewed their rule of the country through traditional indirect rule in which a constitutional monarch headed the country as an integral part of the French Union (Kershaw, 2001). While the monarch had little formal power, he provided legitimacy to French rule and at the same time reminded the population and the French about the separate nature of Laos in relation to the other Indochinese possessions.

The conflagration in Vietnam led by the Vietminh gave rise to communist parties in Cambodia and in Laos (Kershaw, 2001; Neher, 2002). Interestingly enough the founder of the communist party in Laos (Pathet Laos) was a prince of the royal family (Kershaw, 2001). Due to the international goal of the communists in North Vietnam of freeing the entire Indochinese region from French rule under a communist system, the political situation of the country came to be linked to the independence struggle in the rest of the region. To complicate matters even more the fighting spread to the border areas of Laos and Cambodia and the Pathet Lao started to fight against the Royal Lao Government based in Vientiane. The result of the struggle was an uneasy agreement between the two sides in which they would share power under a constitutional monarchy (Heidhues, 2000).

Nevertheless developments in the rest of the region strengthened the hand of the Pathet Lao and sapped the resolve of the Royal Government. Serious harassment of right wing ministers in the early 1970s led to them fleeing the country and leaving the reins of power in the hands of the Pathet Lao. After their departure the Pathet Laos consolidated their control of the country by setting up people's assemblies in villages and by asking the King for a letter of abdication (Kershaw, 2001). Thus the revolution was completed relatively peacefully. From that moment on Laos embarked on the path of socialism under the Vietnamese sphere of influence (Neher, 2002).

After the fall of communism in the Soviet Union and the weakening of their Vietnamese benefactors, the Lao leadership decided to move towards guided capitalism in the 1990s. One way to do so was to increase cooperation with Thailand and also by joining the Association of Southeast Asian Nations (ASEAN) in 1997 (Simon, 2008). Some of the challenges faced by Laos are the transportation of goods due to its lack of a seaport, the return of Hmong refugees from Thailand, and a lack of modern infrastructure.

With a GDP per capita of US$ 2,100, Laos is considered to be one of the most underdeveloped countries in the world (CIA, 2010b). Nevertheless Laos has seen impressive economic growth since it opened up its economy in the late 1980s. GDP has grown by an average of 6 percent per year and the poverty rate has halved in the last decade from about 40 percent to 26 percent (CIA, 2010b). In addition to that foreign direct investment has increased in the construction, mining, and hydropower sectors. Eighty percent of the population is still employed in the agricultural sector while twenty percent work in the industrial and service sectors (CIA, 2010b).

Unemployment is minimal, hovering around 2.5 percent of the workforce. Agriculture continues to be the most important sector of the economy with rice serving as the staple product. It is interesting to note that in terms of GDP composition services has become the most important sector, accounting for 37 percent of the GDP. The main activity driving the growth of the service sector is tourism. Industry follows with 33.1 percent of the GDP. Mining, construction, and some textile production account for the growth of the industrial sector. Finally, agriculture accounts for 29.9 percent of the GDP, however its importance is due to the large percentage of the population that it employs (CIA, 2010b).

Laos faces important challenges such as improving its infrastructure. Roads in the countryside are unpaved and substandard which makes transportation of products difficult. The telecommunications infrastructure only covers major urban centres and suffers from instability. Laos also faces considerable challenges in other aspects of human development. In terms of health the country has a relatively low life expectancy of 62. Infectious diseases such as typhoid, hepatitis A, dengue, and malaria are endemic and the public health system is very basic and insufficient to tackle the challenge (CIA, 2010b; UNDP, 2010b).

Education is also low in the country with a total literacy rate of 73 percent and a considerable gap between the rate for men, 83 percent, and women, 63 percent (UNDP, 2010b). It is also important to note that most of the population lives in rural settings, only 31 percent of the population lives in cities. The rate of urbanization is 5.6 percent which means that the major urban centre will have to prepare for a considerable inflow of people from the countryside putting further strain on the meagre infrastructure.

In terms of governance, Lao remains a one party communist country (Neher, 2002). Minorities, specially the Hmong, suffer discrimination by the central government and there is no freedom of speech. On the other had there are some good signs from the government such as the recent, 2009 repatriation of hundreds of Hmong from the Thai border without any signs of government repression or abuse of the returning population. At one point, the Hmong aided the United States during the Vietnam war and were thus connected to the opposition by the communist government, however now that the war is long past and that the country is looking forward to joining the World Trade Organization, the skills and labour of the Hmong may be viewed as an asset by the government.

Laos' human development index is 0.497 placing it 122nd in the world (UNDP, 2010b). It is clear that Laos has a long way to go in order to develop enough to be removed from the list of least developed countries. Nevertheless the government has shown some positive signs by opening up the economy, promoting foreign direct investment, gradually improving the infrastructure, and seeking membership in the World Trade Organization.

Socialist Republic of Vietnam

The Socialist Republic of Vietnam is considered to be one

of the members of ASEAN with the best future prospects for economic growth (Vu-Tung, 2007). Vietnam, a former French colony won its independence from France in 1954 and was then unified by the communist north in 1975 (Kissinger, 1994; Neher, 2002). The result of many years of war was a centralized economy with a clear need for restructuring. Central planning in the Stalinist mould was abandoned in 1986 when the "doi moi" policy of renovation was introduced by the government (Heidhues, 2000; Neher, 2002). "Doi moi" included the progressive liberalization of the market, the courting of foreign direct investment, and the promotion of exports. The country negotiated membership in the World Trade Organization for more than a decade and was finally successful in 2007 when it joined the organization (CIA, 2010g). Membership in the WTO allowed Vietnam to join the global economy and to access the American and European markets.

In terms of natural resources, Vietnam has proven reserves of oil and of natural gas and thus has the considerable advantage of having virtual energy independence (CIA, 2010g). Nevertheless with a population of 89 million and a half people, the country faces considerable development challenges such as unemployment, absolute poverty, and rural development. In addition to the previously mentioned challenges, joining the international economy has also brought about previously unknown economic fluctuations cases by changes in the international market. Nevertheless Vietnam has a relatively good infrastructure and is one of the ASEAN countries with the largest industrial sectors.

With a GDP per capita of US$ 2,900, Vietnam is ranked 167th in the world (CIA, 2010g). However, it should be noted that the low GDP per capita is due to the exponential population growth of the last few decades the hides the considerable economic clout of the country in the region with a GDP of approximately US$ 257 billion, placing it in 42nd place in the world. Thus, Vietnam faces a very similar challenge to that of China in that its economy is large by any standards and it is growing at a considerable pace but a booming population tends to dilute the results at the per capital level of analysis.

One sign of a modern economy is the strength of the industrial and service sectors in terms of their contribution to the total GDP. Agriculture accounts for 21.3 percent of the total GDP while industry contributes 40 percent and the service sector 32.7 percent. The share of the GDP contributed by agriculture has been decreasing at a rate of almost 2 percent per year for the last decade. On the other hand agriculture still employs a large section of the population, 51.8 percent while industry employs 15.4 percent and services accounts for 32.7 percent of jobs (CIA, 2010g). This shows that industry in Vietnam is very capital intensive and that while industry is growing as share of GDP, the service sector is absorbing the jobs left behind by the contraction of the agricultural sector.

In terms of unemployment, it has increased in the past few years. In 2008 it stood at 4.7 percent and it rose to 6.5 percent in 2009 (CIA, 2010g). The increase in unemployment is one of the side effects of the liberalization of the economy and also reflects the effects of the global recession of 2008-2009. Nevertheless the government has been able to keep a relatively low percentage of the population under the poverty line, 12.3 percent, due to the generous social services provided by the government.

One example of those social services includes health care and is reflected by the country's high life expectancy rate of almost 75 years. In terms of other indicators of quality of life and development such as education, Vietnam has made considerable progress. The total literacy rate is of just over 90 percent while the average years of schooling is 11 (CIA, 2010g). Both literacy and average years of schooling vary according to gender with men having a considerable advantage.

In summary Vietnam has pursued a bumpy road towards development. The period of centralized economic development reached its high point during the 1970s and allowed the country to establish a vast array of heavy industries such as steel, mining, and machinery production. In addition to that social services and basic development of human capital in terms of elementary education and literacy took place under the protective direction of the central government. Nevertheless, the end of the Cold War and the fall of the Soviet bloc encouraged the Communist government to gradually open the economy and to join the world market.

The result of the "doi moi" policy has been positive in terms of the promotion of economic growth and has brought much needed foreign capital in order to modernize the country's infrastructure and create new jobs. On the negative side the opening of the economy has also exposed the country to the fluctuations of the global economy and has made it harder for the government to provide the generous social services that it has historically provided. One thing is clear and that is that Vietnam will continue to attract foreign capital investment and that it will become one of the major industrial centres in ASEAN.

With a stable political environment, a highly educated population, and relatively developed infrastructure, Vietnam seems to be reaping the benefits of decades of investment in human capital and in a powerful industrial base. At this point it looks like the future of textile production is in Vietnam rather than in the more unstable Thailand or the more developed Malaysia. The human security index for Vietnam is of 0.572 placing it 113th in the world and showing that the country still has a long road to go towards the ideal of sustainable development (UNDP, 2010c).

The Kingdom of Cambodia

The Kingdom of Cambodia is considered to be the successor of the Khmer Empire which dominated great swaths of Southeast Asia during the 10th to 13th centuries (Heidhues, 2000). During the late 19th century Cambodia become a French protectorate and joined French Indochina. After the Japanese occupation during World War II, the country declared independence and followed a foreign policy based on non-alignment. Led by the charismatic King Sihanouk, the country followed a socialist path which created resentment on some quarters and was considered insufficient by others (Kershaw, 2001).

During the 1970s the Khmer Rouge, an extremist Maoist movement, took over the government and drove everyone away from the cities and towns in order to force massive collectivization of farming (Short, 2004). The period was one of the most traumatic in the country's history. The genocide and human suffering that was brought about by the Khmer Rouge takeover was put to an end by a Vietnamese invasion in 1978 (Gottesman, 2003). As a result of the invasion a prolonged civil war ensued between the Vietnamese backed communist regime in the capital, the Khmer Rouge, Royalist forces led by Prince Sihanouk, and forces loyal to the Republic overthrown by the Khmer Rouge. In 1993 the Paris Peace Accord put an end to the fighting and resulted in a weak constitutional monarchy. Prime Minister Hun Sen, originally installed by the Vietnamese after the invasion, become the key figure in Cambodian politics and continues to rule the country to this day (Gottesman, 2003; Kissinger, 1994).

With a population of approximately fourteen and a half millions, Cambodia is one of the poorest countries in Southeast Asia. The damaged inflicted by the Khmer Rouge interregnum in addition to the prolonged civil war that followed it reversed decades of development and virtually obliterated the country's human capital. Cambodia's low GDP per capita is of US$ 1900, placing the country in 188th place in the world (CIA, 2010d). In terms of the composition of the GDP, industry contributes 30 percent, services account for 41 percent, and agriculture for 29 percent.

The country's major industries include construction and garment production. In relation to services, tourism has grown to become a significant sector of the economy. In terms of agriculture, other than staple products such as rice, rubber is the main export commodity. It should be noted that while industry and services contribute the highest percentages to the total GDP, in terms of labour, agriculture outstrips both by far. 67.9 percent of Cambodians work in the agricultural sector, mostly at the subsistence level. Industry employs 12.7 percent of the population, mostly in the garment production industry, and services accounts for 19.5 percent of jobs (CIA, 2010d).

With more than half of the population under the age of 25, Cambodia has a serious demographic bulge necessitating fast economic growth and job creation. Lack of skills and inappropriate or inexistence of infrastructure in the provinces means that it is very difficult for millions of youths to find gainful employment. Cheaper labour costs in countries such as Vietnam and China also threaten the budding garment industry. Construction, which saw a boom during the 1990s has also slowed down due to a shortage of credit in addition to investor fears related to the political stability of the country and the ability of the government to provide the necessary infrastructure. A low literacy rate of 73.6 percent is just one example of the low level of human capital in the country (CIA, 2010d).

Health is also a major challenge in Cambodia. Life expectancy at birth hovers around 62.28 years and diseases such as malaria, dengue, and cholera are widespread (CIA, 2010d). Hepatitis A and typhoid fever are also common. In addition to the previously mentioned diseases, Cambodia has a rising rate of HIV infections which while still relatively low in comparison to the regional average, may become a serious challenge in the future due to the age bulge and the possibility of contagion among young people.

There is a wide gender gap in Cambodia and men have considerably higher levels of education than women, 84.7 percent literacy rate versus 64.1 percent, in addition to a female/male ratio of population with at least a secondary education of 0.563 (CIA, 2010d; UNDP, 2010a). The overall gender inequality index for Cambodia is relatively high standing at 0.641 (UNDP, 2010a). This disparity is aggravated by the higher percentage of the population under the poverty line, 31 percent (CIA, 2010d). Women suffer disproportionately from poverty and the shortage of adult men due to the long civil war means that many women are heads of households taking care of several children with little support from the community.

It is clear that Cambodia has a long way to go in terms of development. The country has to recover decades of lost development due to the political violence and at the same time handle a difficult transition to a market economy. Cambodia is a good example of the beneficial and detrimental consequences of joining the world market. While the 1990s saw high levels of economic growth and a boom in the construction industry, the country was seriously affected by the economic downturn of 1997 as well as the global economic recession that started in 2008 (CIA, 2010d).

It is hard to calculate the human costs of each one of the economic downturn but taking into consideration that more than a third of the population lives under the poverty line and the government does not have the means to provide appropriate social services, it is an understatement to say that thousands of families are living in conditions near starvation. A relatively high rate of urbanization, 4.6 percent per annum, further aggravates the situation (CIA, 2010d). With a weak infrastructure, few opportunities of gainful employment in the major urban centres, and a highly vulnerable agricultural sector, the result has been the exponential sprawling of illegal settlements at the margins of the cities.

In summary, Cambodia is one of the most underdeveloped countries in the world and faces formidable challenges. With a human development index of 0.494, it ranks 124th in the world (UNDP, 2010a). Nevertheless the country has taken considerable steps in the last two decades in terms of developing its infrastructure, strengthening the rule of law, and promoting tourism. Joining the global economy through ASEAN and agreements with the WTO are also positive steps in the bumpy path to development.

The Wider Operating Environment

ASEAN's economy is extremely porous and still in an inchoate state of regional integration. It should be noted that for most members of ASEAN their major trading partners are extra regional (Simon, 2008). This means that the economy of ASEAN is by no means self contained or even self directed. In other words, the economy of the region is mostly guided by bilateral agreements and trading relationships with the major global economies. The result of this is that ASEAN members are highly sensitive to what happens in their surrounding environment.

The end of the Cold War marked the beginning of globalization for the region. While the phenomenon actually started in the 1980s, the trade for the region was largely determined by geopolitical considerations and alliances rather than the market (Heidhues, 2000; Neher, 2002). Examples of this include the economic aid and foreign direct investment pumped into Thailand during the Vietnam War and the Cambodian crisis. Vietnam received help from the Soviet bloc and mostly traded with communist countries. Even the so-called Non Aligned Movement (NAM) gravitated towards trade with the Soviet bloc and preferential trade depended on political expediency and ideology rather than on the quality of products or the complementarities of the economies in question (Kissinger, 1994).

After the end of the Cold War, ASEAN faced new and previously unknown challenges. Japan's economy was slowing down in comparison to China and other Newly Industrializing Countries such as South Korea and Taiwan (Hook, Gilson, Hughes, & Dobson, 2005; Hwang, 2006). International trade was becoming more important and more complex as a path to development. Other developing countries starting to offer stiff competition in the light industrial sector, such as in textiles.

To make things even more complicated labour costs started to rise in some ASEAN member states without the necessary economic growth and human capital development in order to make the transition from heavy and light industry to information technology and services. This is a particular challenge to countries such as Thailand and Indonesia which have relatively high labour costs but lack the human capital and infrastructure to compete in high value added sectors such as electronics and financial services. An important regional trading partner, Japan, started to move factories to China in order to take advantage of cheap labour costs, political stability, and infrastructure (Sakamoto, 2008).

Some countries such as Singapore took advantage of its strategic location and multicultural population to become a strategic node in the global financial system (Lee, 2000). Malaysia managed to develop a strong sector in electronics and to be competitive at the global level. Other countries such as the Philippines, Indonesia, and Thailand lost their lustre and stagnated at a level of development that made them too costly in terms of labour in comparison to other developing countries such as India and China and not advanced enough to undertake research and development and higher value added services. Other countries such as Vietnam, Laos, and to a certain extend Cambodia are taking advantage of their low labour costs to attract foreign capital and to boost exports.

It is clear that the more complex international environment has complicated the political economy of ASEAN's member states. More is needed now to secure a good trade agreement than the rhetorical adherence to democracy and freedom. A more detailed discussion of the interaction of ASEAN's members in a complex global economy and a competitive regional environment will be provided in chapters 6 and 7. Chapter 6 deals with the main trade barriers and obstacles found in the region while chapter 7 applies structural dynamics to the analysis of the present trade structure and the blueprint for an ASEAN Economic Community.

End Note

1. Adriesse classifies Thailand's economic system as "embedded mercantilism" in that the private sector cooperates with the public sector in order to promote exports while simultaneously attempting to co-opt weaker sectors such as agriculture (Andriesse & Westen, 2008, p. 172). Nevertheless Thailand's "embedded mercantilism" is of the "managed type" in that powerful interest groups enter the government and use their influence but without a coherent central policy such as the one found in Malaysia. Other less sympathetic scholars have called this system "crony capitalism" (Feigenblatt, 2009d; Handley, 2006; Ungpakorn, 2007, 2010).

References

Akaha, T. (2009). Human Security in East Asia. *Journal of Human Security, 5*(3), 11-34.

Andriesse, E., & Westen, G. v. (2008). Varieties of embedded mercantilism and regional development in the Thailand-Malaysia Borderlands. *Journal of Development Alternatives and Area Studies, 27*(3/4), 165-187.

ASEAN. (2008). *ASEAN ECONOMIC COMMUNITY BLUEPRINT.* Retrieved. from http://www.aseansec.org/5187-10.pdf.

Battersby, P., & Siracusa, J. M. (2009). *Globalization & Human Security* (Hardcover ed.). Lanham: Rowman & Littlefield Publishers, Inc.

Bitzinger, R. A. (2010). A New Arms Race? Explaining Recent Southeast Asian Military Acquisitions. *Contemporary Southeast Asia, 32*(1), 50-69.

Chottmann, S. (2006). Melayu Islam Beraja: The Politics of Legitimisation in a Malay Islamic Monarchy. *Review of Indonesian and Malaysian Affairs 40*(2), 111-139.

CIA. (2009a). The World Factbook: Singapore. Retrieved October 12, 2010, from https://www.cia.gov/library/publications/the-world-factbook/geos/sn.html.

CIA. (2009b). The World Factbook: Thailand. Retrieved October 14, 2010, from https://www.cia.gov/library/publications/the-world-factbook/geos/th.html.

CIA. (2010a). The World Fact Book: Burma. Retrieved November 5, 2010, from https://www.cia.gov/library/publications/the-world-factbook/geos/bm.html.

CIA. (2010b). The World Fact Book: Laos People's Republic Retrieved November 9, 2010, from https://www.cia.gov/library/publications/the-world-factbook/geos/la.html.

CIA. (2010c). The World Factbook: Brunei. Retrieved October 27, 2010, from https://www.cia.gov/library/publications/the-world-factbook/geos/bx.html

CIA. (2010d). World Factbook: Cambodia. Retrieved November 29, 2010, from https://www.cia.gov/library/publications/the-world-factbook/geos/cb.html

CIA. (2010e). The World Factbook: Indonesia. Retrieved September 16, 2010, from https://www.cia.gov/library/publications/the-world-factbook/geos/id.html.

CIA. (2010f). The World Factbook: Malaysia. Retrieved September 27, 2010, from https://www.cia.gov/library/publications/the-world-factbook/geos/my.html

CIA. (2010g). The World Factbook: Socialist Republic of Vietnam. Retrieved November 13, 2010, from https://www.cia.gov/library/publications/the-world-factbook/geos/vm.html.

CIA. (2010h). The World Factbook: The Philippines. Retrieved October 8, 2010, from https://www.cia.gov/library/publications/the-world-factbook/geos/rp.html.

DRESSEL, B. (2009). Thailand's Elusive Quest for a Workable Constitution, 1997-2007. *Contemporary Southeast Asia, 31*(2), 296-325.

Falise, T. (2010). On the Run: In Burma's Jungle Hell. *World Policy Journal, 27*(1), 57-64.

von Feigenblatt, Otto F. (2009a). Comparing the 2006 Military Coup in Thailand and the 2009 Coup in Honduras: Internal Socio-political Similarities and External Normative Differences. *Infinity Journal, 1*(4), 3-9.

von Feigenblatt, Otto F. (2009b). Human Security and the Responsibility to Protect: A Holistic Approach to Dealing with Violent Conflict in Southeast Asia. *Journal of Social Sciences,*

11(1), 27-40.

von Feigenblatt, Otto F. (2009c). Some lessons from the White Rajahs of Sarawak: Identifying and strengthening local capacities for peace in the deep South of Thailand. *Journal of Law and Conflict Resolution, 1*(6), 117-121.

von Feigenblatt, Otto F. (2009d). The Thai Ethnocracy Unravels: A Critical Cultural Analysis of Thailand's Socio-Political Unrest. *Journal of Alternative Perspectives in the Social Sciences, 1*(3), 583-611.

von Feigenblatt, Otto F. (2010a). *Human Security in the Asia Pacific Region: Security Challenges, Regional Integration, and Representative Case Studies* (Hardcover ed.). Jaipur: YKING BOOKS.

von Feigenblatt, Otto F. (2010b, April 09, 2010). Thailand's Struggle over Legitimacy. *UPI Asia.com,* pp. 1-3. Retrieved April 9, 2010, from http://www.upiasia.com/Politics/2010/04/09/thailands_struggle_over_legitimacy/2024/

von Feigenblatt, Otto F. (2010c, May 27, 2010). UNCERTAINTY AND FEAR IN THAILAND. *Insight on Conflict.* Retrieved May 27, 2010, from http://www.insightonconflict.org/conflicts/thailand/stories/uncertainty-fear-thailand/

von Feigenblatt, Otto F., Suttichujit, V., Shuib, M. S., Keling, M. F., & Ajis, M. N. e. (2010). Weapons of Mass Assimilation: A Critical Analysis of the Use of Education in Thailand. *Journal of Asia Pacific Studies, 1*(2), 292-311.

Galtung, J. (1969). Violence and Peace. *Journal of Peace Research,* 167-191.

Glassman, J. (2005). The "War On Terrorism" Comes To Southeast Asia. *Journal of Contemporary Asia, 35*(1), 3-28.

Gottesman, E. (2003). *CAMBODIA After the Khmer Rouge: Inside the Politics of Nation Building.* New Haven: Yale University Press.

Handley, P. M. (2006). *The King Never Smiles: A Biography of Thailand's Bhumibol Adulyadej.* New Haven Yale University Press.

Heidhues, M. S. (2000). *Southeast Asia: A Concise History.* London: Thames & Hudson.

Hew, D. (2008). The Malaysian Economy: Developments and

Challenges. *Southeast Asian Affairs*, 207-222.

Hook, G., Gilson, J., Hughes, C. W., & Dobson, H. (2005). *Japan's International Relations: Politics, economics and security* (2nd Edition ed.). London: Routledge.

Hwang, H.-d. (2006). APEC and emerging regionalism in North East Asia. *Asia Europe Journal, 4*(4), 499-510.

Katanyuu, R. (2006). Beyond Non-Interference in ASEAN: The Association's Role in Myanmar's National Reconciliation and Democratization. *Asian Survey, 46*(6), 825-845.

Keling, M. F., Saludin, M. N., von Feigenblatt, Otto F., Ajis, M. N. e., & Shuib, M. S. (2010). A Historical Approach to Myanmar's Democratic Process. *Journal of Asia Pacific Studies, 1*(2), 132-148.

Keong, C. Y. (2006). Behind Malaysia's "Miracle": A Veblenian Perspective on Mahathir's Era of Economic Modernization. *Journal of Economic Issues, 40*(4), 861-875.

Kershaw, R. (2001). *Monarchy in South-East Asia: The Faces of Tradition in Transition* (First ed.). London: Routledge.

Kershaw, R. (2003). Partners in Realism: Britain and Brunei Amid Recent Turbulence. *Asian Affairs (London), 34*(1), 46-53.

Kissinger, H. (1994). *Diplomacy* (Paperback ed.). New York: Simon & Schuster.

Ku, S. C. Y. (2010). Brunei in 2009: Maturity in Doubt? *Asian Survey, 50*(1), 260-264.

Lee, K. Y. (2000). *From Third World to First: The Singapore Story: 1965-2000* (First ed.). New York: HarperCollins Publishers.

Lintner, B. (2009). The Battle for Thailand: Can Democracy Survive? *Foreign Affairs, 88*(4), 108-118.

Liow, J. C. (2006a). International Jihad and Muslim Radicalism in Thailand? Toward an Alternative Interpretation. *Asia Policy* (2), 89–108.

Liow, J. C. (2006b). *Muslim Resistance in Southern Thailand and the Southern Philippines: Religion, Ideology, and Politics*. Washington, D.C.: East-West Centre.

MacFarlane, S. N., & Khong, Y. F. (2006). *Human Security and the UN: A Critical History* (1st Edition ed.). Indianapolis: Indiana University Press.

McCargo, D. (2008). *Tearing Apart the Land: Islam and Legitimacy in Southern Thailand* (First ed.). Ithaca: Cornell University Press.

McCargo, D. (2009). The Politics of Buddhist identity in Thailand's deep south: The Demise of civil religion? *Journal of Southeast Asian Studies, 40*(1), 11-32.

Means, G. P. (2009). *Political Islam in Southeast Asia* (Paperback ed.). London: Lynne Rienner Publishers.

Millard, M. (2004). *Jihad in Paradise: Islam and Politics in Southeast Asia*. Armonk: East Gate Books.

Mulder, N. (1996). *Inside Southeast Asia: Religion, Everyday Life, and Cultural Change*. Chiang Mai: Silkworm Books.

Neher, C. D. (2002). *Southeast Asia in the New International Era*. Boulder: Westview Press.

Payne, R. (1995). *The White Rajahs of Sarawak*. Kuala Lumpur: Oxford University Press.

Pitsuwan, S. (2010). ASEAN central to the region's future. *East Asia Forum Quarterly, 2*(2), 4-5.

Sakamoto, T. F. C. T. (2008). *Japan Since 1980*. New York: Cambridge University Press.

Sen, A. (1999). *Development as Freedom*. New York: Anchor Books.

Shatkin, G. (2006). Colonial Capital, Modernist Capital, Global Capital: The Changing Political Symbolism of Urban Space in Metro Manila, the Philippines. *Pacific Affairs, 78*(4), 577-600.

Short, P. (2004). *Pol Pot: Anatomy of a Nightmare*. New York: Henry Holt and Company.

Simon, S. (2008). ASEAN and Multilateralism: The Long, Bumpy Road to Community. *Contemporary Southeast Asia, 30*(2), 264-292.

Singh, D. (2008-2009). Southeast Asian Security: An Overview. In D. Nair & L. P. Onn (Eds.), *Regional Outlook: Southeast Asia 2008-2009* (pp. 3-7). Singapore: Institute of Southeast Asian Studies.

Stockwell, A. J. (2004). Britain and Brunei, 1945-1963: Imperial Retreat and Royal Ascendancy. *Modern Asian Studies, 38*(4), 785-819.

Than, M., & Thein, M. (2007). Transitional Economy of Myanmar: Present Status, Developmental Divide and Future Prospects. *ASEAN Economic Bulletin, 24*(1), 98-118.

Thawnghmung, A. M. (2009). Responding to Strategies and Programmes of Myanmar's Military Regime: An Economic Viewpoint. *Southeast Asian Affairs, 2008*, 274-290.

Trinidad, D. D. (2010). Domestic Actors, Market Reform and Regional Integration in Southeast Asia. *Asia Pacific World, 1*(1), 95-115.

UNDP. (2009a). Human Development Report 2009: Brunei Darussalam. Retrieved October 28, 2010, from http://hdrstats.undp.org/en/countries/country_fact_sheets/cty_fs_BRN.html.

UNDP. (2009b). Human Development Report 2009: Indonesia. Retrieved September 17, 2010, from http://hdrstats.undp.org/en/countries/country_fact_sheets/cty_fs_IDN.html.

UNDP. (2009c). Human Development Report: Malaysia. Retrieved September 27, 2010, from http://hdrstats.undp.org/en/countries/country_fact_sheets/cty_fs_MYS.html.

UNDP. (2009d). Human Development Report: Singapore. Retrieved October 13, 2010, from http://hdrstats.undp.org/en/countries/country_fact_sheets/cty_fs_SGP.html.

UNDP. (2009e). Human Development Report: Thailand. Retrieved October 14, 2010, from http://hdrstats.undp.org/en/countries/country_fact_sheets/cty_fs_THA.html.

UNDP. (2009f). Human Development Report: The Philippines. Retrieved October 8, 2010, from http://hdrstats.undp.org/en/countries/country_fact_sheets/cty_fs_PHL.html.

UNDP. (2009g). Myanmar: Country Profile of Human Development Indicators. Retrieved November 9, 2010, from http://hdrstats.undp.org/en/countries/profiles/MMR.html.

UNDP. (2010a). Country Profile of Human Development Indicators: Cambodia. Retrieved November 29, 2010, from http://hdrstats.undp.org/en/countries/profiles/KHM.html.

UNDP. (2010b). Country Profile of Human Development Indicators: Lao People's Republic. Retrieved November 9, 2010, from http://hdrstats.undp.org/en/countries/profiles/LAO.html.

UNDP. (2010c). Country Profile of Human Development Indicators: Viet Nam. Retrieved November 13, 2010, from http://hdrstats.undp.org/en/countries/profiles/VNM.html.

Ungpakorn, G. J. (2007). *A Coup for the Rich: Thailand's Political*

Crisis. Bangkok: Workers Democracy Publishing.

Ungpakorn, G. J. (2010). *Thailand's Crisis & the Fight for Democracy*. London: WD Press.

Vu-Tung, N. (2007). Vietnam's Membership of ASEAN: A Constructivist Interpretation. *Contemporary Southeast Asia, 29*(3), 483-505.

Winfield, J. C. (2010). Buddhism and Insurrection in Burma, 1886-1890. *Journal of the Royal Asiatic Society, 20*(3), 345-367.

Wyatt, D. K. (2003). *Thailand: A Short History* (Thailand ed.). Chiang Mai: Silkworm Books.

6

Intra-regional Trade Barriers and Extra-regional Trade Challenges

The present chapter provides an overview of the main intraregional trade barriers present in ASEAN. Based on the five core elements of the blue print for an ASEAN Economic Community, namely free flow of goods, free flow of services, free flow of investment, freer flow of capital, and free flow of skilled labour, barriers and obstacles to their achievement will be identified and explained. An obstacle of paramount importance, asynchronous and asymmetric intra and inter member development will also be discussed at length. The chapter concludes with a discussion on the measures currently underway in ASEAN, designed to tackle some of the barriers and obstacles identified in the chapter.

Introduction

Second to regional security, economic integration is the most important purpose of the Association of Southeast Asian Nations (Pitsuwan, 2010). Moreover, while member states disagree on issues of democratization, human rights, and regional security, they all agree on the need to cooperate in order to improve the economic competitiveness of the region in an increasingly integrated global economy (Simon, 2008). The expected economic benefits of regional integration have motivated otherwise isolated nation-states such as Myanmar, Vietnam, and Laos to join the international organization (Than & Thein, 2007; Vu-Tung, 2007).

In other words economic issues are what keep most members at the table during difficult conversations on other more controversial issues (Katanyuu, 2006). Thus, economic integration and the common threats faced by regional economies from East Asia, Latin America, and Eastern Europe move them towards greater cooperation on issues of trade, financial flows, and economic integration. Therefore ASEAN's Economic Pillar is expected to be one of the strongest of the three pillars of the ASEAN Community (ASEAN, 2008c). The expectations of ASEAN members are high regarding the benefits that will accrue from economic integration and the plethora of plans, programs, projects, and initiatives included in the blue print for the economic community is astounding. Not only the sheer complexity of the effort is surprising but also the obstacles and barriers that must be overcome in order to successfully implement the plans is daunting to say the least.

As repeatedly mentioned throughout this book, ASEAN includes member states at considerably different developmental stages. The development gap is not only present between member states but also within the states themselves. Development in the region is asynchronous and asymmetrical and this is evident in the wide gaps in terms of infrastructure, banking systems, human capital development, and legal systems, *inter alia* (Eades & Cooper, 2010; Komori, 2009; Neher, 2002). One obvious example of the gap in terms of the development of the banking system and financial services between member states is the wide difference between the Singaporean financial sector and that of Myanmar.

Singapore is a global financial hub almost at the same level as London and New York while Myanmar has one of the most underdeveloped banking systems in the world with very few legal safeguards (Keling, Saludin, von Feigenblatt, Ajis, & Shuib, 2010; Lee, 2000; Thawnghmung, 2009). An example of asynchronous and asymmetric development within member states themselves is the gap between the periphery and the centre in Thailand (von Feigenblatt, 2009d; Ungpakorn, 2007, 2010). The modern capital, Bangkok, is decades ahead in terms of development compared to the Northeast or the Deep South of the country for example (Liow, 2006; Perkasa, 2008;

Wyatt, 2003). Differences are present not only in obvious sectors such as infrastructure but more importantly in human capital and transportation.

Thus, the gap between the periphery and the centre in Thailand is as wide as that between advanced member states and some of the least developed ones such as Myanmar. Up to this point development gaps have been discussed as if they were immobile, snapshots in time however time is an integral dimension of development and economic growth. Asynchronous development also means that one area or country is developing faster than another in terms of chronological time. Thus, Myanmar can be considered to be thirty years behind Singapore in terms of development. The same is true in periphery-centre gaps such as the one previously mentioned in Thailand or the one found in the Philippines between metro Manila and Mindanao (Yegar, 2002).

The importance of the previous passage dealing with asynchronous development in relation to obstacles and barriers to trade is that ASEAN's goal to integrate the regional economic through a plethora of projects involves considerable trade liberalization (ASEAN, 2008c). This liberalization in turn requires countries to open their economies to foreign competition in terms of services, goods, and labour. According to Adam Smith's original conception of the market, each country or "economy" would thus concentrate on a sector in which it enjoys a competitive advantage (Tannebaum & Schultz, 2004). Thus in the case of the European Union Germany might have an advantage in computers and information technology while the United Kingdom has a strong financial services sector (McCormick, 2005).

Greater competition would compel each country to concentrate on strong sectors which would complement the strong sectors of other countries. Thanks to free trade both countries would enjoy a complementary relationship in which the quality of the services and products will be better than they would be if each country tried to produce and provide all services on its own. Some industries will suffer from greater competition but the growths in the sectors enjoying a competitive advantage will more than makeup up for the loss in terms of jobs and profits lost due to liberalization.

Nevertheless it should be noted that in this obviously simplified scenario both countries must have at least one sector that enjoys a competitive advantage in relation to the other country. Otherwise, liberalization would open the weaker economy to competition and lead to the demise of its indigenous industry. Unemployment would follow in addition to a serious trade deficit in which good which were previously produced nationally would now have to be imported from abroad. For economies with a weak industrial sector and a high reliance on the agricultural sector, there is another important challenge. If countries trading with each other produce similar products but one does so at a lower cost it will discourage national farmers from producing them and ultimately may result in less food security for the country as a result of reduced self-sufficiency.

The following sections will discuss some of the main barriers and obstacles that stand in the way of ASEAN economic integration and the ultimate goal of establishing a successful ASEAN Economic Community. Obstacles and barriers are varied and include differences in infrastructure, legal systems, banking systems, inter alia. Nevertheless it should be clear to the reader that asynchronous development is an overarching commonality shared by most obstacles. Finally, external pressures and the dynamic interaction with the global economy can also be considered to pose important barriers and obstacles to the fulfilment and integration of the ASEAN Economic Community.

Barriers and Obstacles to the Free Flow of Goods

One of the most basic considerations when assessing the level of integration of economic integration of a region is the relative easy in terms of movement of goods (products). The degree of easy of movement of goods depends on several important factors including but not limited to tariff barriers, non-tariff barriers, transportation, standards and technical barriers, legal regimes (patents and copyrights laws), differences in trade and customs procedures, and asynchronous development. Some barriers represent physical limitations that may hamper the flow of trade. Other barriers deal with legal, bureaucratic, and macroeconomic issues of equal importance.

It is important to note that political capital is necessary in order to carry out and implement any policy. Trade liberalization presents many risks to national political elites who may depend on the legitimacy brought about by economic growth and improving living standards (Than & Thein, 2007; Trinidad, 2010). Thus political elites back and support trade liberalization with the hope that the process will bring economic growth relatively quickly so as to compensate the usual negative externalities of economic liberalization and free trade in general. In other words, there is an important political factor involved in the process which involves high expectations and at the same time considerable fears about the possible effects on the national economies. Authoritarian regimes such as the ones in Singapore, Brunei, Vietnam, Myanmar, and to a certain extend Thailand increasingly rely for their legitimacy on their economic performance and their ability to improve living standards (Chang, Chun, & Park, 2007; Than & Thein, 2007; Ungpakorn, 2007, 2010).

Now that "political will" has entered our discussion of asynchronous development and trade barriers let's consider what happens when ASEAN members are asked to lower trade barriers such as tariffs in addition to other liberalization measures. The least developed countries in the region tend to have weak industrial sectors and depend heavily on the agricultural sector (CIA, 2010a, 2010b). Examples of this include Cambodia, Myanmar, and the Philippines. As shown in chapter 5, countries that derive most of the GDP from agriculture and the export of natural resources tend to be poorer and to have lower scores on most indicators of socio-economic development.

Those that attempted to develop an indigenous industry encounter a vast array of challenges and obstacles such as the need to invest on a modern infrastructure, human capital development, and technology transfer. A sudden opening of the market in a country with a nascent national industrial sector may cause the sudden demise of the industrial sector and a further dependence on the export of staple agricultural products and natural resources with very little value added. As explained in the introduction to this chapter, the demise of national industry would then require the importation of finished products from more advanced neighbours.

Since agricultural products have very little value added in comparison to finished products, there would be a net outflow of money and a subsequent trade deficit. At a more macro-level dependency would ensue in that the less developed country would need the more developed country to supply products which are not produced at home because of their lack of competitiveness vis-à-vis those of produced in the more developed neighbour. This is the argument posed by Wallerstein's famous world system's theory and the related dependency theory (Wallerstein, 1976).

Advocates of free trade point to the benefits of cooperation in terms of technology transfer, increased productivity, improved product quality, and increased regional competitiveness in the global market (Bhattacharyay, 2010). As mentioned in the introduction, free trade works best when the countries engaged it in have similar levels of development which is not the case of ASEAN. One example of an early onset of economic dependence is Laos. The country imports most finished products from Thailand and only exports a few agricultural products which are not really competitive since they are also found in Thailand (CIA, 2010b). Everything from caffeinated drinks such as Pepsi to cameras is imported from the richer neighbour. Laotian agricultural products are only competitive due to the low labour costs and thus have little value added.

Nevertheless it should be noted that economic integration can be introduced in stages as recommended by the blue print for an ASEAN Economic Community which will be discussed in a later section of this chapter (ASEAN, 2008c). Asynchronous development between countries can lead to problems as shown in the previous paragraphs but its negative externalities can be ameliorated through interstate agreements and exceptions. What about intra state asynchronous development? Development differences between regions of a single country are more difficult to address effectively when negotiating trade liberalization. An example of the difficulties can be easily grasped by thinking about the effect the process may have on different provinces of Thailand.

Provinces with an important stake in the high-tech industry will undoubtedly benefit from the greater market access provided by trade liberalization while other weaker or less competitive industries such as textiles may suffer and subsequently disappear. This internal economic restructuring is part of the "creative destruction" of the market and does lead to the best allocation of resources in terms of production and GDP. Nevertheless the human costs for those involved in weak sectors of the economy are very high and traumatic (Akaha, 2009; Sen, 1999). Internal migrations to the cities from the countryside are just one of the many symptoms of the malaise (Hew, 2008). A decrease in job security for those formerly employed in the agricultural sector is another example.

Political elites in ASEAN member countries have to take into consideration the human costs of the restructuring that naturally follows economic integration even under the best of circumstances (Suharto, 2009). Thus, there is always a fear of possible political instability due to the possible displeasure and opposition of those interest groups that may be adversely affected by trade liberalization (Collins, 2008; Trinidad, 2010).

The movement for fair trade that developed as an early response to the tentative steps toward market liberalization is just one example of how new obstacles and barriers to the free movement of goods may appear after the process has started (Ungpakorn, 2007, 2010).

Another important aspect of asynchronous development is that self-sufficiency in some non-competitive sectors of the economy may have to be surrendered (Than & Thein, 2007; Trinidad, 2010). For those ASEAN countries with higher levels of development and strong industrial bases their fear is that their agricultural sectors may be obliterated by the in pour of cheap agricultural products from their poorer neighbours.

The result is that staple foods will become cheaper in advanced countries but at the cost of having to import them from abroad. This brings to the fore the fear of possible food shortages in times of crisis such as wars in addition to national fears of a loss of a certain degree of independence (von Feigenblatt, 2009a). Asynchronous development and development asymmetry are two important and pervasive obstacles in the way of the free flow of goods in ASEAN.

Some of the negative externalities of trade liberalization raise issues of food security, socio-economic unrest, and regime legitimacy (Battersby & Siracusa, 2009; von Feigenblatt, 2009a). In a world characterized by the ubiquitous presence of information and the prevalence of international norms favouring human rights and democracy, authoritarian regimes in the region are becoming increasingly dependent on economic performance as a way to shore up their legitimacy (Chang, Chun et al., 2007; von Feigenblatt, 2009c). The previously mentioned factor makes trade liberalization a dangerous necessary evil for that kind of regime since economic growth is needed while at the same time the process may destabilize the system and bring about unwanted socio-political unrest (Katanyuu, 2006; Keling et al., 2010; Kershaw, 2003; Vu-Tung, 2007).

Non-tariff Barriers

It might seem peculiar to address the issue of non-tariff barriers before the more traditional and highly visible tariff barriers, however in an era in which most nation-states in ASEAN are members of the World Trade Organization, non-tariff barriers have become more important obstacles on the way to effective trade liberalization and economic integration (ASEAN, 2008c). Non-tariff barriers come in many forms and refer to all of those regulations, rules, standards, and requirements which can impede the flow of goods from one country to another. Examples of visible non-tariff trade barriers include language requirements in the labelling of products intended for some markets. Quality controls can also be used as non-tariff barriers.

A third example deals with certificates of origin. Non-tariff barriers tend to be very difficult to overcome since they are not as visible and straight forward as tariffs and are sometimes used by regimes to protect or favour some vulnerable sectors of the economy. Since trade liberalization requires greater trust and cooperation between the parties, non-tariff barriers are often perceived as serious stumbling brooks in the negotiation process. Other states view non-tariff barriers as signs that the regime is not serious about trade liberalization or worse that the regime is attempting to trick the other country into opening their market to their products while at the same time protecting its own market from the other country's products. Thus the varied nature of non-tariff barriers makes it very difficult to tackle them effectively in the effort to integrate the regional economy.

A clear sign that the governments of the member states are aware of the problem posed by non-tariff barriers is that different groups of countries have different deadlines to eliminate non-tariff barriers. While it is understandable that the CLMV (Cambodia, Laos, Myanmar, and Vietnam) countries were given a longer grace period, 2018, the Philippines, one of the original members, asked for a similar moratorium

(ASEAN, 2008c). The work of interest groups in requesting the grace periods is clear in the case of the Philippines, a democracy.

Tariff Barriers

A more traditional, yet still important barrier to the free flow of goods is tariff barriers. The Common Effective Preferential Tariffs for ASEAN Free Trade Area (CEPT-AFTA) has managed to gradually lower tariffs in the region (ASEAN, 2008c). Nevertheless the decrease in tariffs has not been even. There are several lists of sensitive products which are exempted from the tariff requirement benchmarks, at least for the next decade. This means that success in lowering tariffs has been most effective in secondary products in which there is little intra regional trade anyway (Trinidad, 2010). It is very important to eliminate intraregional import duties and to phase out the duties for those products on the sensitive lists.

A more daunting challenge is to phase out the tariffs for highly sensitive products. Since most member states share the same staple products as their agricultural base, with the possible exception of Singapore, then there is an inherent lack of complementarity (ASEAN, 2008c). In addition to that there is the fear of a loss of food security by opening up the market for competition from foreign agricultural products and the possibility that agriculture will be affected by it. On the other hand the challenge is that the sensitive lists include such as vast array of products that even if all of other tariffs were removed there would still be a long way to go towards a truly free market.

One clear example of how development differences among member states poses a challenge in terms of tariff barriers is how there are different timelines for the members in terms of the elimination of trade barriers (ASEAN, 2008c). Import duties for products outside of the sensitive lists should be removed by 2010 for the original six members, the ASEAN-6. While the timeframe for CLMV countries ranges from 2015 to

2018, with possible extensions (ASEAN, 2008c). [1] It is understandable that some protection is accorded to weaker economies such as the ones of the CLMV countries, however such flexible timeframes encourage free riding and protectionism.

Differences in Trade and Customs Procedures

It is very important for ASEAN member states to integrate custom procedures. The different requirements, complex procedures, and in some cases, corruption in customs slows trade and discourages intraregional commerce (Bhattacharyay, 2010). Lack of clear custom procedures also pose challenges to trade with extra-regional partners due to the plethora of regulations and challenges faced by foreign countries or partners attempting to introduce their products to the region (ASEAN, 2008c). At this point there are challenges in several areas related to customs integration.

First of all, custom structures are independent, disorganized, and difficult to navigate. Tariff classifications vary from country to country making it difficult to understand the process. Custom clearance tends to be tedious and time consuming. There is considerable corruption in this sector and substandard human resources. Moreover, there is a lack of coordination with international organizations in the area of trade. The development of customs is asymmetric and asynchronous in the region in that some countries such as Singapore have very advanced systems while others such as Myanmar are decades behind and using outdated methods (Than & Thein, 2007; Thawnghmung, 2009).

In summary it is difficult to navigate the complex situation in terms of customs in ASEAN member states. Clearing cargoes is tedious and can be very costly due to the loss of time, corruption, and repetitiveness of the process. The situation is similar to Europe before the Napoleonic wars. Each time a trader reached a border customs had to be cleared, following different standards and requiring different paperwork (Roberts, 1997). The result of this is that trade slows down considerably and that it makes it less attractive to foreign partners willing to enter the ASEAN market as a whole (Bhattacharyay, 2010).

ASEAN is working on a vast array of measures to tackle the previously mentioned challenges. The first measure is a region wide plan to modernize customs techniques based on international standards as expressed in the ASEAN Cargo Clearance and ASEAN Customs Declaration Document in 2007 (ASEAN, 2008c, p. 8). Modernization of custom techniques goes hand in hand with harmonization of the system of tariff classification as well as greater information exchange and an ASEAN e-Customs system (ASEAN, 2008c, p. 9). The flagship project in this area is the ASEAN Single Window. This project will allow for the integration of regional custom system with the added benefits of a "single submission of data and information, a single and synchronous processing of data and information and a single decision-making for customs clearance of cargo" (ASEAN, 2008c, p. 9). The ASEAN Single Window is a very ambitious project which requires considerable cooperation between ASEAN member states as well as some flexibility in terms of timeframes.

Intellectual Property

ASEAN member states have very different approaches regarding the protection of intellectual property which makes it difficult for some corporations to operate in certain member states. Intellectual property is particular important in high value added products that require considerable investments in research and development (Gleditsch, 2008; E. C. Murphy, 2009). Since most of the value of the previously mentioned kind of products arises from the design and development of the product, producers have a major interest in protecting those designs as a form of intellectual property. A very clear example of this is the movie industry and DVDs.

More than 99 percent of the cost of producing a DVD

movie involves intellectual property rather than the cost of the materials to make the actual physical DVD. Filming the movie, marketing the product, and most importantly writing the script for the original idea, account for most of the value. Thus if a Disney DVD sales for US$ 19, less than US$ 0.50 of that is the cost of the physical DVD. The same is true of designer clothes, books, video games, and even pharmaceutical drugs. In the case of designer clothes considerable investment had been made by the producer in marketing a brand which is then packaged and sold as a lifestyle.

Southeast Asia is famous among international tourists as a counterfeit goods paradise. Tourists can buy the copies of the newest Rolex watches for US$ 40 in Bangkok, Louis Vuitton purses for less than US$ 100, Lacoste polo shirts for US$ 5, and copies of virtually any edition of lonely planet travel guides for less than US$ 3. Thai college students can borrow any book from the library and have the entire book copied for the cost of the paper. The situation for DVDs and CDs is similar. It is possible to purchase the newest movies for US$ 3 as well as the latest album of your favourite pop band. The reason behind this is simple.

Movies in DVD format derive most of their value from the cost of filming not from the actual production of the physical copies of the DVD. Therefore it is very inexpensive to copy them and sell them to the public at a fraction of the cost and still make a huge profit. The same is true with copies of designer clothes. Some of the same regional producers who sell the textiles used by the big designer brands can easily create virtually identical copies and sell them for a huge profit in for the local market. Sometimes it is a matter of adding a label costing less than US$ 0.05 and copying the design, such as in the case of designer men's suits.

A similar challenge is faced by pharmaceutical companies. Drugs that require millions of dollars in research and development can be produced at a fraction of the cost in a generic version. The result of this practice is that drugs can be provided at a much lower cost but it also discourages international pharmaceutical companies from making the necessary investment in research and development necessary to discover and produce new drugs. This paradox is particularly problematic in relation to the drugs needed to treat HIV such as the latest retroviral treatments.

Intellectual property rights are not only important to extra regional trade partners but also to regional members as well. Countries such as Malaysia and Singapore have advanced research and development capabilities in technology and in the pharmaceutical sector. Other ASEAN members are in the process of strengthening their research and development in order to move the economy towards higher value added products.

Technological transfer is related to the issue of intellectual property rights in that it both limits and facilitates the transfer of technological know-how. Strict laws protecting intellectual property rights make it harder for local industries to copy foreign products and to attempt to produce their own versions of them. On the other hand a proper intellectual property rights regime provides the needed protection for foreign enterprises to move their production facilities to ASEAN countries and in the process creating many positive externalities such as human capital development, investment in advanced infrastructure, and a certain degree of basic technology transfer. Thus, if implemented properly a functioning intellectual property rights regime can facilitate technological transfer rather than hamper it (Lee, 2000).

There are some important barriers to the standardization and harmonization of intellectual property rights in ASEAN. As always asynchronous and asymmetric development are at the core of most of the challenges. Less developed countries such as Cambodia, Laos, Myanmar, and Vietnam may have short to midterm interests in the weak protection of intellectual property rights. One example of this is in the health sector. A strict intellectual property rights regime would make it impossible to produce a large number of drugs in their generic versions. This would increase the cost of medicine in the short term which would put considerable strain on the health care sectors of ASEAN countries. This problem is even more difficult due to the regime types of the less developed ASEAN members which have historically favoured a welfare state. The fear of the possible loss of legitimacy due to a rise in the cost of healthcare makes it unlikely that CMLV countries will move quickly in the direction of strict protection of intellectual property rights.

Another example of a sector that would suffer in the short term would be higher education. Due to the diverse array of cultures present in the region and the relatively recent decolonization of most ASEAN members, most books in university libraries are written in foreign languages, usually French or English. This means that most books are imported from the West. Since it would be very expensive for students to purchase original copies of the imported books, universities prefer to purchase a few copies for the library and then to allow students to photocopy the entire book. The practice is so institutionalized that there is usually a copy centre outside of each faculty with staff ready to assist students with their copying needs. It should be noted that while the copied version is still expensive for students it is considerably cheaper than purchasing the actual book.

Strict intellectual property protection would pressure universities to discontinue this practice and would lead to two equally undesirable scenarios. One possible scenario would be that since students lack the purchasing power to buy the books and they are not allowed to copy them, then professors will just provide brief summaries of the books and increase their reliance on standalone articles. A second scenario would be that the cost of education would increase exponentially and make it increasingly difficult for members of the lower and working classes to attend college. Both possible results would slow down the development of human capital and weaken the university systems of the less developed members of ASEAN. On the other hand, lax protection of intellectual property rights also discourages regional academics from writing textbooks since there would be little profit to be made and textbooks are not considered to be serious academic research. Thus, the results of both lax and strict intellectual property rights are mixed and include considerable benefits as well as some important negative externalities.

The difficulty in harmonizing and integrating regional policy regarding intellectual property rights is reflected by the ambiguous pronouncements of ASEAN regarding possible reform. There are two main ASEAN processes dealing with intellectual property rights, namely the ASEAN IPR Action Plan and the Work Plan for ASEAN Cooperation on Copyrights (ASEAN, 2008c, p. 19). Both processes are ambiguous and flexible. The ASEAN IPR Action Plan encourages cooperation between the Intellectual Property in ASEAN member countries in terms of filing, information sharing, and coordination. Cooperation, coordination, and information exchange between enforcing agencies is also recommended by the plan. At the core of the plan there is an ambitious proposal for a central filing system which mirrors the ASEAN Single Window for Customs.

Nevertheless, the plan for the proposed central filing system is at an inchoate stage in comparison to the ASEAN Single Window. On the other hand, there is greater agreement in terms of copyright protection for traditional knowledge, genetic resources, and cultural traditional expressions (ASEAN, 2008c, p. 20). The protection of traditional knowledge has become more important due to the popularization of traditional medicine both inside and outside of the region. Genetic resources are very important for countries with large agricultural sectors.

One example of this is Thailand's protection of jasmine rice and the much publicized genetic theft and subsequent adaptation of the grain to other regions. The result of this was that jasmin rice, or rather an improved version of it, was registered and produced outside of Thailand by an American scientist. Cultural traditional expressions are also important for the tourism sector and history shows that they can be copied, modified, and commoditized. An example of this would be traditional dances and ritual in Bali which are the trademark attraction of the region in terms of tourism. Therefore, there are some areas in which ASEAN member agree that the protection of intellectual property rights is necessary while other areas remain problematic.

Barriers and Obstacles to the Free Flow of Services

One of the most important goals in terms of economic integration is the free flow of services inside the ASEAN region. This includes a vast array of services such as financial services, architectural services, accounting, surveying, and medical services, *inter alia*. The obstacles in terms of allowing their free flow are many and varied. First of all due to the different levels of development of ASEAN member states, the quality of professionals in one country greatly varies in comparison to those of another. One important step would be to harmonize and allow for the mutual recognition of professional credentials. This is something that is already underway in four priority sectors, namely "air transport, e-ASEAN, healthcare, tourism, and logistics services" (ASEAN, 2008c, p. 10). Each priority sector faces particular barriers and obstacles on the difficult path to liberalization.

Tourism and Air Transport

Tourism is a sector of increasing importance for many ASEAN members. It is one of the most effective ways to accumulate foreign currency and a great way to create new jobs (Richards, 2010). Nevertheless tourism and air transport have been historically well guarded sectors (Than & Thein, 2007). Lading rights and control over the tourism sector has been considered important by nationalist governments due to their increasing economic importance. It is also believed by some nationalist governments that allowing foreign private sector actors to acquire a stake in the tourism sector facilitates the outflow of resources. In other words, if a large part of the tourism and air transport sector is owned by foreign companies, then a large proportion of the profits will be repatriated to the holding company's country of origin. Another parallel effect could be that a large number of the jobs created by tourism would be filled by foreign workers.

The previously mentioned protectionist tendencies are exacerbated by more emotional issues of national pride. Having a national airline owned by either the government or citizens of that country is considered a symbol of national pride and of development (von Feigenblatt, 2009d). This explains the continued existence of national flag carriers such as Thai Airways which operate at a loss but enjoy considerable government support. Opening the air transport sector to foreign competition by liberalizing it exposes national carriers to greater foreign competition. Foreign national flag carriers and also private budget carriers can slowly carve away from the customer base of the national flag carrier. There is also a security related obstacle in that internal transportation from province to province is slowly provided by private carriers under foreign control.

On the other hand there are clear benefits to the liberalization of tourism and air transport. Tourism is greatly enhanced by the availability of reliable and affordable transportation from destination to destination. Having more airlines increases competition, and also forces national flag carriers to improve their services in order to remain competitive.

Moreover the resulting integration makes tourism a regional affair rather than simply national. It allows a tourist to consider taking a tour of three or four ASEAN countries knowing that standards are similar and transportation is reliable and safe. In terms of human capital it eases the shortage of qualified tour operators, pilots, and other professionals in the tourism and air transport sector by allowing foreign professionals to practice in any ASEAN member. Language proficiency is a challenge in some ASEAN member states and an important skill in the tourism sector. Countries such as Myanmar and Laos would benefit from the inflow of some qualified Filipino tour guides for example.

Healthcare

Healthcare is a very important sector for ASEAN countries, not only due to its importance in terms of quality of life but also due to its growth as a niche in the international tourism sector. Countries such as Thailand and Malaysia have advanced health sectors which attract foreign tourists looking for quality treatment at a fraction of the cost of the same treatment in their countries of origin. However the quality of the healthcare sector is asymmetric both within and between ASEAN member countries. For example, Thailand's advanced healthcare sector in the capital can be contrasted to the very limited services available in the provinces. Moreover, healthcare is not free in Thailand, putting it beyond the reach of the majority of the population (Ungpakorn, 2010). Differences are also present between countries. Singapore has a healthcare sector rivalling those of the United States and the United Kingdom (Lee, 2000). On the other hand, countries such as Myanmar and Laos have a shortage of qualified trained physicians and nurses.

Obstacles in terms of the free flow of services in the healthcare sector involve two main issues, namely the recognition of foreign credentials and the fear of human capital flight (ASEAN, 2008c). The first obstacle involves the varying degrees of quality in terms of medical training. Needless to say a physician trained in Myanmar is not as well trained as one trained in Singapore or the Philippines. Thus there is the fear that by allowing for the mutual recognition of credentials, under qualified professionals would be allowed to practice is countries with a stronger healthcare sector. A related fear is human capital flight due to the difference is medical fees from country to country. Since vocational education in fields such as medicine is heavily subsidized in most Southeast Asian countries, governments expect graduates to stay and practice in the country as a way to repay the assistance they received from taxpayers. If the free flow of services is implemented there is the possibility that the best physicians and nurses will move to countries with better working conditions and better pay for their services.

Financial Services

Financial services represent a critical sector affecting the liberalization of all other parts of the broadly conceived service sector. Nevertheless financial services are probably the most sensitive sector in terms of liberalization. The Asian Financial Crisis of 1998 in addition to regime fears of economic instability represents considerable challenges to liberalization. Singapore and the Philippines have relatively open financial sectors in which foreign equity is permitted beyond the fifty percent mark (Lee, 2000). Most other countries have considerable restrictions regarding foreign equity as well as restrictions on currency exchange and capital flows in general (Trinidad, 2010).

Restrictions in terms of financial services derive from two main fears. The first fear is in relation to loss of national control over an important part of the economy. This results in restrictions to foreign ownership of majority equity. A second fear is in relation to the instability of the international market and the possibility of capital flight (Drysdale, 2010). Colonialism and the Asian Financial Crisis figure prominently in the historical memory of Southeast Asian policymakers (Hew, 2008; Neher, 2002).

Relaxing ownership restrictions would allow foreign companies and investors to gain a controlling stake in a vast array of enterprises and financial devices including but not limited to: bonds, financial companies such as banks, publicly traded stock, mortgages, and saving plans, *inter alia*. Nationalist policy makers fear that foreign ownership of a majority stake would subvert the wellbeing of the national economy in favour of short term profits (Hew, 2008; Shuib, Saludin, von Feigenblatt, Keling, & Ajis, 2010; Than & Thein, 2007; Trinidad, 2010).

This fear was exacerbated by the events connected to the Asian Financial Crisis during which considerable capital flight occurred and regional currencies lost a large share of their values due to international trading (Lee, 2000; Simon, 2008). While this oversimplifies what actually happened during the crisis, regional elites tend to blur the border between the cause and the effect of the crisis and attribute causal force to the symptoms such as capital flight rather than treating them as the effects that they actually were. Perceptions aside, the effects were difficult to manage in a way that would ameliorate the landing partly due to the relatively large degree of control over the regional economies that was handed over to the international market during the gradual process of liberalization (Hew, 2008).

On the other hand ASEAN members recognize the importance of having a modern and dynamic regional financial system (ASEAN, 2008a, 2008b, 2008c; Drysdale, 2010; Hwang, 2006). Capital flows are becoming more important than ever for the region's future growth. Competition from China and from South Asia due to low labour costs means that in order for ASEAN to remain competitive considerable investments in human capital and infrastructure will be necessary (Bhattacharyay, 2010).

Foreign Direct Investment is becoming harder to attract than ever before with traditional sources such as Japan looking at China as a new manufacturing centre for their industries (Hook, Gilson, Hughes, & Dobson, 2005; Hwang, 2006). This means that ASEAN needs to attract a different kind of capital which is not tied to long term mega projects nor to any particular company or country. One way to do so is to garner the power of the international market in shorter term investment such as bonds, currency exchanges, and stock.

In order to attract and keep the flow of this kind of capital it is necessary to have a modern financial sector which allows investors to move and withdraw their investments with a moment's notice. A banking sector that can provide modern international services and that is integrated to the great financial centres of New York, Tokyo, and London is becoming a necessity rather than a luxury. Thus, greater integration and liberalization is the answer rather than more restrictions (Drysdale, 2010). The challenge is that the flexibility and opening that is needed involves a certain degree of loss of control over part of the economy.

It implies that international banks would enter previously protected markets and that those banks will manage the savings of regional citizens even if they are owned by foreigners. Control over savings accounts and other financial flows means that it would become harder for governments to regulate the exchange rates for their currencies and that they would "float" according to the international market (Than & Thein, 2007). [2] Moreover, the liberalization of capital flows would expose member states to the ups and downs of the international market (Skidelsky, 2010). It is clear that there is a lack of consensus as to the way forward in terms of capital liberalization. The Blueprint for the ASEAN Economic Community is very ambiguous regarding the path towards the liberalization of financial flows (ASEAN, 2008c).

There is agreement on the need and desirability of liberalization but as a result of the "ASEAN way" of decision making the Blueprint represents the least common denominator of agreement reached by the member states (von Feigenblatt, 2009a). Directly following statements asserting the need for greater liberalization of capital flows there are statements extolling the need for some protections and the inclusion of the ASEAN–X formula shows that true consensus was not reached. ASEAN-X refers to the practice of allowing countries that agree to move forward even if some do not. This eliminates the veto power entailed by strict consensus while at the same time allows recalcitrant states to remain engaged in the overall process. The ASEAN-X formula is usually included in cases in which it was impossible to deal with certain objections from member states dealing with important issues of principle. Thus, the case of the liberalization of financial flows shows that while it is considered to be desirable, there is considerable disagreement as to the way forward.

Barriers and Obstacles to the Free Flow of Investment

Closely related to the liberalization in financial sector is the free flow of investment. Since the main obstacles and barriers and obstacles to the free flow of capital have been discussed in the previous subsection, this section will concentrate on other barriers such as: weak legal safeguards; investor-state disputes; political instability; difficulty of transfer and repatriation of capital, profit, and dividends; and red tape with the concomitant lack of transparency in terms of rules and regulations. The previously mentioned set of barriers and obstacles are also affected by the development divide of the region as well as by political issues such as nationalism and control over natural resources.

The first obstacle deals with the weak legal safeguards currently in place in most ASEAN member states. As in everything else, the quality of safeguards vary widely from member to member with countries like Singapore and the Philippines having relatively strong safeguards and countries like Myanmar and Thailand having weaker ones.

Legal safeguards refer to legal protections to investments. Most ASEAN countries have strict rules regulating foreign ownership of enterprises and of real estate. Some countries such as Myanmar forbid any form of direct foreign ownership while others like Cambodia grant citizenship to foreign investors who invest more than US$ 100,000 and thus circumvent citizenship requirements. Legal safeguards are very important in that foreign entities and investors need to know that their investment is safe from government expropriation or other legal challenges.

While a complete liberalization of ownership requirements is not absolutely necessary in order to satisfy the condition of legal safeguards, it is important for foreign entities to have clear legal channels available to protect their investments from extralegal challenges. This includes clear ownership registration rules as well as clear ownership rules. Investors should be aware of their rights and duties at the time of investment so that they can plan accordingly. This step would lower risk and increase trust, thus attracting foreign investment.

One positive initial step would be the strengthening of legal safeguards for intraregional investors. In terms of the resources needed as well as of the political capital required, this small step would lead to greater intraregional cooperation and would move needed capital from richer to poorer members, leading to region wide development and growth. For this to happen, important steps need to be taken in terms of the harmonization of legal systems (at least in terms of legal safeguards for investments) as well as clear ownership rules and dispute resolution systems.

This leads to a closely related barrier, the possibility of investor-state disputes. While investor-state disputes are nothing new and are present even in advanced liberal economies such as the United States, they present a considerable risk in unstable developing countries. The risk associated with expropriation or undue government interference makes investment in unstable developing countries very costly and problematic.

Needless to say the risk varies depending on the type of investment, stock or infrastructure, but it nonetheless discourages investment due to the magnitude of possible losses. Investor-state disputes can cover a range of issues but some of the most notable ones involve nationalization, expropriation, licenses, and management-workers relationships. In order for investor-state disputes to be handled fairly there must be a clear mechanism to deal with them (Ury, Brett, & Goldberg, 1993). The mechanism must be free from political pressure such as from local interest groups. Thus, independence is important in terms of dealing with investor-state disputes.

Moreover, the criteria by which to adjudicate disputes must be clearly agreed to before disputes arise (Fisher & Ury, 1991). One of the reasons why investor-state disputes are such an important obstacle to investment in Southeast Asia is the relatively recent transition by some ASEAN members from a state-run economy to the free market economy as well as weak legal systems (von Feigenblatt, 2009a; Gottesman, 2003; Heidhues, 2000; Short, 2004; Than & Thein, 2007). This means that foreign investment both intra and extra regional must deal with the possibility of backtracking in terms of liberalization as well as possible government interference in issues usually outside of the purview of government authorities. Thus, issues of control over natural resources as well as management-employee relations can become overly complicated and acrimonious due to the shadow of colonialism as well as the possible political considerations such as a rise in nationalist sentiments as well as union pressures.

In other words, investors must be protected from arbitrary government actions affecting their investments. Two extreme negative externalities of a weak dispute management system are government expropriations during which the state forces the investor to sale all assets and to turn control of the enterprise over to the government in exchange of an artificially low price, and the revocation of licenses due to political pressure which make it impossible for investors to put their capital to work. Both externalities are extremely costly to investors and due to the oftentimes exponential sunk costs required for certain types of productive investments, an exit strategy is very challenging and costly.

Certain ASEAN members such as Laos, Myanmar, Cambodia, and Vietnam have abandoned a state-run economy relatively recently and their governments maintain a considerable stake in the economy (CIA, 2010b, 2010c, 2010d; Vu-Tung, 2007). It is very important to set up processes allowing investors to deal with state-investor disputes fairly and through neutral objective procedures. This is an issue that can be addressed by the ASEAN Secretariat by providing binding arbitration for investor-state disputes.

Political instability is a regional challenge that is harder to tackle. Extra-constitutional regime changes are nothing new in the region and are sources of considerable uncertainty in terms of the investment environment (Chang, Chu, & Park, 2007; von Feigenblatt, 2009a, 2009b; Katanyuu, 2006; Keling et al., 2010; Lintner, 2009; Neher, 2002; Ockey, 2007; Ungpakorn, 2007). Due to the weakness of the legal protections accorded to foreign investments in some ASEAN members, political instability exponentially increases the uncertainty of doing business across borders. ASEAN countries mostly avoid legalism in favour of trust and informal agreements similar to those studied in Chinese business networks which are based on informal networks (Augsburger, 1992).

A consequence of this is that business is carried out according to personal relationships and trust. Thus, if a Singaporean investor decides to invest in a certain business venture in Thailand based on the connections a Sino-Thai friend with government links, the venture depends on the trust the Singaporean investor has on his Sino-Thai friend, who in turn depends on his relationship to members of the government. Therefore, legalism is avoided in favour of personal relationships and networks based on reputation and trust. This system works very well as long as relationships are stable and transitions are predictable such as in South Korea, Taiwan, China, and Japan.

Nevertheless the system faces considerable difficulties in countries facing considerable political instability outside of the constitutional framework. An example of this is the recurrent military coups in Thailand which are usually followed by witch hunts, accusations of corruption, and a run for the spoils of power (DRESSEL, 2009; C. Murphy, 2009). In this unstable scenario, it is difficult for a foreign investor to know whether his or her connection in the country will have friends in the government when the next coup takes place.

While instability and transfers of power are also part of democracy the difference is that changes are not as punitive as extra-constitutional changes of regime and the rule of law provides a certain degree of protection from the whims of the new elites. Political instability is especially problematic when dealing with investments with considerable sunk costs such as in the energy sector and in infrastructure projects. A change in government can bring about the nationalization or revocation of costly licenses and operating rights.

It is ironic that the greater political stability in terms of investment protection is found in either the most authoritarian or the least authoritarian countries of the region. An example at the authoritarian end is Vietnam which is committed to the protection of the market economy and is actively courting foreign direct investment (CIA, 2010d; Vu-Tung, 2007). A change in the top leadership positions will not cause any considerable changes for investors since the entire party favours the protection of foreign investment.

On the other extreme countries like the Philippines have turbulent democracies but transitions tend to be constitutional and most political parties favour the free market and defend private investment (CIA, 2010e). This means that regardless of a change in government, policies regarding foreign investment remain relatively stable (Shatkin, 2006). The greater challenges are faced by semi-authoritarian countries such as Thailand and Cambodia which show the worst of both extremes, instability without the rule of law. There is no clear institution to chart a path but rather opportunistic elites protecting their own short term interests.

In Thailand, the network monarchy aligns itself with whichever civilian or military faction is in the ascendancy and thus provides little stability for foreign investors (Handley, 2006; Ungpakórn, 2007, 2010). The same is true in Cambodia where the only stability is brought about by the continued rule of Hun Sen (Gottesman, 2003). A lack of a clear government ideology and at the same time a weak level of the rule of law make investing in those countries highly risky. Political instability is an issue which presents a considerable challenge to ASEAN due to its time honoured principle of non-intervention in the internal affairs of member states (von Feigenblatt, 2009a).

Nevertheless, there have been instances in which ASEAN has exerted diplomatic pressure to bring some measure of stability to the region, the case of Cambodia is a good example of this (Katanyuu, 2006; Severino, 2007). The organization has also voiced greater concerns regarding the human rights record of Myanmar and its path towards democracy, on the other hand considerable challenges remain and extralegal coups such as the one that took place in Thailand in 2006 receive little criticism nor result in any concrete actions (von Feigenblatt, 2009b; Keling et al., 2010). It remains to be seen whether the Security pillar of the ASEAN Community makes any headway in this direction through preventive diplomacy and ultimately through more active engagement (Heller, 2005; Nair, 2008; Yzawa, 2006). ASEAN has the potential to establish international norms at the regional level which could make extralegal takeovers more costly and thus discourage the opportunistic support of regional elites for such changes.

The experience of other regions is that political stability is rewarded by the market and that it increases the attractiveness of the region to prospective foreign investors (Friedman, 2000). Central America benefited from the regional peace brought about by the end of its civil wars during the late 1980s and saw two decades of growth (Barry, 1991; Leonard, 1991; Perez-Brignoli, 1989). A similar result was achieved by Eastern Europe after the end of the cold war (Roberts, 1997).

The normative pressure exerted by its proximity to the European Union and the requirements for entry in the regional block raised the costs of political instability and thus discouraged extra-constitutional coups (McCormick, 2005). Greater political stability means that uncertainty becomes risk and that risk is greatly reduced thus lowering the cost of doing business in the region. The improvement in terms of political stability resulted in Eastern European countries attracting considerable foreign direct investment from Western Europe and from the United States. Investments were not limited to volatile fluid ones with short term exit strategies but rather in long term investments with considerable sunk costs in infrastructure. A lower risk translated into a greater willingly of foreign investors to put their money into longer term projects.

Other challenges in the area of the liberalization of investments in ASEAN member states is the freedom of investors to repatriate profits, the elimination or amelioration of red tape, and the clarity of rules and regulations. The three previously mentioned challenges have been discussed in previous sections in relation to capital flows but will be briefly explained in relation to investments. It is very important for investors to be able to repatriate their profit which is sometimes prevented by red tape, unclear regulations, and clear prohibitions. Limitations regarding to the flow of profits is related to other restrictions of capital flows.

Thus, the liberalization of capital flows should lead to an improvement in terms of this obstacle. Nevertheless, the freedom of movement of profits derived from productive investments should be given priority in terms of liberalization since they do not represent a loss to the national economy but rather are a sign of economic growth and can help attract more foreign direct investment. Foreign investors, both extra and intra regional, need to know that they will be able to make use of their profits as they see fit, and this includes the possibility of the repatriation of the profits to their country of origin. In order to facilitate the process to foreign investors, it is important to eliminate complicated red tape through simple and clear procedures which lower transaction costs and show foreign investors that there is a sincere policy of liberalization of capital flows.

Red tape represents one of the most problematic and challenging non-tariff obstacles to trade and its elimination is important in all sub-sectors of the economy. Finally, having clear regulations regarding investments is very important because it lowers risk by making the process more predictable. Investors prefer stability over uncertainty and therefore they would like to know the rules of the game in advance before entering the game. One simple step towards this goal would be to have clear investment rules available in several languages.

Needless to say, ASEAN has taken some tentative steps to deal with the aforementioned challenges in the area of investment. Three broad agreements encompass the efforts in this area, namely the Framework Agreement on the ASEAN Investment Area (AIA), 1998, the ASEAN Agreement for the Promotion and Protection of Investment, 1987, also known as ASEAN Investment Guarantee Agreement (IGA) (ASEAN, 2008c, p. 14). The AIA grants industries from intra regional countries national treatment in terms of investment at the "pre-establishment and the post-establishment stages" (ASEAN, 2008c, p. 14). There are several exceptions to this rule which include industries and occupations in the Temporary Exclusion Lists (TEL) as well as the Sensitive Lists (SL).

The goal is to phase out the TEL and the review the SL in the future. It should be clear that one weakness in this approach is that the meaning of national treatment varies greatly from country to country. ASEAN recognizes this challenge and favours harmonization through the IGA but leaves actual implementation to the countries themselves.

While there are several useful guidelines included in the ASEAN Blueprint for an Economic Community such as the harmonization of applications and the adoption of international standards, concrete steps remain elusive and thus effective implementation is lacking. Greater attention is devoted to the promotion of the region as a safe place to invest.

This is important because it shows that ASEAN is aware of the importance of its international image in order to attract foreign direct investment. Production chains are also encouraged by addressing the challenge of double taxation in the ASEAN region (ASEAN, 2008c, p. 16). A change in this respect would allow foreign investors to produce some components in one country and to assemble them in a second one without having to deal with paying taxes two times. The important idea here is that foreign direct investment can be attracted as a single region rather than as separate countries.

Barriers to the Free Flow of Skilled Labour

By this point we have discussed the liberalization of most factors of production with the exception of labour. The free flow of labour is part of the ideal of liberalization and free trade (Friedman, 2000) however its realization is among the most difficult goals of the economic integration process. Even successful trading blocs such as the North American Free Trade Agreement (NAFTA) have encountered serious obstacles along the road towards the liberalization of the flow/trade of labour (Kolodziej, 2005).

Unemployment, nationalism, different skill levels, and language barriers are just some of the obstacles preventing the full liberalization of the flow of labour in NAFTA. One of the few successful examples of the liberalization of labour can be found in the European Union where the goal was achieved through several stages of liberalization and several agreements recognizing professional qualifications (McCormick, 2005). While a goal of complete liberalization of the free flow of labour is unrealistic and possibly undesirable for ASEAN, the organization has recognized the desirability of allowing the free flow of skilled labour in the region (ASEAN, 2008c).

This is an important goal since labour is an important factor of production, together with capital and land, and true economic integration requires the free flow of all factors of production. The free flow of labour also presents other benefits such as technology transfer from more to less developed countries as well as the harmonization of regional professional standards making regional skilled labour more competitive in the international market. Needless to say there are also some considerable barriers to the free flow of skilled labour in the ASEAN region. A wide development gap between and within member States presents considerable challenges to the flow of labour such as differences in qualifications, language barriers, and different working conditions (Suharto, 2009). Related to the previously mentioned obstacles two broader phenomena can be found namely nationalism and the fear of brain drain.

Since this chapter concentrates on the barriers to liberalization this subsection will focus on the obstacles as well as the barriers rather than on the benefits of the free flow of skilled labour in the region, however the benefits should be kept in mind. The most obvious barrier is the difference in professional qualifications and standards. Licensing is prevalent in some vocational professions such as medicine and law while accredited university degrees serve a similar purpose in other disciplines. Each country has its own system to issue licenses to practice as well as different levels of educational quality at the tertiary level.

Therefore a license to practice medicine in Myanmar does not represent the same skill level as a similar license in Singapore. The same can be said of university degrees, while the region has some of the world's top universities such as the National University of Singapore, Chulalongkorn University in Thailand, and other elite universities in Malaysia, there are also a great number of substandard universities in countries such as Cambodia, Myanmar, and Laos. This gap in quality means that degrees cannot be accepted at face value as a certification of a similar level of knowledge on a subject area.

One relative advantage enjoyed by most countries in the region is that they have mostly adopted the British educational system which clearly divides undergraduate from graduate education. While there are a few anomalies such as the Thai medical degree which is a bachelor's with a long practicum and is incorrectly labelled a medical doctorate and some vocational fields such as physical therapy which are really associate degrees and are incorrectly granted as bachelor's degrees, most countries use a common nomenclature for their degrees. It is understandable that the more advanced members of ASEAN have some reservations about recognizing foreign credentials as acceptable to practice in their territory.

Nevertheless differences in skill levels and quality controls can be established in order to harmonize academic credentials in the region. There are several ways to do this including setting up a supranational authority to accredit universities, a highly unlikely eventuality, or a loose approach similar to the Bologna process in Europe which involves the universities themselves in monitoring each other. Cooperation among universities is in an early stage through the ASEAN University Network (AUN) but there is considerable support from policy elites for an increase in the mobility of students and staff within the region (ASEAN, 2008c, p. 18).

Up to now the emphasis has been on the facilitation of liberalization in the services sectors such as the financial and health sectors but there are plans to do the same in other sectors by the year 2015. At this point progress in terms of the harmonization and homologation of academic credentials depends on the level of cooperation that can be reached by university authorities and intellectual elite.

Several obstacles are present in terms of cooperation between universities such as considerable differentials in freedom of speech, turf wars between different schools, and the different levels of autonomy and development of universities in different ASEAN Members.

Universities tend to serve a vast array of purposes in ASEAN member States which range from serving as the training groups of technicians, physicians, dentists, and other vocational professions, educating future civil servants and political elites, and as oasis for the pursuit of knowledge (Lee, 2000; Ungpakorn, 2007, 2010). The different roles of universities are sometimes at cross purposes with each other which explain the sometimes adversarial relationship of ASEAN governments with universities. An extreme example of this is the closing down of universities in Myanmar by the Military Junta (CIA, 2010a; Keling et al., 2010).

Other less extreme examples include the prosecution of prominent Academics in Thailand for criticizing the monarchy and the antagonistic relationship of conservative elements in the Philippines with the left leaning universities (von Feigenblatt, 2009d; von Feigenblatt, Suttichujit, Shuib, Keling, & Ajis, 2010; Heidhues, 2000; Ungpakorn, 2010). Thus, ASEAN member States view universities as central to the development of the region but also as possible destabilizing forces. The role that universities play as intellectual centres for socio-political movements as Islamism in Malaysia, communism and republicanism in Thailand, and communism and social-democracy in the Philippines is undeniable (Means, 2009; Neher, 2002; Ungpakorn, 2007, 2010; Wyatt, 2003).

The reason why the competing purposes of universities is a challenge for cooperation at the ASEAN level is that both students and academics from different universities are accustomed to different levels of academic freedom and to different levels of emphasis on rote learning over critical thinking (von Feigenblatt et al., 2010). Thus some governments might be wary of having academics from freer universities teaching in their countries. The problem is compounded by the fact that advancement in the applied sciences requires critical analysis which is incompatible with social control and censorship. Furthermore the promotion of research and development implies the need for greater academic freedom in all fields. Moreover, academics in the different ASEAN members play different social roles and their levels of independence vis-à-vis politics and government varies greatly from country to country and also within countries themselves.

Therefore the promotion of cooperation between ASEAN Universities could be derailed by the political role of certain academics involved in the process. This phenomenon of political co-optation of academics is not unique to the region but it is particularly widespread in developing countries due to the lack of autonomy of the university system. Nevertheless, the countervailing influence of the need to promote the training of vocational fields will balance out any trepidation that the political elites might feel about greater cooperation among ASEAN Universities. Furthermore, the successful Singaporean experience with their outstanding university system shows that in some instances it is possible to have some measure of political control over universities while still allowing enough freedom for them to thrive (Lee, 2000).

Another obvious obstacle to the free flow of skilled labour is language. The vast array of languages spoken in the region makes cooperation at the professional level difficult (HSIN-HUANG, HSIAO, & WAN, 2007). A common language is a sine qua nom of greater integration in terms of research and development and an important tool in order to facilitate the flow of both students and researchers inside the ASEAN Region. While several ASEAN member States have had French colonial experiences, English has arisen as the lingua franca of the region, and is recognized as such by ASEAN itself (Heidhues, 2000; Neher, 2002).

Needless to say the language's official status on paper does not reflect the situation on the ground and only very small elite is fluent in the language with the notable exceptions of the Philippines and Singapore (Neher, 2002). Several countries have started to take steps in order to improve English language proficiency among its elite, such as the mushrooming of international programs in Thailand and Malaysia and the exponential increase of language schools all over the region. While greater English proficiency is a goal that is recognized as valuable by most member States it is also controversial due to nationalist reasons. Almost half of the ASEAN member States have had British colonial experiences, there is also a feeling that English is connected to American led globalization and neo-imperialism, and there is fear by conservative national elites that greater emphasis on the teaching and usage of the English language will detract from the importance of their national languages.

Nationalism is not only a barrier in relation to the adoption of a lingua franca for the skilled labour of the region but also in and of itself. The greater flow of skilled labour can be perceived as a threat by certain national professional associations as well as by nationalists in all spheres of society. Thus, the increased presence of skilled foreign workers might be resented by unskilled local labour and blamed for their continued low socio-economic status. Therefore, it is very important for governments to show that greater flow of skilled labour benefits everyone and not just the foreign skilled professionals working in the country. Moreover, the emphasis on welcoming only skilled professionals may alienate unemployed local professionals, especially those holding minimum entry level qualifications. The spread of education at the undergraduate level in certain ASEAN member States has resulted in a high proportion of unemployed or underemployed professionals at the entry level.

Thus, an increase in the number of highly qualified professionals from abroad may be seen as a threat and as unfair by the previously mentioned group. Nationalism always affects the outflow of skilled labour. This refers to the famous "brain drain" phenomenon in which the "best and the brightest" leave the country looking for greener pastures. The liberalization of the labour market in the ASEAN region will certainly result in some uneven flows due to the development differential between member States and most importantly by the difference in working conditions from country to country. Since most ASEAN member States have subsidized the education of their elites in one way or another, their departure to other countries for better working conditions may be seen as a net loss to their countries.

Even if one ignores the subsidized education, the loss of talent can be considered a drain in a country's human capital. It is likely that a blanket liberalization of the flow of skilled labour would result in the most highly qualified workers moving to member States with high GDPs Per Capita such as Singapore and to a certain extend Malaysia. The consequences of this outflow of talent vary considerably depending on the starting point of each Member State. For a country such as Laos it would be devastating to the country if most of its very limited skilled workforce were to leave the country. On the other hand, the Philippines can afford to temporarily export some of its skilled labour (Neher, 2002). It is clear that some governments will view the possibility of a massive outflow of talent as an important threat and would expect some measures to be put in place in order for less advanced countries to also benefit from the flow of skilled labour.

ASEAN has taken some tentative steps to facilitate the flow of skilled labour such as by making it easier to apply for visas and employment passes to engage in cross-border trade and financial services (ASEAN, 2008c, p. 17). There are also plans to facilitate educational exchanges between regional universities and also to allow faculty members to spend some time teaching or conducting research at another university in the region. Nevertheless, the challenges and barriers remain along the road towards the liberalization of the free flow of skilled labour.

Probably the most important challenge is keeping nationalism in check and garnering the needed political capital to keep the momentum going. While ASEAN members agree on the need to facilitate the flow of skilled labour in order to make the region more competitive and in order to move towards the goal of greater economic integration, there is little agreement as to the way and the pace to be taken in order to achieve the ultimate goal. In the short run, greater interaction between the professional and intellectual elites of the region may be the best starting point towards a more specific implementation plan. The promotion of English as the region's lingua franca is another relatively uncontroversial step that can support the entire process of liberalization and integration of the region's economy.

Economic Relations and ASEAN Centrality Principle

An important challenge for ASEAN members is to increase the proportion of trade that takes place intra-regionally versus extra-regionally. Greater economic integration entails greater intra-regional economic interdependence and a good measurement of this is the level of intraregional trade taking place. As of 2010 ASEAN had a total trade volume of 1.54 billion USD. 24.5 percent of the total trade volume represents intra-ASEAN trade while 75.5 percent is made up of extra-ASEAN trade (ASEAN, 2010). It is clear that ASEAN members still conduct most of their trade extra-regionally rather than within the ASEAN bloc.

This state of affairs is partly due to the region's history of division during the Cold War and the different bilateral trading arrangements that arose due to that. A second explanation is the challenge of finding complementarities between the products of the member States. Especially at the early stages of economic development most products tend to be agricultural and there is little differentiation. The problem for developing countries in Southeast Asia is that due to similar climatic conditions and geographic proximity, their products tend to be quite similar. While this presents considerable challenges and obstacles during early stages of development, it is less of a problem as a country develops and products with a greater value added are traded.

It should be noted that three broad historical trading groups can be found among ASEAN Member States. Certain countries such as Thailand, Singapore, Malaysia, Brunei, and the Philippines have depended mostly on trade with the United States and its allies during the post-war period. A second group is more heterogeneous in nature and represents countries which followed the Non-Aligned Movement (NAM) or that favoured China during the Cold War. Members of the second group include Indonesia, Myanmar, Cambodia (before the fall of the Khmer Rouge).

Countries in this second group trade with both the Soviet bloc as well as with China and the West. Their trading relationships were more opportunist than the first group and depended on the needs of the moment. Finally, the third group was the pro Soviet bloc which included Vietnam, Cambodia (after the Khmer Rouge), and Laos. This third group conducted most of its trade with the Eastern Bloc in Europe. ASEAN Member States have for the most part expanded their trading relationships since the end of the Cold War and thus the previously mentioned groups are no longer as neatly defined as they once were. Nevertheless the groups are still useful as a heuristic device to understand the present arrangement based on bilateral trade agreements.

The first group continued to have a strong trading relationship with the United States, Japan, and Western European members of the European Union while at the same time expanding trade to previously ignored regional powers such as China and Indochina. In order to protect their access to the American market some countries such as Singapore signed free trade agreements with the United States, others took advantage of preferential trade terms related to American security concerns, for example Thailand.

This group's relationship with Japan differed in that their products were integrated into the Japanese production chain as sources of basic raw materials and as production sites for intermediate products for Japanese industry. Thus, this group has historically relied heavily on its trading relationship with Japan and with the United States. Notwithstanding the group's continued relationship with its traditional trading partners, members have reacted to China's economic growth by actively promoting trade with the giant while at the same time attempting to move up the value chain in order to forestall Chinese competition.

The second group is more heterogeneous and its members have taken different paths after the end of the Cold War. Indonesia continued its opportunistic policy while increasingly being integrated into the Japanese production chain. The country also increased its trade with China and with the United States. Myanmar continues to rely on trade with China as well as with other regional economies such as Thailand. Finally, Cambodia moved to the third group for a while after the Vietnamese occupation and then expanded its trade with the West after the United Nations intervention that ended the civil war.

The greatest changes can be seen in the third group which reacted to the fall of the Soviet Union by completely revamping their trading policies. Vietnam followed the Chinese path towards a market economy with its "Doi Moi" policy and expanded its trade with the West and with members of the first group. This policy culminated with the country joining the World Trade Organization in 2007 (WTO, 2007). Laos followed a similar path but with less impressive results and its trade with Thailand increased exponentially over the decades following the fall of the Soviet Union (CIA, 2010b).

A more detailed looked at the import/export trends of ASEAN members shows that countries low at the development continuum tend to have a higher proportion of their total exports inside of the ASEAN region in comparison to with extra-regional partners. Two clear examples of this are Myanmar and Laos with 50.4 percent and 80.6 percent respectively of their exports remaining in the ASEAN region

(ASEAN, 2010). Other than the two previously mentioned exceptions, the average share to total exports to extra-regional partners is of 75.4 percent (ASEAN, 2010). This shows that while there is greater economic interaction between ASEAN members, extra-regional partners continue to dominate the export market.

Figure 14: Intra-ASEAN and Extra-ASEAN Exports

Country	Intra-ASEAN exports		Extra-ASEAN exports		Total Exports
	Value	Share to total exports	Value	Share to total exports	
Brunei	1,229.3	17.1	5,939.3	82.9	7,168.6
Cambodia	644.6	12.9	4,341.2	87.1	4,985.8
Indonesia	24,623.9	21.1	91,886.1	78.9	116,510.0
Lao PDR	997.4	80.6	239.8	19.4	1,237.2
Malaysia	40,365.1	25.7	116,525.8	74.3	156,890.9
Myanmar	3,196.7	50.4	3,144.8	49.6	6,341.5
Philippines	5,838.4	15.2	32,496.2	84.8	38,334.7
Singapore	81,646.5	30.3	188,186.0	69.7	269,832.5
Thailand	32,490.6	21.3	120,006.6	78.7	152,497.2
Vietnam	8,554.8	15.1	48,136.2	84.9	56,691.0
ASEAN	199,587.3	24.6	610,901.9	75.4	810,489.2

Source: Data taken from ASEAN Stat Table 18, July, 2010. Values are in US$ million (ASEAN, 2010).

A similar trend can be observed in terms of imports. With the exception of Brunei Darussalam most members of ASEAN import more from extra-regional partners than from other intra-regional members. The case of Brunei is due to the high reliance of the export sector on oil and on a small industrial base. Two good examples of this trend are Thailand and Vietnam which import 80.0 and 80.4 percent of their total imports from extra-regional partners. The regional average for intra-regional imports is of 24.3 percent while the average for extra-regional imports is of 75.7 percent.

It is clear that the averages are almost identical to the total shares for exports showing that ASEAN members continue to rely on extra regional partners not only to sell their products abroad but also to satisfy local demand. There are several possible explanations for ASEAN member's reliance on regional partners for trade including both exports and imports. Two possible explanations were discussed previously and deal with a lack of complementary of products and the legacy of the cold war, however there is a third explanation related to free trade agreements (FTAs) and the promotion of globalization.

Figure 15: Intra-ASEAN and Extra-ASEAN Imports

Country	Intra-ASEAN imports		Extra-ASEAN imports		Total Imports
	Value	Share to total exports	Value	Share to total exports	
Brunei	1,242.8	51.8	1,156.8	48.2	2,399.6
Cambodia	1,453.3	37.3	2,447.6	62.7	3,900.9
Indonesia	27,742.4	28.7	69,086.8	71.3	96,829.2
Lao PDR	1,480.8	85.8	244.2	14.2	1,7399.5
Malaysia	31,700.2	25.7	91,630.2	74.3	123,330.5
Myanmar	2,065.7	53.7	1,784.1	46.3	3,849.9
Philippines	11,561.1	25.4	33,972.9	74.6	46,533.9
Singapore	59,047.6	24.0	186,737.1	76.0	245,784.7
Thailand	26,759.5	20.0	107.010.1	80.0	133,769.6
Vietnam	13,566.7	19.6	55,664.2	80.4	69,230.9
ASEAN	176,620.1	24.3	549,734.0	75.7	726,354.1

Source: Data taken from ASEAN Stat Table 18, July, 2010. Values are in US$ million (ASEAN, 2010).

As Dennis Arnold aptly explains in his insightful article dealing with the role of free trade agreements in Southeast Asia, the stalled condition of the WTO talks led the United States to pursue a parallel strategy to promote its economic interests abroad, namely bilateral free trade agreements (Arnold, 2006). Thus multilateralism gave way to bilateralism for several reasons. First of all, the WTO process was slowing down and facing considerable opposition from some developing countries (Zagl, 2008).

Secondly, it is much easier for the United States to extract trade concessions when dealing with a small developing country rather than with a grouping due to the power differential. Geopolitical factors also play a role in that the war on terror and support on other American foreign policy priorities could be linked to trade as both an incentive to support American goals and in order to put extra pressure on some countries to open their markets to American products (Ellis, 2009; Glassman, 2005).

The measuring stick for free trade agreements in Southeast Asia is the United States-Singapore Free Trade Agreement (USSFTA) which has become the model for all other planned FTAs in the region (Arnold, 2006, p. 23). The USSFTA has put pressure on other Southeast Asian countries to start negotiating FTAs with the United States with the result that five other ASEAN members (Brunei, Malaysia, the Philippines, and Thailand) have signed trade and investment facilitation agreements (TIFA) with the United States (Arnold, 2006, pp. 23-24).

The previously mentioned fragmented state of affairs is a challenge for the future economic integration of the ASEAN region. Bilateral Free Trade Agreements stress the national interest of the intra-regional Member State and those of the extra-regional trading partner without taking into consideration the interests of the ASEAN region as a whole. Moreover, the bilateral process circumvents ASEAN entirely and thus weakens the ability of the region to negotiate and operate as a single economic block. It is clear that negotiation on a bilateral basis lowers the negotiating/bargaining power of ASEAN member which are mostly developing countries vis-à-vis the more powerful extra-regional trading partners.

Positive externalities such as cooperation and integration of the production chain are also missed due to the narrow focus of bilateral trade negotiations. Thus it is a tactic that follows the traditional imperial technique of "divide and conquer". Nevertheless one should not jump to conclusions and blame this fragmented state of affairs on an American imperial conspiracy since the United States is also attempting to deal with the challenges posed by a stalled WTO process and with a resurgent China with similarly self interested plans in the region (Bush, 2010).

Therefore, the challenge is for ASEAN members to follow the principle of "ASEAN Centrality". This very ambiguous principle is included in the Charter and in the Blue Print for the ASEAN Economic Community and it represents the lowest common denomination or broad consensus reached by ASEAN members as to the relatively importance or precedence that ASEAN should have in terms of investment and trade (ASEAN, 2008b, 2008c). "ASEAN Centrality" claims that the ASEAN process should serve as the anchor to all other efforts. ASEAN is meant to serve as the central node of the network rather than as a parallel structure to the more influcntial bilateral trade agreements.

As always there is a gap between the broad principles espoused by ASEAN members and their implementation and this is particularly stark in the area of trade and investment. As was shown by the brief overview of trade, imports, and exports in the region, ASEAN does not enjoy "centrality" at this time and the rise in the number of bilateral trade and investment agreements does not augur well for the region's ability to function as a single integrated economic bloc.

The Way Forward

This chapter has covered some of the barriers and obstacles that are faced by ASEAN in relation to its goal of achieving economic integration. The planned ASEAN Economic Community is a very ambitious project involving a vast array of policy areas and requiring considerable coordination and cooperation by ASEAN Member States. As was shown in the previous sections, the obstacles and barriers are many and complex. Notwithstanding the challenges, there is somc basic consensus regarding the desirability of the liberalization of trade and investment in the ASEAN region.

Some of the measures taken by ASEAN to overcome the obstacles and barriers that were identified in this chapter have been discussed and some of the most important structural conflicts have been alluded to. The following chapter moves from the specific to the general in an effort to identify the structural conflicts stalling the integration process. Emphasis is placed on structure and on the competing tensions affecting the organization. While the many challenges faced by ASEAN have been identified this should not be interpreted as an inevitable path to failure but simply a detailed assessment of possible problems that have to be resolved in order to move the organization towards a deeper stage of integration and cooperation. This is what the next two chapters aim to do. Chapter 7 applies structural dynamics to tackle ASEAN's economic and trade oscillation while chapter 8 provides some conclusions regarding the region's economic development.

End Notes

1. CLMV countries refer to Cambodia, Laos, Myanmar, and Vietnam.
2. Myanmar's financial system is one of the least advanced ones in the region. Exchange rates are complicated and three rates coexist simultaneously, the black market rate, the official rate, and a semi-official one released by the government. As expected, the existence of several exchange rates makes it very difficult to do business in Myanmar. For more information about Myanmar's deficient banking system see Than & Thein (2007).

References

Akaha, T. (2009). Human Security in East Asia. *Journal of Human Security, 5*(3), 11-34.

Arnold, D. (2006). Free Trade Agreements and Southeast Asia. *Journal of Contemporary Asia, 36*(2), 195-207.

ASEAN. (2008a). *2007-2008 Annual Report: One Vision, One Identity, One Community*. Retrieved November 30, 2008. from http://www.aseansec.org/AR-08.pdf.

ASEAN. (2008b). *ASEAN Charter*. Retrieved November 30, 2008. from http://www.aseansec.org/ASEAN-Charter.pdf.

ASEAN. (2008c). *ASEAN ECONOMIC COMMUNITY BLUEPRINT*. Retrieved. from http://www.aseansec.org/5187-10.pdf.

ASEAN. (2010). Intra- and extra-ASEA trade as of 15 July 2010. In T. 18 (Ed.). Jakarta: ASEAN.

Augsburger, D.W. (1992). *Conflict Mediation Across Cultures: Pathways and Patterns* (First ed.). Louisville: Westmister/John Knox Press.

Barry, T. (1991). *Central America Inside Out: The Essential Guide to Its Societies, Politics, and Economies* (First ed.). New York: Grove Weidenfeld.

Battersby, P., & Siracusa, J.M. (2009). *Globalization & Human Security* (Hardcover ed.). Lanham: Rowman & Littlefield Publishers, Inc.

Bhattacharyay, B. N. (2010). Infrastructure for ASEAN Connectivity and Integration. *ASEAN Economic Bulletin, 27*(2), 200-221.

Bush, G. W. (2010). *Decision Points*. New York: Crown Publishers.

Chang, Y.-t., Chu, Y.-h., & Park, C.-M. (2007). Authoritarian Nostalgia in Asia. *Journal of Democracy, 18*(3), 71-80.

Chang, Y.-t., Chun, Y.-h., & Park, C.-M. (2007). Authoritarian Nostalgia in Asia. *Journal of Democracy, 18*(3), 71-80.

CIA. (2010a). The World Fact Book: Burma. Retrieved November 5, 2010, from https://www.cia.gov/library/publications/the-world-factbook/geos/bm.html

CIA. (2010b). The World Fact Book: Laos People's Republic Retrieved November 9, 2010, from https://www.cia.gov/library/publications/the-world-factbook/geos/la.html.

CIA. (2010c). World Factbook: Cambodia. Retrieved November 29, 2010, from https://www.cia.gov/library/publications/the-world-factbook/geos/cb.html

CIA. (2010d). The World Factbook: Socialist Republic of Vietnam. Retrieved November 13, 2010, from https://www.cia.gov/library/publications/the-world-factbook/geos/vm.html.

CIA. (2010e). The World Factbook: The Philippines. Retrieved October 8, 2010, from https://www.cia.gov/library/publications/the-world-factbook/geos/rp.html.

Collins, A. (2008). A People-Oriented ASEAN: A Door Ajar or Closed for Civil Society Organizations? *Contemporary Southeast Asia, 30*(2), 313-332.

DRESSEL, B. (2009). Thailand's Elusive Quest for a Workable Constitution, 1997-2007. *Contemporary Southeast Asia, 31*(2), 296-325.

Drysdale, P. (2010). APEC's Achievements and Challenges Today: Keynote Address, APEC Economic Committee Roundtable, Beppu, Oita, Japan, 7 August 2010. *Asia Pacific World, 1*(2), 33-44.

Eades, J.S., & Cooper, M.J.M. (2010). Introduction. The Asia Pacific World: A Summary and an Agenda. *Asia Pacific World, 1*(1), 1--22.

Ellis, D.C. (2009). U.S. Grand Strategy Following the George W. Bush Presidency. *International Studies Perspectives, 10*(4), 361-377.

von Feigenblatt, Otto F. (2009a). ASEAN and Human Security: Challenges and Opportunities. *Ritsumeikan Centre for Asia Pacific Studies Working Paper, No. 09-5*(July), 1-22.

von Feigenblatt, Otto F. (2009b). Comparing the 2006 Military Coup in Thailand and the 2009 Coup in Honduras: Internal Socio-political Similarities and External Normative Differences. *Infinity Journal, 1*(4), 3-9.

von Feigenblatt, Otto F. (2009c). Human Security and the Responsibility to Protect: A Holistic Approach to Dealing with Violent Conflict in Southeast Asia. In A. K. Pandey, S. Verma, R.P. Pathak, B. Paranjape, N.K. Mishra, Gangatharan, D. Pande & B.K. Choudhary (Eds.), *Repositioning 'Subalternity' in Globalized India: The Dynamics of Social Inclusion* (pp. 130). Delhi: Macmillan.

von Feigenblatt, Otto F. (2009d). The Thai Ethnocracy Unravels: A Critical Cultural Analysis of Thailand's Socio-Political Unrest. *Journal of Alternative Perspectives in the Social Sciences, 1*(3), 583-611.

von Feigenblatt, Otto F., Suttichujit, V., Shuib, M.S., Keling, M.F., & Ajis, M.N. e. (2010). Weapons of Mass Assimilation: A Critical Analysis of the Use of Education in Thailand. *Journal of Asia Pacific Studies, 1*(2), 292-311.

Fisher, R., & Ury, W. (1991). *Getting to Yes: Negotiating Agreement Without Giving In* (Second ed.). New York: Penguin Books.

Friedman, T.L. (2000). *The Lexus and the Olive Tree: Understanding Globalization* (Revised ed.). New York: Farrar Straus Giroux.

Glassman, J. (2005). The "War On Terrorism" Comes To Southeast Asia. *Journal of Contemporary Asia, 35*(1), 3-28.

Gleditsch, N.-P. (2008). The Liberal Moment Fifteen Years On. *International Studies Quarterly, 52*(4), 691-712.

Gottesman, E. (2003). *CAMBODIA After the Khmer Rouge: Inside the Politics of Nation Building*. New Haven: Yale University Press.

Handley, P.M. (2006). *The King Never Smiles: A Biography of Thailand's Bhumibol Adulyadej*. New Haven Yale University Press.

Heidhues, M.S. (2000). *Southeast Asia: A Concise History*. London: Thames & Hudson.

Heller, D. (2005). The Relevance of the ASEAN Regional Forum (ARF) for Regional Security in the Asia-Pacific. *Contemporary Southeast Asia, 27*(1), 123-145.

Hew, D. (2008). The Malaysian Economy: Developments and Challenges. *Southeast Asian Affairs*, 207-222.

Hook, G., Gilson, J., Hughes, C.W., & Dobson, H. (2005). *Japan's International Relations: Politics, economics and security* (2nd Edition ed.). London: Routledge.

HSIN-HUANG, HSIAO, M., & WAN, P.-S. (2007). The Experiences of Cultural Globalizations in Asia-Pacific. *Japanese Journal of Political Science, 8*(3), 361-376.

Hwang, H.-d. (2006). APEC and emerging regionalism in North East Asia. *Asia Europe Journal, 4*(4), 499-510.

Katanyuu, R. (2006). Beyond Non-Interference in ASEAN: The Association's Role in Myanmar's National Reconciliation and Democratization. *Asian Survey, 46*(6), 825-845.

Keling, M.F., Saludin, M.N., Feigenblatt, O.F. v., Ajis, M.N. e., & Shuib, M.S. (2010). A Historical Approach to Myanmar's Democratic Process. *Journal of Asia Pacific Studies, 1*(2), 132-148.

Kershaw, R. (2003). Partners in Realism: Britain and Brunei Amid Recent Turbulence. *Asian Affairs (London), 34*(1), 46-53.

Kolodziej, E.A. (2005). *Security and International Relations*. New York: Cambridge University Press.

Komori, Y. (2009). Asia's Institutional Creation and Evolution. *Asian Perspective, 33*(3), 151-182.

Lee, K.Y. (2000). *From Third World to First: The Singapore Story: 1965-2000* (First ed.). New York: HarperCollins Publishers.

Leonard, T.M. (1991). *Central America and the United States: The Search for Stability*. Athens: The University of Georgia Press.

Lintner, B. (2009). The Battle for Thailand: Can Democracy Survive? *Foreign Affairs, 88*(4), 108-118.

Liow, J.C. (2006). *Muslim Resistance in Southern Thailand and the Southern Philippines: Religion, Ideology, and Politics*. Washington, D.C.: East-West Centre.

McCormick, J. (2005). *Understanding the European Union* (3rd ed.). New York: Palgrave Macmillan.

Means, G.P. (2009). *Political Islam in Southeast Asia* (Paperback ed.). London: Lynne Rienner Publishers.

Murphy, C. (2009). Populism Erodes Thailand's Old Order. *Far Eastern Economic Review, 172*(5), 7-12.

Murphy, E.C. (2009). Theorizing ICTs in the Arab World: Informational Capitalism and the Public Sphere. *International Studies Quarterly, 53*(4), 1131-1153.

Nair, D. (2008). Regionalism in the Asia Pacific/East Asia: A Frustrated Regionalism? *Contemporary Southeast Asia, 31*(1), 110–142.

Neher, C. D. (2002). *Southeast Asia in the New International Era*. Boulder: Westview Press.

Ockey, J. (2007). Thailand in 2007: The Struggle to Control Democracy. *Asian Survey, 48*(1), 20-28.

Perez-Brignoli, H. (1989). *A Brief History of Central America* (R.B. Sawrey & S. Sawrey, Trans.). Los Angeles: University of California Press.

Perkasa, K. (2008). *Patani: Behind the Accidental Border*. Los Angeles: KijangMas Perkasa.

Pitsuwan, S. (2010). ASEAN central to the region's future. *East Asia Forum Quarterly, 2*(2), 4-5.

Richards, G. (2010). Metropolitan Tourism: Competition, Collaboration and Creativity. *Asia Pacific World, 1*(1), 75-94.

Roberts, J.M. (1997). *The Penguin History of Europe* (Paperback ed.). London: Penguin Books.

Sen, A. (1999). *Development as Freedom*. New York: Anchor Books.

Severino, R.C. (2007). ASEAN Beyond Forty: Towards Political and Economic Integration. *Contemporary Southeast Asia, 23*(3),

406-423.

Shatkin, G. (2006). Colonial Capital, Modernist Capital, Global Capital: The Changing Political Symbolism of Urban Space in Metro Manila, the Philippines. *Pacific Affairs, 78*(4), 577-600.

Short, P. (2004). *Pol Pot: Anatomy of a Nightmare*. New York: Henry Holt and Company.

Shuib, M.S., Saludin, M.N., Feigenblatt, O.F. v., Keling, M.F., & Ajis, M.N. e. (2010). The Role of Malaysian Leaders in Nation Building Process (1957-2003). *Arts and Social Sciences Journal, 2010*, 1-17.

Simon, S. (2008). ASEAN and Multilateralism: The Long, Bumpy Road to Community. *Contemporary Southeast Asia, 30*(2), 264-292.

Skidelsky, R. (2010). *Keynes: The Return of the Master* (Paperback ed.). New York: Public Affairs.

Suharto, E. (2009). Social Protection Systems in ASEAN: Social Policy in a Comparative Analysis. *Social Development Issues, 31*(1), 1.

Tannebaum, D.G., & Schultz, D. (2004). *Inventors of Ideas: An Introduction to Western Political Philosophy*. Singapore: Thomson Wadsworth.

Than, M., & Thein, M. (2007). Transitional Economy of Myanmar: Present Status, Developmental Divide and Future Prospects. *ASEAN Economic Bulletin, 24*(1), 98-118.

Thawnghmung, A.M. (2009). Responding to Strategies and Programmes of Myanmar's Military Regime: An Economic Viewpoint. *Southeast Asian Affairs, 2008*, 274-290.

Trinidad, D.D. (2010). Domestic Actors, Market Reform and Regional Integration in Southeast Asia. *Asia Pacific World, 1*(1), 95-115.

Ungpakorn, G.J. (2007). *A Coup for the Rich: Thailand's Political Crisis*. Bangkok: Workers Democracy Publishing.

Ungpakorn, G. J. (2010). *Thailand's Crisis & the Fight for Democracy*. London: WD Press.

Ury, W. L., Brett, J.M., & Goldberg, S. B. (1993). *Getting Disputes Resolved: Designing Systems to Cut the Costs of Conflict*. Cambridge: The Program on Negotiation at Harvard Law School.

Vu-Tung, N. (2007). Vietnam's Membership of ASEAN: A Constructivist Interpretation. *Contemporary Southeast Asia,*

29(3), 483-505.

Wallerstein, I. (1976). the Modern World-System. In C. Lemert (Ed.), *Social Theory: The Multicultural and Classic Readings* (Third ed., pp. 391-397). Boulder: Westview Press.

WTO. (2007). Viet Nam joins WTO with Director-General's Tribute for true grit. Retrieved Jan 07, 2011, from http://www.wto.org/english/news_e/news07_e/acc_vietnam_11jan07_e.htm

Wyatt, D.K. (2003). *Thailand: A Short History* (Thailand ed.). Chiang Mai: Silkworm Books.

Yegar, M. (2002). *Between Integration and Secession: The Muslim Communities of the Southern Philippines, Southern Thailand, and Western Burma/Myanmar*. New York: Lexington Books.

Yzawa, T. (2006). The Evolution of Preventive Diplomacy in the ASEAN Regional Forum: Problems and Prospects. *Asian Survey, 46*(5), 785-804.

Zagl, B. (2008). Judicialization Matters! A Comparison of Dispute Settlement Under GATT and the WTO. *International Studies Quarterly, 52*(4), 825-854.

7

Economic Organizational Conflict in ASEAN: Overcoming Economic and Trade Oscillation through Structural Dynamics

---

While chapter 6 provided a detailed overview of trade liberalization in ASEAN, chapter 7 concentrates on the macro level trends affecting the structure of the organization. Economic Integration and Trade Oscillation are emphasized due to their centrality in the project to create an ASEAN Economic Community. Throughout the chapter the theoretical framework used is similar to the one applied in chapter 2, namely, structural dynamics and systems design. Six tension-resolution systems are explained in detail and are then paired into three structural conflicts.

Introduction

In order for ASEAN to overcome some of the barriers and obstacles to economic integration described in the previous chapter it is necessary for the organization to consider how the individual policies and measures interact with the region's structural dynamics. Each measure is both a cause and effect of structural characteristics of both the region itself as well as of its operating environment. One way to understand the broad trends affecting the organization's path towards the goal of establishing a working ASEAN Economic Community is to follow a holistic approach such as systems theory or structural dynamics. This chapter applies the theoretical framework introduced in chapter 2 and applies it to economic integration.

Since the theory of structural dynamics was explained in detail in the introduction to chapter 2, it will suffice to say that the theory is holistic and aims to identify basic structural conflicts inherent in the organization's design (Fritz, 1996). Thus, structural dynamics avoids piecemeal solutions or measures in favour of system-wide redesign. It should be noted that redesign does not necessarily imply changes in the official institutional structure of the organization but rather organization wide changes altering the overall structure in a way in which the effects of all parts on the performance of the entire system is taken into consideration. At the core of structural dynamics is the concept of structural tension (Fritz, 1996). Structural tension is defined as the force moving the organization from an undesirable present situation towards a desired state. Thus, tension is created when the desired state differs from the present situation of the organization. The interaction between a desired state and an actual state is called a tension-resolution system.

Tension-resolution systems are useful in that they help explain the relationship between the present state of a certain part of an organization's structure and a desired state. It should be noted that the gap between the two parts of the tension-resolution system is called structural tension. As explained in chapter 2, structural dynamics posits that the discrepancy between the actual state and the desired state moves the system towards a resolution which should be as close as possible to the desired state.

Nevertheless, tension-resolution systems tend to be open to several ways to achieve movement towards a desired state. That flexibility is what determines the possible unintended externalities of movement towards a resolution for a particular tension-resolution system. One example provided in chapter 2 will help clarify this point. An empty stomach is an undesirable state for most people which in turn is related to a desired state of satiation. Thus, the discrepancy between an empty stomach and a full stomach causes structural tension which in this case is experienced as hunger. Hunger moves the system towards a resolution which would possibly result in the individual eating until he or she feels satisfied. At this point this particular tension-resolution system can be considered resolved.

Structural dynamics is a holistic approach and therefore the interaction between any one tension-resolution system and other tension-resolution systems must be taken into consideration. The resolution of one tension-resolution system may activate a second incompatible tension-resolution system and thus reserve some of the measures taken due to the tension in the first system. This would result in movement akin to a rocking chair, called structural oscillation. Gains in one area are reversed by movement in a different area. This phenomenon can only be avoided by dealing with the entire structural conflicts (encompassing at least two interacting tension-resolution systems) in a holistic way. Redesign is the goal so that the structure stops causing unwanted oscillation and instead fosters structural advancement. For a more in depth explanation of the way in which structural conflict and tension-resolution systems interact please read the first section of chapter 2 of this text.

Three Core Economic Conflicts Faced by ASEAN

The obstacles and barriers faced by ASEAN in terms of its goal of economic integration are varied and complex as explained in the previous chapter, however three core structural conflicts are central to the organization's endemic structural oscillation. Superficially random and irrational behaviour such as policy reversals in terms of trade liberalization, opening of the banking sector, *inter alia*, can be explained in a variety of ways. Elite theory blames the region's shaky democratic record and changing interests of the region's elites for the sudden policy reversals. According to group theory reversals represent the changing balance of power between competing interest groups (Anderson, 2006).

Rational choice theory would explain the oscillation by pointing out the changing international economic environment and the sudden policy changes would be considered emergency management or crisis responses (Anderson, 2006). Structural dynamics provides a much deeper insight into the workings of the region's economic structure. Short-term and mid-term policy oscillation is understood as a result of the interaction between incompatible tension-resolution systems. In other words, while agency is not rejected, structure is emphasized. Since policy reversals and oscillation are caused by structural incompatibilities a change in the organization's structure is the only way to overcome the resulting negative externalities.

A cursory look at the economic policies of ASEAN Members during the last three decades shows sudden policy reversals and considerable oscillation from periods of greater protectionism to others of greater liberalization (Arnold, 2006; Bhaskaran, 2010). Chapters 5 and 6 show how individual member States introduced measures in the economic realm that were later reversed or considerably restricted. Some examples include the rollback of liberalization that occurred in Malaysia immediately after the Asian Financial Crisis of 1997, Myanmar's intermittent Bank reform, and Thailand's restrictions of certain financial flows (Heidhues, 2000; Neher, 2002; Than & Thein, 2007; Thawnghmung, 2009; Trinidad, 2010).

Let us turn to the first core structural conflict which is made up of two very important tension-resolution systems. The present state of the economy for most ASEAN members is one of protectionism in terms of trade through a mix of tariff and non-tariff barriers (Bhattacharyay, 2010). While most ASEAN members recognize the importance of trade especially in terms of exports, they are still wary of opening their markets to competition from foreign products and services. The result has been a state of affairs very similar to what happened in Japan in the 1970s and 1980s (von Feigenblatt, 2007; Hook, Gilson, Hughes, & Dobson, 2005; Morton & Olenik, 2005; Sakamoto, 2008; Smith, 1997).

During those decades Japan attempted to protect the domestic market and to guide exports through a relatively centralized economic policy. The goal was to have a certain measure of control over the economy and to transform uncertainty into calculable risk. Most ASEAN members attempted to emulate the Japanese example but with much less success. Following the Japanese model resulted in other countries also closing their markets to ASEAN products and to a decrease in the flow of Foreign Direct Investment. In other words the region became less competitive vis-à-vis other developing regions. Thus protectionism (control over the national economy) was the actual state of affairs in most ASEAN members, with the possible exception of Singapore (Lee, 2000).

ASEAN countries started to realize that they wanted to have a more flexible economy in order to benefit from international trade and to be more competitive in attracting much needed foreign direct investment. Therefore the desired state became liberalization as espoused in the ASEAN Charter and in the Blue Print for the ASEAN Economic Community (ASEAN, 2008a, 2008b). Due to the discrepancy between the actual state and the desired state, structural tension started to build up, moving the organization towards the desired state. Some of the measures adopted by ASEAN in order to liberalize the flow of goods and services were discussed in detail in chapter 6.

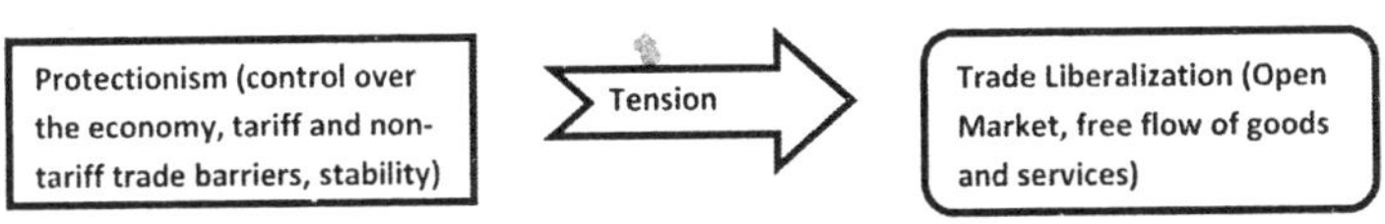

Figure 16. Tension-Resolution System G: Protectionism and Liberalization

Tension-Resolution System G: Protectionism and Liberalization: The structural tension that builds up between the actual and the desired state compels ASEAN members to pass measures to move towards the desired state. Measures in this field in include lowering or removing both tariff and non-tariff barriers, allowing greater foreign ownership of the economy, making it easier for foreign professionals to work in other ASEAN Members, *inter alia.*

Closely related to tension-resolution system G one finds a system dealing with financial and investment flows. Trade liberalization requires a concomitant liberalization and modernization of financial and investment flows. In other words, the liberalization of financial flows and investment flows goes hand in hand with trade liberalization. So as tension-resolution system G moves from the actual to the desired state there is greater liberalization of financial and investment flows. Thus, the resolution of tension-resolution system G becomes the new "actual" state. The new "actual" state involves greater movement of capital across borders, a greater foreign ownership of the economy, and increased competition in the field of financial services.

The liberalization of financial and investment flows introduces a certain degree of uncertainty and loss of control over important parts of the economy. ASEAN Member States have given up a certain measure of control over their national economies in the process of liberalization which has increased uncertainty and economic instability (Arnold, 2006). With a faster flow of both capital and investments, ASEAN governments come under greater strain and pressure to regulate those flows.

It becomes harder to follow the myriad new investments and financial instruments and thus planning becomes increasingly difficult. In addition to that the ups and downs of the business cycle can no longer be smoothed out by the government since control over a considerable part of the economy has been surrendered to the private sector. The result of all of the previously mentioned challenges involved in the liberalization of financial and investment flows is that governments start yearning for greater control over the economy as a way to reduce uncertainty and to be able to tackle the negative social externalities of the fluctuation of the business cycle. Governments also want to have the ability to protect their countries, from the effects of the sudden changes in the international economy. Therefore there is a new desired state which involves greater regulation of both investment and financial flows.

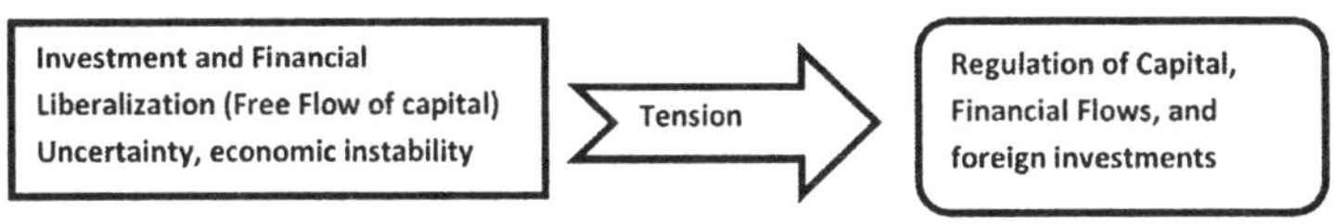

Figure 17. Tension-Resolution System H: Investment and Financial Liberalization; and Regulation

Tension-Resolution System H: Investment and Financial Liberalization; and Regulation: Tension-resolution system H shows the relationship between the actual state of a freer flow of capital and investment and the desired state of greater regulation of capital and foreign investments in order to lower uncertainty and to make planning easier. The way system H works is that as there is greater liberalization in terms of investment and financial flows there is also a concomitant loss of control over an important part of the economy. It becomes much harder to control exchange rates and to cushion the economy from the ups and downs of the financial market.

In addition to that greater foreign investment also means that an important part of the country's productive capacity will come under the control of foreign enterprises. Therefore there is a loss of economic sovereignty. Due to the negative externalities of investment and financial liberalization ASEAN Members have a new desired state which involves greater regulation of capital and financial flows and some limits to foreign investments. The desired state involves greater control over the economy in order to reduce uncertainty and to protect the economy from fluctuations in the international economy.

It should be noted that systems G and H are related in that

the resolution of system G becomes part of the actual state of system H. In other words, the resolution of system G is greater trade liberalization which is parallel to liberalization in financial flows and investment. Thus the resolution of system G becomes the actual state in system H. Nevertheless the new actual state is accompanied by some important unintended consequences and negative externalities. First of all, the free flow of investment and financial liberalization increase uncertainty due to the loss of control over important sectors of the economy. Greater integration in the global economy also results in greater vulnerability to the ups and downs of the international market.

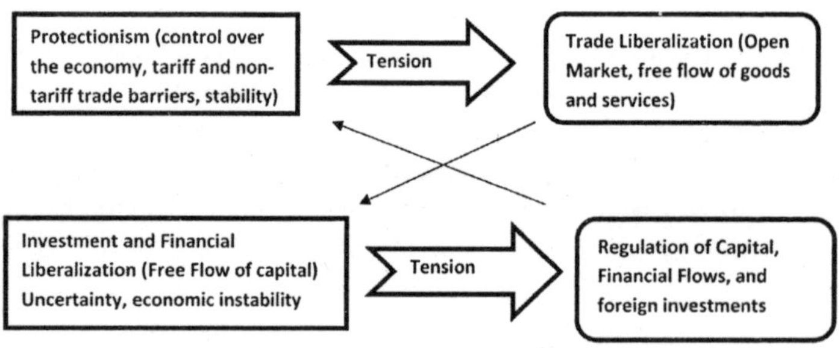

Figure 18. Structural Oscillation in ASEAN due to Incompatibility of tension-resolution systems G and H: (Fluctuation between Protectionism and Liberalization in terms of Financial and Investment Flows)

The resolutions of systems G and H are incompatible since trade liberalization is incompatible with the regulation of capital. The result of this is that the two systems compete against each other. When system G is resolved, pressure builds up in system H and the structural tension moves the system towards its resolution. As system H reaches its resolution, pressure builds up again for system G and structural tension in that system moves the organization towards its resolution which is greater trade liberalization. More overtly the structure moves from periods of greater trade liberalization to periods involving greater regulation of capital and of financial flows.

Therefore the structure oscillates between the two periods

and there is considerable backtracking from the organizational goal of greater economic integration. Thus progress made during the first period is partially or completely reversed during the second period. Movement does not lead to success but rather to oscillation. This partly explains the recurrent reversals in economic policy undertaken by ASEAN Member States during the 1990s and the early years of the twenty first century. It is important to emphasize that the policy reversals are the result of the previously described structural oscillation caused by the interaction of tension-resolution systems G and H and therefore can only be overcome through a redesign of the structure so that this kind of structural conflict is avoided.

Structural oscillation in terms of ASEAN's economic policy is not only the result of the interaction of tension-resolution systems G and H but also includes other systems such as the one revolving around issues of intellectual property and technological transfer.

The first system in this second structural conflict involves an actual/present state with little foreign investment in high value added products due to the weak protection of intellectual property rights. This leads ASEAN governments to desire greater foreign direct investment in high value added industries which requires stronger protections for intellectual property rights. In the language of structural dynamics, the discrepancy between the present state and the desired state results in structural tension which moves the system towards a resolution involving greater protection of intellectual property rights and a higher proportion of foreign direct investment in high value added industries.

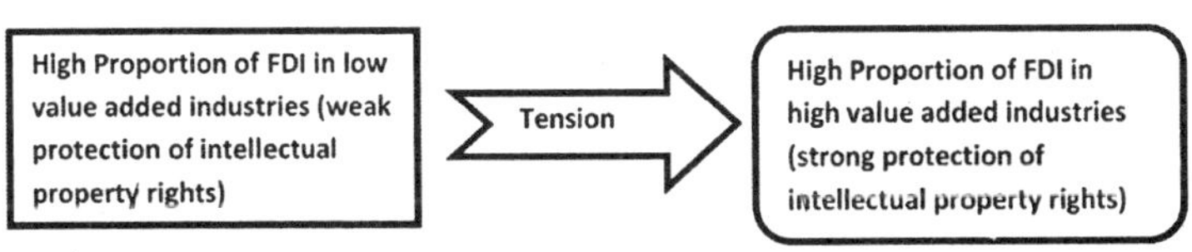

Figure 19. Tension-Resolution System I: Investment and Financial Liberalization; and Regulation

Tension-Resolution System I: Investment and Financial Liberalization and Regulation: The resolution of tension-resolution "I" forces governments to implement stronger protections for intellectual property as a way to attract a higher proportion of FDI in high value added industries. Needless to say there are important tradeoffs to implementing strong protections for intellectual property.

First of all, there is the considerable cost of enforcing laws penalizing the theft of intellectual property. Secondly, the government makes certain products more expensive for its own domestic market. The traditional example of one such product is pharmaceuticals. Strengthening intellectual property rights means that generic versions of major drugs cannot be produced anymore and that only those versions licensed by the pharmaceutical companies can be sold. While the price of the generic version does not include the costs of research and development that were involved in the creation of the drug, the licensed version includes a portion of those costs in addition to those of marketing. Thus the cost of healthcare increases for the government as well as for the entire population. In addition to that, there is a political cost involved in that higher price for a basic need such as healthcare is highly unpopular.

A similar effect takes place in relation to other products such as music records, foreign movies, certain industrial parts and textbooks. Therefore, there are considerable negative externalities accompanying the benefits of the greater protection of intellectual property rights. Technological development goes hand in hand with greater FDI in high value added industries. One of the alleged benefits of FDI is the transfer of technological know-how from more advanced countries to less advanced ones. This leads us to the next tension-resolution system in which there is a present state of low technological development and a desired state of high technological development. In the short term the easiest way for developing countries to advance technologically is to adapt, copy, and reproduce knowledge developed in the more advanced countries.

Thus, before original research and development can take place it is necessary for the developing country to reach a certain baseline of technological development which is very costly to acquire through traditional methods such as buying patents, hiring outside consultants to train local professionals, or import the entire technological base for entire industries. Other than resource rich countries such as Brunei in Southeast Asia, and the Emirates of the Middle East, purchasing the entire industrial infrastructure is not a realistic option. Moreover the inability to afford official methods of gaining the baseline technological base needed in order to produce its own research and development capability puts developing countries in a difficult development trap. Tension resolution system J shows the relationship between a present state of low technological development and a desire to achieve high technological development in the short term.

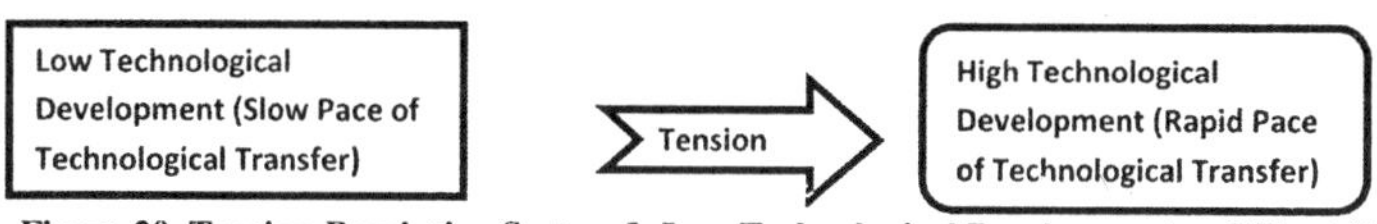

Figure 20. Tension-Resolution System J: Low Technological Development and Short Term Technological Transfer

Tension-Resolution System J: Low Technological Development and Short Term Technological Transfer: Tension-resolution system J starts with an undesirable state of low technological development with a slow pace of technological transfer and moves towards a desired state of high technological development with a rapid pace of technological advancement. Since most members of ASEAN are developing countries the only way in which they can achieve a rapid pace of technological transfer in the short run is to relax the protection of intellectual property rights and to copy and adapt foreign technology. Thus the tension between the actual state and the desired state leads the structure towards a weakening of intellectual property rights and to a faster pace in the adaptation of foreign technology to local needs. Therefore the resolution has the benefits of a faster pace in terms of the transfer of technology but also some negative externalities such as the weakening of intellectual property rights.

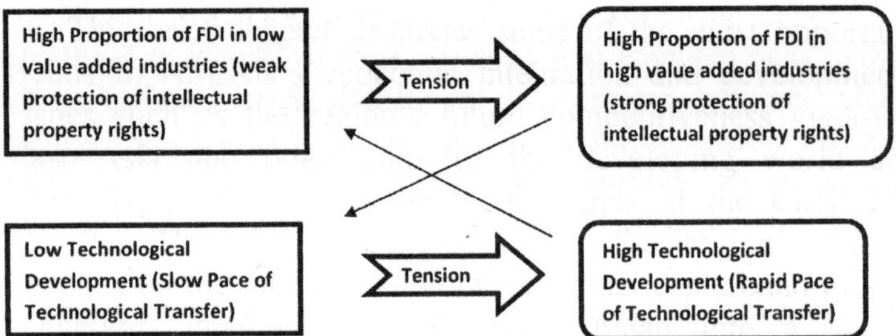

Figure 21. Structural Oscillation in ASEAN due to Incompatibility of tension-resolution systems I and J: (Fluctuation between Strong and Weak Protection of Intellectual Property)

Incompatibility of Tension-resolution Systems I and J: The structural oscillation that takes place due to the structural conflict brought about by the incompatible resolutions of tension-resolution systems I and J. Tension-resolution system "I" results in the greater protection of intellectual property rights as a side effect of attracting foreign direct investment in high value sectors which the resolution of tension-resolution system J is higher short term technological development through a faster pace of technological transfer which entails a weakening of the protection of intellectual property rights. At any one time one system prevails until enough structural tension builds up so that the other tension-resolution system becomes dominant.

The result of this is considerable structural oscillation between periods in which the attraction of FDI in high value sectors is prioritized and other periods in which the main goal is to achieve a high technological development in the short term through a faster pace of technological transfer. From a public policy perspective, the previously described structural conflict explains why ASEAN member States fluctuate from periods in which intellectual property laws are applied stringently to periods in which they are either ignored or repealed.

Fluctuations do not reflect irrational behaviour by decision makers but rather the competing structural tension of tension-resolutions I and J. The challenge of this structural conflict is that until it is resolved, oscillation will continue and backtracking will be present. Thus progress made on one front, for example in attracting FDI in high value added sectors, will be undermined or rolled back by progress on a second front, a faster pace of technological transfer for example. While backtracking is the most obvious disadvantage of this structural conflict, there may be even more serious long term consequences such as a permanent loss of reputation for the country leading to a higher cost for attracting FDI in high value added sectors.

Moreover, the instability and sudden policy changes caused by the structural conflict may be interpreted as irrational and politically motivated by foreign investors and thus the country may be deemed politically unstable and thus the price of capital would increase. The previously described structural conflict is at the core of one of the most common development traps experienced by developing countries and can only be overcome through a redesign of the underlying structure causing the conflict in the first place. A piecemeal approach simply does not work since it only leads to a momentary solution rather than leading to long term advancement.

Therefore ASEAN member States find themselves in a situation in which they need to achieve a certain level of technological development before they can proceed with their own research and development. In order to achieve that level of technological development they have to either invest in very costly training and/or import the technology from more advanced countries or simply copy and adapt foreign technology through a process akin to reverse engineering. This is a challenged that is faced by most developing countries including China, whose J-22 Stealth Fighter was allegedly reverse engineered from parts of a downed American Stealth fighter found in Kosovo.

Developing the technology to create a "stealth" fighter that can evade radar detection would take years and billions of Yuan to develop locally and purchasing the technology from the United States would be prohibitively expensive and in some cases prohibited by American laws limiting the export of advanced technology. ASEAN Member States find themselves in a very similar situation to China with the added disadvantage of having a much smaller local market for their products and less bargaining power due to their smaller economic clout.

The speed of growth and development is another important issue in ASEAN's Economic Community. How fast should the region develop? How much economic growth should there be in the short term versus the long term? The natural reaction of regional governments is to want higher economic growth in the short term. Regime and social stability are both partly dependent on the speed of economic growth since globalization has brought about an exponential increase in expectations which puts greater pressure on regional governments to bring about the desired benefits of faster growth and the subsequent increase in consumption. Thus, regional governments have a strong desire to change the present state of sluggish economic growth into one of fast economic growth. The discrepancy between the actual state and the desired state creates structural tension which in this case is very strong due to the popular desire for faster economic growth and a simultaneous increase in purchasing power. Tension-resolution system K shows this relationship.

Tension-Resolution System K: Slow Economic Growth and Fast Economic Growth: Figure 22 shows that there is a discrepancy between an actual state of slow economic growth with economic inflexibility and a desired state of fast economic growth and economic dynamism. The tension between the two states is that ASEAN governments pass measures to speed up economic growth in the short term. Some of the measures involve deregulation of a vast array of sectors and in some cases privatization of some industries. As the system moves towards its resolution there is greater economic growth and greater economic dynamism.

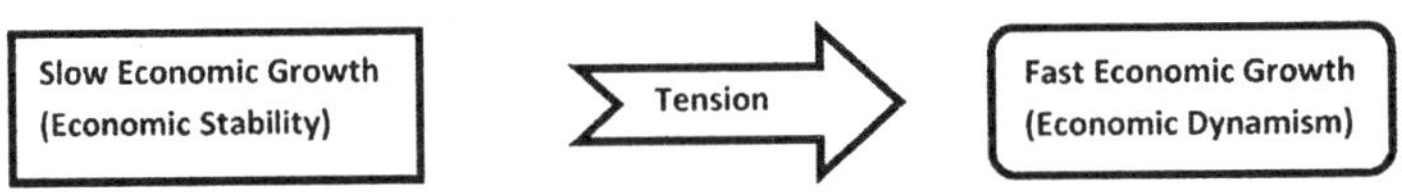

Figure 22. Tension-Resolution System K: Slow Economic Growth and Fast Economic Growth

A related tension-resolution system deals with the relationship between the dynamism brought about by the resolution of tension-resolution system K and a new desired state of greater economic stability and control. In other words, one negative externality of greater economic dynamism and liberalization is a loss of control over the economy and greater economic instability. This new actual state leads to a new desired state of greater economic stability and greater government oversight over the economy.

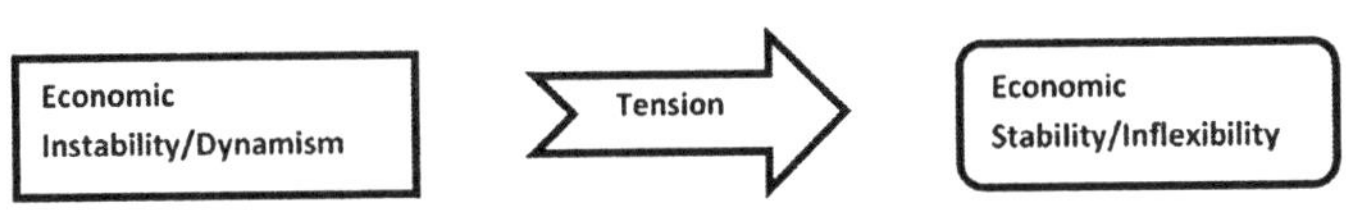

Figure 23. Tension-Resolution System M: Economic Instability/Dynamism and Economic Stability/Inflexibility

Tension-Resolution System M: Economic Instability/Dynamism and Economic Stability/Inflexibility: The interaction of systems K and M creates a structural conflict causing considerable structural oscillation for ASEAN. For example the economic dynamism attained as part of the resolution to tension-resolution system K is reversed by the resolution of tension-resolution system M which is greater economic stability and thus inflexibility. Therefore the way in which the structural conflict works is that the structure of the organization moves from an undesirable actual state of slow economic growth to one of fast economic growth.

The transition between the two states is caused by the structural tension caused by the discrepancy and is facilitated by measures passed in order to achieve the desired state. In this case most measures would include a certain degree of deregulation and liberalization which would lead to greater economic growth in the short term through a more dynamic economy. At the same time the increase in the speed of economic growth and its accompanying measures have the negative externality of greater economic instability.

Furthermore, the resolution of system K will become a new undesirable state of economic instability and vulnerability. This undesirable present state will lead to a new desired state of greater economic stability and predictability and the tension built up by the discrepancy between the two states will move the system towards the new desired state of greater economic stability. Some of the measures taken to achieve this desired state include greater regulation and protectionism. Thus the system will oscillate from periods in which short term economic growth and dynamism are prioritized to periods in which economic stability is given primacy.

Incompatibility of Tension-resolution Systems K and M: The problem with this is that as one system becomes dominant over the other, some of the measures passed by the other system are reversed or cancelled. Therefore, the gains made in the field of liberalization and privatization may be reversed by the gains made in achieving economic stability through greater regulation. In other words, the resolutions of the two systems are incompatible and lead to backtracking. As noted throughout this book and in earlier sections of this chapter, the backtracking and sudden policy reversals are not due to any inherent irrationality on the part of policymakers but are due to the structural dynamics of the organization.

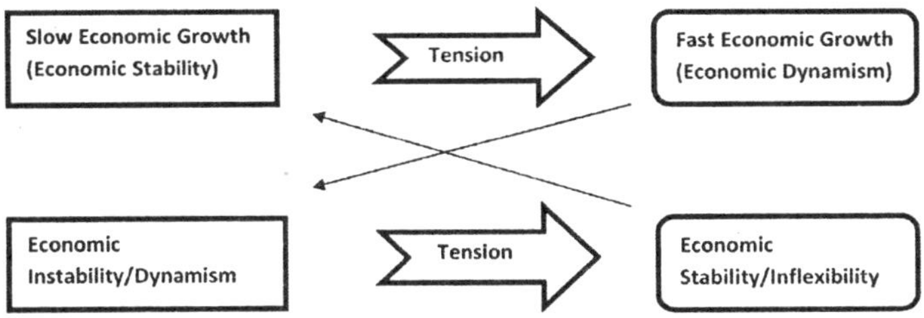

Figure 24. Structural Oscillation in ASEAN due to Incompatibility of tension-resolution systems K and M: (Fluctuation between Deregulation and Regulation)

The measures passed to achieve a resolution are perfectly logical and do support the goals of each individual system, however they are in competition with those passed by the other system. The gains achieved in one system are then partially or sometimes completely reversed by those achieved in another system. Therefore the problem is with the structure itself and cannot be resolved through short term localized measures but rather requires a more holistic redesign of the structure in order to foster real organizational advancement instead of oscillation. The final section of this chapter will tackle each one of the core structural conflicts and provide some possible solutions.

Overcoming Structural Oscillation and Engendering Sustainable Structural Advancement

Before going into the details of how to tackle each one of the core structural conflicts covered in this chapter it is important to remind the reader of the hierarchy of goals introduced in chapter 2 of the present volume. Organizations are made up of many layers and their goals should also be multilayered so as to reflect the multi-synchronous nature of the organization's goals as well as the different degrees of prioritization accorded to them. Thus, an organization has an overarching purpose which is stated at a macro level and is usually considered to be a long term goal.

Directly supporting an organization's purpose is the organization's strategy which deals with macro and meso level issues and time frames. The implementation of an organization's strategy is undertaken by managerial and local goals which are more limited in nature and usually deal with short to midterm time frames. This organizational hierarchy of goals can be envisioned as a pyramid in which lower levels support higher levels and each local action serves to support a management goal, which in turn helps implement the organization's strategy. Ultimately all of the other layers of the hierarchy of goals should support the organization's long term purpose.

The first core structural conflict discussed in this chapter deals with the oscillation of ASEAN from periods in which liberalization is actively promoted to periods of considerable retrenchment, and with the subsequent regulation of financial and investment flows. Before venturing to provide any possible alternatives to resolve the first structural conflict it is important to classify the components of each tension-resolution system according to their position in the organization's hierarchy of goals. Trade liberalization is a strategic goal since it servers the purpose of promoting sustainable development in the region. On the other hand, financial flows and investment and their regulation is a managerial goal at a lower level of the hierarchy of goals.

Therefore, the first core structural conflict involves two goals which are at different levels and thus possess different levels of importance. It should be noted that lower level goals should support higher levels goals so that all organizational actions support the ultimate purpose of the organization which in this case is promoting sustainable development in Southeast Asia. Since the regulation and control of financial and investment flows is a managerial goal and trade liberalization is a strategic goal, the latter should support the former.

This means that the actions at the managerial level should

support the achievement of goals at the strategic level even if there are some negative externalities in the short term. Therefore, one logical way so solve the first structural conflict is to prioritize the resolution of tension-resolution system G by clearly decoupling tension-resolution system H. This can be done by downgrading and operationalizing the starting state of tension-resolution system H as simply an automatic managerial step necessary to achieve the higher strategic goal of liberalization. By decoupling the two systems, they would not be operating at the same structural levels and thus they would cease to compete since the tension in system H would be operating at a lower level of the organization.

While it is easy to see how this proposed decoupling and downgrading would separate the two systems into two different hierarchical levels it does not address the issue of the tension aiming to move system H towards greater regulation of investment and financial flows. The answer to this is that the tension moving system G towards greater liberalization would be much greater than that moving system H towards its resolution since it is a system operating at a much higher structural level. This would mean that system G would be permanently dominant over system H and liberalization would be promoted at the lower managerial level through the liberalization of financial and investment flows. Therefore, structural oscillation would be avoided and organizational advancement would be fostered.

The second core structural conflict involves goals in two different timeframes. Attracting FDI in High value added sectors is a managerial goal for the midterm while achieving a high degree of technological advancement in the short term is a short term strategic goal. Nevertheless it should be noted that there is a clear incompatibility between some of the negative externalities caused by tension-resolution system "I" and tension-resolution system J. Both systems aim to support higher organizational goals such as regional integration and improving the international competitiveness of regional industries, however it is important to consider whether their resolutions are sustainable and whether there are any alternative methods to achieve similar goals.

The goal of system "I" is to attract FDI in high value added sectors so as to benefit from the possible transfer of technology from more advanced countries. On the other hand the goal of system J is to attain technological know-how in the short term through reverse engineering and copying of foreign products. FDI in high value added sectors attains technological transfer in the midterm while reverse engineering attains it in the short term. One way to compare the suitability of the two methods of achieving the higher goal of technological development is by comparing their benefits and their costs.

Attracting FDI in high value added sectors is more costly in the short term but more sustainable in the long term while weakening the protection of intellectual property laws in order to copy foreign technology is effective in the short term but very costly in the long term. Due to the social negative externalities of the strict protection of intellectual property rights, this option also poses considerable political challenges to regional governments. Therefore, the challenge behind the second core conflict is dealing with the negative externalities of system "I" while also promoting technological transfer.

One way to deal with this structural conflict is by decoupling the two systems and by redesigning tension-resolution system J. Tension-resolution system J can be redesigned by identifying managerial goals that can achieve a certain degree of technological transfer in the short term. For example, greater cooperation between regional universities and a fund to send bright regional students to study abroad and then return to teach in regional universities is one way to decrease the tension in tension-resolution system J. Needless to say, a decrease in tension due to a moderate increase in the short term transfer of technology does not permanently resolve the incompatibility of systems "I" and J but it does weaken the latter system and thus makes "I" dominant over J. This is desirable since tension-resolution system J is a more important managerial goal leading to sustainable development while the resolution of system J is a short term managerial goal.

It should be noted that even thought "I" would now be dominant and J would be weakened, there would still be some movement towards the resolution of system J and a certain degree of short technological transfer would take place. At this point it is important to remember that the structural tension that builds up due to the discrepancy between an actual and a desires state does not determine the means to attain a resolution but simply moves the system towards a certain goal. This can be interpreted to mean that one way to redesign a system is to tamper with the means of achieving a desired state rather than necessarily attempting to change the nature of the desired state itself. In the case of tension-resolution system J, the desired state is short term technological transfer and the least costly and most effective way to do so is by weakening intellectual property laws and by promoting reverse engineering and other forms of copying foreign technology.

Even though the previously described method is the least costly way to move from the actual to the desired state in tension-resolution system J, its resolution conflicts with the resolution of system "I" which is stronger intellectual property laws so as to attract FDI in high value added industries. If the process of moving from the actual to the desired state of tension-resolution system J is redesigned so as to eliminate the conflicting elements of its resolution then the structural conflict would be resolved and the subsequent organizational oscillation avoided.

Greater regional cooperation in research and development as well as an increase in human capital trained abroad can achieve a certain degree of technological transfer in the short to midterm timeframe while at the same time leaving the protection of intellectual property rights intact. The result of this process of redesign of the second core structural conflict would be an attenuated resolution in tension-resolution J and a full resolution of system I. Most importantly the resolutions of both systems would now be compatible and complementary.

The third core structural conflict is one of the most widespread and possibly obvious paradoxes in development. Governments want to have fast economic growth which requires movement towards a more decentralized economy and results in greater economic dynamism and flexibility. On the other hand deregulation and decentralization is also tantamount to a loss of control over an important part of the economy and also a greater vulnerability to the fluctuations of the business cycle of the international economy. Tension-resolution system K shows how there are an actual state of relatively slow economic growth and a desired state of fast economic growth.

Since the "creative destruction" of liberal capitalism is considered to be one of the most effective methods of achieving economic growth, measures are passed in order to achieve this strategic goal. Nevertheless the weak democratic credentials of most governments in the Southeast Asian region make them hesitant to give up control of an important sector of the economy. Tension-resolution system M deals with that hesitation and the automatic government reaction to turn back deregulation and to take back control over parts of the economy. The result of this rollback of deregulation is that the economy losses its dynamism and economic growth slows down.

Since regional governments depend on economic growth in order to garner legitimacy, they start deregulating the economy again in order to speed up economic growth. The result is oscillation between periods of government retreat from the economy to periods of active government intervention in the economy. It should be noted that tension-resolution system K is a higher order system than tension-resolution system M. System K is an important managerial goal supporting the strategic goal of promoting regional development. On the other hand system M deals with short term externalities of liberalization. Applying a similar method to the one applied to the previous core structural conflicts, it is possible to lower the priority accorded to system M while strengthening system K. This is what the Chinese government has done since its movement towards market liberalization.

Even though the Chinese government is a one party communist regime, it recognizes the importance of achieving economic growth so as to raise the living standards of the majority of the population. As a result of this the Chinese government has dealt with the negative externalities by greater government intervention in other areas of governance rather than slowing down economic growth.

A similar approach could be adopted in ASEAN and it would resolve the third structural conflict caused by the interaction of systems K and M. For example, greater government intervention in the provision of certain social services would effectively deal with some of the negative externalities of deregulation. In other words, the provision of a safety net would lower the intensity of the tension moving system M towards its resolution and if coupled with greater government control of certain other spheres of social activity would also weaken any trepidation governments might feel about losing control over greater parts of the economy.

The result of the previously mentioned measures would be to change the nature of tension-resolution system M by making the goal of greater government control over the economy less desirable. A lower level of desirability would in turn reduce the discrepancy between the actual state and the desired state and tension between the two ends of the system would virtually be eliminated.

Resolving the three core structural conflicts discussed in this chapter would eliminate organizational oscillation and would engender sustainable organizational advancement. Therefore progress made in the different areas of economic integration would lead to greater progress in other related areas. Measures at the local, tactical, managerial, and strategic levels would all support ASEAN's purpose of fostering sustainable development in the region and maintaining security. Eliminating unnecessary structural oscillation would also improve the region's international image by transforming uncertainty into calculable risk. Finally, considerable resources would be saved and put to work in a more efficient manner. ASEAN's productivity would move closer to the region's actual production capability's curve which is the ultimate goal of regional economic integration.

This chapter has discussed some of the most important structural conflicts affecting ASEAN's economic development and integration; however there are many other important structural conflicts which were not discussed both due to space constraints as well as to their interaction with other policy areas such as the socio-cultural realm. It should be noted that structural dynamics is a holistic approach and that therefore the separation of economic, security, and cultural issues is simply a heuristic device rather than a reflection of reality.

Thus, the structural conflicts discussed in this chapter interact and are affected by tension-resolution systems in other policy areas such as security and socio-cultural issues. While this relationship is acknowledged, this chapter has discussed the three core economic structural conflicts in isolation so as to provide a more parsimonious explanation of the basic structural dynamics behind complex econo-political regional behaviour. The goal was to isolate a few important variables and to analyze how they are affected by structural changes. Chapter 8 discusses some of the issues underlying the three core structural conflicts discussed in this chapter in a more holistic manner so as to provide context and a certain degree of detail to the theoretical discussion of this chapter. Some tentative conclusions and trends are also discussed in chapter 8 so as to provide a broad overview of the future of ASEAN's Economic pillar.

References

Anderson, J.E. (2006). *Public Policymaking* (6th ed.). Boston:

Houghton Mifflin Company.

Arnold, D. (2006). Free Trade Agreements and Southeast Asia. *Journal of Contemporary Asia, 36*(2), 195-207.

ASEAN. (2008a). *ASEAN Charter*. Retrieved November 30, 2008. from http://www.aseansec.org/ASEAN-Charter.pdf.

ASEAN. (2008b). *ASEAN ECONOMIC COMMUNITY BLUEPRINT*. Retrieved. from http://www.aseansec.org/5187-10.pdf.

Bhaskaran, M. (2010). Review of Southeast Asian Economic Developments. *Southeast Asian Affairs*, 23-44.

Bhattacharyay, B.N. (2010). Infrastructure for ASEAN Connectivity and Integration. *ASEAN Economic Bulletin, 27*(2), 200-221.

von Feigenblatt, Otto F. (2007). *Japan and Human Security: 21st Century ODA Policy Apologetics and Discursive Co-optation* (2nd ed.). Delray Beach: Academic Research International.

Fritz, R. (1996). *Corporate Tides: The Inescapable Laws of Organizational Structure* San Francisco: Berrett-Koehler Publishers

Heidhues, M. S. (2000). *Southeast Asia: A Concise History*. London: Thames & Hudson.

Hook, G., Gilson, J., Hughes, C.W., & Dobson, H. (2005). *Japan's International Relations: Politics, economics and security* (2nd Edition ed.). London: Routledge.

Lee, K. Y. (2000). *From Third World to First: The Singapore Story: 1965-2000* (First ed.). New York: HarperCollins Publishers.

Morton, W. S., & Olenik, J. K. (2005). *Japan: Its History and Culture* (4th ed.). New York: McGraw Hill.

Neher, C.D. (2002). *Southeast Asia in the New International Era.* Boulder: Westview Press.

Sakamoto, T.F.C.T. (2008). *Japan Since 1980*. New York: Cambridge University Press.

Than, M., & Thein, M. (2007). Transitional Economy of Myanmar: Present Status, Developmental Divide and Future Prospects. *ASEAN Economic Bulletin, 24*(1), 98-118.

Thawnghmung, A.M. (2009). Responding to Strategies and Programmes of Myanmar's Military Regime: An Economic Viewpoint. *Southeast Asian Affairs, 2008*, 274-290.

Trinidad, D.D. (2010). Domestic Actors, Market Reform and Regional Integration in Southeast Asia. *Asia Pacific World, 1*(1), 95-115.

8

ASEAN and Development: Conclusions

This brief chapter discusses some of the most important trends in ASEAN's economic integration and development. Issues such as the region's future competitiveness vis-à-vis East Asia and other parts of the developing world are discussed in relation to the broad trends of the early 21st century. The chapter concludes that the region's future depends on the modernization of its human capital and on the successful integration of Southeast Asian into a single production base.

Introduction

Section three of the present volume has discussed in detail the development and growth of the Southeast Asian region. Chapter 5 provided a broad overview of the major development challenges and opportunities of the members of ASEAN. Chapter 6 then moved on to identify and explain some of the obstacles and challenges faced by ASEAN in its process towards the establishment and implementation of an ASEAN Economic Community. Finally chapter 7 applied a powerful theoretical framework, structural dynamics, in order to identify and analyze the main structural conflicts affecting the functioning of ASEAN's economy. This final chapter connects the findings from the previous three chapters and attempts to provide a glimpse at the economic future of the region. In other words, this chapter answers the question "What now?"

It is clear from the detailed description of the individual economies of the member States that ASEAN is a very diverse region with considerable development gaps between and within countries (von Feigenblatt, 2009; Heidhues, 2000;

Neher, 2002). The region is home to some of the most dynamic economies in the world such as Singapore as well as to some of the most backward dictatorships in existence, Myanmar (Keling, Saludin, von Feigenblatt, Ajis, & Shuib, 2010; Lee, 2000). Nevertheless most other member States fall somewhere in between the two extremes of the continuum and are actively aiming to move towards sustainable development.

A good indicator of the region's general direction is exemplified by Vietnam's and Laos' development models. Both are one party communist country which have moved towards a market economy and have accepted the need to cooperate with the other Southeast Asian nations (CIA, 2010a, 2010b). Vietnam joined the World Trade Organization and Laos is actively working towards that goal (WTO, 2007).

Cambodia's pragmatic leaders also discarded their former communist robes and jumped in the liberalization bandwagon (Gottesman, 2003). Even Myanmar's erratic and superstitious leaders have started to move their country in fits and starts towards a market economy (Thawnghmung, 2009). Some of the reasons for this seemingly inevitable trend include China's rise through the late adoption of a market based economy and an aggressive campaign to attract FDI, the rise in regionalism in Europe and America, and the failure of other models to achieve the necessary economic growth to raise the living standard of the majority of the population (Callahan, 2008). All of the previously mentioned factors served as very strong incentives for Southeast Asian countries to strengthen the only working region-wide organization and to use it as the main institutional vehicle to achieve greater regional economic integration.

Challenges for the Future

The challenges for the future are many; however the future is also full of opportunities for the Southeast Asian region. Achieving the goal of economic integration is probably the most important challenge faced by the region. Chinese competition, increasing labour costs, and the global economic recession are other important challenges faced by ASEAN members in the immediate future. Other challenges are structural in nature and involve overcoming structural conflicts preventing the organization from working as an integrated whole towards common goals. Thus regional governance is an important challenge in its own right (Jones & Smith, 2007).

It is worth discussing the challenge of Chinese competition for ASEAN Member States. China's sudden economic and political rise caught the region relatively by surprise and presented considerable challenges and opportunities (Nair, 2008). On the economic front the challenges far surpassed the opportunities due to the fact that most regional products compete against Chinese substitutes in the international market. Thus, low value added agricultural products such as rice and certain fruits in addition to inferior manufacturing products such as basic electronic devices and plastic utensils faced increasing competition from Chinese products. In addition to that due to China's sheer size and strong government guidance of the economy, the Chinese were increasingly successful in attracting FDI.

China still has a long way to go in order to become a developed country which means that it will continue to grow at a relatively fast rate for the next few decades. Due to China's virtually unlimited labour supply, costs of manufactured products can be kept low. Beijing's policy of undervaluing the Yuan in order to artificially lower the price of Chinese products makes competition even more difficult for Southeast Asian nations. China has successfully flexed its political muscle to keep the international community's call to allow the Yuan to float, at bay.

ASEAN members do not have the option of undervaluing their currencies to make their products more competitive in the international market nor have they been able to benefit from negotiating trade agreements as a single block (Arnold, 2006). China's aggressive trade policies will continue to pose a serious challenge to the region's competitiveness for the foreseeable future and ASEAN will have to learn how to negotiate as a single block in order to get more favourable trade agreements with other economic blocks.

On the other hand China's challenge also presents some opportunities for ASEAN member States such as a possible export market, some complementary products such as winter fruits, and a buyer for natural resources and energy. China's challenge at the lower end of the value chain also provides a strong incentive for ASEAN Member States to move to strengthen their services sector and to concentrate on higher value added products such as electronics and automobiles.

Harnessing the considerable human capital present in the region towards a common goal of moving higher in the value chain is certainly a formidable challenge due to the necessary cooperation and coordination that is required in other to achieve it. Nevertheless greater interaction between the region's governing elites and the spread of region wide epistemic communities sharing a common lingua franca can successfully achieve coordination as has been proven by the success of the European Union (McCormick, 2005).

Probably the most important challenge for the future will be integrating production in ASEAN. Due to climatic and geographic characteristics, ASEAN members tend to produce very similar products (Arnold, 2006). An integrated economic community would require that each Member State concentrate on products for which it has a competitive advantage. Thus some members would concentrate on producing certain parts of advanced electronic devices which would then be assembled in another country and then shipped from others. This approach would spread production in order to get as close as possible to the production possibilities frontier of the entire region. Needless to say, this integration would require considerable changes to the national economies of most countries; resulting in some industries disappearing and others booming.

The agricultural sector would also have to be liberalized and restructured which would mean that countries would have to give up their food security in exchange for interdependence. All of the previously mentioned challenges require considerable political capital and strong leadership. Certain necessary measures will be very unpopular while also crucial for the region's mid to long term development. Therefore achieving strong and enlightened political leadership will be an important challenge for ASEAN.

A Glimpse at the Future

The art of forecasting is fraught with considerable dangers and clouded by a thick veil of uncertainty. Nowhere is this more accurate than in the incredibly dynamic Southeast Asian region. The challenge of making any statements about the region's economic future is exacerbated by political uncertainty, serious security challenges, and the exponential speed of change in the international economy as a whole. If one concentrates solely on economic and development trends, *ceteris paribus*, then the region is expected to show considerable economic growth in the near future, higher value added products will slowly displace agricultural products and textiles as the main regional exports and a much higher proportion of FDI will be intraregional.

Thus, everything else being equal, the region's economies will grow considerably in the next few decades due to aggressive market oriented policies as well as due to the starting development levels of most ASEAN member States. Developing states tend to show very high growth rates in the stages between take-off and maturity. While stages of development are very broad and often criticized heuristic devices they serve the useful purpose of allowing one to group countries according to certain important development indicators. Some ASEAN members such as Malaysia, Thailand, and possibly Vietnam are moving towards a development stage similar to that of Taiwan in the 1980s, other

ASEAN members are still developing a basic industrial base in order to reach the level of the previous group. Early stages of economic and industrial development are characterized by relatively high growth rates of between 6 percent to 12 percent.

In the real world there is a great number of confounding variables which may derail some of the expected events included in the previous forecast. Political instability is the major confounding factor in Southeast Asia. It is impossible to predict what will happen to the region's economic integration if there is a wave of popular uprisings in the region, something that is increasingly likely as seen in the events currently taking place in the Middle East.

Even elite conflict might distort the expected trends due to sudden policy changes. Modernizing elites in Thailand, Malaysia, the Philippines, and other ASEAN members are actively contesting power from traditional elites which bodes political instability in the near future. There might be waves of conservative retrenchment during which traditional elites attempt to slow down the liberalization process.

Broadly conceived there is a regional cleavage between elites controlling traditional sectors such as real estate, agriculture, and banking versus newly rich entrepreneurs concentrating in services, international trade, *inter alia*. Movement towards economies based on high value added products and services depending on highly skilled human capital is sure to weaken traditional sectors which is expected to engender considerable opposition from conservative quarters.

Capital tends to dislike political instability and thus regime changes will lower the regional appeal as a possible destination for extra-regional FDI. China's size and authoritarian stability will also present considerable competition for international capital. On the other hand, Japan, Western Europe, and the United States will continue to view the region as a good supplier of raw materials which may actually delay some countries' development due to excessive reliance on revenues resulting from the export of natural resources.

In this respect, bilateral trade agreement will pose a major challenge due to the incentives that members have to "defect" and strike a deal on their own (Arnold, 2006). The United States will probably continue to use this approach in order to strengthen its economic position in Southeast Asia as a possible bulwark to China's growing regional influence. Needless to say this will make cooperation and the pursuit of an integrated regional trade policy very. Disjointed action will weaken the bargaining position of regional members and could result in lower than expected growth rates for ASEAN.

Another important factor is that the region will increasingly be viewed as a desirable end market for East Asian and American products. The growth of a wider middle class will result in an exponential increase in regional demand for consumer products. Due to the sluggish growth rate of developed countries, traditional exporting countries such as Korea, Japan, and Taiwan will increasingly concentrate on access to ASEAN's growing market.

This increase in the region's attractiveness as an end market will mean that developed countries will increasingly court ASEAN Members to sign advantageous bilateral trade agreements so as to secure market access for their products. The result of this trend will be a proliferation of bilateral trade agreements with extra regional partners and the subsequent weakening of ASEAN's bargaining power as a singular trading block (Arnold, 2006). Nevertheless in the mid to long term, ASEAN members will probably realize that bilateral agreements tend to favour the stronger party and that they can get a fairer bargain if they negotiated as a bloc.

In terms of intra-regional development gaps, certain countries will start catching up to the more advanced members of the Southeast Asian region. For example, Vietnam is expected to catch up to Thailand and Malaysia in the next decade. Brunei will undergo a painful transition from being dependent on oil exports to a service intensive economy.

Cambodia still has a long way to go due to its very low levels of human capital and also due to the considerable investment in infrastructure that the country needs but is also expected to show considerably high growth rates throughout the next decade. Laos faces considerable challenges due to its geographical location, weak infrastructure, and low levels of human capital but can also be expected to show high growth rates although not as high as those of Vietnam. Malaysia is likely to move towards its goal of becoming a developed country while facing considerable challenges in maintaining its competitive edge in the high tech sector.

On the other hand Singapore will probably show low levels of economic growth due to its aging population and increased competition from other regional financial centres. Indonesia and the Philippines face considerable challenges in terms of speeding economic growth and considerable development challenges such as Islamic fundamentalism and several insurgencies. The democratic nature of both countries actually adds to the possibility of political instability and makes it more unlikely that there will be strong leadership in moving the economy towards market led growth.

Nevertheless, Indonesia will continue to be an important source of raw materials for Japan and for other developed countries while the Philippines has a very strong base in terms of human capital and its service sector has the potential to grow considerably in the next few years. Finally, Myanmar's future is clouded by a very thick veil of uncertainty. The country's military rulers tend to react to short term needs and events rather than following a long term development plan.

Thus, Myanmar's future depends on a vast array of factors including but not limited to: a possible democratic transition, the possibility of prolonged civil strife, the possibility of a civil war, and the military junta's possible retrenchment in North Korean fashion as a response to international pressure for political change. Due to the previously mentioned reasons, Myanmar has the worse economic prospects and whatever growth takes place will be mostly dependent on the sale of natural resources and government linked industries.

Conclusions

Southeast Asia is home to countries at all stages of the development continuum. The region has shown high growth rates in the last few years and several new members of ASEAN have started moving their economies towards a market based model. While the region faces considerable development challenges such as wide development gaps both within and between ASEAN Members, the region also shows great potential due to its large population base, natural resources, and strategic location. It remains to be seen whether ASEAN will be able to overcome the main structural conflicts influencing its economic development.

The organization considers the second pillar of the ASEAN Community, namely the Economic Pillar, to be one of the most important ones and thus the stakes are high in terms of overcoming the structural oscillation resulting from the structural conflicts described in the previous chapter. Greater cooperation, increasing interdependence, and greater coordination between ASEAN members hold the key to success in terms of dealing appropriately with the challenges identified in this section of this volume.

It is clear that ASEAN would benefit from a structural view of its economic integration which would clarify some of the previously misunderstood phenomena in terms of backtracking of liberalization as well as other measures which are part of structural oscillation. The previous chapters provide a structural road map to deal with some of the more pressing core structural conflicts and can be used for policy discussion as well as for activism. While this second part of the volume concentrates on the Economic Pillar of ASEAN it is important to remember that the three Pillars are interconnected and interdependent and thus should be treated as an indivisible whole. The third section of this volume deals with the Socio-cultural Pillar of ASEAN and also touches on some issues of importance for the region's development.

References

Arnold, D. (2006). Free Trade Agreements and Southeast Asia. *Journal of Contemporary Asia, 36*(2), 195-207.

Callahan, W. A. (2008). Chinese Visions of World Order: Post-hegemonic or a New Hegemony? *International Studies Review, 10*(4), 749-761.

CIA. (2010a). The World Fact Book: Laos People's Republic Rctricvcd Novcmbcr 9, 2010, from https://www.cia.gov/library/publications/the-world-factbook/geos/la.html.

CIA. (2010b). The World Factbook: Socialist Republic of Vietnam. Retrieved November 13, 2010, from https://www.cia.gov/library/publications/the-world-factbook/geos/vm.html.

von Feigenblatt, Otto F. (2009). ASEAN and Human Security: Challenges and Opportunities. *Ritsumeikan Centre for Asia Pacific Studies Working Paper, No. 09-5*(July), 1-22.

Gottesman, E. (2003). *CAMBODIA After the Khmer Rouge: Inside the Politics of Nation Building*. New Haven: Yale University Press.

Heidhues, M. S. (2000). *Southeast Asia: A Concise History*. London: Thames & Hudson.

Jones, D.M., & Smith, M.L.R. (2007). Making Process, Not Progress ASEAN and the Evolving East Asian Regional Order. *International Security, 32*(1), 148-184.

Keling, M.F., Saludin, M.N., von Feigenblatt, Otto F. , Ajis, M.N. e., & Shuib, M.S. (2010). A Historical Approach to Myanmar's Democratic Process. *Journal of Asia Pacific Studies, 1*(2), 132-148.

Lee, K. Y. (2000). *From Third World to First: The Singapore Story: 1965-2000* (First ed.). New York: HarperCollins Publishers.

McCormick, J. (2005). *Understanding the European Union* (3rd ed.). New York: Palgrave Macmillan.

Nair, D. (2008). Regionalism in the Asia Pacific/East Asia: A Frustrated Regionalism? *Contemporary Southeast Asia, 31*(1),

110–142.

Neher, C. D. (2002). *Southeast Asia in the New International Era.* Boulder: Westview Press.

Thawnghmung, A.M. (2009). Responding to Strategies and Programmes of Myanmar's Military Regime: An Economic Viewpoint. *Southeast Asian Affairs, 2008*, 274-290.

WTO. (2007). Viet Nam joins WTO with Director-General's Tribute for true grit. Retrieved Jan 07, 2011, from http://www.wto.org/english/news_e/news07_e/acc_vietnam_11jan07_e.htm.

Part III
A Structural Analysis of Socio-cultural Integration in ASEAN

Part III deals with ASEAN's progress towards socio-cultural integration. Chapter 9 provides a brief overview of the main socio-cultural cleavages and commonalities present in the region as well as covering some of the main goals of the ASEAN Blue Print for a Socio-Cultural Community. Challenges and socio-cultural incompatibilities are covered in chapter 10 while chapter 11 concentrates on socio-cultural conflict and on how to overcome the oscillation caused by that conflict. Finally, chapter 12 provides some tentative conclusions regarding the region's socio-cultural integration and discusses possible trends that may be present in the region's future path toward and more integrated socio-cultural community. It should be noted that many of the social issues covered by ASEAN's Blue Print for a Socio-Cultural community were discussed in the previous part of the book in relation to development and the Economic Community and because of that they will not be discussed in this part of the book. Therefore, this part of the book will concentrate on social issues from a different perspective which includes human rights, social safety nets, and civil rights. The previously mentioned issues are inextricably linked to cultural issues and will therefore be discussed in and analyzed in conjunction with important cultural debates such as the one regarding the universality of human rights and the relatively importance of "Asian Values".

9

Socio-cultural Integration in ASEAN: An Overview

This chapter provides a brief introduction to the complex issues encompassed by socio-cultural integration broadly conceived. ASEAN's main cultural and social trends are discussed from a regional perspective and a brief historical background is provided for the region's major cultural categories. Some of the region's main socio-cultural debates are briefly explained and their importance in relation to the region's progress towards the achievement of a Socio-Cultural Community is discussed.

Introduction

The Socio-Cultural Pillar of the ASEAN Community is probably the most ambitious and ambiguous of the three pillars (Collins, 2008). It aims to cover a wide array of issues ranging from social development to regional cultural integration and identity formation (ASEAN, 2009). Since the economic dimension of development has been discussed in detail in part II of this volume, this chapter will only deal with the cultural dimension of social development. The meaning of social issues as encompassed by the Socio-Cultural Pillar of the ASEAN Community mostly concentrates on certain kinds of social safety needs and on human capital development broadly conceived.

There is clearly a strong connection between human capital development and issues of cultural integration and identity formation since culture represents the worldview used to interpret the world (Pieterse, 2009). Needless to say, ASEAN declarations for ASEAN unity in moving towards a Socio-Cultural Community tend to be extremely broad and navigate between statements calling for greater convergence of values and also call for the protection of local differences and respect for each country's distinct cultures. Cultural issues tend to be controversial due to their connection to issues of human rights and the debate between universal norms and local values (Akaha, 2009; Blau & Moncada, 2009; Huntington, 2003; Kim, Fidler, & Ganguly, 2009; MacFarlane & Khong, 2006).

Historical Background

Southeast Asia can be broadly divided in half according to the early cultural influence dominating each sub region. The two most important early historical influences on the region include China and India (Heidhues, 2000). Thailand, Indonesia, Malaysia, Brunei, the Philippines, Cambodia, Burma, and Laos were greatly influenced by Hinduism while Vietnam was closer to the Chinese sphere of influence (Heidhues, 2000; Neher, 2002). Buddhism and Brahmanism spread from India to the Southeast Asian region were it mixed with local animistic beliefs (Mulder, 1996).

Sunni Islam was then brought to the region by traders from India and the Middle East in during the 15th Century and it became the official religion of the ruling elites of the Malay world, most of Indonesia, and certain parts of the Philippines. The conversion of the Malay world to Islam started with the conversion of Melaka's ruler in 15th century (Means, 2009). Prince Parameswara adopted the Muslim name of Megat Iskandar Shah and with it the Islamic system of governance (Means, 2009, p. 21). Islam's spread was uneven which led to a syncretic mix of religious and cultural elements combining Hinduism, Islam, and animism (Means, 2009; Millard, 2004; Mulder, 1996). Islam's success in the region can be attributed to its adoption by the ruling families of several sultanates and the subsequent diffusion of the religion to the rest of the population (Heidhues, 2000; Means, 2009).

The process was slow and uneven but had a profound

influence on the current socio-cultural makeup of Southeast Asia. Catholicism made considerable inroads in the Philippines due to its Spanish colonial heritage (Mulder, 1996; Neher, 2002). Thus the Philippines shares many cultural characteristics with Latin America and differs considerably from other countries in the region in terms of social structure and values. This transformation of a previously animistic and temporarily Muslim region into a culturally Latin area is due to the type of colonialism practice by Spain in comparison to that practiced by France, the United Kingdom, and the Netherlands (Roberts, 1997). Spanish colonialism was not based on indirect rule but rather aimed at the complete assimilation of the conquered culture into the Spanish worldview (Eakin, 2007; Williamson, 1992).

Religion, language, dress, and other cultural factors were also influenced during the colonial period. The prominent role of Catholic missionaries during the conquest and subsequent consolidation of the empire resulted in much higher levels of assimilation and also to a faster rate of Westernization of the local inhabitants (Banyai, 2010; Yegar, 2002). Testimony to this is the names of Filipinos and the pride of some elite families in having Spanish ancestors. Catholicism also made some inroads into other regions of Southeast Asia such as Vietnam and Laos but the end of the Vietnam War led to the forced exile of much of the Catholic community (Neher, 2002).

Other important cultural influences on the region include American colonialism in the Philippines, British colonialism in Malaysia, and Japanese influence after the end of World War II (Hook, Gilson, Hughes, & Dobson, 2005; Kissinger, 1994; Lee, 2000; Morton & Olenik, 2005; Neher, 2002; Stockwell, 2004). American colonialism in Southeast Asia started after the Spanish-American War of 1898 when the Philippines became an American colony (Kissinger, 1994). The American occupation involved considerable reforms in terms of governance, education, and the pacification of the remaining unconquered territories (Yegar, 2002). Thus the result of the American occupation was the further consolidation of power by the Catholic Manila elites. This patters further polarized the division between the Muslim inhabitants and the Westernized Catholics (Yegar, 2002).

British colonialism was based on indirect rule and had a weaker effect on the cultural of the subject populations (Chottmann, 2006; Rober Kershaw, 2003; Stockwell, 2004). Nevertheless the influence of British culture on regional elites is worthy of notice. During most of the colonial period great swaths of territory were administered as a seamless whole and the key to survival depended on understanding the British colonial government (Chottmann, 2006; Lee, 2000). Thus many members of the traditional ruling elites sent their children to study in the United Kingdom. For those who could not study in England the next best thing was enrolling in one of several British learning centres in Southeast Asia such as Raffles College in Singapore which later on became the prestigious National University of Singapore (Lee, 2000).

Therefore, while British colonialism exerted little to no influence on popular culture, it exerted an important influence on the high culture of the elites which would subsequently lead the newly independent nations. French colonialism also exerted some influence on regional culture as can be attested by Vietnam's discarding of Chinese characters in favour of adopting the Roman alphabet (Neher, 2002). There are still some trances of French culture in modern day Cambodia as can be seen in the names of government buildings and the use of French in certain official documents (Gottesman, 2003).

Japan's influence in the region is harder to pin down due to its intermittent and diffuse nature (Bix, 2000; von Feigenblatt, 2007; Hook et al., 2005; Lind, 2009; Morton & Olenik, 2005). It is widely accepted that Japan's occupation of the region during World War II strengthened independence movements in Indonesia and Vietnam (Neher, 2002; Smith, 1997). Japan's influence also fuelled a resurgent nationalism in the region both as a result of the foreign occupation itself and also due to Japan's status as an Asian power standing up to the Western Powers (Bix, 2000). The end of the War led to a pause in Japanese influence which resumed and considerably increased during the late 1970s up to the 1990s (Peng-Er, 2006; Togo, 2005).

Southeast Asia was integrated into Japan's economy through the flying geese model which led to considerable Japanese investment in the region (Hook et al., 2005; Smith, 1997). Japan's economic influence was described in the previous section of the book but its cultural influence also deserves some notice. Japanese food, language, and other cultural products spread throughout Southeast Asia during that period (Sakamoto, 2008; Smith, 1997). This increase in interest in Japanese culture reflected Japan's economic power but was also part of a demonstration effect. Japan proved that a country could remain culturally Asian and at the same time develop economically (Morton & Olenik, 2005).

The 21st century is a time of broadly contested cultural influences in Southeast Asia. American influence continues to be present in the region, Japanese economic power can still be felt, but other cultural centres are starting to influence the cultural development of the region. China's rise has resulted in a heightened interest in Chinese language and culture and to a cultural realignment of the region's Chinese population towards the mainland (Hew, 2008; Kiong & Bun, 2001; Lee, 2000). South Korea is also a new cultural centre to be reckoned with. Korean Soap Operas and music are becoming increasingly popular in Southeast Asia. Other important cultural influences on the elite include Australia, New Zealand, and the United Kingdom. Due to the lower requirements to study at the university level in those countries, increasingly numbers of middle and upper class students from Southeast Asia are choosing to study there rather than in Japan and the United States.

Southeast Asia is characterized by its cultural syncretism

and diversity (Mulder, 1996; Neher, 2002). The region is a smorgasbord of socio-cultural groups sharing many values but also possessing an equal number of divergent beliefs. Cultural borders are impossible to pin down since they are diffuse, dynamic, and in a constant state of flux. Moreover, the compression of time and space brought about by globalization makes the territorial analysis of culture even more problematic (Pieterse, 2009). Culture is being deterritorialized by the spread of the internet and the greater mobility of people and products (Battersby & Siracusa, 2009; Friedman, 2000; HSIN-HUANG, HSIAO, & WAN, 2007). Therefore, this study concentrates on the tension between a very complex deterritorialized cultural reality characterized by crisscrossing sets of overlapping spheres of culture and an artificially narrow conception of culture and ethnicity as defined by the postcolonial nation-state.

Socio-Cultural Debates

At this point the debate between universal human rights and regional "Asian Values" should be introduced due to the influence it has exerted over the framing of socio-cultural issues in ASEAN. This debate is basically about the applicability of the values and norms represented by human rights to ASEAN members (Kim et al., 2009; Lee, 2000; Tow, Thakur, & Hyun, 2000). It should be noted that human rights advocates claim that the human rights accepted by the United Nations have universal validity and applicability (Blau & Moncada, 2009; MacFarlane & Khong, 2006; Scott Cooper, 2008). Their argument is that all humans share some fundamental needs and yearn for a certain degree of freedom.

The Human Rights regime can be broadly divided into the rights included in the Covenant on Civil and Political Rights and those included in the International Covenant on Economic, Social and Cultural Rights (August, 1995; Blau & Moncada, 2009). While the division seems arbitrary it reflects the cleavage between supporters of a very basic number of human rights related to physical survival and those supporting a broader conception of basic needs including freedom of speech as well as religious freedom (Bellamy, 2009; von Feigenblatt, 2010a). The 1990s were years of active debate over the universality of both sets of rights and several ASEAN members actively promoted the view that regional cultural values were incompatible with certain rights claimed as universal by the United Nations (Kim et al., 2009; Lee, 2000).

Regional leaders such as Lee Kuan Yew of Singapore, Mahathir of Malaysia, Myanmar's Military Junta, and some prominent Thai Intellectuals and Royalists argued that ASEAN members had differently historical experiences from the West which had resulted in a set of authoritarian and patriarchal values loosely labelled "Asian Values" (von Feigenblatt, 2009a; Lee, 2000; Ungpakorn, 2007, 2010). The exact nature of "Asian Values" is hard to pin down since its definition was watered down by its proponents as a way to include countries as diverse as Japan, Singapore, Malaysia, and Thailand into a single cultural fold, however there was agreement regarding a few common characteristics (Albritton & Bureekul, 2004; Chang, Chu, & Park, 2007).

According to proponents of "Asian Values", ASEAN's peoples respect authority, respect their elders, prefer order and harmony, and prioritize the needs of the collectivity rather than those of the individual (von Feigenblatt, 2009a; Lee, 2000). There is a clear Confucian undercurrent in this debate blended with Malay and Thai Kingship (Chottmann, 2006; Handley, 2006; Roger Kershaw, 2001). Thus, the proponents of "Asian Values" claimed that there was some room for Economic, Social, and Cultural Rights in their countries but that the values encompassed in the Covenant on Civil and Political Rights are incompatible with "Asian Values" and that therefore they should either be revised or qualified so as to drop that claims for their universality (von Feigenblatt, 2009a; Lee, 2000).

The height of the debate was reached at the time of the

World Conference on Human Rights which was held in 1993 in Vienna, Austria (Akaha, 2009; Blau & Moncada, 2009; MacFarlane & Khong, 2006). One of the central issues of the Conference was the continued claims to universality of human rights. While proponents of "Asian Values" and other developing countries formed a strong coalition in order to resist the "universality" claim, an unexpected defection greatly weakened the coalition. Japan supported the "universality" of Human Rights and due to its centrality in the humanitarian and development world in addition to its identity as an East Asian country with a Confucian background, its support for universal human rights carried the day and the final report of the Conference upheld the universality of Human Rights (von Feigenblatt, 2007; MacFarlane & Khong, 2006). While the debate did not end on that day, it certainly represented the apex of the struggle. After that moment the coalition in favour of "Asian Values" weakened and a wave of democratic transitions in the late 1990s further discredited this position (Collins, 2008; Katanyuu, 2006; Yzawa, 2006).

It should be noted that culture is a term with considerable political baggage in the Southeast Asian context (von Feigenblatt, 2009c; von Feigenblatt, Suttichujit, Shuib, Keling, & Ajis, 2010; McCargo, 2008; Perkasa, 2008). The concept is linked to colonialism due to the importance of appearing civilized during the colonial period in order to enjoy full rights according to international law (Chottmann, 2006; Cuasay, 1998; Payne, 1995; Wyatt, 2003). This aspect of culture is clearly present in the emphasis placed by Southeast Asian governments in showing that there is a clear national culture with a proud historical legacy through political historiography (Roux, 1998; Ungpakorn, 2007). The goal is to rewrite the past so as to reflect western characteristics of what was then considered to be a "civilized culture" (von Feigenblatt, 2010b).

This aspect of the cultural debate is clearly visible in Thailand's historical revisionism and propaganda (von Feigenblatt, 2009c; Perkasa, 2008). A second aspect of "culture" in the Southeast Asian context closely related to the first is nationalism and the formation of a "national culture". Former colonies adopted the political philosophy of their colonial rulers in the form of the virulent strand of nationalism of the late 19th century (Liow, 2006). In other words the system of independent nation-states was artificially imposed in a very diverse and permeable region as a way to cement the control over territory of the postcolonial state.

The result of this was that certain historical narratives, languages, and religions were reified and imposed on a vast array of ethnic groups so as to force order on a very disorganized and complex reality (von Feigenblatt, 2009b; Funston, 2010). This trend in turn led to what I call post-colonial colonialism in which postcolonial Southeast Asian states ruled by dominant ethnic groups attempted the forceful assimilation of their ethnic minorities in order to forge a national identity based on the history and cultural traits of the dominant group (von Feigenblatt, 2009b, 2009c, 2010).

Malaysia is a clear example of this as shown by the privileges and power held by the Malays over other ethnic groups (Hew, 2008; Shuib, Saludin, von Feigenblatt, Keling, & Ajis, 2010). In the Philippines, the Catholic majority gained control over the government apparatus and attempted to pacify and assimilate the Muslim regions of the country (Means, 2009; Yegar, 2002). Burma's experience is similar with the Burmese majority dominating a large number of ethnic minorities (Abdullahi, 2009; Falise, 2010; Keling, Saludin, von Feigenblatt, Ajis, & Shuib, 2010).

The experiences of Vietnam, Laos, and Cambodia followed a similar path and even the single Southeast country to have avoided foreign colonial domination, Thailand, became an example of virulent nationalism and postcolonial colonialism through its invasion of the Malay Muslim region in the country's south (Cuasay, 1998; Roger Kershaw, 2001; McCargo, 2008). Cultural indoctrination and bitter struggles for cultural survival are the legacy left by the previously described trend. Thus, cultural issues can be very sensitive in Southeast Asia due to their connection to politico-economic issues such as sovereignty over territory and control over natural resources.

The Socio-Cultural Pillar of the ASEAN Community aims to sidestep some of the previously mentioned difficulties by concentrating on both the local and the regional while avoiding the national. This is a strategy that proved to be relatively successful in the European Union but is still in an inchoate state in Southeast Asia. Thus the emphasis is on people to people links so as to avoid the dangerous dynamics of state to state diplomacy. Nevertheless, it should be noted that ASEAN's strategy to promote this new regional awareness remains incomplete and to a certain extend contradictory. The next chapter provides a brief overview of the present contours of the ASEAN Socio-Cultural Community as described in the Blue Print for its development in addition to explaining some of the main structural conflicts hampering its further development.

References

Abdullahi, N. (2009). Myanmar's Unwanted Boat People [Electronic Version]. Retrieved February 15, 2009, from http://english.aljazeera.net/news/asia/2009/02/20092451910503370.html

Akaha, T. (2009). Human Security in East Asia. *Journal of Human Security, 5*(3), 11-34.

Albritton, R.B., & Bureekul, T. (2004). Developing Electoral Democracy in Developing Nations: Thailand [Electronic Version]. *A Comparative Survey of Democracy, Governance and Development, Working Paper Series*, 1-33. Retrieved September 20, 2009, from http://www.asianbarometer.org/newenglish/publications/workingpapers/no.17.pdf.

ASEAN. (2009). *ASEAN SOCIO-CULTURAL COMMUNITY BLUEPRINT*. Retrieved August 11, 2010. from http://www.aseansec.org/5187-19.pdf.

August, R. (1995). *Public International Law: Text, Cases, and*

Readings (Paperback ed.). New Jersey: Prentice Hall.

Banyai, C.L. (2010). Community Capacity Building and Local Policy: An Example from Pagudpud, the Philippines. *Asia Pacific World, 1*(2), 83-108.

Battersby, P., & Siracusa, J.M. (2009). *Globalization & Human Security* (Hardcover ed.). Lanham: Rowman & Littlefield Publishers, Inc.

Bellamy, A.J. (2009). Realizing the Responsibility to Protect. *International Studies Perspectives, 10*(2), 111-128.

Bix, H.P. (2000). *Hirohito and the Making of Modern Japan* (Paperback ed.). New York: Perennial.

Blau, J., & Moncada, A. (2009). *Human Rights: A Primer*. Boulder: Paradigm Publishers.

Chang, Y.-t., Chu, Y.-h., & Park, C. M. (2007). Authoritarian Nostalgia in Asia. *Journal of Democracy, 18*(3), 71-80.

Chottmann, S. (2006). Melayu Islam Beraja: The Politics of Legitimisation in a Malay Islamic Monarchy. *Review of Indonesian and Malaysian Affairs 40*(2), 111-139.

Collins, A. (2008). A People-Oriented ASEAN: A Door Ajar or Closed for Civil Society Organizations? *Contemporary Southeast Asia, 30*(2), 313-332.

Cuasay, P. (1998). Borders on the Fantastic: Mimesis, Violence, and Landscape at the Temple of Preah Vihear. *Modern Asian Studies, 32*(4), 849-890.

Eakin, M.C. (2007). *The History of Latin America: Collision of Cultures* (Paperback ed.). New York: Palgrave Macmillan.

Falise, T. (2010). On the Run: In Burma's Jungle Hell. *World Policy Journal, 27*(1), 57-64.

von Feigenblatt, Otto F. (2007). *Japan and Human Security: 21st Century ODA Policy Apologetics and Discursive Co-optation* (2nd ed.). Delray Beach: Academic Research International.

von Feigenblatt, Otto F. (2009a). ASEAN and Human Security: Challenges and Opportunities. *Ritsumeikan Centre for Asia Pacific Studies Working Paper, No. 09-5*(July), 1-22.

von Feigenblatt, Otto F. (2009b). Some lessons from the White Rajahs of Sarawak: Identifying and strengthening local capacities for peace in the deep South of Thailand. *Journal of Law and Conflict Resolution, 1*(6), 117-121.

von Feigenblatt, Otto F. (2009c). The Thai Ethnocracy Unravels: A Critical Cultural Analysis of Thailand's Socio-Political Unrest.

Journal of Alternative Perspectives in the Social Sciences, 1(3), 583-611.

von Feigenblatt, Otto F. (2010a). International Policymaking: The Case of the Norm of the Responsibility to Protect. *Entelequia: Revista Interdisciplinar, Spring 2010*(11), 267-272.

von Feigenblatt, Otto F. (2010b). Resisting Universalistic Feminist and Queer Hegemonic Discourses: An Emic Model of Thai Gender and Sexuality. *Ritsumeikan Centre for Asia Pacific Studies Working Paper, No. 10-1*(July), 1-19.

von Feigenblatt, Otto F. (2010). The Malay Minority in Southern Thailand: A "Small People" Facing Existential Uncertainty. *Ritsumeikan Journal of Asia Pacific Studies, 27*(February), 53-63.

von Feigenblatt, Otto F., Suttichujit, V., Shuib, M. S., Keling, M. F., & Ajis, M.N. e. (2010). Weapons of Mass Assimilation: A Critical Analysis of the Use of Education in Thailand. *Journal of Asia Pacific Studies, 1*(2), 292-311.

Friedman, T.L. (2000). *The Lexus and the Olive Tree: Understanding Globalization* (Revised ed.). New York: Farrar Straus Giroux.

Funston, J. (2010). Malaysia and Thailand's Southern Conflict: Reconciling Security and Ethnicity. *Contemporary Southeast Asia, 32*(2), 234-258.

Gottesman, E. (2003). *CAMBODIA After the Khmer Rouge: Inside the Politics of Nation Building*. New Haven: Yale University Press.

Handley, P.M. (2006). *The King Never Smiles: A Biography of Thailand's Bhumibol Adulyadej*. New Haven Yale University Press.

Heidhues, M.S. (2000). *Southeast Asia: A Concise History*. London: Thames & Hudson.

Hew, D. (2008). The Malaysian Economy: Developments and Challenges. *Southeast Asian Affairs*, 207-222.

Hook, G., Gilson, J., Hughes, C.W., & Dobson, H. (2005). *Japan's International Relations: Politics, economics and security* (2nd Edition ed.). London: Routledge.

HSIN-HUANG, HSIAO, M., & WAN, P.-S. (2007). The Experiences of Cultural Globalizations in Asia-Pacific. *Japanese Journal of Political Science, 8*(3), 361-376.

Huntington, S.P. (2003). *The Clash of Civilizations and the Remaking of World Order* (Paperback Edition 2003 ed.). New

York: Simon & Schuster Paperbacks.

Katanyuu, R. (2006). Beyond Non-Interference in ASEAN: The Association's Role in Myanmar's National Reconciliation and Democratization. *Asian Survey, 46*(6), 825-845.

Keling, M.F., Saludin, M.N., von Feigenblatt, Otto F., Ajis, M. N. e., & Shuib, M. S. (2010). A Historical Approach to Myanmar's Democratic Process. *Journal of Asia Pacific Studies, 1*(2), 132-148.

Kershaw, R. (2001). *Monarchy in South-East Asia: The Faces of Tradition in Transition* (First ed.). London: Routledge.

Kershaw, R. (2003). Partners in Realism: Britain and Brunei Amid Recent Turbulence. *Asian Affairs (London), 34*(1), 46-53.

Kim, S.W., Fidler, D.P., & Ganguly, S. (2009). Eastphalia Rising? Asian Influence and the Fate of Human Security. *World Policy Journal, 26*(2), 53-64.

Kiong, T.C., & Bun, C.K. (Eds.). (2001). *Alternate Identities: The Chinese of Contemporary Thailand.* Singapore: Brill Times Academic Press.

Kissinger, H. (1994). *Diplomacy* (Paperback ed.). New York: Simon & Schuster.

Lee, K.Y. (2000). *From Third World to First: The Singapore Story: 1965-2000* (First ed.). New York: HarperCollins Publishers.

Lind, J. (2009). The Perils of Apology: What Japan Shouldn't Learn from Germany. *Foreign Affairs, 88*(3), 132-146.

Liow, J.C. (2006). International Jihad and Muslim Radicalism in Thailand? Toward an Alternative Interpretation. *Asia Policy*(2), 89–108.

MacFarlane, S.N., & Khong, Y.F. (2006). *Human Security and the UN: A Critical History* (1st Edition ed.). Indianapolis: Indiana University Press.

McCargo, D. (2008). *Tearing Apart the Land: Islam and Legitimacy in Southern Thailand* (First ed.). Ithaca: Cornell University Press.

Means, G.P. (2009). *Political Islam in Southeast Asia* (Paperback ed.). London: Lynne Rienner Publishers.

Millard, M. (2004). *Jihad in Paradise: Islam and Politics in Southeast Asia.* Armonk: East Gate Books.

Morton, W.S., & Olenik, J.K. (2005). *Japan: Its History and Culture* (4th ed.). New York: McGraw Hill.

Mulder, N. (1996). *Inside Southeast Asia: Religion, Everyday Life, and Cultural Change*. Chiang Mai: Silkworm Books.

Neher, C.D. (2002). *Southeast Asia in the New International Era.* Boulder: West view Press.

Payne, R. (1995). *The White Rajahs of Sarawak.* Kuala Lumpur: Oxford University Press.

Peng-Er, L. (2006). Japan's Human Security Role in Southeast Asia. *Contemporary Southeast Asia, 28*(1), 141-159.

Perkasa, K. (2008). *Patani: Behind the Accidental Border*. Los Angeles: KijangMas Perkasa.

Pieterse, J. N. (2009). *Globalization & Culture: Global Melange* (Second ed.). Plymouth: Rowman & Littlefield Publishers, Inc.

Roberts, J.M. (1997). *The Penguin History of Europe* (Paperback ed.). London: Penguin Books.

Roux, P. L. (1998). To be or not to be: The Cultural Identity of the Jawi (Thailand). *Asian Folklore Studies, 57*(2), 223-255.

Sakamoto, T.F.C.T. (2008). *Japan Since 1980*. New York: Cambridge University Press.

Scott Cooper, D.H., Wade Jacoby, and Daniel Nielson. (2008). Yielding Sovereignty to International Institutions: Bringing System Structure Back In. *International Studies Review, 10*(3), 501-524.

Shuib, M.S., Saludin, M.N., von Feigenblatt, Otto F. , Keling, M. F., & Ajis, M.N. e. (2010). The Role of Malaysian Leaders in Nation Building Process (1957-2003). *Arts and Social Sciences Journal, 2010*, 1-17.

Smith, P. (1997). *Japan A Reinterpretation.* New York: Random House.

Stockwell, A.J. (2004). Britain and Brunei, 1945-1963: Imperial Retreat and Royal Ascendancy. *Modern Asian Studies, 38*(4), 785-819.

Togo, K. (2005). *Japan's Foreign Policy 1945-2003: The Quest for a Proactive Policy* (Second Edition ed.). Leiden: Brill.

Tow, W.T., Thakur, R., & Hyun, I.-T. (Eds.). (2000). *Asia's emerging regional order: Reconciling traditional and human security*. Tokyo: United Nations University Press.

Ungpakorn, G.J. (2007). *A Coup for the Rich: Thailand's Political Crisis*. Bangkok: Workers Democracy Publishing.

Ungpakorn, G.J. (2010). *Thailand's Crisis & the Fight for Democracy*. London: WDPress.

Williamson, E. (1992). *The Penguin History of Latin America*

(Paperback ed.). London: Penguin Books.

Wyatt, D.K. (2003). *Thailand: A Short History* (Thailand ed.). Chiang Mai: Silkworm Books.

Yegar, M. (2002). *Between Integration and Secession: The Muslim Communities of the Southern Philippines, Southern Thailand, and Western Burma/Myanmar*. New York: Lexington Books.

Yzawa, T. (2006). The Evolution of Preventive Diplomacy in the ASEAN Regional Forum: Problems and Prospects. *Asian Survey, 46*(5), 785-804.

10

ASEAN Blue Print for Socio-cultural Community

This chapter explains some of the most important challenges in the Blue Print for an ASEAN Socio-Cultural Community. The main plans for the establishment of this community are reviewed and evaluated critically so as to identify the main challenges to be encountered during its implementation. Consensus building and negotiation results in ambiguous policy documents such as the Blue Print, however the careful study of such policy papers reveals important regional cleavages as well as areas of agreement in terms of socio-cultural integration.

The policy making process can be reconstructed from a careful analysis of policy papers and thus a greater and deeper understanding of the official deliberations that took place in order to conceive and plan for the ASEAN Socio-Cultural Community can be attained. This chapter concludes that the diffuse nature of ASEAN's conception of a Socio-Cultural Community blurs the distinction between aspects of socio-economic development and the more controversial issues of deeply held cultural values. Moreover, a greater and stronger role for the Secretary General is interpreted as a good sign in the path towards regional integration, in particular in terms of the fostering of a regional identity.

Introduction

Chapter 9 provided a general overview of the region's complex history and a brief introduction to some of the most prominent cultural debates. This chapter continues where chapter 9 left off by analyzing ASEAN's Blue Print for a Socio-Cultural Community (ASEAN, 2009). ASEAN Official

Policy Papers are rich sources of information regarding the thinking of the region's policy elites. Hidden policy debates and regional cleavages can be distilled from the tersely worked broad generalizations of official policy papers. Clues as to those debates are internal contradictions, different levels of specificity from one subsection to another and random statements reinforcing the original principles of the organization, *inter alia.* Due to the informal nature of negotiation in the Southeast Asian region and the carefully worded official statements of government officials, policy papers provide the best evidence for contestation and policy debates at the governmental level.

Needless to say, the debates of policy elites and government officials do not tell the entire story regarding the region's socio-political cleavages and debates; however, their importance cannot be denied in a region with various levels of democratic participation and in an intergovernmental organization with a long history of respect for absolute sovereignty (von Feigenblatt, 2009a; Narine, 1997). The two perspectives are not necessarily contradictory but rather tell different parts of a more complex story. Elites react to the yearnings and needs of the people while at the same time they also help shape those "needs" and "wants" (Anderson, 2006). Chapter 9 attempted to provide a brief glimpse as to some of the historic-cultural factors affecting the peoples of ASEAN while this chapter will concentrate mostly on how the policymaking elites deal with those socio-cultural forces.

This entire book has shown how structure affects institutional outputs and this chapter follows the same theoretical framework so as to identify and explain the underlying structural conflicts causing structural oscillation in the socio-cultural realm. It should be noted that socio-cultural structural conflicts represent the interaction of purely institutional characteristics and conditions in tandem with broader socio-cultural regional characteristics. Thus, this chapter aims to provide a plausible model for an immensely complex socio-cultural system. Southeast Asia is a region characterized by its cultural and social heterogeneity (Heidhues, 2000; Mulder, 1996). Furthermore, the region is in a constant state of flux and therefore socio-cultural factors are not stable but rather part of a process possibly leading to what Pieterse calls "cultural syncretism" (Pieterse, 2007).

A Critical Analysis of the ASEAN Blue Print for a Socio-cultural Community

ASEAN's Blue Print for a Socio-Cultural Community (ASCC) is the most ambitious and ambiguous of the three Blue Prints dealing with the three pillars of the ASEAN Community (ASEAN, 2009). The eight characteristics and elements of the Blue Print show the vast array of concerns included in the Socio-cultural community as well as some of the internal contradictions present in the remainder of the official document. "Forging a common identity" is the topic of the first characteristic which also includes the goal of building a people-cantered community based on the values of caring and harmony (ASEAN, 2009, p. 1).

A second element deals with the micro elements of sustainable development while the third one covers important issues of human rights and culture. Human rights, gender equality, and social justice are included in the third element as part of a "culture of regional resilience" (ASEAN, 2009, p. 1). It should be noted that this is one of the few instances of the inclusion of human rights in an official ASEAN document. Nevertheless it is also telling that the fourth element deals with cultural respect and how it should be treated according to "present realities" (ASEAN, 2009, p. 1).

This element can be interpreted as a concession to cultural relativism and to the proponents of "Asian Values". It is supposed to serve as a qualifier to the previous element dealing with human rights and social justice. The sixth element deals with closing the development gap among members thus emphasizing economic rights over civil and political ones.

Finally, the eight point lists the main characteristics of the ASCC as being: "human development, social welfare and protection, social justice and rights, ensuring environmental sustainability, building the ASEAN identity, and narrowing the development gap" (ASEAN, 2009, p. 1).

The first page of the Blue Print introduces some of the tensions and debates behind the Socio-Cultural Community. In terms of style, the wording is ambiguous and grandiloquent. The topical movement from the first to the eight elements shows a rhetorical adherence to popular concepts in the fields of international development and international governance while also including traditional concerns such as economic development and cultural relativism. It is also important to pay particular attention to the qualifiers inserted throughout the elements.

Words like "present realities", "opportunities", and "challenges" greatly weaken the commitment to lofty goals such as the achievement of social justice, human rights, and the development of a people-cantered community. Nevertheless one must not jump to the conclusion that the intercalation of traditional economic development goals and civil and political rights is simply a cunning discursive rhetorical device to appease regional NGOs and international donors but rather the result of ASEAN's process of consensus building. Thus, the eight elements represent the percolated positions of the members of ASEAN after considerable negotiations and concessions.

Therefore, the result is the lowest common denominator plus qualifiers inserted so as to make new elements such as human rights and certain freedoms more palatable to recalcitrant members. In other words, the contradictory and ambiguous nature of the resulting eight elements is a result of the process used by the members to draft the document.

The first page of the Blue Print is a good example of the rest of the document in terms of the presence of qualifiers, the insertion of unrelated economic concerns, and the undercurrent of cultural relativism that permeates the policy paper. Thus submitting the policy document to content analysis is a useful first step in order to understand some of the underlying conflicts and debates taking place regarding the ASEAN Socio-Cultural Community. As mentioned at the beginning of this chapter, policy papers represent the voice of governmental elites and not necessarily the wishes of the people. This is especially true in ASEAN which has historically favoured the nation-state as the most important instrument of regional governance; however this does not make the endeavour any less important as an initial step at elucidating the deeper structural conflicts causing the oscillation afflicting the region.

Human Development

Section A of the Blue Print concentrates on social development issues under the category of human development. This section includes issues as diverse as the use of Information Technology and Human Capital development together with education (ASEAN, 2009, p. 1). While the three previously mentioned issues are part of social development they also contain an important cultural aspect. Information Technology can be a powerful force for cultural integration due to its pivotal function in rapidly spreading information and in facilitation region wide communication. The same is true of Human Capital development which includes professional training and vocational programs designed to modernize the workforce. Since the socio-economic aspects of the aforementioned issues have been discussed in previous chapters of this book, this discussion will concentrate on cultural aspects.

Education

Education is a very sensitive area in terms of regional integration due to the important role it plays in the socialization of the population (von Feigenblatt, Suttichujit, Shuib, Keling, & Ajis, 2010). Important values are transmitted from generation to generation through primary and secondary education. Moreover, important political values are also included in the curriculum (Pitiyanuwat & Sujiva, 2005). The teaching of social studies and history are considered to be very important by ASEAN governments due to their emancipator potentials. Thus subjects such as civics are carefully monitored by the Ministries of Education so as to produce submissive and loyal subjects/citizens (Pitiyanuwat & Sujiva, 2005).

Therefore schools are important centres for the indoctrination of the population into a certain worldview preferred by ASEAN governments (Liow, 2006; Perkasa, 2008; Wang, 2008). As should be clear by now, ASEAN members have a diverse array of political systems with varying degrees of civil and political freedoms (Kim, Fidler, & Ganguly, 2009; Neher, 2002). Those differences are manifested in school curricula. Moreover, the region's traumatic experience with colonialism and its adoption of European late 19th Century nationalism as the core of its nation-building efforts, has also had a profound effect on the way history is taught in schools.

The Blue Print's section on education begins with the very ambitious goal of achieving "universal access to primary education across ASEAN by 2015" (ASEAN, 2009, p. 2). Other important goals delineated in this section include emphasizing the eradication of illiteracy, promoting gender equality in education, and eliminating differential access according to ethnicity and social class. Achieving equal access for all ethnic and social groups will prove a challenging goal to achieve due to the history of ethnic struggle in certain ASEAN members.

For example, Malaysia has a preferential system in terms of higher education which makes it much easier for members of the Malay ethno nationality to attend institutions of higher learning in the country (Hew, 2008; Lee, 2000). Other ethnic groups such as the Chinese and Indian communities find it difficult to gain acceptance and therefore have tended to send their children to study abroad if they can afford it. While this is one of the few overt barriers to equal access to education in ASEAN there are countless other covert ones. The University system in Thailand is a great example of the many hidden barriers minorities and the poor face when attempting to get an education (von Feigenblatt et al., 2010; Ungpakorn, 2007).

University students are not expected to be older than 25 years old, they cannot be married, cannot have children, and must pass highly biased and flawed entrance examinations designed to favour those who can pay cram schools and tutors in order to gain acceptance into the best Public Universities. Thailand has some of the best Universities in the region which are highly subsidized with incredibly low tuitions for those who get accepted, however the barriers to entry including the lack of appropriate education at the secondary level in the provinces makes it very difficult to those in the lower class and peasants to gain acceptance. Since the university system is paid for by the taxes paid by the entire population and only the children of the middle class can gain access to this service, there is a kind of reverse taxation on the poor in order to subsidize the education of the rich. In terms of gender discrimination, barring entrance to married women and women with children is a clear obstacle to entry.

Due to local traditions and culture, women in the provinces marry younger than in the cities and once married are expected to have children, thus not allowing them to attend college for that reason unjustly limits the educational options of a large proportion of the population. While this state of affairs is well known and has been challenged on several occasions, the piecemeal approach to reform has been to establish open universities with much more limited budgets and with minimal reputations. Degrees from those universities count for the equivalent of a high school diploma from a selective Bangkok high school.

A very interesting goal in the section dealing with education is the inclusion of distance education and the use of

ICT as a way to achieve the goals of reducing illiteracy and promoting vocational training (ASEAN, 2009, p. 3). E-learning has incredible potential in Southeast Asia due to the relatively low cost of this approach to education in comparison to traditional education which requires a considerable investment in infrastructure. Due to the spread of satellite technology, internet cafes, and cell phones, distance learning is more appealing than ever in order to spread education to remote and underserved areas of the region. An emphasis on vocational programs, as recommended by the Blue Print, would reduce any trepidation regional governments may have regarding the possible use of education for political propaganda or democratization.

Probably the most controversial and innovative proposal in the section on education is the inclusion of teaching materials dealing with the common cultural heritage of ASEAN (ASEAN, 2009, p. 3). The goal is to create a common identity by teaching ASEAN studies at the elementary, secondary, and tertiary levels. Needless to say this section is very ambiguous regarding the possible content to be included in ASEAN studies as well as regarding how those materials are going to be developed. As mentioned in previous sections of this chapter, education is a very sensitive area for regional governments and the inclusion of courses dealing with ASEAN studies may be viewed with suspicion by some governments. Even the goal of building a regional identity remains controversial as evidenced by the assertions of the importance of local culture and practices throughout the Blue Print.

Other interesting proposals in the education section include the promotion of exchange programs at the tertiary level as well as the strengthening of regional university networks (ASEAN, 2009, p. 3). Regional youth networks, are also part of the effort to integrate the region. ASEAN Members recognize the need to increase the English proficiency of their populations so as to promote direct communication between countries. Due to the region's exponential language diversity, English is recognized as the best possible lingua franca (ASEAN, 2009, p. 3; Lee, 2000; Neher, 2002). Communication is at the core of establishing a common identity through greater interaction between the populations of ASEAN's members. Increasing the population's English proficiency also has some hidden dangers such as their possible exposure to a greater range of sources of information and news which might have a destabilizing potential in terms of political stability.

Section A.2. briefly returns to the topic of human resource development. This topic was discussed in the Blue Print for the ASEAN Economic Community but some aspects dealing with social and cultural issues are included in the Blue Print for a Socio-Cultural Community as well (ASEAN, 2009, p. 3). For example, the importance of English proficiency is emphasized as well as the implementation of measures to help women, minorities, and people with disabilities in terms of training and integration in the workforce.

Developing the skills needed for high value industries is also emphasized in this section echoing similar recommendations in the Blue Print for an Economic Community. The brevity of this subsection shows that while human resource development has some socio-cultural aspects, it is mainly an economic issue. Challenges in terms of the goals for human resource development include cultural barriers to the incorporation of women in the work place, barriers to the spread of English as the language of choice for business, as well as discrimination against people with disabilities and minorities.

It should be noted that ageism is widespread in Southeast Asia which means that those in senior positions are usually more conservative than young people and may have reservations regarding the use of English in the workplace as well as regarding the integration of women and minorities in the workforce. One concrete case is the discrimination faced by transgender individuals in Thailand who want to enter the teaching profession. Sexual orientation is officially pathologized in order to ban the entry into certain professions of certain minority groups (Jackson, 1997).

The promotion of "decent work" is the topic of section A.3. Issues such as work safety, the promotion of entrepreneurship as part of work culture, improvement of industrial relations, and working towards mutual skills recognitions are discussed in this section (ASEAN, 2009, p. 4). Issues of work safety are clearly important since they vary greatly among ASEAN members and directly affect the quality of life of millions of people.

Work safety includes aspects such as the quality of the equipment used, availability of medical services in case of emergencies, as well as appropriate infrastructure for the industry in question. Improvement of industrial relations is an important aspect of the general topic of "decent work" since it alludes to the need for proper procedures for conflict management in the workplace. Two terms included in the section regarding the previously mentioned goal raise some issues regarding the ultimate aim of the effort. "Industrial harmony" and "higher productivity" are goals that can be achieved in various ways and that may or may not improve the quality of life and the working conditions in ASEAN member States.

The first term is especially problematic because it implies that the status quo should be protected and that change is destabilizing and inherently dangerous. While the same term might not have such negative connotations in a different context, Southeast Asia has a long history of authoritarianism which instinctively brings association of government crackdowns on workers and activists (Collins, 2008). "Harmony" also alludes to the issue of Asian values and its neo-confucian current.

Thus, the juxtaposition of the word "harmony" and the goal of "higher productivity" in a context of authoritarianism bring to the fore strong suspicions as to the true intentions of the proposed improvement in "industrial relations" recommended at the beginning of the section. The use of very ambiguous terms is a trademark of the ASEAN way of consensus building and while some members might have interpreted the previously discussed terms in emancipatory and progressive ways others might have attributed a very different meaning to the same set of terms. Therefore, this is a clear example of some of the difficulties of content analysis of policy papers produced by ASEAN.

Information and Communication Technology (ICT)

Information and Communication Technology (ICT) is an important subject area for ASEAN (ASEAN, 2009, p. 5). Most regional governments recognize the importance of ICT for the region's development (Bhattacharyay, 2010). The importance of this topic is reflected by the subsection dealing with ICT included in the Blue Print for the ASEAN Socio-Cultural Community (ASEAN, 2009). It should be noted that a section on ICT was also included in the Blue Print for the Economic Community which shows that this is an important area from both a social and an economic point of view (ASEAN, 2008).

Section A.4. concentrates on the human capital development necessary in order to take advance of ICT. Thus the emphasis here is on the necessary skills required in order to take advance of the tools provided by ICT. There is a clear link between this point and education which is mentioned in the Blue Print. The document recommends the promotion of ICT literacy among not only the traditional workforce but also women, the elderly, and people with disabilities (ASEAN, 2009, p. 5). Moreover, there is an emphasis on the teaching of these skills in elementary and secondary schools. The internet is mentioned as a particular area of interest.

ICT is a double edged sword in that it can be used to destabilize governments as well as to increase productivity. Moreover, the faster flow of information has an important integrative effect at the regional level. News travel faster and remote areas are brought into the socio-cultural fold of the country. Southeast Asian governments are aware of the dangers of greater computer literacy and especially of the spread of the use of the internet ("The 15 Enemies of the Internet and Countries to Watch," 2005). Singapore, Myanmar, and Thailand use filtering software in order to block and censor sensitive information in the internet (AHRC, 2009; von Feigenblatt, 2009c; Le-Coz, 2009; Lee, 2000; Than & Thein, 2007).

Singapore has developed some of the most advanced software to filter online content in order to avoid political dissent and content deemed immoral by the government authorities. Myanmar has purchased software from Singapore and Thailand in order to filter opposition web-sites and thus to control the flow of information. In the case of Myanmar even foreign news are filtered in addition to e-mail accounts (Keling, Saludin, von Feigenblatt, Ajis, & Shuib, 2010; Thawnghmung, 2009). Thailand also has a long history of censoring the media and in particular the internet (Le-Coz, 2009; Ungpakorn, 2007, 2010). Thousands of web-sites have been blocked by the government due to their support for exiled Prime Minister Dr. Thaksin Shinawatra or due to opposition to the monarchy (Ungpakorn, 2010). Thailand also filters pornographic web-sites and other information considered improper by the government.

Issues of censorship are becoming more salient for other Southeast Asian governments as their populations become more literate and as access to the internet becomes more widespread. It should be noted that most countries in Southeast Asia filter the internet with the possible exception of the Philippines. Another possible danger of the spread of ICT in Southeast Asia is the use of the technology by Islamist and terrorist groups (Glassman, 2005).

This has already happened to a certain extend in Indonesia and in parts of the Philippines. ICTs facilitate communication between terrorist networks and make it much easier for them too plan and coordinate attacks (Millard, 2004). Thus, regional governments have to deal with a vast array of risks and challenges related to the spread of ICTs.

Facilitating Access to Science and Technology

Another important goal included in the Blue Print is facilitating access to Science and Technology (ASEAN, 2009, p. 4). As discussed in the section of the book dealing with economic integration, ASEAN member States are very interested in the possibility of technology transfers. There are many ways in which technology transfers can take place but one of the most inexpensive and basic ones is by cooperating with other members in conducting basic research and by having greater interaction between research centres.

The Blue Print contains another interesting proposal which is a Virtual Institute of Science and Technology (AVIST) which makes use of information and communication technology in order to increase cooperation among ASEAN scientists (ASEAN, 2009, p. 4). Greater rotation and movement of scientists and researchers is also recommended. Challenges in this respect include the disparity in terms of scientific and technological advancement of ASEAN members. More advanced members would be expected to transfer some of their technology to less advanced ones.

Improving the Civil Service

The final goal in the section of the Blue Print dealing with human capital is about civil service capability (ASEAN, 2009, p. 5). Disparities between the professionalism of the civil service in ASEAN Member States are stark. The civil service of countries such as Indonesia and Vietnam are famous for being corrupt and those of Myanmar for being incompetent. Therefore, member states recognize the importance of standardizing the quality of civil service in terms of governance. This can be done in a variety of ways but due to the great differences separating the countries' bureaucracies such as ideology, development, and funding, training by a pool of regional experts is deemed to be one of the best options.

Point eight of this goal stresses the importance of developing a civil service that is responsive to the needs of the people, respects human rights, gender equality, and is sensitive to the needs of the poor (ASEAN, 2009, p. 5). This is a tall order for a region known for corrupt and authoritarian bureaucracies but according the Blue Print the key is to increase citizen feedback and out-put based performance ratings. Thus, the Blue Print recommends adopting some of the practices of the private sector in order to increase the region wide quality of civil service.

Standardizing the professionalism of civil service in ASEAN is a great challenge. Different bureaucracies have diverse professional cultures and operate in different power contexts. Thus, the operating environment of a bureaucrat in Vietnam is not the same of one in the Philippines. Moreover, those different world views or cultures lead bureaucrats to behave in different ways and to interpret their missions differently.

For example, a government official in a Burmese province may not consider his mission to include the protection of human rights. A Thai bureaucrat in the border provinces may not consider his role to be to respond to the needs of the local community but rather to serve the interests of the central government (von Feigenblatt, 2009b).

Therefore, the proposal implies that there is a need for a region wide cultural shift towards a more professional culture of service based on private sector standards such as out-put based performance ratings and informed by global norms such as human rights and gender equality. Considerable resistance to this shift can be expected from all levels of the regional bureaucracy and in order to overcome this resistance political will be necessary on the part of decision makers.

Social Welfare and Protection

Part B of the Blue Print covers the very broad topic of social welfare and protection (ASEAN, 2009, p. 6). This section is in turn subdivided into subsections dealing with a range of topics ranging from poverty alleviation, food security, access to healthcare, ensuring a drug free region, disaster resilience, and social safety nets. As discussed at the beginning of this chapter most of these issues were also discussed in the section of the book dealing with economic integration however some aspects of these issues fall under the rubric of socio-cultural integration and therefore these aspects will be discussed here. The first subtopic, namely poverty alleviation is intimately related to social safety nets. This subtopic deals with the possible negative externalities of globalization and economic integration.

Economic restructuring and changes in the employment market due to the growing integration of services and production processes in the ASEAN region cause considerable social problems such as internal displacement of people in search of jobs, unemployment in certain sectors of the economy, and important changes in consumption patterns. ASEAN governments are aware of the social and cultural challenges posed by globalization and economic integration and agree on the need to put in place a certain level of social safety needs including but not limited to, measures for poverty alleviation such as the promotion of microfinance and the improvement of rural infrastructure (ASEAN, 2009, p. 6).

On the cultural side of the issue, measures include the monitoring of the use of the internet in order to prevent its use in order to incite ethnic hatred and discrimination. This is an interesting proposal inserted between a range of social issues. It shows that ASEAN governments are aware of the cultural shifts that may be brought about by the internet and other forms of information and communications technology. The internet has the potential to connect ethnic groups dispersed in several nation-states and thus weaken the fabric of the nation-state. In other words, the internet can be used to spread alternative narratives about a people's history and about its future.

Another important proposal is the establishment of social insurance for the informal sector. This proposal is important because of the large number of people employed in the informal sector. The changes brought about by greater economic integration will undoubtedly bring about some unemployment and hardship to certain sections of the informal sector but while most other sectors have access to social insurance and other social safety nets, members of the informal sector do not. ASEAN members are aware of the considerable socio-political consequences of ignoring such a large sector during an important and difficult process towards regional integration and because of that want to ameliorate the negative externalities of the process by protecting the most vulnerable sectors of the population. Notwithstanding the good intentions behind this proposal, the challenges for its successful implementation are daunting.

Different political systems entail different levels of social protection and government intervention. Moreover, even if ASEAN members could agree on an ideal level of protection the resources available for ASEAN members vary considerably. This problem is particularly salient for the CLMV countries which are undergoing the most radical changes socio-economically. CLMV countries lack the resources to institute the social safety nets necessary in order to cushion the majority of the population from painful but necessary transitions from command economies to regionally integrated free markets. This situation is unfortunate since the populations that would suffer the most from the negative externalities of globalization and economic integration will enjoy the least protection.

Another interesting proposal deals with the promotion of rural development through the help of young volunteer professionals (ASEAN, 2009, p. 6). This is something that was attempted in Thailand during the 1970s and early 1980s with good results. While the logistics of this proposal may be complex the idea makes good use of available resources and also has the important positive externality of integrating the intellectual elite with the rural population.

Political cleavages in Thailand, for example, tend to polarize the country into an educated urban middle class and an uneducated rural majority (Ungpakorn, 2007, 2010). Young professionals need not be from the same country as the rural population they work with since socio-cultural integration from the local to the regional level would be facilitated by these exchanges. Therefore, the mobilization of considerable qualified human resources in the cities, which are currently underutilized due to unemployment and underemployment, would help mobilize the region's most important resource the huge rural population waiting to have the skills and opportunities to develop its capabilities.

Social Justice and Rights

Part C of the Blue Print deals with the important topic of Social Justice and Rights (ASEAN, 2009, p. 11). This section covers a vast array of important issues such as the protection of women, the elderly, the disabled and migrant workers. Some measures proposed in the Blue Print include the strengthening of an ASEAN network of social workers, the implementation of measures supporting important declarations and conventions dealing with the rights of women and children, such as the Declaration on the Elimination of Violence Against Women, the Convention on the Rights of the Child, *inter alia* (ASEAN, 2009, p. 12). Another proposal stresses the importance of the collection of sex-disaggregated data to promote awareness of gender inequality. A gender perspective should be included in policymaking as recommended by the Blue Print. It is also recommended to increase the percentage of women on all fields including politics and business (ASEAN, 2009, p. 12).

Some of the challenges in implementing the rights included in the previous paragraph have been discussed in early sections of this chapter. The main obstacle is the debate regarding culture and its relationship to universal human rights. Many of ASEAN members have cultural practices which discriminate women and which limit their career opportunities. Divorce laws in Malaysia for example, greatly favour men who can divorce their wives by saying it in public three times while women have to go through a much more complicated process to do the same thing. Moreover, cultural practices in certain sub-regions condone domestic violence under the rubric of domestic discipline. There is a tension between traditional practices and international human rights (Merry, 2006).

Since gender relations are something that affects the very fabric of society starting with the family, it is an area of considerable contestation in terms of guiding norms (Bem, 1993). Those opposed to change challenge Human Rights on the grounds of cultural incompatibility and the protection of local traditional practices. Thus, the universalism of Human Rights is compared to the relativism of local culture (Blau & Moncada, 2009; Merry, 2006). Due to the sensitive nature of this debate, the Blue Print, avoids concrete plans and instead attempts to concentrate on broad principles through the selective avoidance of thorny issues that may be divisive such as the possible standardization of "marriage laws" and other legal regimes that may be perpetuating inequality in ASEAN member States.

Another sensitive issue is the rights of migrant workers (ASEAN, 2009, pp. 12-13). ASEAN has history of considerable population movements for work (Ajis et al., 2010; Neher, 2002). Malaysian workers often cross the border to Singapore to work, Burmese migrate to Thailand to work in factories, Vietnamese trade in Cambodia, and Filipinos have a long history of working overseas and in other ASEAN members (Green, Jacobsen, & Pyne, 2008; Lee, 2000; Wyatt,

2003). This reflects the fact that borders in ASEAN are porous and ill defined (Tagliacozzo, 2001). Borders are liminal areas in which different ethnic groups blend and governance takes place through a combination of formal and informal structures (Pieterse, 2007; Vaughan-Williams, 2008).

On the other hand the "violent imaginaries" of the recent efforts to impose the concept of the nation-state on the peoples of Southeast Asia have had some effect in socializing certain sectors of society and thus increased xenophobia against migrant workers and nationalism (Ajis et al., 2010). Thus there are two opposing forces at work in terms of how migrant workers are viewed and the relative influence of those forces affects the way foreign workers are treated.

Due to the seriousness of certain cases of abuse of migrant workers, the topic of migrant rights has received growing attention (Green et al., 2008). Cases of modern day slavery, human trafficking and dreadful working conditions have brought to the attention of policy elites the need to tackle this issue. Some of the most pressing issues include the protection and regulation of the recruitment of foreign workers so that innocent people are not tricked into servitude under infrahuman working conditions (Green et al., 2008). Other cases involve the deceitful recruitment of women to work in garment factories who are then forced into prostitution (Haritaworn, 2007).

Even for those workers who are recruited into a legitimate industry, their working conditions tend to be much worse than for local employees (Ajis et al., 2010). At this point there is an ASEAN Declaration on the Protection Promotion of Rights of Migrant Workers but it has not been operationalized (ASEAN, 2009, pp. 12-13). Some of the proposed measures to protect migrant workers include the strengthening of consular functions so as to aid migrant workers in distress, greater data sharing about working conditions and abuses, and more dialogue about the topic through the ASEAN Forum on Migrant Labour (ASEAN, 2009, pp. 12-13). It is clear that the measures are weak and probably ineffective while the principles are lofty and well informed. The problem is that there is a lack of political will to take strong measures to protect migrant workers (Ajis et al., 2010).

Decades of propaganda promoting nationalism have made the middle classes very protectionist and xenophobic in certain ASEAN members such as Thailand (Ungpakorn, 2007, 2010). Since the middle classes are politically very active, the protection of migrant workers could be politically very costly. Moreover, unemployment in certain ASEAN members makes migrant workers unpopular also among the lower classes. Nevertheless since ASEAN is a region wide organization with the goals of security, economic, and socio-cultural integration, it is important to take steps to ameliorate some of the dangers of such a process on migrant workers. This issue will become increasingly important and salient as more skilled workers rotate from ASEAN member to member.

The expanded employment possibilities for the previously isolationist and protectionist middle classes may cause a positive change in the political environment in favour of increased protection for migrant workers. While skilled workers will also need protections, unskilled labour tends to be the most vulnerable in terms of bad working conditions and other abuses.

Closely related to better working conditions is the concept of corporate social responsibility (CSR). This is an issue that is tackled in section C.3. of the Blue Print and represents a socio-cultural approach to important economic issues (ASEAN, 2009, p. 13). It should be noted that this section tackles good corporate practices from the point of view of international norms such as the ones included in ISO 26000 (ASEAN, 2009, p. 14). The goal is to exert normative pressure on the private section in ASEAN so as to compel companies to adopt best practices without the need of government intervention and supervision (Kollman, 2008).

This approach requires a cultural change at the corporate

level and mirrors the desired changes at the broader social level. Thus ASEAN members expect the private sector to become a good regional citizen following internationally accepted standards of conduct. Therefore one of the main proposals in this section is the adoption of a regional code containing the standards of ISO 26000 so as to mainstream the instrument in the region and thus make it a normal part of doing business. CSR is a very broad concept that includes the goals and principles of sustainable development as applied to private enterprises (Kollman, 2008).

One final proposal in this subsection mentions the need to foster sustainable relations between the private sector and the communities where they operate. This alludes to the need to use the resources of the private sector to promote local development in partnership with communities (ASEAN, 2009, p. 14). Moving the private sector towards CSR will take considerable resources in terms of educational campaigns for executives as well and consumer education. In order to increase the effectiveness of informal norms such as CSR it is important to have a well informed and sophisticated consumer group.

Thus, regional governments would need to make a considerable investment in educating the public about good corporate practices as well as about the negative externalities cause by the private sector when it disregards the public good.

This would provide an informal market mechanism to punish those companies that do not adhere to CSR while also providing incentives to those that do. One proposal that was not included in the Blue Print but that would be very useful in operationalizing the goal of promoting CRS is to adopt the European practice of adding a label to products that adhere to certain standards such as CRS as well as environmental protection. This would make those products more appealing to educated consumers and would punish those companies that refuse to adopt the recommended code of conduct.

Environmental Issues

Section D of the Blue Print deals with environmental issues ranging from transboundary haze pollution to the promotion of environmental education (ASEAN, 2009, pp. 15-16). It should be noted that most issues discussed in this section could have been included under security or economics but due to their social importance they were included in the Blue Print for the ASEAN Socio-Cultural Community. Since environmental issues were discussed in the section of the book dealing with economic issues, this section will deal with the cultural and social aspects related to environmental awareness. An entire subsection is devoted to the importance of environmental education in order to achieve sustainable development (ASEAN, 2009, p. 16).

There is a connection between an increase in public awareness of environmental issues and greater public participation in dealing with them. Thus, one of the proposals in the Blue Print is an Environmental Education Action Plan which would undertake other related activities such as an evaluation of the current environmental content in school curricula and in teacher training (ASEAN, 2009, p. 16). Other related proposals and projects include the production of region wide educational materials dealing with environmental issues and sustainable development.

The goal of this set of proposals is the mainstreaming and integration of environmental issues into all realms of life including governance and education. The Blue Print puts considerable emphasis on the education of relevant stakeholders including teachers, government officials, the private sector, and the general public. Therefore, awareness raising is at the core of the socio-cultural elements of sustainable development and the ultimate goal is to foster a shift in values towards environmentally friendly ones in line with sustainable development. As explained in previous sections of this chapter, any proposal dealing with a change in the curriculum can prove to be controversial however environmental issues tend to enjoy considerable support throughout the region.

Building an ASEAN Identity

Section E of the Blue Print is at the core of the ASEAN Socio-Cultural Community and deals with the ambitious goal of "Building an ASEAN Identity" (ASEAN, 2009, p. 20). This section of the Blue Print is subdivided into the following subsections: "promotion of ASEAN awareness and sense of community", "preservation and promotion of ASEAN cultural heritage", "promotion of cultural creativity and industry", and "engagement with the community" (ASEAN, 2009, pp. 20-23). Section E is pivotal for the socio-cultural integration of the region and thus will be discussed in detail in the following pages.

The first subsection deals with the "promotion of ASEAN awareness and sense of community" (ASEAN, 2009, p. 21). This subsection's main strategic goal is to foster a sense of community in the ASEAN region through a greater understanding of the region's history and cultures. At the core of this effort is the ASEAN logo and symbols. As the organization behind the integration effort, the first step in the process towards a sense of community is for the people of member countries to recognize and be able to identify the symbols of the organization. At the core of this effort is the Regional and National Communication Plan which coordinates the creation and dissemination of materials informing the public about ASEAN (ASEAN, 2009, p. 21).

This plan includes the promotion of ASEAN identity by government officials in addition to partnering with the media in order to publicize ASEAN programs with an emphasis on those dealing with culture and the arts. Other parts of the plan involve the promotion of ASEAN Day in schools as well as the fostering of people to people interaction in Southeast Asia. One program deals with establishing cultural links between different towns and cities in ASEAN so as to cooperate in terms of the promotion of arts and culture. Another interesting program in this subsection encourages the cooperation of media personnel from different ASEAN members in order to promote cultural tolerance and a greater understanding of cultural diversity.

Similar exchanges are expected in the television industry so as to have a more balanced media content in addition to spreading information about the cultures and arts of other member countries. Cooperation between libraries is also encouraged in order to exchange resources and to promote the diversity and breadth of content available. Finally the subsection encourages youth exchanges as part of efforts to increase people to people interaction. The goal of this subsection of the Blue Print is to spread the work about ASEAN as a first step in the process of building a regional identity. This is followed by the need to increase the mutual understanding of ASEAN members about each other's cultures and traditions in order to at least achieve a greater level of tolerance.

Therefore the spread of information about other ASEAN members is pivotal in this effort but is also fraught with challenges. The media operates under very different levels of censorship in the different ASEAN member States and therefore cooperation on joint projects such as the production of original programming for television would run into challenges such as the proper depiction of certain historical events, the role of religion, freedom of speech, etc. Even the simple expansion of programming to include content produced in other ASEAN members would also have to screened and censored in certain countries due to national sensibilities and governmental policy.

One way to avoid this would be to avoid thorny issues and to concentrate on the most superficial aspects of culture such as certain forms of art and some rituals however this would also detract from the experience and from the possible improvement in the cultural proficiency of the general public.

Exchanging books is an even more problematic endeavour due to very stringent censorship laws and also due to language barriers. ASEAN is a region with a vast array of languages and the majority of the population is not fluent in English. Thus an exchange of books written in English would simply benefit the educated elite and would include mostly volumes written by scholars outside of the ASEAN region. Most books written in English in Southeast Asia are written for an extra-regional audience and tend to be either extremely superficial or conformist or tend to be books written to be extremely critical of government policies.

The first genre is usually government sanctioned and supports the tourism industry by providing an ideal picture of the country and its people while the second tends to be written in order to gain international support against a government or interest group. This means that the first genre would only provide a superficial understanding of the culture and society of other ASEAN members while the second would most likely be banned and removed from circulation. Thus, the exchange of collections between ASEAN libraries would have a very weak effect in terms of increasing awareness about other cultures since few people can read in English outside of the capitals.

There is also the challenge of a possible nationalist backlash to foreign content in the media. Even though foreign content will be of ASEAN origin it may be regarded as alien by certain nationalist groups and thus may be heavily criticized. This is something that has already happened to a certain extend with Thai content in Cambodian Television. Nationalist groups in Cambodia including the ruling party have criticized the high proportion of Thai content in Cambodian Television. A rumour that was spread about a Thai Soap Opera actress claiming that Angkor Wat should belong to Thailand created such a furore that the Thai embassy in Cambodia was torched to the ground by a mob of Cambodian nationalists (Hinton, 2006).

Thus a rumour related to popular culture, soap operas, was linked to a historical antagonism over ownership of Angkor Wat which in turn reignited the flames of nationalism and xenophobia in both Thailand and Cambodia. This example shows that seemingly innocuous cultural artefacts can have considerable consequences in a region historically characterized by its fractiousness and instability.

The second part of this section deals with the "preservation and promotion of ASEAN cultural heritage" (ASEAN, 2009, p. 22). This includes the preservation of both physical and intangible cultural heritage such as festivals and traditional dances. The proposed measures to preserve and promote cultural heritage include some very common standard procedures such as the use of the media to increase public awareness about the importance of certain cultural sites and practices in addition to the physical protection of certain sites through better legislation and security. Another important measure is to make it harder to take out cultural artefacts from Southeast Asia. This is an important measure since it deals with a problem that is rampant in Southeast Asia and has resulted in the illicit sale of thousands of important historical artefacts all over the world (Tagliacozzo, 2001).

The previously described measures for the "preservation and promotion of ASEAN cultural heritage" are linked by the ulterior motive of promoting tourism at the regional level. Thus there are plans to open ASEAN Cultural offices in dialogue partners, who are important sources of tourists, and to produce audiovisual materials to promote ASEAN's diverse cultures while at the same time fostering a regional identity (ASEAN, 2009, p. 22). There is also a strong emphasis in protecting "living traditions" through fostering community participation and by providing incentives through government and private initiatives.

There are important challenges related to this subsection of the Blue Print. One of the most obvious challenges is the lack of the necessary resources to undertake such an ambitious campaign. ASEAN Members have considerably different levels of capacity in terms of governance and thus can provide different levels of protection for heritage sites and cultural artefacts. In addition to that there is an important political undercurrent to what is and is not considered to be a living tradition. Since having a cultural practice labelled as a "living tradition" would attract government funding and tourism to a group then it is logical to assume that there will be competition over limited resources and media attention. This would be a problem in multiethnic societies in which there has been a struggle over what is considered part of national culture versus minority culture.

Even if governments decide to promote minority cultural artefacts in order to attract tourism, there is also the political risk of weakening majority claims to primacy in terms of national culture (Funston, 2010). To complicate matters even more there is the fact that ASEAN's borders are relatively recent and do not reflect ethnic lines which means that some cultural sites will be located in member States with a different majority culture from the one that created the cultural site. Moreover, there are cultural sites that were created by defunct nation-states and others whose ownership changed over the years from one ASEAN Member to another (Cuasay, 1998; Hinton, 2006). One salient example of one such dispute over a cultural site is the conflict over the listing of Preah Vihear Temple as a World Heritage Site in 2008 (Gallis, 2009).

The temple was in dispute between Thailand and Cambodia until it was awarded to Cambodia by the International Court of Justice (Chan, 2004). Thailand protested the decision but finally agreed to remove its flag from the Temple and to hand control over the Temple to Cambodia. Nevertheless, the flag was removed in standing position and Thailand continued to assert its claim over the Temple (Cuasay, 1998). During the late 1990s Cambodia decided to apply to UNESCO to have the site listed as a World Heritage Site but the signature of both countries was needed to do so. In

2008 the Thai government at the time agreed to sign the application and the Temple was added as a World Heritage Site (Gallis, 2009). However, a silent coup removed the government that had supported Cambodia's application and insisted that the application signed by the previous government was illegal since it had not been approved by parliament. This led to considerable protests along the border, to military skirmishes, and to the closing of the border. Thus the protection of a cultural site resulted in conflict between two ASEAN Members.

The third subsection of the Blue Print dealing with the creation of a regional ASEAN identity deals with the "promotion of cultural creativity and industry" and is more present and future oriented than the previous subsection (ASEAN, 2009, p. 23). This relatively brief subsection deals with the promotion of cooperation of ASEAN members in the cultural industry. While the term "cultural industry" is left undefined in the Blue Print, the term refers to small to medium sized industries that market and produce tangible and intangible cultural products. This is a very broad category that includes certain sectors of the tourism industry such as heritage tourism as well as small village level enterprises selling handicrafts.

Dance troupes and certain forms of local theatre can also be included in this category. Another way to understand this concept is to think of the commercialization of "living culture". Local practices and knowledge can be processed so as to make it a commodity. Regional governments are eager to encourage local and regional entrepreneurs to protect and promote this kind of industry. The Blue Book recommends cooperation at the regional level so as to form medium sized enterprises that make use of young people so as to reduce unemployment (ASEAN, 2009, p. 23). Thus, training programs are also encouraged.

There is also a proposal for the promotion of this industry both intra and extra regionally through regional marketing campaigns and the active participation of ethnic groups. It should be noted that the content of these cultural products need not be unchanging and reflecting the past but rather a creative mixture between traditional local elements and new creations. Therefore, creativity is highly encouraged in terms of the packaging and marketing of new cultural products.

The previous subsection is also fraught with challenges and possible obstacles. While some of the challenges discussed in relation to the previous subsection such as majority versus minority cultural clashes are also present in this case, there is a greater challenge which is the possibility of cultural appropriation of local practices by powerful economic interests. This issue is closely related to intellectual property rights which was discussed in part II of this volume. Certain aspects of "living culture" which can be packaged and sold as commodities for a large profit are difficult to protect as intellectual property since there is no single owner or creator.

It is usually a village or ethnic group that creates the core of the product which is then packaged in a creative way and promoted by a larger enterprise usually controlled by an outside group. The problem with this is that the part of "living culture" is appropriated by an external agent and few of the benefits of its commercialization flow to those who actually gave rise to the product.

Closely related with the participatory nature of the previous subsection is the final subsection of section E which deals with engagement with the community. This is the shorted subsection in the entire Blue Print which shows that it is not an area that is considered particularly important by ASEAN Members. Moreover, certain ASEAN member States such as Myanmar are ambivalent or at times even clearly opposed to the role and influence of civil society organizations. While there certain processes such as the ASEAN Social Forum, the ASEAN Civil Society Conference, and a list of ASEAN affiliated non-governmental organizations, most of these venues tend to be at the margins of the ASEAN structure.

Thus, there is a minimum consensus about the need to get civil society organizations involved in one way or another but there is also agreement that ASEAN is a state-centric organization and that the role of non-state parties will remain peripheral. Collins concludes that the door to grassroots participation in ASEAN is actually closed and that meaningful participation in the policy making process is not welcomed by ASEAN member States (Collins, 2008). Nevertheless there is also a need for ASEAN to reach out to civil society organizations and community groups in order to facilitate the implementation of its projects.

Thus, ASEAN member States want communities and civil society to be involved in the implementation of its projects but fears greater involvement in the planning stages. This functionalist view of the role of civil society organizations aims to take advantage of the greater legitimacy of those organizations and their resources for the benefit of ASEAN. This aspect of civil society participation was discussed in the first section of this volume in relation to non-traditional security issues.

ASEAN's current approach to civil society participation can be divided into two parts. Independent civil society groups with a grassroots following are used in order to gain legitimacy and to facilitate the implementation of ASEAN projects while at the same time being sidelined in terms of actual input in terms of planning and strategy. On the other hand there are a group of non-governmental organizations that enjoy a close relationship with ASEAN through a neo-corporatist arrangement. These organizations are mostly trade associations, chambers of commerce, and professional associations.

ASEAN has virtually engulfed these semi-independent organizations which have overlapping memberships with ASEAN's governing elites and share some of the same goals and values. It should be noted that these second type of civil society organizations are not grassroots organizations but instead represent narrow upper and middle class interests in a fashion resembling the guilds of Renaissance Europe. Both ASEAN and these professional associations benefit from this relationship in that the interests of the groups are usually narrow and politically innocuous while ASEAN can mobilize the support of powerful interest groups in ASEAN member States and also claims that there is an active engagement with civil society organizations.

While most intergovernmental organizations tend to have ambivalent and at times strained relationships with civil society organizations the case of ASEAN is particularly interesting in the way in which it shows the two extreme poles of possible relationships with non-governmental organizations. A corporatist arrangement implies that the recognized corporations will jointly develop policy with the government will do so jointly rather than attempt to pressure policymakers from the outside. Thus, those organizations in this arrangement become insiders in exchange for a certain degree of submission to the needs of ASEAN Member States.

In other words, the relationship is not one of opponents anymore bur rather of team members or factions of a single system. On the other hand the relationship with most other NGOs is antagonistic and resembles more closely the relationship of social movements and official governments and organizations. There is a clear problem with this arrangement in that the power of certain interests in individual nation-states is projected to the regional level. Thus the "division of labour" at the nation level is mirrored at the regional level. Opportunities for NGOs to participate in the ASEAN process provide asymmetrical access to NGOs aiming to influence policymakers and through them regional policy.

Therefore, inequalities at the national level are simply transposed to the regional level and the promise of meaningful participation and popular empowerment is lost. While this analysis of civil society's relationship with ASEAN is not shared by a majority of grassroots civil society groups in the region, some NGOs have started to complain about differential access to important meetings and the lack of NGO input in regional policy (Collins, 2008).

Narrowing the Development Gap

The final substantive section of the Blue Print for the ASEAN Socio-Cultural Community deals with development issues (ASEAN, 2009, pp. 23-24). It is a very ambiguous section with the intention of "narrowing the development gap". Aspects of this goal have been discussed in the second part of this volume in relation to economic development and therefore only a brief overview of this issue will be provided here. The main concern of this section is in narrowing the social development gap between ASEAN Members. There is a special emphasis on cooperation platforms in order to help the CLMV countries bring up their social development standards through joint projects with the more developed members of ASEAN.

Most projects related to this section include economic corridors, development triangles, and other such arrangements (ASEAN, 2009, p. 24). Nevertheless it should be noted that the main thrust of those projects is economic development and that social development is expected to follow economic growth. This is a questionable assumption that shows how there is a lack of agreement regarding the best way to achieve social development. Some ASEAN members subscribe the "trickle down" model of development while others hold a model that promotes economic and social development concurrently.

Implementation and Evaluation

The Blue Print concludes with a section dealing with the implementation and evaluation of progress regarding the ASEAN Socio-Cultural Community (ASEAN, 2009, pp. 24-26). This section is subdivided into a subsection dealing with the implementation mechanism, another one dealing with resource mobilization, one dealing with the communication strategy, and finally concluding with the review mechanism. The implementation strategy follows the traditional ASEAN way of operating.

A Council is set up to oversee and coordinate the broad initiative, in this case called the ASEAN Socio-Cultural Community Council. The next layer involves the Ministerial meetings and the pertinent national bodies. Mainstreaming and integrating the projects and principles included in the Blue Print is the next step of the strategy. This layer is very diffuse and depends on the good will and political capital available in each member State. It is important to note however that the Secretary General has been empowered to receive reports regarding the progress made in terms of the implementation of the Blue Print. On the other hand it is also noteworthy that the Secretary General can receive those reports but cannot request them.

The subsection dealing with resource mobilization is even briefer and more ambiguous than the previous one and simply states the obvious fact that member States and dialogue partners should set aside funds to implement the projects described in the Blue Print. This section also includes the private sector as well as foundations as important sources of funding. Closely related to resource mobilization is the communication strategy which explains the importance of spreading the word about the initiatives included in the Blue Print in order to facilitate their implementation in addition to helping mobilize necessary resources. In traditional ASEAN style, the document provides few specific details and concludes in an equally ambiguous way by stating that a mid-term review will be prepared "whenever necessary" and that the Secretariat will "develop and adopt indicators" in order to monitor progress (ASEAN, 2009, pp. 25-26).

Conclusions

The Blue Print for the ASEAN Socio-Cultural Community is the outcome of a political process that utilizes consensus building in the tradition of the "ASEAN way". Internal inconsistencies, ambiguities, contradictions, and omissions area all evidence for the negotiations that took place in order to reach this superficial level of agreement. Nevertheless, some important steps along the path toward integration are also reflected in the Blue Print. The stronger role of the Secretary General of the organization should be noted.

While the Secretary General lacks the administrative authority of his counterparts in order intergovernmental organizations, he or she represents the entire organization and thus holds an important symbolic position that if used widely can mobilize political capital towards greater regional integration or other important goals of the organization. Moreover, the secretariat is one of the few ASEAN bodies that hold its authority directly from the organization rather than from the member states. Needless to say the power and effectiveness of the office will greatly depend on the person who holds that office as has been observed in studies dealing with Secretary Generals of the United Nations and their leadership styles.

The next chapter will identify and explain the three core socio-cultural structural conflicts ASEAN currently faces. Each structural conflict will be explained in detail and a few examples will be provided to illustrate how the conflict operates in the region. A few suggestions as to how the core structural conflicts could be overcome in the mid and long term in order to avoid organizational oscillation and foster sustainable advancement will be provided in the second part of the next chapter.

References

The 15 Enemies of the Internet and Countries to Watch [Electronic. (2005). Version], *2009*, from http://www.rsf.org/The-15-enemies-of-the-Internet-and.html.

AHRC, A. (2009). The Rise of the Internal-Security State and Decline of Human Rights in Thailand [Electronic Version], from http://www.ahrchk.net/statements/mainfile.php/2009statements/1888.

Ajis, M.N. e., Saludin, M.N., Ismail, A., von Feigenblatt, Otto F., Shuib, M.S., & Keling, M.F. (2010). Managing Foreign Workers in Southeast Asian Countries. *Journal of Asia Pacific Studies, 1*(3), 481-505.

Anderson, J.E. (2006). *Public Policymaking* (6th ed.). Boston: Houghton Mifflin Company.

ASEAN. (2008). *ASEAN ECONOMIC COMMUNITY BLUEPRINT.* Retrieved. from http://www.aseansec.org/5187-10.pdf.

ASEAN. (2009). *ASEAN SOCIO-CULTURAL COMMUNITY BLUEPRINT.* Retrieved August 11, 2010. from http://www.aseansec.org/5187-19.pdf.

Bem, S.L. (1993). *The Lenses of Gender: Transforming the Debate on Sexual Inequality*. New Haven: Yale University Press.

Bhattacharyay, B.N. (2010). Infrastructure for ASEAN Connectivity and Integration. *ASEAN Economic Bulletin, 27*(2), 200-221.

Blau, J., & Moncada, A. (2009). *Human Rights: A Primer*. Boulder: Paradigm Publishers.

Chan, P.C. W. (2004). Acquiescense/Estoppel in International Boundaries: Temple of Preah Vihear Revisited. *Chinese Journal of International Law, 3*(2), 421-439.

Collins, A. (2008). A People-Oriented ASEAN: A Door Ajar or Closed for Civil Society Organizations? *Contemporary Southeast Asia, 30*(2), 313-332.

Cuasay, P. (1998). Borders on the Fantastic: Mimesis, Violence, and Landscape at the Temple of Preah Vihear. *Modern Asian Studies, 32*(4), 849-890.

von Feigenblatt, Otto F. (2009a). ASEAN and Human Security: Challenges and Opportunities. *Ritsumeikan Centre for Asia Pacific Studies Working Paper, No. 09-5*(July), 1-22.

von Feigenblatt, Otto F. (2009b). Some lessons from the White Rajahs of Sarawak: Identifying and strengthening local capacities for peace in the deep South of Thailand. *Journal of Law and Conflict Resolution, 1*(6), 117-121.

von Feigenblatt, Otto F. (2009c). The Thai Ethnocracy Unravels: A Critical Cultural Analysis of Thailand's Socio-Political Unrest. *Journal of Alternative Perspectives in the Social Sciences, 1*(3), 583-611.

von Feigenblatt, Otto F. , Suttichujit, V., Shuib, M.S., Keling, M.F.,

& Ajis, M.N. e. (2010). Weapons of Mass Assimilation: A Critical Analysis of the Use of Education in Thailand. *Journal of Asia Pacific Studies, 1*(2), 292-311.

Funston, J. (2010). Malaysia and Thailand's Southern Conflict: Reconciling Security and Ethnicity. *Contemporary Southeast Asia, 32*(2), 234-258.

Gallis, A. (2009). Symposium: International Commercial Arbitration: Fifty Years after New York Convention: UNESCO Documents and Procedure: The Need to Account for Political Conflict When Designating World Heritage Sites. *Georgia Journal of International and Comparative Law, 38*(Spring), 1-27.

Glassman, J. (2005). The "War On Terrorism" Comes To Southeast Asia. *Journal of Contemporary Asia, 35*(1), 3-28.

Green, M., Jacobsen, K., & Pyne, S. (2008). Invisible in Thailand: documenting the need for protection [Electronic Version]. Retrieved February 16, 2009, from http://www.humansecuritygateway.info/documents/FMR_Burma_InvisibleInThailand.pdf.

Haritaworn, J. (2007). Beautiful beasts. Ambivalence and distinction in the gender identity negotiations of multiracialised women of Thai descent. *Women's Studies International Forum, 30*(5), 391-403.

Heidhues, M.S. (2000). *Southeast Asia: A Concise History*. London: Thames & Hudson.

Hew, D. (2008). The Malaysian Economy: Developments and Challenges. *Southeast Asian Affairs*, 207-222.

Hinton, A. (2006). Khmerness and the Thai 'Other': Violence, Discourse and Symbolism in the 2003 Anti-Thai Riots in Cambodia. *Journal of Southeast Asian Studies, 37*(3), 445-469.

Jackson, P.A. (1997). Thai Research on Male Homosexuality and Transgenderism and the Cultural Limits of Foucaultian Analysis. *Journal of the History of Sexuality, 8*(1), 52-85.

Keling, M.F., Saludin, M.N., Feigenblatt, O. F. v., Ajis, M.N. e., & Shuib, M.S. (2010). A Historical Approach to Myanmar's Democratic Process. *Journal of Asia Pacific Studies, 1*(2), 132-148.

Kim, S.W., Fidler, D.P., & Ganguly, S. (2009). Eastphalia Rising? Asian Influence and the Fate of Human Security. *World Policy Journal, 26*(2), 53-64.

Kollman, K. (2008). The Regulatory Power of Business Norms: A

Call for a New Research Agenda. *International Studies Review, 10*(3), 397-419.

Le-Coz, C. (2009). "His Untouchable Majesty" Thailand Censorship and Emprisonment: The Abuses in the Name of Lese Majeste [Electronic Version]. *Reporters Sans Frontiers*, 1-16. Retrieved September 20, from http://www.rsf.org/IMG/pdf/rapport_en_ok-2.pdf

Lee, K.Y. (2000). *From Third World to First: The Singapore Story: 1965-2000* (First ed.). New York: HarperCollins Publishers.

Liow, J.C. (2006). *Muslim Resistance in Southern Thailand and the Southern Philippines: Religion, Ideology, and Politics*. Washington, D.C.: East-West Centre.

Merry, S.E. (2006). *Human Rights & Gender Violence: Translating International Law into Local Justice*. Chicago: The University of Chicago Press.

Millard, M. (2004). *Jihad in Paradise: Islam and Politics in Southeast Asia*. Armonk: East Gate Books.

Mulder, N. (1996). *Inside Southeast Asia: Religion, Everyday Life, and Cultural Change*. Chiang Mai: Silkworm Books.

Narine, S. (1997). ASEAN and the ARF: The Limits of the "ASEAN Way". *Asian Survey, 37*(10), 961-978.

Neher, C.D. (2002). *Southeast Asia in the New International Era*. Boulder: Westview Press.

Perkasa, K. (2008). *Patani: Behind the Accidental Border*. Los Angeles: KijangMas Perkasa.

Pieterse, J.N. (2007). *Ethnicities and Global Multiculture: Pants for an Octopus* (Hardcover ed.). Plymouth: Rowman & LIttlefield Publishers, Inc.

Pitiyanuwat, S., & Sujiva, S. (2005). *Civic Education in Thailand: Policies and Practices in Schools* (1st ed.). Bangkok: Chulalongkorn University Press.

Tagliacozzo, E. (2001). Border Permeability and the State in Southeast Asia: Contraband and Regional Security. *Contemporary Southeast Asia, 23*(2), 254-275.

Than, M., & Thein, M. (2007). Transitional Economy of Myanmar: Present Status, Developmental Divide and Future Prospects. *ASEAN Economic Bulletin, 24*(1), 98-118.

Thawnghmung, A.M. (2009). Responding to Strategies and Programmes of Myanmar's Military Regime: An Economic Viewpoint. *Southeast Asian Affairs, 2008*, 274-290.

Ungpakorn, G.J. (2007). *A Coup for the Rich: Thailand's Political Crisis*. Bangkok: Workers Democracy Publishing.

Ungpakorn, G.J. (2010). *Thailand's Crisis & the Fight for Democracy*. London: WD Press.

Vaughan-Williams, N. (2008). Borders, Territory, Law. *International Political Sociology, 2*(4), 322-338.

Wang, Z. (2008). National Humiliation, History Education, and the Politics of Historical Memory: Patriotic Education Campaign in China. *International Studies Quarterly, 52*(4), 783-806.

Wyatt, D.K. (2003). *Thailand: A Short History* (Thailand ed.). Chiang Mai: Silkworm Books.

11

Socio-cultural Conflict in ASEAN: Overcoming Socio-cultural Oscillation through Structural Dynamics

This chapter introduces three core socio-cultural structural conflicts afflicting ASEAN. The three structural conflicts are analyzed in detail by applying structural dynamics so as to understand the source behind the overt structural oscillation observed in ASEAN. Human Rights, the flow of information, and nationalism are the core concepts underlying the three structural conflicts to be discussed in this chapter and are inextricably connected to other structural conflicts discussed in parts 1 and 2 of this volume. Finally, a few suggestions are provided as to how to overcome the three socio-cultural structural conflicts introduced in early sections of the chapter.

Introduction

Chapters 9 and 10 have served as an introduction as to some of the most important socio-cultural debates taking place in Southeast Asia. Chapter 10 covered some of the main policy proposals being discussed in relation to the ASEAN Socio-Cultural Community. It is clear that socio-cultural issues tend to be ambiguous and have far reaching consequences in other policy areas. Therefore, even though the different aspects of the ASEAN Community are discussed separately, this is merely a heuristic device with the sole aim of facilitating the analysis of a complex intergovernmental structure superimposed on an even more complex and fluid reality on the ground. Thus, it will be obvious to the reader that some of the structural conflicts discussed in previous sections of this book are connected to the ones in this chapter dealing with socio-cultural issues. The reason for this is manifold and reflects the fact that culture and social practices provide the frame of reference for all other policy areas (Anderson, 2006). In other words, culture provides the "worldview" through which all other policy areas are discussed and debated. This means that the order in which the parts of this book are presented, progressing from political to economic and finally to cultural issues, is arbitrary and could easily be reserved. Nevertheless saving the discussion on culture for last can be helpful in order to pull together some of the seemingly disconnected issues that have been discussed up to now.

The relative importance of social and cultural issues varies according to the theoretical stand of the reader (Kevin Avruch, 1998). Those favoring an elite view of politics and society will consider political and security issues to precede cultural and economic ones. On the other hand economic determinists in the Marxian tradition will consider economic issues to precede the other two and would consider cultural and social issues to be a reflection of the economic structure (a superstructure) (Ritzer, 2008). Nevertheless a sociological approach influenced by constructivism recognizes the importance of cultural and social values and how it shapes other spheres of life (Augsburger, 1992; Kenvin Avruch & Black, 2001; Dubinskas, 1992). Regardless of the theoretical preferences of the reader, this chapter serves as the glue linking the other aspects of the ASEAN Community. The structural conflicts to be discussed have far reaching consequences for other policy areas and are therefore of interest to economists and to political analysts in addition to those directly interested in cultural and social issues.

The next section provides a brief introduction of the three core concepts behind the three socio-cultural structural conflicts that are considered to be the most important for ASEAN. Each structural conflict is discussed in detail and examples are provided of evidence of overt and covert structural oscillation that they have caused in addition to diagrams of the structural mechanics behind them.

Structural Dynamics and Socio-Cultural Integration

This section applies the same theoretical framework that has been applied throughout the book in order to make sense of some of the most important structural conflicts afflicting the organization. For an in-depth discussion of the theory of structural dynamics readers are asked to refer to part I of the book. Nevertheless a brief explanation of the theoretical framework is appropriate. Structural dynamics is a holistic framework that explains organizational outcomes through structural analysis (Fritz, 1996). An organization's structure is considered to limit and to determine what outcomes are possible while operating in a certain environment. Thus agency is not denied nor underplayed however agency is channeled into creative energy shaping the structure of an organization. Organizations are deemed to be propelled towards a goal by a basic force called structural tension which is simply the tendency of a system to move from an undesirable state to a desired state (Fritz, 1996). Each combination of an undesirable existing state to a desired condition is called a tension-resolution system. When the outcomes of two tension-resolution systems are incompatible with each other the result is a structural conflict which causes structural oscillation. When the outcomes of two or more tension-resolution systems are compatible then organizational advancement takes place. As was explained in previous parts of this volume, structural oscillation is not only wasteful but also represents an important challenge for an organization. Backtracking is the main characteristic of structural oscillation while progress and forward movement are the main ones of organizational advancement. Needless to say the goal of every organization should be structural advancement rather than structural oscillation. Structural advancement can be achieved when the outputs of interacting tension-resolution systems at the same organizational level are compatible or complementary (Fritz, 1996). This helps garner the momentum of each part of the structure towards common goals such as the organization's mission, vision, strategy, etc.

Parts I and II of this volume explained and analyzed some of the most important structural conflicts in terms of security, economics, and political development. This section introduces three core structural conflicts dealing with socio-cultural integration. As was briefly mentioned in the introduction to this chapter, cultural and social issues tend to overlap with economic and political ones and thus can be viewed as the overarching framework of the entire ASEAN integration project. Some of the structural conflicts identified in previous parts of this book will be reflected by similar ones in the realm of socio-cultural issues and this is not a coincidence. Structural conflicts are crosscutting and separating them by policy area is a helpful heuristic but hides the continuous nature of issues. Thus a structural conflict may be present in all three domains in one way or another while another one is more strongly represented in the security realm. The important concept here is that some of the structural conflicts that will be discussed in this section seem very similar to other ones discussed in previous sections of the book but the difference is that the explanatory thrust of this section concentrates on the socio-cultural dimension of these structural conflicts rather than the economic and security dimensions that was emphasized in previous parts of the volume.

Three Core Socio-Cultural Structural Conflicts in ASEAN

There are three topics that stand out as contentious issues in terms of ASEAN's Socio-cultural integration. One of the most salient ones is the issue of Human Rights and their role in the region (Akaha, 2009; ASEAN, 2008b). A second one is the flow of information at the regional level (Bhattacharyay, 2010). Lastly nationalism remains a force to be reckoned with (von Feigenblatt, 2009f; Lee, 2000). While the three previously mentioned issues are not the only contentious ones in terms of socio-cultural integration they are at the core of three of the most central and influential structural conflicts in terms of socio-cultural integration. Most other issues in this realm can be discussed as parts of the previously mentioned three. Each one of the contentious issues deemed central to socio-cultural structural integration will be explained in detail in the following sections of this chapter.

Human Rights and Socio-Cultural Integration

The topic of human rights tends to be a contentious one in Southeast Asia (Kim, Fidler, & Ganguly, 2009; Simon, 2008). Important proponents of the "Asian Values" movement such as Lee Kuan Yew of Singapore and Mahathir Mohammad of Malaysia equated human rights with an ethnocentric Western intervention (Keong, 2006; Kim et al., 2009; Lee, 2000). Other regional notables such as the King of Thailand proposed softer variants of the "Asian Values" approach disguised as developmental approaches such as his pseudo theory of "self sufficiency economy" (Handley, 2006; Ungpakorn, 2007, 2010). While the core principles of the "Asian values" movement were discussed in chapters 9 and 10 a brief summary of their main arguments will be provided here. "Asian values" refers to a group of values which are supposedly shared by most people of Asian origin (von Feigenblatt, 2009b). Those values include respect for elders and for hierarchy, collectivism, discipline, and harmony. According to proponents of "Asian values", those values are shared by Southeast and Northeast Asians and are incompatible with some of the core values of the international human rights regime. One of the clearest incompatibilities, according to proponents of "Asian values", is the emphasis on individual rights versus the rights of the group (Kim et al., 2009; MacFarlane & Khong, 2006; Merry, 2006). In addition to that, the Human Rights approach tends to depend on the assertion of those rights by individuals which tends to disturb harmony and thus runs counter to one of the core principles of "Asian values" (Merry, 2006). Moreover, the strict equality accorded to individuals by the human rights regime runs counter to the hierarchical approach to social relations encompassed by "Asian values". Discrimination based on status, age, and official rank are considered to be part of the "Asian values" that are necessary in order to maintain harmony. Thus "Asian values" favor the status quo rather than change (von Feigenblatt, 2009b). While the previously mentioned ideological debate over values presented a temporary challenge to Human Rights at the international level, it eventually lost traction at the global level but continued to be a force to contend with at the regional level (Blau & Moncada, 2009; von Feigenblatt, 2009b; MacFarlane & Khong, 2006; Merry, 2006).

Another important challenge to human rights is more functional in nature and relates to the different political systems present in the region (Neher, 2002). Southeast Asia is home to military dictatorships, semi-authoritarian constitutional monarchies, socialist republics under one party rule, absolute monarchies, liberal democracies, and mixtures of the previous ideal types (Heidhues, 2000; Heller, 2005; Limaye, 2007; Neher, 2002; Thayer, 2010; Vu-Tung, 2007). Thus some governments are apprehensive about the adoption of international norms based on the rights of citizens in a liberal democracy (Akaha, 2009). This explains the strong resistance of certain countries such as Myanmar and Vietnam to interference in their internal affairs even by a regional organization such as ASEAN (Jones & Smith, 2007; Katanyuu, 2006; Keling, Saludin, von Feigenblatt, Ajis, & Shuib, 2010; Selth, 2009; Simon, 2008; Vu-Tung, 2007). Recent popular protests in Thailand and the Middle East are making regional governments even more apprehensive about granting greater political freedom since this could lead to regime change and would thus lead to their loss of power (von Feigenblatt, 2010d; Hewinson, 2010; Murphy, 2009).

The first tension-resolution system related to human rights starts with the unwanted state of having a bad human rights record and suffering international criticism due to this. As discussed in part two of this volume political instability and a bad human rights record can cause a decrease in tourism and foreign direct investment in addition to lower levels of official development assistance (von Feigenblatt, 2007). Due to this regional governments want to have the best international reputation in terms of human rights possible. This does not mean that their desired condition is having a better human rights record but rather to be perceived as having one is the actual goal. Thus the actual state for many regional governments is one in which they are criticized for not doing enough to protect the human rights of their citizens (Kim et al., 2009). Many regional governments are suffering from a mix of economic sanctions, international shaming, lowered tourism, and restricted official development assistance due to their bad reputations in terms of human rights (Chang, Chu, & Park, 2007; Lintner, 2009; Selth, 2009; Thayer, 2009). The perceived benefits of having a good reputation in terms of respect for human rights moves the system from the actual state to the desired state. It should be noted that the desired state is a good reputation in terms of human rights and the actual state is a bad reputation. Regional governments will then take action in order to improve their reputations. Some of the most common actions taken by governments include the establishment of human rights commissions, increasing the freedom of the press, establishing new departments or agencies to promote the rights of women and the disabled, as well as launching propaganda campaigns to spread the word about the previously mentioned programs (Merry, 2006). ASEAN as a whole followed a similar path and also established several committees dealing with human rights (ASEAN, 2008a).

Tension-Resolution system N shows how structural tension moves the system from a present state of having a poor human rights reputation to one in which regional governments have good human rights reputations. As discussed in the previous paragraph it should be noted that the change that governments desire is in terms of reputation not in terms of the actual respect of human rights.

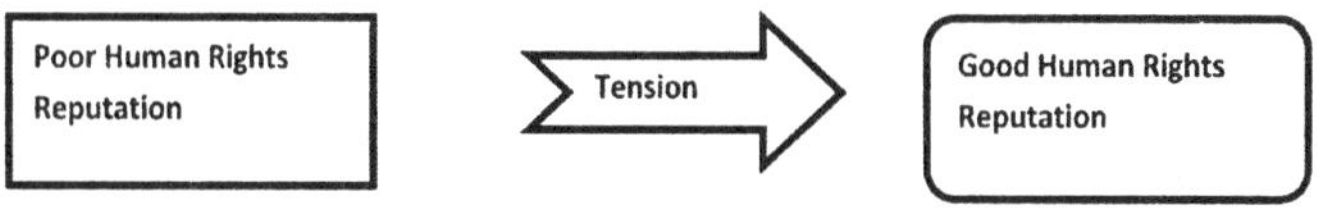

Figure 25. Tension-Resolution System N: Poor Human Rights Reputation/Good Human Rights Reputation

Closely related to this system is the one dealing with an unwanted level of civil strife and political unrest due to greater civil society activism and a desired state of social harmony and stability. This second tension-resolution system, system O, is closely related to the "Asian Values" debate and the importance accorded to social harmony over individual rights. Civil society activism includes confrontation for the rights of certain groups such as gender minorities, ethnic minorities, the disables, the poor, *inter alia* (Collins, 2008; von Feigenblatt, 2009d; Omelicheva, 2009). Most regional governments in addition to a large portion of the middle classes dislike violent confrontation and are biased against narrow interest even when they are worded in the language of human rights (Ungpakorn, 2007). The result of this unwanted state of affairs is that regional governments try to limit the activities of civil society organizations as well as of individuals clamoring for change. This is done through strict censorship, intimidation, as well as other more coercive measures depending on the government in question (Chang, Chun, & Park, 2007; Le-Coz, 2009).

As shown in figure 26, the result of tension-resolution system O is that the activities of civil society organizations as well as of individuals clamoring for reform and for human rights are limited by regional governments (sometimes with the support of the middle class) in order to achieve a desired state of social harmony characterized by low levels of civil strife as well as by an emphasis on the needs of the group (in this case defined as the entire nation-state) over those of the individual.

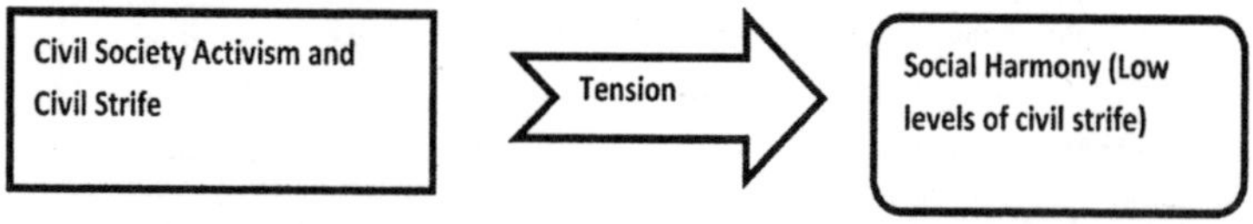

Figure 26. Tension-Resolution System O: Civil Society Activism and Civil Strife/Social Harmony

It is clear from figures 25 and 26 that tension-resolution systems N and O interact. Tension-resolution system N results in a resolution characterized by a better human rights reputation which is usually achieved by a greater opening to civil society participation in one way or another. Nevertheless the outcome of tension-resolution system N becomes the unwanted state in tension-resolution system O due to the greater social strife brought about by the measures passed by regional governments in order to improve their human rights reputation. In other words the social strife brought about by the governmental attempts to improve its human rights reputation leads to higher levels of civil strife and thus to a situation in which a vast array of civil society groups call for change and reform through various tactics including protests as well as other more violent methods.

Figure 27 shows the interaction of tension-resolution systems N and O and how they form one of the core socio-cultural structural conflicts in ASEAN. Tension-resolution system N is resolved by an improvement in a country's human rights reputation which entails an opening to civil society participation as well as greater freedom of expression. The outcome of tension-resolution system N in turn has the unintended consequence of civil society activism and a higher incidence of civil strife which becomes the unwanted starting state for tension-resolution system O.

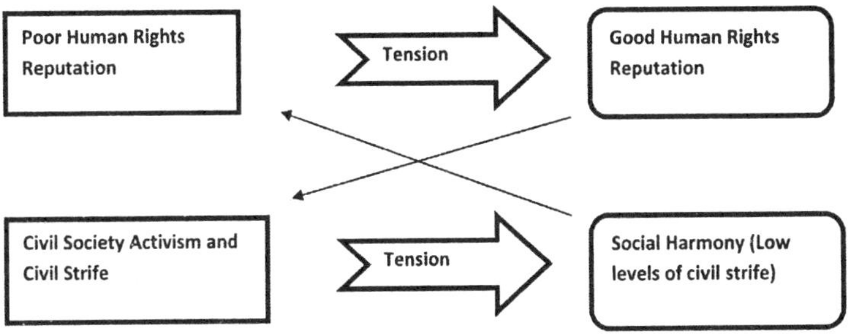

Figure 27. Structural Oscillation in ASEAN due to Incompatibility of tension-resolution systems N and O: (Fluctuation between Respect for Human Rights and Limited Liberties in order to achieve Social Harmony)

This system has the desired state of social harmony and low levels of civil strife and thus there is movement in that direction due to the structural tension that builds up in the system. The result of tension-resolution system O is greater social control through various means such as greater censorship and limits on civil society participation. Needless to say the constraints on freedom of assembly and of speech caused by the resolution of tension-resolution system O will result in a bad human rights reputation which will in turn restart tension-resolution system N. From a policy perspective this means that the measures that will be instituted in order to resolve tension-resolution system N will be partly reversed by the measures passed in order to resolve tension-resolution system O. Thus the dynamic force that is produced by the discrepancy between the actual and desired states in both systems is dissipated due to the incompatibility of the outcomes of both systems. The result of this incompatibility is not stasis but rather structural oscillation in which periods of advancement are followed by periods of retrenchment and backtracking.

An example of this structural conflict in action is ASEAN's limited steps in order to facilitate civil society participation (Collins, 2008; CSCAP, 2008). Periods of active engagement with civil society organizations are followed by periods of isolation from civil society influence (Collins, 2008). The same process is paralleled in terms of active engagement over human rights with member states. Collins has described the way in which regional NGOs find that even the accommodations and access provided to civil society organizations tends to fluctuate from Ministerial Meeting to Ministerial Meeting (Collins, 2008). Periods of greater opening are followed by periods of antagonism and coercion. This backtracking on ASEAN's commitment to meaningful civil society participation and respect for human rights in general has costly consequences such as the decrease in terms of trust of the region's civil society about ASEAN's sincerity in its wish for greater engagement with non-governmental organizations. It should be noted that while this core structural conflict is present in the previously mentioned examples it is also present in other ASEAN processes such as in the organization's level of respect for the principle of absolute sovereignty and its stance in relation to military coups (von Feigenblatt, 2009c; Katanyuu, 2006; Simon, 2008). Some of the processes connected to this core structural conflicts are discussed in greater detail in parts I and II of this volume such as in relation to security and the "ASEAN Way".

Ease of Information Flows in ASEAN Member States

The second core socio-structural conflict revolves around the issue of the flow of information in the region. ASEAN's integration has increased the speed and amount of information that flows in the region. This exponential increase in the regional information flow has had varied consequences. The economic benefits of this greater flow of information are widely recognized by ASEAN Member States as well as its dialogue partners (ASEAN, 2008a, 2008c; Bhattacharyay, 2010; Collins, 2008). In addition to that the faster flow of information has also helped the region share information about security threats such as terrorist plots more effectively which was discussed in part I of this volume (Means, 2009; Millard,

2004; Storey, 2008). The greater flow of information has also helped in the region's integration from a socio-cultural perspective. There is greater awareness about the culture of other member states as well as a growing regional identity (von Feigenblatt, 2010b; Trinidad, 2010). News travel much faster which also helps establish a sense of greater integration and closeness to ones neighbors (Bhattacharyay, 2010). Nevertheless the greater flow of information at the regional level has other unintended consequences such as the exposure of the population to foreign ideas about a vast array of issues such as democracy, human rights, the role of the citizen, family structure, and consumption patterns (von Feigenblatt, 2010b).

The first tension-resolution system in the second structural conflict starts with an unwanted condition of limited information sharing characterized by a lack of information about other regional countries, slow flow of information about economic and social trends in neighboring countries, as well as a slow pace of technological transfer due to a lack of communication between regional epistemic communities. This leads to a desired state of a greater flow of information in order to make it easier for the region to function as a single socio-economic bloc. Regional governments want their populations to be aware of their policy goals in terms of regional economic integration as well as other policy areas such as social development, and disaster prevention. In order to achieve this desired state they need to facilitate the flow of information which usually includes improving accessibility (Bhattacharyay, 2010). Accessibility includes both expanding telecommunication networks as well as easing certain restrictions to foreign content. Some of the measures related to facilitating the flow of information were reviewed in chapter 10 including exchanges of library holdings between ASEAN members, the rotation of faculty and students at the university level, as well as the promotion of English as a regional language (ASEAN, 2009). All of those previously mentioned measures are intended to facilitate the flow of information which would in turn help ASEAN achieve many of its other goals such as economic integration.

Figure 28 shows how an unwanted condition characterized by a slow and limited flow of information and the discrepancy with the desired goal of a fast and unlimited flow of information creates structural tension moving the system from the starting point to its resolution. Measures passed by governments in order to facilitate the flow of information include an expansion of the information technology infrastructure, lifting certain restrictions on foreign content such as television programming, the promotion of English so that the wider population can access information from other countries, as well as the promotion of cooperation between epistemic communities. All of those measures result in easier and faster access to information which in turn supports important strategic goals such as technological transfer and capacity building in addition to helping construct a common ASEAN identity.

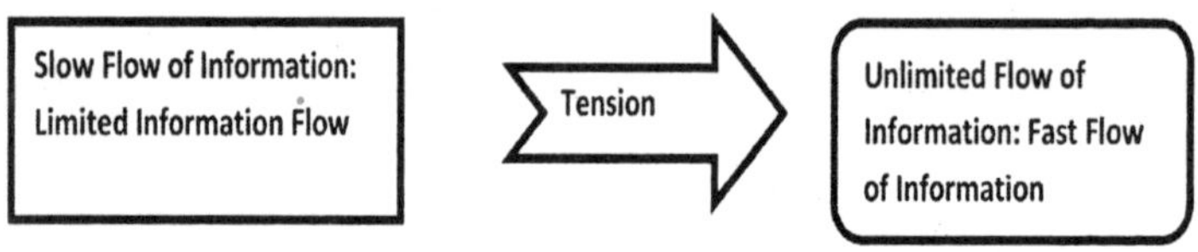

Figure 28. Tension-Resolution System P: Information Flow in ASEAN

A related tension-resolution system deals with some of the negative externalities of the unlimited flow of information. Due to the increased access to information brought about by regional integration, economic development, and globalization in general, regional populations are suddenly exposed to foreign consumption patterns, new philosophical ideas, different family structures, and to a vast variety of cultures. The way in which all these new information is processed depends on the level of sophistication of the population as well as to their socio-political situation. Nevertheless the results are very difficult to predict and even harder to control. One simple example of this is the visible change in family patters in the urban capitals of ASEAN due to exposure to foreign ideas about romantic love (von Feigenblatt, 2010a). This has resulted in women getting married later and in some cases remaining single due to the higher expectations for marriage. In terms of consumption patterns some of the results are quite obvious. Witnessing higher living standards increases a person's expectations and levels of consumption. Another example is exposure to more egalitarian authority structures which is particularly problematic for certain socio-cultural groups since it disrupts social relationships and leads to overt conflict (Kenvin Avruch & Black, 2001; von Feigenblatt, 2010d). Thus an increased flow of information leads to change which disrupts harmony and in turn threatens the status quo. This can result in greater political strife, problems in the family structure such as prostitution due to consumerism, as well as new forms of vices (von Feigenblatt, 2009a). From a social perspective there are also important consequences for the elderly due to changing family patters which require greater government support for their welfare due to the decrease in the number of expanded families living together in relation to nuclear families. This new actual state is considered undesirable by ASEAN member states and therefore a new desired condition characterized by social harmony and stability is constructed. Some of the measures aim to control the quality and quantity of information flows so as to control the pace of change.

Figure 29 shows how the discrepancy between the desired goal of social harmony and stability and the present condition characterized by rapid social change creates structural tension moving the system towards the desired goal. Regional governments then pass measures intended to limit the flow of information and thus achieve social harmony and stability by slowing down the pace of change. Some of the measures related to this system are quite visible such as censorship in Singapore, Thailand, Brunei, Myanmar, and Vietnam (Chang, Chun et al., 2007; Katanyuu, 2006; Keling et al., 2010; Le-Coz, 2009; Vu-Tung, 2007). Particular kinds of censorship intended to slow down change are the *lese majeste* laws in Thailand and Brunei as well as the tight control over history books in most ASEAN member states (Chottmann, 2006; Handley, 2006; Ungpakorn, 2007, 2010). The goal of some of the previously mentioned measures is to stop the flow of information questioning traditional authority such as the monarchy in Brunei and Thailand, and one party rule in the case of Myanmar and Vietnam. Thus there are various controls to the flow of information which can be felt in both print and visual media such as books and television programming. In some cases there are limits on foreign content for television programming as well as the banning of television programming considered immoral or politically sensitive.

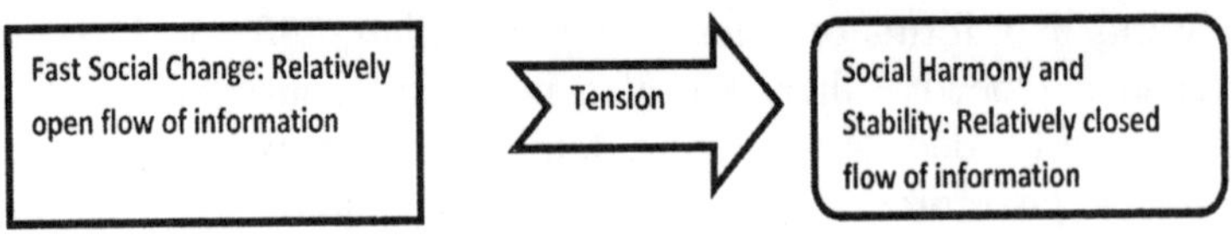

Figure 29. Tension-Resolution System Q: Rate of Social Change due to Information Flows

The second structural conflict is caused by the incompatibility between tension-resolution systems P and Q. ASEAN members react to the need to facilitate the flow of information in order to aid the integration process by passing measures easing the flow of information. Nevertheless the result of the consequent open flow of information is a much faster rate of social change which comes with an increase in social instability. This new state of social instability leads to a new desired state characterized by social harmony and stability which then encourages governments to control the flow of information in order to slow down the pace of change. A slower flow of information makes other ASEAN goals harder to achieve which restarts the cycle all over again. The result is structural oscillation characterized by backtracking in terms of policies. Periods of greater openness to information flows are followed by periods of censorship and tight media controls. This backtracking is costly for ASEAN member states since considerable resources are used in order to filter and censor information (Chang, Chu et al., 2007; von Feigenblatt, Suttichujit, Shuib, Keling, & Ajis, 2010).

There are also considerable indirect costs to controlling information such as delays in the flows of important information in a vast array of policy areas as well as the damage to the reputation of the governments in question. It

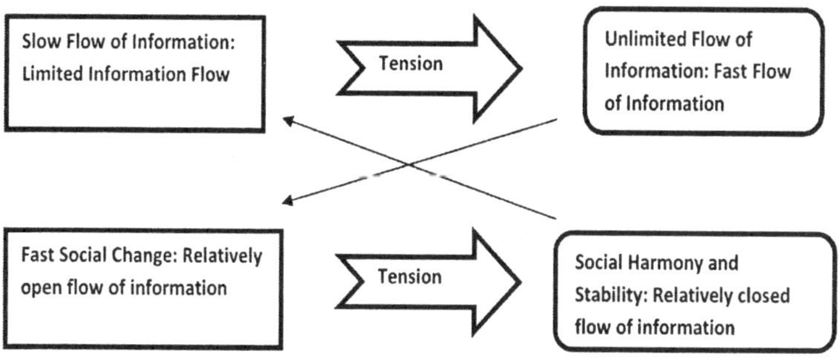

Figure 30. Structural Oscillation in ASEAN due to Incompatibility of tension-resolution systems P and Q: (Fluctuation between and Open Flow of Information and a Circumscribed Flow of Information)

should be noted that it is very difficult to filter certain information without slowing down the flow of all information. The filtering process is time consuming and thus information that is considered important for economic and social policies is also slowed down by restrictions. Examples of attempts to slow down the flow of information have been provided in other sections of this volume and include censorship of the media in Thailand, Burma, Singapore, and Brunei (Chang, Chu et al., 2007; von Feigenblatt, 2009f). Considerable efforts are spent to filter web-sites with information considered inflammatory or in opposition to the monarchy in Thailand (von Feigenblatt, 2009f; Le-Coz, 2009). Similar measures are in place in Singapore and Myanmar in order to filter information that may be politically sensitive (Katanyuu, 2006; Keling et al., 2010; Lee, 2000). Problems with internet filtering include the filtering of useful web-sites by mistake. In the case of Myanmar the filtering is so thorough that it slows the entire network and few e-mail providers can be used. The result is a loss of connectivity. A similar process is now in place in order to monitor financial transactions so as to trace the funding for terrorist networks. While this practice increases security by helping fight terrorism it also slows down the entire system in addition to creating considerable expenses (Glassman, 2005). A final example is the greater monitoring of international mail which has also increased security but at considerable costs.

Nationalism and Socio-Cultural Openness

The final structural conflict that will be discussed in this section of the volume is centered on the concept of nationalism. There is a tension between a growing cosmopolitanism and a resurgent nationalism (Millard, 2004; Mulder, 1996; Neher, 2002). Nevertheless it is not simply a dichotomy between the global and the local but rather a complex interaction between the national, the local, the regional, and the global (Merry, 2006; Pieterse, 2007). From the point of view of ASEAN Member States it is more useful to understand this tension as one between official nationalism and a new fluid syncretism. The first part of this final structural conflict involves the tension between an unwanted condition of socio-cultural isolationism and a desired condition characterized by socio-cultural openness. ASEAN Member States recognize the importance of fostering a regional identity in order to implement some of the other policy goals such as economic integration (ASEAN, 2008c, 2009). Thus a socio-cultural worldview characterized by isolationism becomes an important barrier to regional integration. This unwanted condition is contrasted with a desired one characterized by socio-cultural openness which would ease the formation of a regional identity. Therefore socio-cultural isolationism makes regional integration difficult on a very basic cultural level which in turn leads regional governments to desire greater openness so as to ease other policy goals such as technological transfer, human capital formation, economic integration, etc. The discrepancy between the actual condition and the desired condition gives rise to structural tension which moves the system towards its resolution. Regional governments pass measures aimed at fostering a greater socio-cultural openness such as ASEAN Games, the inclusion of courses dealing with regional history, cultural exchanges, study abroad programs, and greater foreign media content (ASEAN, 2009). The result of all of those measures is a slow shift towards a more open worldview.

Figure 31 shows how tension-resolution system R starts with an unwanted condition characterized by isolationism and moves towards a resolution of socio-cultural openness. As discussed in previous sections of this chapter, socio-cultural views are of considerable importance due to their role in the interpretation of information and stimuli (Kevin Avruch, 1998; Kenvin Avruch & Black, 2001; Dubinskas, 1992; von Feigenblatt, 2010c). Thus the relative openness in terms of worldview has far reaching consequences in other policy areas including security, politics, economics, and social welfare. It can be asserted that in order for the entire regional integration process to be successful a certain degree of socio-cultural openness is needed. This is something that has been studied in relation to socio-cultural integration in the European Union (McCormick, 2005). The role of communication and intersubjective understanding in terms of regional integration has been emphasized by prominent scholars such as Harbermas (Jürgen Habermas, 2005; Jurgen Habermas, 2006). A certain degree of cosmopolitanism is required in order for a region characterized by its socio-cultural diversity to start acting as a single integrated unit.

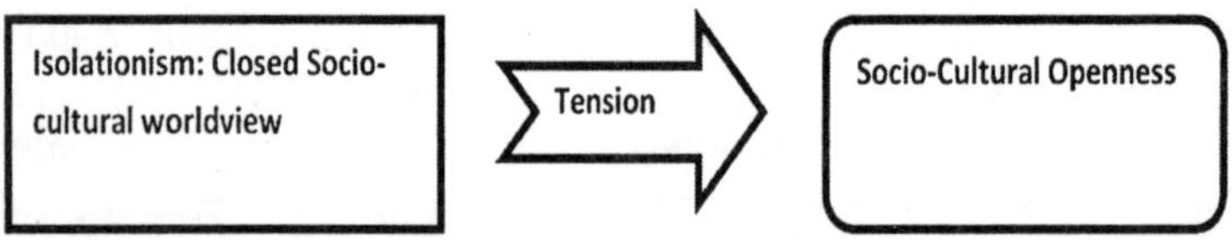

Figure 31. Tension-Resolution System R: Socio-Cultural Openness.

This assumes that thinking precedes action at the normative level. Therefore, in order for the peoples of ASEAN to act for a common purpose a certain openness is required so as to expand one's *mandala* of inclusion further until it becomes concomitant with at least the region's limits. This is particularly important in collectivist cultures which have clearly defined and impermeable borders between those who belong to the in-group and those considered outsiders (Hook, Worthington, & Utsey, 2008; Pruitt & Kim, 2004).

Nationalism as an artificial state-sponsored ideology is at the core of the second tension-resolution system operating in the third and final structural conflict. For the purposes of this study nationalism refers to a reified national ideology claiming a parsimonious shared history and destiny while in many cases also claiming a homogeneous set of cultural values (Pieterse, 2007). Nationalism serves an important purpose in Southeast Asia which revolves around the issue of governance. Ruling over a vast array of ethnic groups with different languages and cultural practices is a challenging endeavor and because of that postcolonial Southeast Asian states invested considerable resources in engendering national ideologies which would in turn supersede other local attachments (Heidhues, 2000; McCargo, 2009; Mulder, 1996). The process was never complete yet it helps the central government maintain its legitimacy and also makes the bureaucratic aspects of governance less complex by centralizing education, in many cases language, and security. It is a process of assimilation attempting to create a homogeneous supra-ethnic consciousness encompassing all of the inhabitants inside the territory of a state (von Feigenblatt et al., 2010; McCargo, 2008). In practice the result is not a completely new invention but rather a mix of traditional cultural values of the dominant ethnic groups and the particular political ideology of the governing elite. The benefits of promoting nationalism were many for regional governments which explain the continued appeal of the practice in Southeast Asia. Thus separatism, ethnic competition over resources, administrative difficulties due to different languages and customs, as well as the weak legitimacy of certain postcolonial governments all led to an undesired condition of cultural diversity and diffuse centers of power. This pre-nationalist stage is characterized by ethnic loyalties and fragmentation which leads to a desired condition characterized by a homogeneous national culture which would in turn make the administration of the population residing within the territory under the control of the particular government easier.

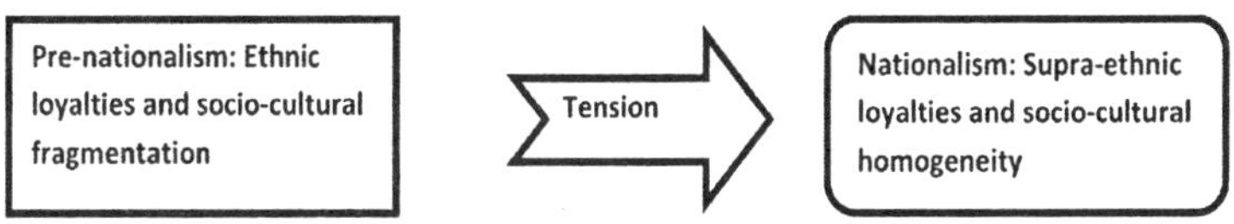

Figure 32. Tension-Resolution System S: Level of Nationalism.

Tension-resolution system S shows how the region's multiethnic makeup and socio-cultural fragmentation was and still is considered to be an undesirable condition by many of ASEAN Member States which leads to a desired condition characterized by a strong supra-ethnic loyalty to the state and a shared intersubjective reality. The discrepancy between the two conditions led to the passing of a considerable number of measures intended to foster a shared national culture legitimizing the primacy of the nation-state (Chottmann, 2006;

Stockwell, 2004; Wyatt, 2003). Some of the measures include the centralization of the education system, propaganda campaigns in the media promoting a single view of history and of a common destiny, censoring alternative views of historical events, promotion of a single language for official government business, *inter alia* (Chottmann, 2006; von Feigenblatt, 2009f; Gottesman, 2003; Handley, 2006; Hinton, 2006). The result of these policies is that there is a greater attachment to the nation-state and a higher degree of socio-cultural homogeneity at least at the superficial level. There are also many unintended consequences such as the domination of one ethnic group over ethnic and cultural minorities. Another possible unintended consequence is an increase in isolationism and xenophobia.

Figure 33 shows the interaction of tension-resolution systems R and S. The resolutions of the two systems are clearly incompatible. Tension-resolution system O is resolved by measures intended to increase socio-cultural openness which strengthens and reinforces ethnic loyalties and socio-cultural fragmentation. Ethnic loyalties and fragmentation make it more difficult for governments to govern their territories which in turn lead to the resolution of tension-resolution system S. The resolution of this second system is the promotion of nationalism as an ideology that includes both traditional and newly created elements intended to foster supra-ethnic loyalties and socio-cultural homogeneity. Due to the negative externality of xenophobia and isolationism the resolution of tension-resolution system S feeds the starting condition of tension-resolution system R creating a serious structural conflict. Periods of greater openness and a certain degree of cosmopolitanism are followed by periods of nationalism and xenophobia. In other cases both tension-resolution systems operate concurrently thus competing against each other and cancelling each other out. One example of this structural conflict in action is policies dealing with the Chinese minority in Southeast Asia.

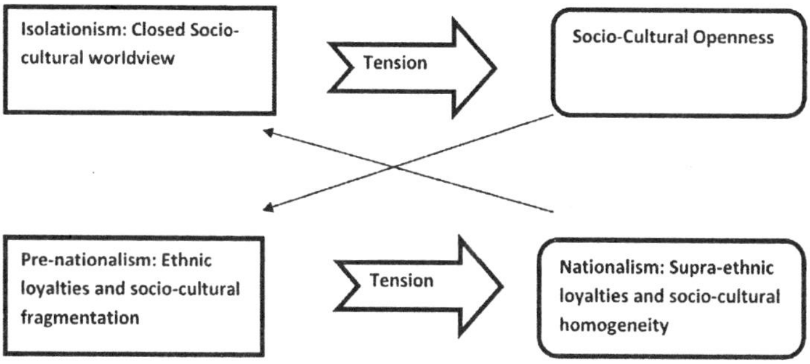

Figure 33. Structural Oscillation in ASEAN due to Incompatibility of tension-resolution systems R and S: (Nationalism and Syncretism)

This community enjoyed considerable freedom of action during the colonial period due to the imperial vision of regional order which mirrored the ethnic syncretism of the area (von Feigenblatt, 2009e; Kiong & Bun, 2001; Payne, 1995; Pieterse, 2007). Independence brought nationalism with it and the struggle for primacy between different ethnic groups (Heidhues, 2000; Means, 2009; Mulder, 1996; Neher, 2002). Due to the porous borders and important population movements that had taken place through the centuries, territories were not inhabited by homogeneous ethnic groups but rather by interdependent and crosscutting ethnic groups (Cuasay, 1998; Ishii, 1994; Tagliacozzo, 2001; Yegar, 2002). The situation in the regional capitals was even more fluid due to the arrival of Indians from the colonies of South Asia and the rise of mixed race communities (Means, 2009; Millard, 2004; Mulder, 1996). Nevertheless the political need to justify a foreign political structure over the region led to efforts to hide or erase the ethnic diversity existing on the ground and instead superimpose an imagined homogeneous vision of society based on the traditions and needs of the dominant ethnic group.

The Chinese community was particularly affected by the nationalist postcolonial turn due to their emphasis on trade and services rather than on the direct control of land (Kiong &

Bun, 2001). It is clear that discrimination against the Chinese increased in most newly independent Southeast Asian countries which in some cases resulted in considerable bloodshed and in one particular case to the independence of a city, Singapore, due to the struggle between the prosperous Chinese community in the former British enclave, and the Malays in the rest of Malaya (Lee, 2000). Separation was not an option in other parts of Southeast Asia since the Chinese were an integral part of the community and lived in the same areas as other ethnic groups (Heidhues, 2000; Mulder, 1996; Wyatt, 2003). Therefore, regional governments attempted several measures in order to erase and control the Chinese community. Initial measures tended to be more coercive and included limits on civil liberties. These initial measures were later on followed by measures intended to assimilate the Chinese community (von Feigenblatt et al., 2010; Handley, 2006). Thus some countries forced people of Chinese ancestry to change their names and to convert to the dominant religion such as in the case of Thailand (Kiong & Bun, 2001; Wyatt, 2003). The education system was used in order to assimilate their children and in order to regulate the school curriculum (von Feigenblatt et al., 2010). Schools teaching Chinese history and languages were closed for many years in certain Southeast Asian countries and their activities were closely monitored when they were allowed to reopen. China's economic growth and increased regional influence changed the cost-benefit of analysis of regional governments which now saw their Chinese communities as powerful transnational networks which could spearhead their countries' integration into the Asia Pacific economic region (Pieterse, 2007). The result of this was that some restrictions were eased such as laws about land holding and Chinese communities were once again allowed to express their ethnic pride in terms of celebrating traditional festivals. Needless to say the path followed in different Southeast Asian countries varies considerably and in some countries there are periods of intense ethnic strife and violence followed by periods of greater openness and cooperation but structural oscillation is present in most Southeast Asian countries with a large Chinese ethnic community. The myriad contradictory policies passed in relation to the Chinese communities in Southeast Asia provide good examples of some of the negative externalities of structural oscillation. Coercive measures against the Chinese community have created considerable distrust and animosity towards regional governments. Moreover, considerable human capital has been lost in important areas of the bureaucracy due to discriminatory policies discouraging ethnic Chinese from entering the civil service. Even softer nationalist policies such as assimilation through education have the unintended consequence of a loss of rich traditions and language ability (von Feigenblatt et al., 2010).

There are myriad other examples dealing with nationalist policies in Southeast Asia but they all have certain elements in common such as the dominance of the traditions of a certain ethnic group as well as a mixture of traditional and newly created elements into a single ideology defending the legitimacy of the nation-state (Liow, 2006; Neher, 2002; Pieterse, 2007). The structural oscillation brought about by the incompatibility between the resolutions of tension-resolution systems R and S is at the core of some of the most important challenges faced by ASEAN along its path towards regional integration. Nationalism is at odds with regional integration while at the same time being an important factor in terms of regional stability and social cohesion. This structural conflict has an important impact on a vast array of policy areas which include regional security, economic integration, technological transfer, and the promotion of a regional identity. The next and final section of this chapter discusses some possible ways to overcome the three core socio-cultural conflicts.

Overcoming Socio-cultural Structural Oscillation

As discussed in previous parts of this volume, there is only one way to overcome structural oscillation which is restructuration. Regardless of the number of piecemeal measures passed by regional governments or by ASEAN as a whole, structural oscillation will continue as long as the structural conflict that causes it remains in place. Thus one of the most important functions of identifying the tension-resolution systems underlying each socio-cultural structural conflict is that it provides the policymaker with a causal map of the mechanisms behind each policy area. Once the structural conflicts are carefully mapped, which was done in the previous sections of this chapter, the next step is to attempt to find a way to either eliminate or neutralize the incompatibilities between the resolutions of the two tension-resolution systems making up each structural conflict. Tension-resolution systems show the flow of structural tension and its dissipation through their interaction in a structural conflict. Therefore, when attempting to overcome a structural conflict it is important to keep in mind that the goal is to garner structural tension in order to foster sustainable organizational advancement.

There are several ways to go about this task. The first one, which was discussed in detail in part I of the volume, concentrates on the different levels of the organization. Policies can be divided into different levels such as strategic, managerial, tactical, and local (Fritz, 1996). Each level is supposed to support higher levels in order to achieve the overall mission of the organization. Therefore, the goal is to have structural tension flow upwards to higher levels of the organization by avoiding having two incompatible tension-resolution systems operating at the same level of the organization. This approach involves prioritizing certain goals over others while downgrading some other tension-resolution systems in order to strengthen the impact of other ones. A second approach deals with the decoupling of two incompatible tension-resolution systems. In other words, the two tension-resolution systems are separated in order to avoid the structural oscillation caused by their interaction. This approach is much harder to apply to an intergovernmental organization such as ASEAN than to a small private enterprise due to the sheer size and complexity of the issues involved. Nevertheless, there are cases in which tension-resolution systems can be decoupled by assigning their implementation to different governmental agencies or regions of the country. Finally a third approach involves the elimination of one of the two tension-resolution system in order to allow the most important one to continue to operate in the desired direction.

The first core socio-cultural structural conflict discussed in early sections of this chapter deals with respect for human rights. In this case there is a clear incompatibility between some of the measures undertaken in order to achieve a good human rights reputation and social harmony. As was discussed in the previous section, the problem is that some of the measures necessary in order to improve the human rights reputation of a government require measures that include greater freedom of speech and greater civil society participation (Akaha, 2009; Blau & Moncada, 2009; Merry, 2006). This in turn leads to an increase in civil strife and less social harmony. Nevertheless it should be noted that social harmony can be achieved in various ways which are not necessarily coercive. Thus, the importance of tension-resolution system O could be downgraded and the measures used in order to resolve this system could be limited to non-coercive measures such as populist ones. Some measures that could be used included development projects aimed to increase support for the government, national festivals, and other measures that could improve the quality of life of the general population. These measures would help maintain a certain level of social harmony while at the same time avoiding harming the human rights reputation of a certain government. Another equally valid approach would involve providing peaceful venues for civil society participation such as regular civil society-government meetings. The goal is to avoid violent civil strife without having to resort to coercive measures which contravene internationally recognized human rights. This is an approach that has been used in Nordic European countries and Japan with great success (Dore, 1997; von Feigenblatt, 2007; MacFarlane & Khong, 2006). The goal, from the point of the view of the government is the co-option of civil society. Rechanneling the creative energy of civil society in a constructive direction would eliminate the incompatibility between tension-resolution systems N and O. Needless to say this is much easier for governments with considerable resources at their disposal such as Brunei and Singapore. These governments attempt to tackle the possible grievances that might be brought to the fore by nongovernmental organizations before they become controversial issues. Thus they weaken civil society through the efficient and effective governance of their territories. While this approach can be criticized on philosophical grounds it is difficult to deny that the majority of the population of those previously mentioned countries support their governments. Therefore, the successful implementation of a developmental state model may foster social harmony while at the same time weakening civil society organizations without the need for coercive measures that may damage the human rights reputation of a government.

The previous discussion of the first core socio-cultural conflict is just a preliminary suggestion as to how to go about redesigning the relationship between tension-resolution systems N and O so as to avoid structural oscillation. Due to the diversity in terms of economic development and socio-cultural makeup of the different ASEAN Member States it is very difficult to generalize. The important point about this discussion is that it is very helpful to look at the source of the structural oscillation and to make changes that affect the structural dynamics of the entire organization so as to achieve structural advancement. In the first socio-cultural conflict the incompatibility between the two systems is due to coercive measures intended to achieve the desired state of social cohesion while at the same time attempting to pass measures that improve the human rights reputation of a country.

Replacing coercive measures with co-optation and improvements in quality of life eliminates the incompatibility between the two resolutions and thus synergy is achieved. This means that structural tension will flow in a single direction leading to higher level goals such as successful regional integration and socio-cultural development. Progress in one area will lead to progress in other areas. In this case improvements in terms of human rights will parallel improvements in social harmony. Measures passed in one policy area will support rather than conflict with measures passed in other related policy areas. One example of this is a government that establishes a human rights commission while at the same time providing cheap access to universal healthcare. The first measure will increase civil society activism which could lead to greater civil strife but the second measure leads to greater social harmony by eliminating a possible grievance that could be used by civil society organizations and opposition groups.

The second core socio-cultural structural conflict deals with the flow of information. Tension-resolution system P is resolved by improving the flow of information. On the other hand tension-resolution system Q involves restrictions on the flow of information in order to maintain social stability. The two resolutions are clearly incompatible. There are several ways to deal with this structural conflict. First of all it is important to identify the ways in which the two outcomes are incompatible. One obvious incompatibility would be that some measures intended to maintain social stability slow down and restrict the flow of information. The speed of change brought about by greater access to large quantities of information is an important factor in this discussion. There is a choice between gradual reform and sudden change. Using time as the dimension to be restructured, system P could be maintained as a high priority short-term goal while system Q could be moved to the mid and long term. This would shift the emphasis from the short term restriction of the flow of information in order to avoid sudden changes to the social fabric, to the mid to long term amelioration and guidance of gradual social changes and reform. This shift would eliminate the structural conflict between the two systems, which would be operating in different time frames and thus would not conflict with each other. The measures required to guide and manage mid to long term change are also less coercive than the ones that would be needed to slow down the flow of information in the short term. Some examples of the measures that could be passed include education campaigns for the general public about the dangers of consumerism, social policies intended to deal with the negative externalities of changes in the family structure such as care for the elderly, and finally an ideological shift which allows the individual to be both a good patriot and a global citizen. Those are just some of the measures that could manage the changes brought about by greater information flows in a constructive way rather than attempting to stop change altogether. It is also important to note that system P is pivotal to the success of other important high level goals of both ASEAN and regional governments. Economic integration can only take place if there is a good telecommunications infrastructure and eased restrictions which in turn would bring about the economic development necessary in order to fund other policy areas (Bhattacharyay, 2010).

Finally, the third core socio-cultural conflict revolves around the concept of nationalism and is probably the most challenging of the three. Nationalism is an important force during the early stages of nation-building but can be counterproductive in more advanced stages of development. Tension-resolution systems R and S are resolved by seemingly incompatible outcomes. System R results in a greater socio-cultural openness which is very important for ASEAN's integration. On the other hand system S is resolved by increased nationalism and loyalty to the nation-state which in turn can transform into isolationism and xenophobia. The main goal of system S is not exactly nationalism but rather supra-ethnic loyalty to the state. This means that the problem is not such much the need for political stability and supra-ethnic loyalty to the central government but rather how that goal is achieved. There are many ways in which loyalty for the state can be achieved and ethnic nationalism is only one of them. Thus there exist vast arrays of nationalisms which do not always revolve around the core cultural traits of a dominant ethnic group. This means that the incompatibility in the third core socio-cultural conflict is not due to the goal of stability itself but rather to the kind of nationalism that has traditionally being employed in Southeast Asia to achieve this.

One very good example of how loyalty to the nation-state can be achieved without a nationalism based on a dominant ethnic group can be found in Singapore (Lee, 2000). The small city-state has a very diverse population including Chinese, Indians, Malays, and Eurasians (CIA, 2009; Millard, 2004). Rather than follow the Malaysian approach to nation-building based on a dominant ethnic group, Singapore created its own nationalism based on a strong work ethic, a global worldview, and a sense of a common destiny (Lee, 2000). In this case the core of the new nationalism was not ethnicity but rather the shared experience of living in a small city-state that had to compete in the global economy not by isolating itself but rather by opening itself to the world in order to learn the best production methods and economic practices. Based on the recurrent ethnic tensions found in almost every other Southeast Asian country, it seems that the Singaporean system is one of the most successful ones in terms of socio-political stability. It should be noted that in this case social stability was not achieved at the expense of isolationism and xenophobia but rather through a philosophy based on lifestyle choices and common challenges. A similar shift could be attempted in other ASEAN Member States at a gradual pace. Needless to say a sudden shift to a nationalism such as the one previously described would require considerable political will from policy elites and would run counter to powerful ethnic interest groups. Thus a gradual shift is more likely. An *emic* approach to this issue could follow the traditional *mandala* cosmological system of pre-colonial times which is based on a system of concentric circles centered on the capital and implying different levels of proximity to the center of power (Harris, 2010). This approach resembles the traditional Chinese view of international relations based on the concept of *tianxia* (Callahan, 2008). The *mandala* and the *tianxia* approaches to intra-national governance and international relations have the advantage of avoiding simple dichotomies in favor of a more nuanced gradualism. Relationships between different groups are characterized by different levels of proximity rather than on a simple in-group and out-group typology. Needless to say both the *mandala* and the *tianxia* approaches imply relations of unequal power between certain groups but on the other hand the borders between groups are considered to be much more permeable (Callahan, 2008; Harris, 2010). A syncretic mix between *emic* and *etic* approaches to regional governance could be used in order to avoid the simplistic nationalism currently in vogue in Southeast Asia. Lessons from the European experience are pertinent and can be adapted to regional cultural needs through a creative merging with local pre-colonial discourses on regional governance.

Conclusions

This chapter has covered a vast array of issues dealing with socio-cultural integration in Southeast Asia. As was discussed in previous sections of this chapter, socio-cultural issues tend to be broad and ambiguous while at the same time of considerable importance to all other policy areas. Culture provides the glue that binds all other aspects of regional governance and thus it can be considered to be constitutive of other policy areas. While this study does not deny the important role played by power and other more traditional concerns of political science such as control over resources, it should be noted that the importance of those resources and the way they are deployed in order to achieve certain strategic goals is interpreted through the frame of culture. Southeast Asia's exponential cultural diversity makes any attempts at providing a regional overview of cultural debates and challenges difficult to say the least. Nevertheless this chapter has attempted to provide some order to the complex and immensely fluid situation on the ground by centering the discussion on three core socio-cultural structural conflicts. The three core debates revolve around issues of nationalism, respect for human rights, and the flow of information. All three structural conflicts have important repercussions in other policy areas such as security and economic development. It is important to note that the approach recommended in the present volume concentrates on the possibility of making changes to the structure of the conflict so as to facilitate the effective and efficient use of resources for a coherent and well integrated set of strategic and managerial goals. Therefore, the main contribution of this chapter to the very complex topic of socio-cultural change and development in the Southeast Asian region is to identify and explain some of the core mechanisms that are causing structural oscillation and backtracking in important policy areas. The three structural conflicts that were identified in this chapter can serve as a useful starting point to tackle more specific policy measures and thus can serve in informing policy debates as well as raising important areas for future research.

The main conclusion reached in this section of the volume is that the Western dichotomies that were borrowed at the turn of the 19th century to promote nation-building in Southeast Asia are now becoming one of the most important root causes of the difficulties faced by ASEAN in achieving regional integration. This is an important finding in that pre-colonial models have been shown to be devoid of simple dichotomies and were rather characterized by nuanced governance models based on either Theravada Buddhism in the case of the *mandala* system, and in Taoism in the case of *Tianxia*.

Moreover, the rise of virulent nationalism in Southeast Asia coincided with the height of the struggle for independence and contravened the political trends in vogue in late 19th century Europe (Heidhues, 2000). Fukuyama has adeptly labeled this problem as being stuck in "history" (Fukuyama, 1992). It is important for regional elites to move beyond the simple governance models that proved useful in early stages of nation-building and to adapt to a more complex regional and international environment characterized by socio-economic interdependence and a fluid security situation. Thus an important cultural shift must take place at the policy elite level before regional integration can be successful in Southeast Asia. The advantage of this approach is that a more diffuse model of governance based on a more nuanced set of categories more closely resembles the way the average Southeast Asian experiences the world (Mulder, 1996). Identity is not only plural but also situational and attempting to force it into a dichotomous straightjacket based on the past political needs of the dominant classes is not only counterproductive but also a futile endeavor in the long term. In conclusion, Southeast Asia must simply look back at the complex web of interactions and relationships of the diffuse polities of the pre-colonial period or even to the well integrated governance under the British Empire to find inspiration for a more nuanced model of regional governance that skews narrow nationalisms in favor of crosscutting cooperation and interdependence.

References

Akaha, T. (2009). Human Security in East Asia. *Journal of Human Security, 5*(3), 11-34.

Anderson, J. E. (2006). *Public Policymaking* (6th ed.). Boston: Houghton Mifflin Company.

ASEAN. (2008a). *2007-2008 Annual Report: One Vision, One Identity, One Community*. Retrieved November 30, 2008. from http://www.aseansec.org/AR-08.pdf.

ASEAN. (2008b). *ASEAN Charter*. Retrieved November 30, 2008. from http://www.aseansec.org/ASEAN-Charter.pdf.

ASEAN. (2008c). *ASEAN ECONOMIC COMMUNITY BLUEPRINT*. Retrieved. from http://www.aseansec.org/5187-10.pdf.

ASEAN. (2009). *ASEAN SOCIO-CULTURAL COMMUNITY BLUEPRINT*. Retrieved August 11, 2010. from http://www.aseansec.org/5187-19.pdf.

Augsburger, D. W. (1992). *Conflict Mediation Across Cultures: Pathways and Patterns* (First ed.). Louisville: Westmister/John Knox Press.

Avruch, K. (1998). *Culture & Conflict Resolution*. Washington, D.C.: United States Institute of Peace Press.

Avruch, K., & Black, P. W. (2001). Conflict Resolution in Intercultural Settings: Problems and Prospects. In P. K. Chew (Ed.), *The Conflict & Culture Reader* (pp. 7-14). New York: New York University Press.

Bhattacharyay, B. N. (2010). Infrastructure for ASEAN Connectivity and Integration. *ASEAN Economic Bulletin, 27*(2), 200-221.

Blau, J., & Moncada, A. (2009). *Human Rights: A Primer*. Boulder: Paradigm Publishers.

Callahan, W. A. (2008). Chinese Visions of World Order: Post-hegemonic or a New Hegemony? *International Studies Review, 10*(4), 749-761.

Chang, Y.-t., Chu, Y.-h., & Park, C.-M. (2007). Authoritarian Nostalgia in Asia. *Journal of Democracy, 18*(3), 71-80.

Chang, Y.-t., Chun, Y.-h., & Park, C.-M. (2007). Authoritarian Nostalgia in Asia. *Journal of Democracy, 18*(3), 71-80.

Chottmann, S. (2006). Melayu Islam Beraja: The Politics of Legitimisation in a Malay Islamic Monarchy. *Review of Indonesian and Malaysian Affairs 40*(2), 111-139.

CIA. (2009). The World Factbook: Singapore. Retrieved October 12, 2010, from https://www.cia.gov/library/publications/the-world-factbook/geos/sn.html.

Collins, A. (2008). A People-Oriented ASEAN: A Door Ajar or Closed for Civil Society Organizations? *Contemporary Southeast Asia, 30*(2), 313-332.

CSCAP. (2008). About Us. Retrieved July 29, 2010, from http://www.cscap.org/index.php?page=about-us.

Cuasay, P. (1998). Borders on the Fantastic: Mimesis, Violence, and Landscape at the Temple of Preah Vihear. *Modern Asian Studies, 32*(4), 849-890.

Dore, R. (1997). *Japan, Internationalism and the UN* (2nd ed.). London: Routledge.

Dubinskas, F. A. (1992). Culture and Conflict: The Cultural Roots of Discord. In D. M. Kolb & J. M. Bartunel (Eds.), *Hidden Conflict in Organizations: Uncovering Behind-the-Scenes Disputes* (pp. 187-208). London: Sage.

von Feigenblatt, Otto F. (2007). *Japan and Human Security: 21st Century ODA Policy Apologetics and Discursive Co-optation* (2nd ed.). Delray Beach: Academic Research International.

von Feigenblatt, Otto F. (2009a). Anomie, Racial Wage, and Critical Aesthetics: Understanding the Negative Externalities of Japanese and Thai Social Practices. *Journal of Asia Pacific Studies, 1*(1), 69-75.

von Feigenblatt, Otto F. (2009b). ASEAN and Human Security: Challenges and Opportunities. *Ritsumeikan Center for Asia Pacific Studies Working Paper, No. 09-5*(July), 1-22.

von Feigenblatt, Otto F. (2009c). Comparing the 2006 Military Coup in Thailand and the 2009 Coup in Honduras: Internal Socio-political Similarities and External Normative Differences. *Infinity Journal, 1*(4), 3-9.

von Feigenblatt, Otto F. (2009d). Disciplinary "Moratorium": Post-Colonial Studies, Third Wave Feminism, and Development Studies. *Journal of Alternative Perspectives in the Social Sciences, 1*(3), 892-896.

von Feigenblatt, Otto F. (2009e). Some lessons from the White Rajahs of Sarawak: Identifying and strengthening local capacities for peace in the deep South of Thailand. *Journal of Law and Conflict Resolution, 1*(6), 117-121.

von Feigenblatt, Otto F. (2009f). The Thai Ethnocracy Unravels: A Critical Cultural Analysis of Thailand's Socio-Political Unrest. *Journal of Alternative Perspectives in the Social Sciences, 1*(3), 583-611.

von Feigenblatt, Otto F. (2010a). A Brief Analysis of Popular Aesthetics in Thailand: Subjective Culture vs. Objective Culture. *Journal of Social Sciences, 22*(1), 61-63.

von Feigenblatt, Otto F. (2010b). *Human Security in the Asia Pacific Region: Security Challenges, Regional Integration, and*

Representative Case Studies (Hardcover ed.). Jaipur: YKING BOOKS.

von Feigenblatt, Otto F. (2010c). Identity and culture: a cultural interpretation of the Hopi-Navajo land dispute. *Vivat Academia, 111*(June), 35-47.

von Feigenblatt, Otto F. (2010d, May 27, 2010). UNCERTAINTY AND FEAR IN THAILAND. *Insight on Conflict*. Retrieved May 27, 2010, from http://www.insightonconflict.org/conflicts/thailand/stories/uncertainty-fear-thailand/

von Feigenblatt, Otto F. , Suttichujit, V., Shuib, M. S., Keling, M. F., & Ajis, M. N. e. (2010). Weapons of Mass Assimilation: A Critical Analysis of the Use of Education in Thailand. *Journal of Asia Pacific Studies, 1*(2), 292-311.

Fritz, R. (1996). *Corporate Tides: The Inescapable Laws of Organizational Structure* San Francisco: Berrett-Koehler Publishers

Fukuyama, F. (1992). *THE END OF HISTORY AND THE LAST MAN*. New York: The Free Press.

Glassman, J. (2005). The "War On Terrorism" Comes To Southeast Asia. *Journal of Contemporary Asia, 35*(1), 3-28.

Gottesman, E. (2003). *CAMBODIA After the Khmer Rouge: Inside the Politics of Nation Building*. New Haven: Yale University Press.

Habermas, J. (2005). The Theory of Communicative Action. In S. F. Moore (Ed.), *Law and Anthropology: A Reader* (pp. 58-61). Oxford: Blackwell Publishing.

Habermas, J. (2006). *The Divided West* (C. Cronin, Trans.). Padstow: Polity.

Handley, P. M. (2006). *The King Never Smiles: A Biography of Thailand's Bhumibol Adulyadej*. New Haven Yale University Press.

Harris, I. (2010). Rethinking Cambodian Political Discourse on Territory: Genealogy of the Buddhist ritual boundary (sīmā). *Journal of Southeast Asian Studies, 41*(2), 215-239.

Heidhues, M. S. (2000). *Southeast Asia: A Concise History*. London: Thames & Hudson.

Heller, D. (2005). The Relevance of the ASEAN Regional Forum (ARF) for Regional Security in the Asia-Pacific. *Contemporary Southeast Asia, 27*(1), 123-145.

Hewinson, K. (2010). Rebellion, Repression and the Red Shirts. *East Asia Forum Quarterly, 2*(2), 14-17.

Hinton, A. (2006). Khmerness and the Thai 'Other': Violence, Discourse and Symbolism in the 2003 Anti-Thai Riots in Cambodia. *Journal of Southeast Asian Studies, 37*(3), 445-469.

Hook, J. N., Worthington, E. L., & Utsey, S. O. (2008). Collectivism, Forgiveness, and Social Harmony. *The Counseling Psychologist, 37*(6), 821-847.

Ishii, Y. (1994). Thai Muslims and the Royal Patronage of Religion. *Law & Society Review, 28*(3), 453-460

Jones, D. M., & Smith, M. L. R. (2007). Making Process, Not Progress ASEAN and the Evolving East Asian Regional Order. *International Security, 32*(1), 148-184.

Katanyuu, R. (2006). Beyond Non-Interference in ASEAN: The Association's Role in Myanmar's National Reconciliation and Democratization. *Asian Survey, 46*(6), 825-845.

Keling, M. F., Saludin, M. N., Feigenblatt, O. F. v., Ajis, M. N. e., & Shuib, M. S. (2010). A Historical Approach to Myanmar's Democratic Process. *Journal of Asia Pacific Studies, 1*(2), 132-148.

Keong, C. Y. (2006). Behind Malaysia's "MIracle": A Veblenian Perspective on Mahathir's Era of Economic Modernization. *Journal of Economic Issues, 40*(4), 861-875.

Kim, S. W., Fidler, D. P., & Ganguly, S. (2009). Eastphalia Rising? Asian Influence and the Fate of Human Security. *World Policy Journal, 26*(2), 53-64.

Kiong, T. C., & Bun, C. K. (Eds.). (2001). *Alternate Identities: The Chinese of Contemporary Thailand.* Singapore: Brill Times Academic Press.

Le-Coz, C. (2009). "His Untouchable Majesty" Thailand Censorship and Emprisonment: The Abuses in the Name of Lese Majeste [Electronic Version]. *Reporters Sans Frontiers*, 1-16. Retrieved September 20, from http://www.rsf.org/IMG/pdf/rapport_en_ok-2.pdf

Lee, K. Y. (2000). *From Third World to First: The Singapore Story: 1965-2000* (First ed.). New York: HarperCollins Publishers.

Limaye, S. P. (2007). United States-ASEAN Relations on ASEAN's Fortieth Anniversary: A Glass Half Full. *Contemporary Southeast Asia, 29*(3), 447-464.

Lintner, B. (2009). The Battle for Thailand: Can Democracy Survive? *Foreign Affairs, 88*(4), 108-118.

Liow, J. C. (2006). International Jihad and Muslim Radicalism in Thailand? Toward an Alternative Interpretation. *Asia Policy*(2), 89–108.

MacFarlane, S. N., & Khong, Y. F. (2006). *Human Security and the UN: A Critical History* (1st Edition ed.). Indianapolis: Indiana University Press.

McCargo, D. (2008). *Tearing Apart the Land: Islam and Legitimacy in Southern Thailand* (First ed.). Ithaca: Cornell University Press.

McCargo, D. (2009). The Politics of Buddhist identity in Thailand's deep south: The Demise of civil religion? *Journal of Southeast Asian Studies, 40*(1), 11-32.

McCormick, J. (2005). *Understanding the European Union* (3rd ed.). New York: Palgrave Macmillan.

Means, G. P. (2009). *Political Islam in Southeast Asia* (Paperback ed.). London: Lynne Rienner Publishers.

Merry, S. E. (2006). *Human Rights & Gender Violence: Translating International Law into Local Justice*. Chicago: The University of Chicago Press.

Millard, M. (2004). *Jihad in Paradise: Islam and Politics in Southeast Asia*. Armonk: East Gate Books.

Mulder, N. (1996). *Inside Southeast Asia: Religion, Everyday Life, and Cultural Change*. Chiang Mai: Silkworm Books.

Murphy, C. (2009). Populism Erodes Thailand's Old Order. *Far Eastern Economic Review, 172*(5), 7-12.

Neher, C. D. (2002). *Southeast Asia in the New International Era*. Boulder: Westview Press.

Omelicheva, M. Y. (2009). Global Civil Society and Democratization of World Politics: A Bona Fide Relationship or Illusory Liaison? *International Studies Perspectives, 11*(1), 109-132.

Payne, R. (1995). *The White Rajahs of Sarawak*. Kuala Lumpur: Oxford University Press.

Pieterse, J. N. (2007). *Ethnicities and Global Multiculture: Pants for an Octopus* (Hardcover ed.). Plymouth: Rowman & LIttlefield Publishers, Inc.

Pruitt, D., & Kim, S. H. (2004). *Social Conflict: Escalation, Stalemate and Settlement* (3rd ed.). New York: McGraw Hill.

Ritzer, G. (2008). *Sociological Theory*. New York: McGraw Hill Higher Education.

Selth, A. (2009). Known Knowns and Known Unknowns: Measuring Myanmar's Military Capabilities. *Contemporary Southeast Asia, 31*(2), 272-296.

Simon, S. (2008). ASEAN and Multilateralism: The Long, Bumpy Road to Community. *Contemporary Southeast Asia, 30*(2), 264-292.

Stockwell, A. J. (2004). Britain and Brunei, 1945-1963: Imperial Retreat and Royal Ascendancy. *Modern Asian Studies, 38*(4), 785-819.

Storey, I. (2008). Securing Southeast Asia's Sea Lanes: A Work in Progress. *Asia Policy*(6), 95–127.

Tagliacozzo, E. (2001). Border Permeability and the State in Southeast Asia: Contraband and Regional Security. *Contemporary Southeast Asia, 23*(2), 254-275.

Thayer, C. A. (2009). Cambodia: The Cambodian People's Party Consolidates Power. *Southeast Asian Affairs, 2009*, 85-101.

Thayer, C. A. (2010). US Rapprochement with Laos and Cambodia. *Contemporary Southeast Asia, 32*(3), 442-459.

Trinidad, D. D. (2010). Domestic Actors, Market Reform and Regional Integration in Southeast Asia. *Asia Pacific World, 1*(1), 95-115.

Ungpakorn, G. J. (2007). *A Coup for the Rich: Thailand's Political Crisis*. Bangkok: Workers Democracy Publishing.

Ungpakorn, G. J. (2010). *Thailand's Crisis & the Fight for Democracy*. London: WDPress.

Vu-Tung, N. (2007). Vietnam's Membership of ASEAN: A Constructivist Interpretation. *Contemporary Southeast Asia, 29*(3), 483-505.

Wyatt, D. K. (2003). *Thailand: A Short History* (Thailand ed.). Chiang Mai: Silkworm Books.

Yegar, M. (2002). *Between Integration and Secession: The Muslim Communities of the Southern Philippines, Southern Thailand, and Western Burma/Myanmar*. New York: Lexington Books.

Part IV

Conclusions and for Further Research

Part IV summarizes the study's main conclusions regarding ASEAN's role in the region's development and conflict. Chapter 12 brings together the themes discussed in the previous three parts of the book while also discussing some possible future trends in terms of Southeast Asia's integration. The research process is the topic of chapter 13 which serves two purposes. First of all, chapter 13 describes the way in which the research leading to the writing of this book was conducted. The researcher is positioned as part of a specific epistemic community operating in a particular place and time under a certain set of theoretical and disciplinary assumptions. Finally, chapter 13 concludes with a few topics proposed for further research as well as a few suggestions regarding the applicability of the research method used in this volume to studies covering diverse regional blocs.

12

Conclusions: ASEAN's Future in the Region's Development and Conflict

This chapter provides a brief summary of the main conclusions reached throughout the study regarding ASEAN's future in the region's development and conflict. Some important future trends in terms of regional integration are discussed in relation to ASEAN's role in their development. Finally, the chapter provides a holistic overview of the region's near term integration prospects based on the observations made in parts I, II, and III of the present volume. The chapter concludes that ASEAN is central to the region's development as well as to its conflict management system.

Introduction

This volume has covered a vast array of issues affecting the diverse Southeast Asian region. Economic development, regional security, socio-cultural integration, and political development are some of the main themes that were discussed in the first three sections of the book. Notwithstanding the diversity of issues that were discussed, there is a common thread connecting them all. ASEAN has served as the anchor for the discussion of all other issues due to its position as the only viable regional intergovernmental organization as well as due to its international visibility as one of the most respected regional groupings in the Asia Pacific region. Since ASEAN has expanded to include every single country geographically located in Southeast Asia, the choice to concentrate on its regional role does not exclude any important population centers or political entities located in the region (von Feigenblatt, 2009a). Moreover, ASEAN has become one of the main vehicles for regional countries to reach out diplomatically to extra-regional partners such as their East Asian neighbors, Japan and China (Heller, 2005; Komori, 2009). Thus, the organization's geographical reach matches the entire Southeast Asian region.

In terms of scope, ASEAN's purview has expanded considerable since its inception to include virtually all areas of policy and regional governance such as economic, political, cultural, and social issues (Narine, 1998; Nem-Singh, 2008; Pitsuwan, 2010; Rolfe, 2008; Severino, 2007). Due to ASEAN's expanded purview it is possible to center a discussion of the region's socio-economic and politico-cultural development on the organization as was done in the first three sections of this study. Moreover, it should be noted that by concentrating on the role of structural dynamics on both the organization's functioning in addition to the region as a whole, it was possible to trace the relationship between the policies of a diverse group of nation-states as well as the influence of the international environment on those policies. Throughout the exploration of the influence of structural dynamics on the policies of regional governments important conclusions were reached regarding the main challenges in the different policy areas. The following sections of this chapter will briefly summarize those conclusions as well as provide a few suggestions regarding possible future developments.

ASEAN's Security Role

ASEAN's role in regional security was discussed in part I of the volume. There are several important aspects to ASEAN's security role. ASEAN's internal conflict management system is important since it is an popular venue for interstate disputes in a region with a history of violent conflict (Rolfe, 2008; Yzawa, 2006). Chapter one provides an in depth analysis of the dispute resolution system currently in place and identifies the core principles underlying the "ASEAN way". Consensus building was identified as the most important conflict management strategy used in ASEAN while dispute avoidance was found to be closely related and usually complementary. The system currently in place, called the "ASEAN way", creates costs and benefits to the organization due to lost opportunities for change as well as the lack of a proper way to deal with serious interstate conflicts without the possibility of at least minimal regional interference (Narine, 1997). Chapter two expands on chapter one's findings by applying structural dynamics to ASEAN's organizational structure. Some of the conclusions reached in terms of ASEAN's organization structure include the existence of three important structural conflicts which cause considerable oscillation and backtracking in terms of organizational development. The emphasis here is on the development of the regional intergovernmental organization. Membership expansion and the widening or narrowing of the organization's purview are at the core of the first structural conflict. There are considerable challenges when a small regional organization attempts to expand its membership while at the same time it considers expanding its purview to include a broader set of policy areas (Collins, 2008; Komori, 2009). The second core structural conflict that was identified explains the fluctuation between a myopic short-term orientation and long term broad principles. Thus the second structural conflict explains the challenges faced by the organization in terms of prioritizing goals in terms of time orientation. Finally, the third core structural conflict revolves around the fluctuation between periods of condensation and periods of diffusion. This third structural conflict can also be understood in terms of the relative level of institutionalization of ASEAN. The three core structural conflicts result in considerable structural oscillation which is costly and prevents the organization from achieving sustainable organizational advancement. Progress in some areas is reversed due to a shift in emphasis to other conflicting areas. In other words different measures work at cross purposes which prevents the organization from achieving long term objectives.

Chapter three provides a proposal to help overcome the three previously mentioned structural conflicts through a new "ASEAN Way". The proposed dispute resolution system applies structural dynamics in that it aims to tackle the incompatibilities identified in chapter two by restructuring the organization in a way in which structural tension can flow unimpeded towards the achievement of progressively higher level organizational goals. The proposed dispute resolution system aims to maintain the strengths of the traditional "ASEAN Way" while also reforming some of its disadvantages. Mediation, arbitration, and negotiation are all conflict resolution methods that are included in the proposed system. Information sharing and consultations are also emphasized so as to make sure that local, managerial, strategic, and organizational goals are well integrated.

The "ASEAN Way" is of pivotal importance to regional security since it represents the only region wide mechanism to deal with interstate disputes (von Feigenblatt, 2009a; Narine, 1998; Yzawa, 2006). Thus, the early discussion of ASEAN's organizational dispute resolution system sets the tone for chapter four's exploration of the ASEAN Political-Security Community. The Blue Book for the proposed community is discussed and analyzed in detail due to the importance of the policy paper as the outcome of intergovernmental consensus building and elite bargaining. As a product of the regional policy making process, the Blue Book, is a key source of clues regarding the level of agreement, disagreement, avoidance, and struggle over certain policy points. The critical content analysis that was undertaken in chapter four revealed considerable disagreements on certain areas such as human rights and on the meaning of sovereignty. Disagreement was also evident in terms of the desired pace of democratization as well as regarding the attributes of democracy (Collins, 2008). There was considerable agreement in terms of the need for greater cooperation to deal with non-traditional security threats such as natural disasters, pollution, and terrorism (Severino, 2007).

Chapter four concludes with a discussion of the regional security environment. Extra-regional actors are particularly important in this respect. American influence in the region as well as China's growing political clout are two issues at the center of regional debates about security (Limaye, 2007; Thayer, 2010). ASEAN is becoming central to the region's security by serving as the core institution in the Asia Pacific (Pitsuwan, 2010; Rolfe, 2008). At this point there is no other organization that can take the lead in terms of security cooperation in the Asia Pacific Region which means that ASEAN will continue to play a central role in any future efforts to tackle transpacific security issues (von Feigenblatt, 2010; Komori, 2009; Pitsuwan, 2010). ASEAN centrality is evident in regional security frameworks such as CSCAP, the ASEAN Regional Forum, and the vast array of ASEAN + arrangements (CSCAP, 2008; Heller, 2005). ASEAN can play an important role equivalent to that traditionally played by middle powers in terms of serving as an important intergovernmental organization with a wide reach in terms of extra regional partners (Heller, 2005; Komori, 2009; Limaye, 2007). In terms of power, ASEAN's power is mostly of the soft type in that it exerts considerable normative pressure on the regional integration process due to its centrality (von Feigenblatt, 2009a; Tow, Thakur, & Hyun, 2000).

Thus, part one of the volume reaches some important conclusions regarding ASEAN's organizational structure as an intergovernmental institution as well as regarding ASEAN's role for regional security. ASEAN is becoming more institutionalized as time goes on as evidenced by the strengthening of the office of the secretary general as well as by the ambitious plans for the organization to play a more active goal in tackling regional non-traditional security threats (ASEAN, 2008a; Pitsuwan, 2010; Severino, 2007). Moreover, ASEAN is central to the wider Asia Pacific Region's fragmented security cooperation framework. Since other intergovernmental organizations such as APEC have avoided dealing with security issues in any meaningful sense and East Asia lags behind in terms of regional integration, ASEAN has taken the lead in terms of institution building and has achieved a central position because of this (Komori, 2009; Nair, 2008).

ASEAN's Role in the Region's Economic Development

Part two of the present volume deals with ASEAN's role in the region's economic development. Chapter 5 provides a broad overview of the region's socio-economic development. A broad approach to development was adopted due to the important role of social development issues for certain aspects of economic development and regional integration. For example, literacy and health are important factors affecting a country's human capital and thus may become important assets in the path towards economic development or obstacles to overcome (Sen, 1999). An overview of each ASEAN member's socio-cultural development was provided in order to set the stage for a more macro discussion of economic integration in subsequent chapters. The main conclusion that can be drawn from chapter 5 is the sheer diversity in terms of socio-economic development that characterizes the members of ASEAN. This diversity presents considerable challenges in terms of socio-economic integration due to the presence of asynchronous development both between and within member states. Chapter 6 concentrates on the main barriers to regional trade by providing a content analysis of the Blue Print for an ASEAN Economic Community. Barriers to trade were divided into non-tariff and tariff barriers. Non-tariff barriers were found to include language differences, certificates of origin, different levels of socio-economic development, and different deadlines for liberalization. On the other hand tariff barriers include high intraregional import tariffs for regional products. The challenges in lowering those tariffs and possibly eliminating them were discussed in detail.

The two most important challenges to economic integration that were identified include asynchronous and asymmetric development of ASEAN's member States. In addition to that the production of similar agricultural products exacerbates the difficulties due to the greater challenges encountered in finding complementarities in trade. Other important challenges that were identified include weak legal protections for foreign investors and deficient infrastructural bases. Financial flows proved to be a challenging area of integration due to the experience of the Asian Financial Crisis of 1997 (Peng-Er, 2006). The easing of regional financial flows may result in macroeconomic instability and requires an advanced monitoring system in order to avoid other negative externalities such as money laundering and capital flight (Sharman, 2008).

Based on the descriptive statistics presented in chapter 6, ASEAN still has a long way to go in order to achieve economic integration. Extra-regional exports make up approximately 75% of all trade which means that intra-regional trade lags behind (ASEAN, 2010). This is a clear indicator that ASEAN must take concrete steps in order to increase intra-regional trade in order to set the stage for greater economic integration (Arnold, 2006). In addition to that it is also important to note that imports are also mostly from extra-regional partners rather than from other ASEAN members (ASEAN, 2010). The goal of achieving a single production base in order to increase regional productivity and competitiveness depends to a large extend on ASEAN's ability to promote intra-regional imports and exports in the near future. This is a difficult goal due to the influence of extra-regional powers on certain members. For example, the United States uses its political influence to encourage extra-regional trade in exchange for official development assistance, market access, and in some cases military support (Arnold, 2006). China is taking a similar approach to trade which combines political and economic issues to the detriment of region-wide economic interests (Emmers, 2001; Hwang, 2006).

Chapter 7 provides the theoretical core of part II of the volume. Three economic structural conflicts are introduced. The first conflict explains the fluctuation between protectionism and liberalization in terms of financial and investment flows. The second conflict centers on the issue of protection of intellectual property rights while the third explains fluctuation in the area of regulation and deregulation. The three previously mentioned structural conflicts explain the mechanics behind some of the most important challenges to ASEAN's economic integration. Protectionism poses an important challenge to integration in the Southeast Asian region but the reasons why certain countries opt for protectionism are important. Asymmetric development and similar agricultural products pose considerable challenges to liberalization due to the vulnerability of less developed countries to an influx of foreign products. This is particularly problematic for CMLV countries which cannot compete against the products of other regional member and whose domestic industries would be decimated by a sudden liberalization. ASEAN has recognized this challenge to a certain extend and has responded with more flexible deadlines for CMLV countries as well as some policy measures in order to promote development in those countries (ASEAN, 2008b). Nevertheless, the use of the ASEAN minus formula is only viable in the short to midterm before it starts to have the negative externality of creating an incentive for other members to defect from the liberalization effort or to set up non-tariff barriers in order to protect their own markets. A similar problem is present in the second structural conflict. Regional members have important reasons for wanting to increase liberalization in terms of financial and investment flows however they also have considerable reservations (Than & Thein, 2007; Trinidad, 2010).

Regional governments fear losing control over large sectors of their economies which in turn leads them to temporary protectionist measures aiming to control financial and investment flows. This stop and go approach to financial and investment flows results in a damaged reputation due to a loss in investor confidence in addition to lost investment opportunities. Finally, the third core economic structural conflicts deals with the broad issue of regulation versus deregulation. This structural conflict centers on the debate regarding the degree of control regional governments should have over their economies. Greater dynamism and growth requires deregulation which in turn leads to a loss of control over important sectors of the economy. This structural conflict can be overcome by adopting an approach similar to that of the People's Republic of China. The provision of considerable social services may ameliorate some of the negative externalities of deregulation and thus remove an important obstacle to economic growth. Singapore has adopted a similar approach in which the economies is largely deregulated and gains in this policy area are then transferred to other areas such as the provision of social services (CIA, 2009; Lee, 2000).

Finally, chapter 8 introduces important trends in the realm of economic integration in addition to identifying some important conclusions regarding the present state of affairs. One of the most important trends is the adoption of a market economy. Even authoritarian states such as Vietnam and Myanmar have slowly moved towards the deregulation of their economies in order to benefit from greater economic growth (CIA, 2010; Than & Thein, 2007; Thawnghmung, 2009; Vu-Tung, 2007; WTO, 2007). A second important trend is the rise of Chinese competition for low value added products and FDI. Southeast Asia has lost its competitive advantage for low value added products and thus FDI is flowing to China rather than the region (Arnold, 2006; Than & Thein, 2007; Trinidad, 2010). It is also important to note that it will become increasingly important for Southeast Asian governments to negotiate trade agreements as a bloc in order to compete against economic power houses such as China as well as other regional blocs such as the European Union and NAFTA (Arnold, 2006). Individually, ASEAN members are minor powers or least developed countries but as a group they represent an important market as well as a strong production base. For ASEAN to be competitive it is important for the region to function as a borderless production base which would make the region more appealing for FDI and would also lower transaction costs and eliminate redundancy. This poses considerable challenges in terms of infrastructure, language barriers, and political will (ASEAN, 2008b; Bhattacharyay, 2010). A final challenge is political instability. Economic growth, integration, and the attraction of FDI require political stability and the rule of law. The region is plagued by political instability in the shape of recurrent military coups, discontinuity due to weak civilian governments, and predatory interest groups (Cock, 2010; DRESSEL, 2009; von Feigenblatt, 2009b; Thayer, 2009; Ungpakorn, 2007). ASEAN can play an important role in avoiding political instability by spreading norms making coups more costly and by serving as a mediator between powerful regional interest groups. ASEAN can also exert considerable diplomatic pressure in order to secure more favorable trading agreements for its members.

ASEAN's Role in the Region's Socio-Cultural Integration

Part III of the present volume covers the topic of socio-cultural integration. This is a very broad topic that includes a vast array of issues ranging from education to technological transfers. Chapter 9 provides a historical background so as to understand the salience of the two most important regional socio-cultural debates. The first socio-cultural debate deals with the topic of human rights versus "Asian Values" (Lee, 2000; Merry, 2006; Tow et al., 2000). A second debate is centered on the issue of nationalism. Both debates are shaped and influenced by the region's recent history of colonialism.

The importance of the previously mentioned debates to the region's socio-cultural integration is due to their centrality in most policy issues. Culture is a frame of reference that helps a person interpret the world. Some of the most important historical influences on the region include, Japanese expansion during World War II and during the 1990s, American influence during most of the Cold War, and China's growing economic and political power in the region (Baird, 2010; Heidhues, 2000; Hook, Gilson, Hughes, & Dobson, 2005; Kissinger, 1994; Sakamoto, 2008; Wyatt, 2003).

Chapter 10 provides a detailed content analysis of the Blue Print for the ASEAN Socio-Cultural Community (ASEAN, 2009). The main findings of the content analysis are that there is considerable ambiguity in the document reflecting the elite bargaining process undertaken in order to produce it. ASEAN's emphasis on consensus building for the drafting process results in very broad principles and ambiguous implementation plans. The Blue Print for the ASEAN Socio-Cultural Community is not exception in this respect however it is even more ambiguous than the Blue Prints for the other two pillars of the ASEAN Community. This ambiguity reflects the lack of agreement on certain important areas such as human rights and nationalism. There is a latent tension in the document when it comes to measures involving the two previously mentioned concepts. One recurrent pattern is the assertion of a broad principle such as the respect for human rights and then the inclusion of several qualifiers such as the respect of local practices and national sovereignty. The document is very weak when it comes to implementation and also lacks cohesion. Some sections are better integrated than others which reflect the level of agreement on certain areas. It should be noted that there appears to be greater agreement on social than on cultural issues since social issues can be framed as part of economic development. The importance of the Blue Print is that it allows the researcher to identify points of agreement and points of divergence among ASEAN Members which provides a window into decision making at the regional level.

Chapter 11 presents the most important findings of part III of the present volume. The three core socio-cultural structural conflicts are identified and explained. Human right as an important debate is represented by the first socio-cultural structural conflict. The fluctuation between periods of respect for human rights and periods of limited liberties is explained as a result of the incompatibility between the need to maintain social harmony while at the same time improving the human rights reputation of a nation-state. Measures intended to improve a country's human rights reputation lead to greater civil society activism and dissention which in turn affects social harmony (Collins, 2008). On the other hand measures intended to restore social harmony limit certain liberties which in turn damages a country's human rights reputation. The second core socio-cultural conflict deals with the flow of information. There is a fluctuation between periods during which the flow of information is eased and periods in which it is circumscribed. Easing the flow of information is important because it aids several policy areas such as economic and social integration. On the other hand easing the flow of information also has unintended consequences such as a sharp rise in expectations, changing family patterns, and political instability. Due to the previously mentioned negative externalities there is alternation between periods of easing the flow of information and periods that limit the flow of information in favor of social stability.

The third and final socio-cultural conflict deals with nationalism. Measures intended to increase cultural openness are important for economic and social integration in Southeast Asia but at the same time they tend to challenge the traditional view of the nation-state. Thus there are periods in which governments promote cultural openness and syncretism which are then followed by periods of narrow nationalism. The resulting fluctuation is costly in many ways. Measures intended to foster cultural openness and cross-cultural understanding are neutralized or rolled back by measures intended to foster nationalism. Some of the negative externalities of nationalism include xenophobia and isolationism. Both of the previously mentioned negative externalities affect other policy areas such as technological transfer and human capital formation. Thus nationalism is one of the most important challenges faced by ASEAN (von Feigenblatt, 2009a; Katanyuu, 2006; Narine, 1997).

Socio-cultural structural conflicts are particularly important because they affect all other policy areas. Therefore, one of the main conclusions of this study is that overcoming nationalism will be one of the most important challenges for ASEAN. Nationalism is particularly strong in a region that experienced colonialism and that is fragmented into a greater number of ethnic and linguistic groups (Heidhues, 2000; Mulder, 1996; Neher, 2002). In addition to that, the region is home to a vast array of religious groups including Buddhists, Christians, Muslims, and thousands of local varieties of animism (Kiong & Bun, 2001; Means, 2009; Millard, 2004; Mulder, 1996; Pieterse, 2007; Yegar, 2002). While ethnic diversity does not naturally lead to nationalism, it does make governance more challenging and thus makes nationalism a tempting alternative for regional governments. Alternatives to narrow nationalism are also present in the region which is characterized by syncretism and blurred group borders. Singapore is a great example of a multicultural and multiethnic society that has avoided the nationalist model in favor or an identity based on shared needs and interests (Lee, 2000). Pre-colonial governance models from Southeast and East Asia can also be used as guiding frameworks for more inclusive governance. The *mandala* system of concentric circles of power and the traditional tributary system that was in operation until the mid 19th century are promising *emic* models of governance which are not based on a narrow ethno-nationalism (Harris, 2010; Syukri, 1985). Based on the

European experience, overcoming nationalism and building a shared regional identity will be essential for the success of regional integration (Habermas, 2006; Reinalda, 2009).

An Uncertain Future

ASEAN faces many challenges and operates in a very unstable international environment. Traditional partners such as Japan are experiencing serious economic challenges while other regional powers are rising to political and economic prominence such as China (Sakamoto, 2008; Simon, 2008). American involvement in the region is also uncertain due to military overstretch and budgetary challenges at home (Emmers, 2001; Lal, 2004; Narine, 1997). In addition to that the international economy is undergoing considerable structural changes (Skidelsky, 2010). Production chains are shifting due to the rise of new production centers in the developing world and the movement of basic services from the developed to the developing world (Friedman, 2000; Than & Thein, 2007; Togo, 2005). This is particularly important for ASEAN due to the Chinese challenge and competition for FDI. Size also matters due to the stalled World Trade Organization (WTO) process regional blocks are becoming more important in order to reap the benefits of international trade and in order to enjoy larger economies of scale.

Due to the different levels of development of ASEAN countries as well as the political instability afflicting the region, it is uncertain whether the region will achieve its goal of achieving integration in the near future (Jones & Smith, 2007). Regional security challenges such as terrorism, border disputes, and recurrent military coups will continue to be important challenges for the region's future socio-economic development and integration. Another important factor will be the political future of the region's authoritarian governments and possible transition of one-party states to multiparty democracies (Chang, Chu, & Park, 2007; Glassman, 2005; Thayer, 2010). The process towards democratization is a very difficult one and may lead to greater political instability and possibly even civil wars in the short term (John, 2005; Kim, Fidler, & Ganguly, 2009; Omelicheva, 2009). Nevertheless the region is more stable and integrated than it was twenty years ago and therefore there are grounds to belief that there will continue to be progress in the future (von Feigenblatt, 2009a; Heidhues, 2000; Neher, 2002).

The role of the United States as well as of China will be very important for the region's future (Bhaskaran, 2010; Ellis, 2009; Limaye, 2007). China's foreign policy tends to exclude human rights and tends to skew normative issues in favor of pragmatic interests (Callahan, 2008; Kim et al., 2009). On the other hand the United States and the European Union emphasize the importance of international norms and universal human rights (Brunnee & Toope, 2006; MacFarlane & Khong, 2006; Merry, 2006). A shift in the relative influence of China and the United States in the Southeast Asian region may have important unintended consequences for the future of the ASEAN Community. Chinese power in the region may weaken international norms and may slow down the pace of democratization (Emmers, 2001; Kim et al., 2009). Moreover, China views Southeast Asia as an important region of its near abroad. Since China aims to be a regional power rather than a global one, it will most likely concentrate its energy on influencing the development of the subregion. American overstretch and global interests dilute the attention that can be devoted to Southeast Asia (Limaye, 2007; Thayer, 2010).

In summary, Southeast Asia is an incredibly diverse and dynamic region which makes it very difficult to provide a forecast of the future. Based on current trends it is possible to identify possible paths that the region may follow. There is the possibility that democratization will sweep the region with regime transitions in Myanmar, Thailand, Cambodia, and Laos. A second possibility is that economic reform will take place without political transitions which is what is currently happening in Laos, Vietnam, and to a certain extend in

Myanmar (Than & Thein, 2007; Thawnghmung, 2009; Thayer, 2010). Socio-economic development will continue to be assymetrical for the near future due to the higher growth rates of certain ASEAN Members and due to the shift to higher value products and services in the more advanced economies of the region (Hew, 2008; Lee, 2000). Finally, structural oscillation and fluctuation will continue to take place in most policy areas. The political capital and centralization/coordination that is needed in order to overcome the structural conflicts identified in this study is not available at this point. Measures will continue to be disjointed efforts in most policy areas with the possible exception of crisis management and possibly economic integration. Policy areas that are considered to be of greater importance for regional elites will be prioritized. Nevertheless as the structural approach applied throughout this book shows, piecemeal reforms are counterproductive since all parts of the organizational structure work together in order to move towards organizational goals. Thus, the disagreement over timeframe, over the relative importance of different policy areas, and over the level of institutionalization desired for ASEAN will all contribute to greater structural oscillation at the national and regional levels.

ASEAN's Centrality in the Asia Pacific Region

ASEAN's importance is not limited to its role in the Southeast Asian sub-region since it is central to larger cooperation efforts at the Asia Pacific level (Drysdale, 2010; von Feigenblatt, 2009a; Heller, 2005; Hwang, 2006). As the most successful regional organization in the Asia Pacific, ASEAN has managed to position itself as an important node in most other regional cooperation efforts such as the East Asia Summit and the vast array of ASEAN + dialogue partners formulas (von Feigenblatt, 2010; Narine, 1997, 1998; Severino, 2007; Simon, 2008; Tow et al., 2000; Yzawa, 2006). While ASEAN does not control the process of regional integration at the Asia Pacific level, it does play a very important role due to its centrality in the loose network of Asia Pacific nation-states (von Feigenblatt, 2010). ASEAN has achieved this due to a variety of factors such as the relative weakness and narrow mandate of the Asia Pacific Economic Cooperation Forum (APEC) (Hwang, 2006). There is also the advantage of ASEAN's membership being mostly developing countries with relations with both Western powers as well as with nation-states in the non-aligned movement (Ba, 2009; Limaye, 2007). In addition to that ASEAN was able to take advantage of having the most advanced organizational structure compared to other regional intergovernmental organizations in the Asia Pacific (von Feigenblatt, 2010; Reinalda, 2009). Finally its broad and flexible mandate allowed it to expand its purview to a vast array of issues including those beyond the immediate vicinity of the organization (von Feigenblatt, 2009a). Thus, ASEAN norms have influenced other regional integration efforts such as the Council for Security and Cooperation in the Asia Pacific (CSCAP) and the ASEAN Regional Forum (ARF) (CSCAP, 2008; Heller, 2005; Yzawa, 2006). Dialogue partners have found it convenient to expand ASEAN to include their concerns rather than to establish a new intergovernmental organization from scratch (Nair, 2008). This explains the eagerness of other regional powers such as Australia, Japan, and China to actively participate in ASEAN driven regional processes (von Feigenblatt, 2007; Limaye, 2007).

Due to the serious cleavages in the rest of the Asia Pacific region it seems highly likely that ASEAN will continue to play a central role in terms of regional integration particularly at the institutional level. Nevertheless ASEAN centrality in the economic realm will be more difficult to achieve due to the divergent interests of ASEAN members and the strategy of divide and conquer used by dialogue partners (Arnold, 2006; Bhattacharyay, 2010; von Feigenblatt, 2007). ASEAN members continue to conduct most of their trade with extra-regional partners (ASEAN, 2010). This presents considerable challenges to the goal of achieving a single integrated ASEAN Economic Community. Moreover, the early steps of economic integration require considerable cooperation and coordination in order to achieve an integrated production base which in turn requires considerable political capital as well as sufficient resources (Bhattacharyay, 2010; Trinidad, 2010). The success of ASEAN in this policy area will depend on the political will of ASEAN Members to cooperate and to negotiate trade agreements as a single bloc rather than individually. This shift would empower the entire organization and would pool the market power of regional economies. Therefore ASEAN has considerable potential to lead regional development while at the same the organization faces considerable internal and external challenges.

References

Arnold, D. (2006). Free Trade Agreements and Southeast Asia. *Journal of Contemporary Asia, 36*(2), 195-207.

ASEAN. (2008a). *ASEAN Charter*. Retrieved November 30, 2008. from http://www.aseansec.org/ASEAN-Charter.pdf.

ASEAN. (2008b). *ASEAN ECONOMIC COMMUNITY BLUEPRINT*. Retrieved. from http://www.aseansec.org/5187-10.pdf.

ASEAN. (2009). *ASEAN SOCIO-CULTURAL COMMUNITY BLUEPRINT*. Retrieved August 11, 2010. from http://www.aseansec.org/5187-19.pdf.

ASEAN. (2010). Intra- and extra-ASEA trade as of 15 July 2010. In T. 18 (Ed.). Jakarta: ASEAN.

Ba, A. (2009). Systemic Neglect? A Reconsideration of US-Southeast Asia Policy. *Contemporary Southeast Asia, 31*(3), 369-399.

Baird, I. G. (2010). Different views of history: Shades of irredentism along the Laos-Cambodia border. *Journal of Southeast Asian Studies, 41*(2), 187-213.

Bhaskaran, M. (2010). Review of Southeast Asian Economic Developments. *Southeast Asian Affairs*, 23-44.

Bhattacharyay, B. N. (2010). Infrastructure for ASEAN Connectivity and Integration. *ASEAN Economic Bulletin, 27*(2), 200-221.

Brunnee, J., & Toope, S. J. (2006). Norms, Institutions and UN Reform: The Responsibility to Protect. *Journal of International Law and International Relations, 2*, 121-137.

Callahan, W. A. (2008). Chinese Visions of World Order: Post-hegemonic or a New Hegemony? *International Studies Review, 10*(4), 749-761.

Chang, Y.-t., Chu, Y.-h., & Park, C.-M. (2007). Authoritarian Nostalgia in Asia. *Journal of Democracy, 18*(3), 71-80.

CIA. (2009). The World Factbook: Singapore. Retrieved October 12, 2010, from https://www.cia.gov/library/publications/the-world-factbook/geos/sn.html.

CIA. (2010). The World Factbook: Socialist Republic of Vietnam. Retrieved November 13, 2010, from https://www.cia.gov/library/publications/the-world-factbook/geos/vm.html.

Cock, A. R. (2010). External Actors and the Relative Autonomy of the Ruling Elite in post-UNTAC Cambodia. *Journal of Southeast Asian Studies, 41*(2), 241-265.

Collins, A. (2008). A People-Oriented ASEAN: A Door Ajar or Closed for Civil Society Organizations? *Contemporary Southeast Asia, 30*(2), 313-332.

CSCAP. (2008). About Us. Retrieved July 29, 2010, from http://www.cscap.org/index.php?page=about-us

DRESSEL, B. (2009). Thailand's Elusive Quest for a Workable Constitution, 1997-2007. *Contemporary Southeast Asia, 31*(2), 296-325.

Drysdale, P. (2010). APEC's Achievements and Challenges Today: Keynote Address, APEC Economic Committee Roundtable, Beppu, Oita, Japan, 7 August 2010. *Asia Pacific World, 1*(2), 33-44.

Ellis, D. C. (2009). U.S. Grand Strategy Following the George W. Bush Presidency. *International Studies Perspectives, 10*(4), 361-377.

Emmers, R. (2001). The Influence of the Balance of Power Factor within the ASEAN Regional Forum. *Contemporary Southeast Asia, 23*(2), 275-291.

von Feigenblatt, Otto F. (2007). *Japan and Human Security: 21st Century ODA Policy Apologetics and Discursive Co-optation* (2nd ed.). Delray Beach: Academic Research International.

von Feigenblatt, Otto F. (2009a). ASEAN and Human Security: Challenges and Opportunities. *Ritsumeikan Center for Asia Pacific Studies Working Paper, No. 09-5*(July), 1-22.

von Feigenblatt, Otto F. (2009b). Comparing the 2006 Military Coup in Thailand and the 2009 Coup in Honduras: Internal Socio-political Similarities and External Normative Differences. *Infinity Journal, 1*(4), 3-9.

von Feigenblatt, Otto F. (2010). *Human Security in the Asia Pacific Region: Security Challenges, Regional Integration, and Representative Case Studies* (Hardcover ed.). Jaipur: YKING BOOKS.

Friedman, T. L. (2000). *The Lexus and the Olive Tree: Understanding Globalization* (Revised ed.). New York: Farrar Straus Giroux.

Glassman, J. (2005). The "War On Terrorism" Comes To Southeast Asia. *Journal of Contemporary Asia, 35*(1), 3-28.

Habermas, J. (2006). *The Divided West* (C. Cronin, Trans.). Padstow: Polity.

Harris, I. (2010). Rethinking Cambodian Political Discourse on Territory: Genealogy of the Buddhist ritual boundary (sīmā). *Journal of Southeast Asian Studies, 41*(2), 215-239.

Heidhues, M. S. (2000). *Southeast Asia: A Concise History*. London: Thames & Hudson.

Heller, D. (2005). The Relevance of the ASEAN Regional Forum (ARF) for Regional Security in the Asia-Pacific. *Contemporary Southeast Asia, 27*(1), 123-145.

Hew, D. (2008). The Malaysian Economy: Developments and Challenges. *Southeast Asian Affairs*, 207-222.

Hook, G., Gilson, J., Hughes, C. W., & Dobson, H. (2005). *Japan's International Relations: Politics, economics and security* (2nd Edition ed.). London: Routledge.

Hwang, H.-d. (2006). APEC and emerging regionalism in North East Asia. *Asia Europe Journal, 4*(4), 499-510.

John, R. B. S. (2005). Democracy in Cambodia - One Decade, US$5 Billion Later: What Went Wrong? *Contemporary Southeast Asia, 27*(3), 406-428.

Jones, D. M., & Smith, M. L. R. (2007). Making Process, Not Progress ASEAN and the Evolving East Asian Regional Order. *International Security, 32*(1), 148-184.

Katanyuu, R. (2006). Beyond Non-Interference in ASEAN: The Association's Role in Myanmar's National Reconciliation and Democratization. *Asian Survey, 46*(6), 825-845.

Kim, S. W., Fidler, D. P., & Ganguly, S. (2009). Eastphalia Rising? Asian Influence and the Fate of Human Security. *World Policy Journal, 26*(2), 53-64.

Kiong, T. C., & Bun, C. K. (Eds.). (2001). *Alternate Identities: The Chinese of Contemporary Thailand.* Singapore: Brill Times Academic Press.

Kissinger, H. (1994). *Diplomacy* (Paperback ed.). New York: Simon & Schuster.

Komori, Y. (2009). Asia's Institutional Creation and Evolution. *Asian Perspective, 33*(3), 151-182.

Lal, D. (2004). *IN PRAISE OF EMPIRES: Globalization and Order* (1st ed.). New York: Palgrave Macmillan.

Lee, K. Y. (2000). *From Third World to First: The Singapore Story: 1965-2000* (First ed.). New York: HarperCollins Publishers.

Limaye, S. P. (2007). United States-ASEAN Relations on ASEAN's Fortieth Anniversary: A Glass Half Full. *Contemporary Southeast Asia, 29*(3), 447-464.

MacFarlane, S. N., & Khong, Y. F. (2006). *Human Security and the UN: A Critical History* (1st Edition ed.). Indianapolis: Indiana University Press.

Means, G. P. (2009). *Political Islam in Southeast Asia* (Paperback ed.). London: Lynne Rienner Publishers.

Merry, S. E. (2006). *Human Rights & Gender Violence: Translating International Law into Local Justice.* Chicago: The University of Chicago Press.

Millard, M. (2004). *Jihad in Paradise: Islam and Politics in Southeast Asia.* Armonk: East Gate Books.

Mulder, N. (1996). *Inside Southeast Asia: Religion, Everyday Life, and Cultural Change.* Chiang Mai: Silkworm Books.

Nair, D. (2008). Regionalism in the Asia Pacific/East Asia: A Frustrated Regionalism? *Contemporary Southeast Asia, 31*(1), 110–142.

Narine, S. (1997). ASEAN and the ARF: The Limits of the "ASEAN Way". *Asian Survey, 37*(10), 961-978.

Narine, S. (1998). ASEAN and the Management of Regional Security. *Pacific Affairs, 71*(2), 195-214.

Neher, C. D. (2002). *Southeast Asia in the New International Era*. Boulder: Westview Press.

Omelicheva, M. Y. (2009). Global Civil Society and Democratization of World Politics: A Bona Fide Relationship or Illusory Liaison? *International Studies Perspectives, 11*(1), 109-132.

Peng-Er, L. (2006). Japan's Human Security Role in Southeast Asia. *Contemporary Southeast Asia, 28*(1), 141-159.

Pieterse, J. N. (2007). *Ethnicities and Global Multiculture: Pants for an Octopus* (Hardcover ed.). Plymouth: Rowman & LIttlefield Publishers, Inc.

Pitsuwan, S. (2010). ASEAN central to the region's future. *East Asia Forum Quarterly, 2*(2), 4-5.

Reinalda, B. (2009). *Routledge History of International Organizations: From 1815 to the present day*. New York: Routledge.

Rolfe, J. (2008). Regional Security for the Asia-Pacific: Ends and Means. *Contemporary Southeast Asia, 30*(1), 99-117.

Sakamoto, T. F. C. T. (2008). *Japan Since 1980*. New York: Cambridge University Press.

Sen, A. (1999). *Development as Freedom*. New York: Anchor Books.

Severino, R. C. (2007). ASEAN Beyond Forty: Towards Political and Economic Integration. *Contemporary Southeast Asia, 23*(3), 406-423.

Sharman, J. C. (2008). Power and Discourse in Policy Diffusion: Anti-Money Laundering in Developing States. *International Studies Quarterly, 52*(3), 635-656.

Simon, S. (2008). ASEAN and Multilateralism: The Long, Bumpy Road to Community. *Contemporary Southeast Asia, 30*(2), 264-292.

Skidelsky, R. (2010). *Keynes: The Return of the Master* (Paperback ed.). New York: PublicAffairs.

Syukri, I. (1985). *History of the Malay Kingdom of Patani* (C. Bailey & J. N. Miksic, Trans.). Athens: Ohio University.

Than, M., & Thein, M. (2007). Transitional Economy of Myanmar: Present Status, Developmental Divide and Future Prospects. *ASEAN Economic Bulletin, 24*(1), 98-118.

Thawnghmung, A. M. (2009). Responding to Strategies and Programmes of Myanmar's Military Regime: An Economic Viewpoint. *Southeast Asian Affairs, 2008*, 274-290.

Thayer, C. A. (2009). Cambodia: The Cambodian People's Party Consolidates Power. *Southeast Asian Affairs, 2009*, 85-101.

Thayer, C. A. (2010). US Rapprochement with Laos and Cambodia. *Contemporary Southeast Asia, 32*(3), 442-459.

Togo, K. (2005). *Japan's Foreign Policy 1945-2003: The Quest for a Proactive Policy* (Second Edition ed.). Leiden: Brill.

Tow, W. T., Thakur, R., & Hyun, I.-T. (Eds.). (2000). *Asia's emerging regional order: Reconciling traditional and human security*. Tokyo: United Nations University Press.

Trinidad, D. D. (2010). Domestic Actors, Market Reform and Regional Integration in Southeast Asia. *Asia Pacific World, 1*(1), 95-115.

Ungpakorn, G. J. (2007). *A Coup for the Rich: Thailand's Political Crisis*. Bangkok: Workers Democracy Publishing.

Vu-Tung, N. (2007). Vietnam's Membership of ASEAN: A Constructivist Interpretation. *Contemporary Southeast Asia, 29*(3), 483-505.

WTO. (2007). Viet Nam joins WTO with Director-General's Tribute for true grit. Retrieved Jan 07, 2011, from http://www.wto.org/english/news_e/news07_e/acc_vietnam_11jan07_e.htm

Wyatt, D. K. (2003). *Thailand: A Short History* (Thailand ed.). Chiang Mai: Silkworm Books.

Yegar, M. (2002). *Between Integration and Secession: The Muslim Communities of the Southern Philippines, Southern Thailand, and Western Burma/Myanmar*. New York: Lexington Books.

Yzawa, T. (2006). The Evolution of Preventive Diplomacy in the ASEAN Regional Forum: Problems and Prospects. *Asian Survey, 46*(5), 785-804.

13

For Further Research: Applying Structural Dynamics to other Governmental and Non-governmental Organizations

---

This final chapter explores some possible topics for further research. The study of structure in intergovernmental organizations combined with supporting theories and methods from other paradigms such as constructivism can serve as a good starting point to conduct research dealing with regional organizations such as ASEAN. Overemphasizing the role of structure should be avoided while at the same time ignoring the important role played by it is also pivotal in order to achieve a holistic understanding of the complex nature of regional IGOs. The present study used a vast array of data gathering techniques which included both qualitative and quantitative research methods. Moreover, content analysis which is usually associated with constructivism was used to support the conclusions reached by structural dynamics. A mixed methods approach which takes into consideration both the structural as well as the agency of the principal stakeholders can provide useful insights into the holistic nature of other regional intergovernmental and non-governmental organizations.

Introduction

This chapter deals with the research process leading to the present volume as well as some of the possible topics for further research that were identified during the process. The idea for writing the present volume came about from a complex process of exploration of the broad field of Southeast

Asian Studies as well as through a personal journey of discovery. A mixed methods approach was chosen to study the Southeast Asian region. Rather than simply conducting a descriptive study of the region, an enhanced case study based on structural dynamics was chosen as the theoretical framework for the volume. The present volume is an enhanced case study in that the goal is to understand the Southeast Asian region in a holistic way but through the lens of structural dynamics. By providing a clear theoretical framework the study serves two purposes. Firstly the case study supports the explanatory power of structural dynamics for the study of intergovernmental organizations and it serves as an interpretative framework to guide the reader through a complex web of socio-political and economic phenomena taking place in a very diverse region of the world. A broad understanding of the region in the tradition of what Max Webber calls "verstehen" is the goal of the present volume (Ritzer, 2008; Willis, 2007). Thus there was a need to a strike a balance between explanatory power through analysis and testing of the hypothesis implied by structural dynamics and the broader need to provide enough contextual information for the reader to grasp the way in which the many policy areas function in Southeast Asia. This explains the alternation of analytical chapters with descriptive ones. The following sections of this chapter explain how the present study was conducted and suggest some topics for further research.

The Research Process

The interest that sparked the idea to write to volume started more than eight years ago in a Muay Thai gym located in the peaceful Central American nation of Costa Rica. More specifically the link between that gym and the present volume is a pair of boxing shorts. The author's interest in martial arts took him from practicing Karate, to Ninjutsu, and finally to Muay Thai also known as Thai boxing. Muay Thai was relatively unknown in Central America at the time in comparison to other martial arts from East Asia. As the author started training in that martial art he realized that he knew very little about its country of origin. About a year or so after he started training he went Japan to finish his undergraduate studies where he continued to practice Muay Thai in its international variety, kickboxing. While in Japan he came in contact with a large community of Thai students as well as students from other Southeast Asian countries. Interaction with the Thai community led to a growing interest in the region which complemented his concentration in Asia Pacific Studies. After completing his undergraduate studies he decided that he wanted to continue his graduate studies in Thailand. The author was lucky to get accepted to the highly selective faculty of political science at Chulalongkorn University, Thailand's most prestigious University. Even though his Master's of Arts was in International Development Studies and his thesis actually dealt with Japanese official development assistance, he had the opportunity to travel widely in Southeast Asia. Observations from those trips as well as more limited research projects conducted while the author was residing in Thailand suggested interesting possibilities for research. Nevertheless the idea to write a volume about Southeast Asia lay dormant for a few years while the author devoted his energies to more specific research projects conducted during the early stages of his doctoral studies in the United States.

Remember the boxing shorts? Years later the author found out that those shorts were manufactured by a firm with its headquarters one block away from the house where he was staying in Thailand. Somehow the shorts had travelled from Thailand, to the United States, to Costa Rica, then to Japan, and then back full circle to their origin. Those shorts sparked the author's imagination regarding trade in the Asia Pacific and also about the numerous potential opportunities presented by Southeast Asia's dynamic economy and unique blend of cultural elements. Explaining the importance of a pair of boxing shorts manufactured in Thailand requires more than simply explaining the way in which they were manufactured. Thus even the most detailed description of the salient characteristics of the garment reduces an important symbol to its material incarnation. The shorts are part of a much greater system which includes the cultural factors blending a traditional martial art and sportswear designed in the West. Trade is also present in the way a product of a small family owned enterprise made its way to Los Angeles and was then imported to Costa Rica by a Costa Rican American who had trained in a Thai owned Muay Thai Gym in California. If we trace the origin of the shorts to its origins there are even more interesting question we may pose. How did a Chinese family end up producing equipment for a sport traditionally dominated by ethnic Thais? Under what socio-political conditions did the company operate during its early years and how did they change over time? Those are just some of the many questions that may be posed in relation to the pair of shorts. The important conclusion that the author reached from thinking about the meaning of those boxing shorts is that in order to understand a part of a system you have to look at the entire system first. This volume reflects the previous realization in that the entire system is the case study and the relationship between its parts is discussed in relation to how they affect the whole.

An Enhanced Case Study

The use of case studies in the field of international studies is not new (Chilberg, 1995; Creswell, 2007; Quesada, 1998). Case studies are known to have the advantage of providing context and detail about a particular setting, time period, or region (Stake, 1995). Most traditional research using the case study approach tends of avoid adopting an overarching framework and rather tends to rely on an inductive approach (Druckman, 2005; Stake, 1995). This has the advantage of allowing the researcher to include a vast array of details and allows "thick description". On the other hand case studies without an overarching theoretical framework tend to be disconnected from the rest of the literature in that their conclusions are valid only for that particular case (Druckman, 2005). As was discussed in the introduction to this chapter, one of the goals of writing the present volume was to achieve a holistic understanding of Southeast Asia's conflict and development. Due to the broad nature of the concepts of conflict and development it was necessary to provide some structure to the study in order to concentrate on those issues that have the greatest impact on the actual functioning of the region. ASEAN was chosen as the starting point due to its broad mandate and inclusive membership. The next step was then to understand how the different policy areas under ASEAN's mandate function. It was thus necessary to study the connection between the organization and its operating environment. Agency was also introduced by narrowing down on individual member states and their possible interests and needs. The outcome of this combination of level of analysis was what Druckman calls an "enhanced case study" (Druckman, 2005). What this means is that ASEAN is the case study and provides the topic for the research project while the case study is enhanced in that there is an overarching theoretical framework that guides the entire research project. In the case of the present study the overarching theoretical framework was provided by structural dynamics. While structural dynamics is not the only holistic theory explaining organizational behavior it has the advantage of its simplicity and explanatory traction (Fritz, 1996). Other holistic theories such as human security tend to be more ambiguous and less reliant on the role of structure (Battersby & Siracusa, 2009; Bhattacharjee, 2007; Kim, Fidler, & Ganguly, 2009; King & Murray, 2001; MacFarlane & Khong, 2006). Therefore, structural dynamics was applied to the case study, in this case ASEAN broadly conceived, in order to provide a birds-eye view of the region while at the same time indentifying underlying trends and allowing for a certain degree of explanation regarding causation. Dealing with conflict and development is a policy oriented endeavor and therefore a theory that can be easily operationalized is very useful.

Another advantage of following the enhanced case study approach is that it has a tradition of using mixed methods of data gathering and analysis (Druckman, 2005). This study used a vast array of data ranging from quantitative indicators to newspaper articles. By gathering data from different kinds of sources it is possible to use triangulation in order to support the validity of certain conclusions and about the quality of the data itself (Deegan, 2007; Willis, 2007). Thus conclusions reached through a basic statistical analysis of economic indicators can be supported by data gathered from secondary sources such as academic articles and articles in trade magazines. In addition to that, having different sets of data dealing with the same issues adds context to the issues and compensates the weakness of certain types of sources. It can be argued that this study even includes participant observation since the author visited almost every single member of ASEAN over a period of several years. Those observations have strengthened certain conclusions and added important details to others.

Reflexivity

Recent trends in progressive fields such as gender studies and international development studies have encouraged the practice of reflexivity by researchers (Ackerly & True, 2008; Lynch, 2008). This involves many factors including but not limited to positioning the author in networks of power, trying to understand the effect of the research on both the researcher and on those who participated in the research, and finally the possible impact of the research on the system as a whole (Doucet & Mauthner, 2008; Edwards & Mauthner, 2008). Some of those factors apply to this project and others do not. The first factor is of particular importance in any study that involves interpretation. Researchers have certain biases, preferences, values, and are part of a vast array of networks including epistemic ones that may influence the way they carry out a particular research project (Gillies & Alldred, 2008). This is no exception to the previous assertion in that the research project was influenced by the author's personal experiences, educational background, and position as a member of transnational networks. The author's international educational background in Spain, Thailand, Japan, USA, Costa Rica, and Thailand certainly influenced his views about the value of cross-cultural communication and the value of syncretism. At the same time the author's position as part of a transnational elite may have facilitated his understanding of certain regional processes while making it more challenging to understand local needs and interests. Finally his identity as an outsider with considerable connections to the region was an advantage in terms of allowing a certain degree of objectivity during the research project while at the same time requiring more effort in order to understand other socio-cultural issues. A factor of particular importance was the author's position as a national of a developing country with experience in both the developing and the developed worlds. This aspect of the author's background influenced his views about the development potential of South to South trade and of the role of education in moving from the periphery to the core of the international system. Reflexivity was practiced during the project in that those possible biases and influences were questioned and countervailing positions were considered in order to provide a more balanced view.

In terms of the effects of the present research project on the region, the goal is for it to increase awareness about the dynamism and potential for growth and development of Southeast Asia not only in the Global North but also in developing countries looking for trading partners and development models to reach their own potentials. Therefore the needs and interests of several target audiences were kept in mind during the research project. Scholars looking for a fresh way to understand the Association of Southeast Asian Nations (ASEAN), advanced undergraduate and graduate students in the social sciences, regional and extra-regional policy makers attempting to learn from the challenges and opportunities faced by ASEAN, and transnational professionals who want to understand a region that is becoming increasingly important.

For Further Research

As with most research projects the present one raised more questions than the ones it answered. Due to the level of analysis of the study as well as due to the broad nature of the case study many interesting issues went unexplored. Each policy area could be analyzed in greater depth using structural dynamics. Moreover, there are countless structural conflicts within each one of the structural conflicts that were identified in the present volume. Future research may involve exploring the structure within each one of the core structural conflicts that were identified in the previous three sections of this volume. A map could be prepared for a structural conflict following the different layers of organizational structure. Thus a core structural conflict that takes place mostly at the strategic level could be then broken down into the structural conflicts taking place at the managerial level, and so on.

One area that could be explored in much more detail using structural dynamics is the role of civil society in ASEAN. The role of non-governmental organizations and social movements is becoming more important in the region and the way they interact with each other and with regional governments will play an important role in the region's development and conflict. This topic could be studied with a similar approach to the one used in the present study. Structural dynamics can allow the researcher to focus on the structural aspects of the relationship between civil society and regional governments. More specific studies could narrow in on particular non-governmental organizations and social movements and on how they operate in Southeast Asia's dynamic socio-political environment. Outside of the region similar studies could be undertaken for other regional organizations such as the Organization of American States and the African Union. A similar methodology and theoretical framework could be used resulting in case studies that could be used as qualitative data for further comparative research. This is the advantage of enhanced case studies, that as a group they add support or weaken an existing theory. In this case further studies using structural dynamics would be comparable and could be used for secondary analysis of both qualitative and quantitative data.

Conclusions

The present study has shown that it is possible to apply structural dynamics to the study of intergovernmental organizations. In addition to that the complexity and dynamism of the Southeast Asian region was explored through an overview of its political, economic, and cultural development and conflict. Southeast Asia is a region rich in tradition but at the same time that tradition is constantly reinvented to fit the needs of a changing regional and global environment. The future for the region is full of challenges but opportunities are also present for the construction of a sustainable future. Southeast Asian countries have shown that they can cooperate and that they can accomplish more together than individually. ASEAN itself is an example of what regional governments can accomplish together. As an intergovernmental organization, ASEAN has shown that it can adapt to changing geopolitical trends and that it can influence wider processes in the Asia Pacific region. ASEAN will continue to exert considerable influence on regional integration and will be central to the region's future development and conflict.

References

Ackerly, B., & True, J. (2008). Reflexivity in Practice: Power and Ethics in Feminist Research on International Relations. *International Studies Review, 10*(4), 693-707.

Battersby, P., & Siracusa, J. M. (2009). *Globalization & Human Security* (Hardcover ed.). Lanham: Rowman & Littlefield Publishers, Inc.

Bhattacharjee, D. (2007). Challenges to the Concept of Human Security. *The Journal of Political Studies, 1.*

Chilberg, J. C. (1995). The Interaction Method: A Case Study in Using Group Facilitation Rules and Roles. In L. R. Frey (Ed.), *Innovations in Group Facilitation: Applications in Natural Settings* (pp. 53-74). New Jersey: Hampton Press, Inc.

Creswell, J. W. (2007). *Qualitative Inquiry & Research Design: Choosing Among Five Approaches* (Second ed.). London: SAGE Publications.

Deegan, M. J. (2007). The Chicago School of Ethnography. In P. Atkinson, A. Coffey, S. Delamont, J. Lofland & L. Lofland (Eds.), *Handbook of Ethnography* (Paperback ed., pp. 11-25). London: Sage Publications.

Doucet, A., & Mauthner, N. (2008). Knowing Responsibly: Linking Ethics, Research Practice and Epistemology. In M. Mauthner, M. Birch, J. Jessop & T. Miller (Eds.), *Ethics in Qualitative Research* (pp. 123-145). London: Sage.

Druckman, D. (2005). *Doing Research: Methods of Inquiry for Conflict Analysis*. Thousand Oaks: SAGE Publications.

Edwards, R., & Mauthner, M. (2008). Ethics and Feminist Research: Theory and Practice. In M. Mauthner, M. Birch, J. Jessop & T. Miller (Eds.), *Ethics in Qualitative Research* (pp. 14-31). London: Sage Publications.

Fritz, R. (1996). *Corporate Tides: The Inescapable Laws of Organizational Structure* San Francisco: Berrett-Koehler Publishers

Gillies, V., & Alldred, P. (2008). The Ethics of Intention: Research as a Political Tool. In M. Mauthner, M. Birch, J. Jessop & T. Miller (Eds.), *Ethics in Qualitative Research* (pp. 32-52). London: Sage.

Kim, S. W., Fidler, D. P., & Ganguly, S. (2009). Eastphalia Rising? Asian Influence and the Fate of Human Security. *World Policy Journal, 26*(2), 53-64.

King, G., & Murray, C. J. L. (2001). Rethinking human security. *Political Science Quarterly, 116*(4), 585-610.

Lynch, C. (2008). Reflexivity in Research on Civil Society: Constructivist Perspectives. *International Studies Review, 10*(4), 708-721.

MacFarlane, S. N., & Khong, Y. F. (2006). *Human Security and the UN: A Critical History* (1st Edition ed.). Indianapolis: Indiana University Press.

Quesada, J. (1998). Suffering Child: An Embodiment of War and Its Aftermath in Post-Sandinista Nicaragua. *Medical Anthropology Quarterly, 12*(1), 51-73.

Ritzer, G. (2008). *Sociological Theory*. New York: McGraw Hill Higher Education.

Stake, R. E. (1995). *The Art of Case Study Research*. Thousand Oaks: SAGE Publications.

Willis, J. W. (2007). *Foundations of Qualitative Research: Interpretive and Critical Approaches*. London: SAGE Publications.

Bibliography

Bibliography

Ackerly, B., & True, J. (2008). Reflexivity in Practice: Power and Ethics in Feminist Research on International Relations. *International Studies Review, 10*(4), 693-707.

Ajis, M. N. e., Saludin, M. N., Ismail, A., von Feigenblatt, Otto F., Shuib, M. S., & Keling, M. F. (2010). Managing Foreign Workers in Southeast Asian Countries. *Journal of Asia Pacific Studies, 1*(3), 481-505.

Akaha, T. (2009). Human Security in East Asia. *Journal of Human Security, 5*(3), 11-34.

Albritton, R. B., & Bureekul, T. (2004). Developing Electoral Democracy in Developing Nations: Thailand [Electronic Version]. *A Comparative Survey of Democracy, Governance and Development, Working Paper Series*, 1-33. Retrieved September 20, 2009, from http://www.asianbarometer.org/newenglish/publications/workingpapers/no.17.pdf.

Albritton, R. B., & Bureekul, T. (2007). Thailand Country Report: Public Opinion and Political Power in Thailand [Electronic Version]. *A Comparative Survey of Democracy, Governance and Development, Working Paper Series*, 1-38. Retrieved September 20, 2009, from http://www.asianbarometer.org/newenglish/publications/workingpapers/no.34.pdf.

Alldred, P., & Gillies, V. (2008). Eliciting Research Accounts: Re/Producing Modern Subjects? In M. Mauthner, M. Birch, J. Jessop & T. Miller (Eds.), *Ethics in Qualitative Research* (pp. 146-165). London Sage.

Andriesse, E., & Westen, G. v. (2008). Varieties of embedded mercantilism and regional development in the Thailand-Malaysia Borderlands. *Journal of Development Alternatives and Area Studies, 27*(3/4), 165-187.

Arnold, D. (2006). Free Trade Agreements and Southeast Asia. *Journal of Contemporary Asia, 36*(2), 195-207.

ASEAN. (2008a). *2007-2008 Annual Report: One Vision, One Identity, One Community*. Retrieved November 30, 2008. from http://www.aseansec.org/AR-08.pdf.

ASEAN. (2008b). *ASEAN Charter*. Retrieved November 30, 2008. from http://www.aseansec.org/ASEAN-Charter.pdf.

ASEAN. (2008c). *ASEAN ECONOMIC COMMUNITY BLUEPRINT*. Retrieved. from http://www.aseansec.org/5187-10.pdf.

ASEAN. (2009a). *ASEAN POLITICAL-SECURITY COMMUNITY BLUEPRINT*. Retrieved July 28, 2010. from http://www.aseansec.org/5187-18.pdf.

ASEAN. (2009b). *ASEAN SOCIO-CULTURAL COMMUNITY BLUEPRINT*. Retrieved August 11, 2010. from http://www.aseansec.org/5187-19.pdf.

ASEAN. (2010). Intra- and extra-ASEA trade as of 15 July 2010. In T. 18 (Ed.). Jakarta: ASEAN.

Askew, M. (2010). Fighting with Ghosts: Querying Thailand's "Southern Fire". *Contemporary Southeast Asia, 32*(2), 117-156.

Atkinson, P., Coffey, A., Delamont, S., Lofland, J., & Lofland, L. (Eds.). (2007). *Handbook of Ethnography* (Paperback ed.). London: SAGE Publications.

Bailey, F. G. (1992). Tertius Luctans: Idiocosm, Caricature, and Mask. In D. M. K. a. J. M. Bartunel (Ed.), *Hidden Conflict in Organizations: Uncovering Behind-the-Scenes Disputes* (pp. 31-83). London: Sage.

Baird, I. G. (2010). Different views of history: Shades of irredentism along the Laos-Cambodia border. *Journal of Southeast Asian Studies, 41*(2), 187-213.

Banyai, C. L. (2010). Community Capacity Building and Local Policy: An Example from Pagudpud, the Philippines. *Asia Pacific World, 1*(2), 83-108.

Bayulgen, O. (2008). Muhammad Yunus, Grameen Bank and the Nobel Peace Prize: What Political Science Can Contribute to and Learn From the Study of Microcredit. *International Studies Review, 10*(3), 525-547.

Bhaskaran, M. (2010). Review of Southeast Asian Economic Developments. *Southeast Asian Affairs*, 23-44.

Bhattacharyay, B. N. (2010). Infrastructure for ASEAN Connectivity and Integration. *ASEAN Economic Bulletin, 27*(2), 200-221.

Birch, M., & Miller, T. (2008). Encouraging Participation: Ethics and Responsibilities. In M. Mauthner, M. Birch, J. Jessop & T. Miller (Eds.), *Ethics in Qualitative Research* (pp. 91-106). London: Sage

Bitzinger, R. A. (2010). A New Arms Race? Explaining Recent Southeast Asian Military Acquisitions. *Contemporary Southeast Asia, 32*(1), 50-69.

Bowen, J. R. (2005). Consensus and Suspicion: Judicial Reasoning and Social Change in an Indonesian Society 1960-1994. In S. F. Moore (Ed.), *Law and Anthropology: A Reader* (pp. 154-173). Oxford: Blackwell Publishing.

Callahan, W. A. (2005). The Discourse of Vote Buying and Political Reform in Thailand. *Pacific Affairs, 78*(1), 95-113.

Callahan, W. A. (2008). Chinese Visions of World Order: Post-hegemonic or a New Hegemony? *International Studies Review, 10*(4), 749-761.

Chachavalpongpun, P. (2009). Diplomacy under Siege: Thailand's Political Crisis and the Impact on Foreign Policy. *Contemporary Southeast Asia, 31*(3), 447-467.

Chambliss, W. J. (1973). Bureaucracy. In W. J. Chambliss (Ed.), *Sociological Readings in the Conflict Perspective* (pp. 327-336): Addison-Wesley.

Chang, Y.-t., Chu, Y.-h., & Park, C.-M. (2007). Authoritarian Nostalgia in Asia. *Journal of Democracy, 18*(3), 71-80.

Cheng, J.-Y.-S. (2006). Latin America in China's Contemporary Foreign Policy. *Journal of Contemporary Asia, 36*(4), 500-528.

Chottmann, S. (2006). Melayu Islam Beraja: The Politics of Legitimisation in a Malay Islamic Monarchy. *Review of Indonesian and Malaysian Affairs 40*(2), 111-139.

Chye, T. S. (2008). Rivalry for Political Change in Thailand [Electronic Version]. Retrieved February 25, 2009, from http://www.humansecuritygateway.info/documents/RSIS_Thailand_RivalryForPoliticalChange.pdf

CIA. (2009a). The World Factbook: Singapore. Retrieved October 12, 2010, from https://www.cia.gov/library/publications/the-world-factbook/geos/sn.html

CIA. (2009b). The World Factbook: Thailand. Retrieved October 14, 2010, from https://www.cia.gov/library/publications/the-world-factbook/geos/th.html

CIA. (2010a). The World Fact Book: Burma. Retrieved November 5, 2010, from https://www.cia.gov/library/publications/the-world-factbook/geos/bm.html

CIA. (2010b). The World Fact Book: Laos People's Republic Retrieved November 9, 2010, from https://www.cia.gov/library/publications/the-world-factbook/geos/la.html.

CIA. (2010c). The World Factbook: Brunei. Retrieved October 27, 2010, from https://www.cia.gov/library/publications/the-world-factbook/geos/bx.html

CIA. (2010d). World Factbook: Cambodia. Retrieved November 29, 2010, from https://www.cia.gov/library/publications/the-world-factbook/geos/cb.html

CIA. (2010e). The World Factbook: Indonesia. Retrieved September 16, 2010, from https://www.cia.gov/library/publications/the-world-factbook/geos/id.html.

CIA. (2010f). The World Factbook: Socialist Republic of Vietnam. Retrieved November 13, 2010, from https://www.cia.gov/library/publications/the-world-factbook/geos/vm.html.

CIA. (2010g). The World Factbook: The Philippines. Retrieved October 8, 2010, from https://www.cia.gov/library/publications/the-world-factbook/geos/rp.html.

Cloke, K. (1991). Conflict Resolution Systems Design, the United Nations, and the New World Order. *Conflict Resolution Quarterly, 19*(4), 215-236.

Cock, A. R. (2010). External Actors and the Relative Autonomy of the Ruling Elite in post-UNTAC Cambodia. *Journal of Southeast Asian Studies, 41*(2), 241-265.

Collins, A. (2008). A People-Oriented ASEAN: A Door Ajar or Closed for Civil Society Organizations? *Contemporary Southeast Asia, 30*(2), 313-332.

CSCAP. (2008). About Us. Retrieved July 29, 2010, from http://www.cscap.org/index.php?page=about-us

Cuasay, P. (1998). Borders on the Fantastic: Mimesis, Violence, and Landscape at the Temple of Preah Vihear. *Modern Asian Studies, 32*(4), 849-890.

Dalpino, C. (2011). Thailand in 2010; Rupture and Attempts at Reconciliation. *Asian Survey, 51*(1), 155 - 163.

Diamond, C. (2006). Mae Naak and Company: The Shifting Duality in Female Representation on the Contemporary Thai Stage. *Asian Theatre Journal, 23*(1), 111-148.

Dore, R. (1997). *Japan, Internationalism and the UN* (2nd ed.). London: Routledge.

DRESSEL, B. (2009). Thailand's Elusive Quest for a Workable Constitution, 1997-2007. *Contemporary Southeast Asia, 31*(2), 296-325.

Drysdale, P. (2010). APEC's Achievements and Challenges Today: Keynote Address, APEC Economic Committee Roundtable, Beppu, Oita, Japan, 7 August 2010. *Asia Pacific World, 1*(2), 33-44.

Eades, J. S., & Cooper, M. J. M. (2010). Introduction. The Asia Pacific World: A Summary and an Agenda. *Asa Pacific World, 1*(1), 1--22.

Emmers, R. (2001). The Influence of the Balance of Power Factor within the ASEAN Regional Forum. *Contemporary Southeast Asia, 23*(2), 275-291.

Falco, M. (2003). Burma: Time for Change [Electronic Version]. Retrieved February 16, 2009, from http://www.humansecuritygateway.info/documents/CFR_TimeForChange_Burma.pdf.

Falise, T. (2010). On the Run: In Burma's Jungle Hell. *World Policy Journal, 27*(1), 57-64.

von Feigenblatt, Otto F. (2009a). ASEAN and Human Security: Challenges and Opportunities. *Ritsumeikan Center for Asia Pacific Studies Working Paper, No. 09-5*(July), 1-22.

von Feigenblatt, Otto F. (2009b). Comparing the 2006 Military Coup in Thailand and the 2009 Coup in Honduras: Internal Socio-political Similarities and External Normative Differences. *Infinity Journal, 1*(4), 3-9.

von Feigenblatt, Otto F. (2009c). Divergent Interpretations of the Conflict in the Southern Provinces of Thailand: National-Liberation or Pan-Islamic Jihad? *Journal of Contemporary Literature, 1*(2), 112-118.

von Feigenblatt, Otto F. (2009d). Hero vs. The Dragon Emperor: Discursive Struggle over China's Place in the World. *Journal of Alternative Perspectives in the Social Sciences, 1*(2), 483-489.

von Feigenblatt, Otto F. (2009e). Human Security and the Responsibility to Protect: A Holistic Approach to Dealing with Violent Conflict in Southeast Asia. In A. K. Pandey, S. Verma, R. P. Pathak, B. Paranjape, N. K. Mishra, Gangatharan, D. Pande & B. K. Choudhary (Eds.), *Repositioning 'Subalternity' in*

Globalized India: The Dynamics of Social Inclusion (pp. 130). Delhi: Macmillan.

von Feigenblatt, Otto F. (2009f). The Importance of Culture in *Emic* Interpretations of the History of Thailand's Southern Separatist Movement: The "Gentlemen's Agreement" of 1943 and the Relationship of Malaysia with the Separatists. *Ritsumeikan Center for Asia Pacific Studies Working Paper, No. 09-7*(October), 1-11.

von Feigenblatt, Otto F. (2009g). Some lessons from the White Rajahs of Sarawak: Identifying and strengthening local capacities for peace in the deep South of Thailand. *Journal of Law and Conflict Resolution, 1*(6), 117-121.

von Feigenblatt, Otto F. (2009h). The Thai Ethnocracy Unravels: A Critical Cultural Analysis of Thailand's Socio-Political Unrest. *Journal of Alternative Perspectives in the Social Sciences, 1*(3), 583-611.

von Feigenblatt, Otto F. (2010a). A Brief Analysis of Popular Aesthetics in Thailand: Subjective Culture vs. Objective Culture. *Journal of Social Sciences, 22*(1), 61-63.

von Feigenblatt, Otto F. (2010b). *Human Security in the Asia Pacific Region: Security Challenges, Regional Integration, and Representative Case Studies* (Hardcover ed.). Jaipur: YKING BOOKS.

von Feigenblatt, Otto F. (2010c). The Importance of Culture in Emic Interpretations of the History of Thailand's Southern Separatist Movement: The "Gentlemen's Agreement" of 1943 and the Malaysian Relationship with the Separatists. *Journal of Alternative Perspectives in the Social Sciences, 2*(1), 46-56.

von Feigenblatt, Otto F. (2010d). Resisting Universalistic Feminist and Queer Hegemonic Discourses: An Emic Model of Thai Gender and Sexuality. *Ritsumeikan Center for Asia Pacific Studies Working Paper, No. 10-1*(July), 1-19.

von Feigenblatt, Otto F. (2010e, April 09, 2010). Thailand's Struggle over Legitimacy. *UPI Asia.com,* pp. 1-3. Retrieved April 9, 2010, from http://www.upiasia.com/Politics/2010/04/09/thailands_struggle_over_legitimacy/2024.

von Feigenblatt, Otto F. (2010f, May 27, 2010). UNCERTAINTY AND FEAR IN THAILAND. *Insight on Conflict.* Retrieved May 27, 2010, from

http://www.insightonconflict.org/conflicts/thailand/stories/uncertainty-fear-thailand.

von Feigenblatt, Otto F. (2010). The Malay Minority in Southern Thailand: A "Small People" Facing Existential Uncertainty. *Ritsumeikan Journal of Asia Pacific Studies, 27*(February), 53-63.

von Feigenblatt, Otto F. , Suttichujit, V., Shuib, M. S., Keling, M. F., & Ajis, M. N. e. (2010). Weapons of Mass Assimilation: A Critical Analysis of the Use of Education in Thailand. *Journal of Asia Pacific Studies, 1*(2), 292-311.

Ferguson, D. S. (2010). "Splendid allies" or "Nor more deadly enemies in the world?", General Sir Ian Hamilton, the British Military and Japan 1902-1914. *Journal of the Royal Asiatic Society, 20*(4), 523-536.

Ford, N. J., & Kittisuksathit, S. (1994). Destinations unknown: the gender construction and changing nature of the sexual expressions of Thai youth. *AIDS Care, 6*(5), 517-532.

Funston, J. (2010). Malaysia and Thailand's Southern Conflict: Reconciling Security and Ethnicity. *Contemporary Southeast Asia, 32*(2), 234-258.

Gallis, A. (2009). Symposium: International Commercial Arbitration: Fifty Years after New York Convention: UNESCO Documents and Procedure: The Need to Account for Political Conflict When Designating World Heritage Sites. *Georgia Journal of International and Comparative Law, 38*(Spring), 1-27.

Glassman, J. (2005). The "War On Terrorism" Comes To Southeast Asia. *Journal of Contemporary Asia, 35*(1), 3-28.

Gottesman, E. (2003). *CAMBODIA After the Khmer Rouge: Inside the Politics of Nation Building*. New Haven: Yale University Press.

Gunaratna, R., & Acharya, A. (2006). Thailand. In D. S. Reveron & J. S. Murer (Eds.), *Flashpoints in the war on terrorism* (pp. 137-156). New York: Routledge.

Hamlin, T. (2009). Bangkok's 2008 Stumble: Time for Reform [Electronic Version]. Retrieved Feb 15, 2009, from http://www.stimson.org/pub.cfm?ID=744.

Handley, P. M. (2006). *The King Never Smiles: A Biography of Thailand's Bhumibol Adulyadej*. New Haven Yale University Press.

Haritaworn, J. (2007). Beautiful beasts. Ambivalence and distinction in the gender identity negotiations of multiracialised women of Thai descent. *Women's Studies International Forum, 30*(5), 391-403.

Harris, I. (2010). Rethinking Cambodian Political Discourse on Territory: Genealogy of the Buddhist ritual boundary (sīmā). *Journal of Southeast Asian Studies, 41*(2), 215-239.

Hazen, J. M. (2008). Armed Violence in Asia and the Pacific: An Overview of the Causes, Costs and Consequences [Electronic Version]. *United Nations Development Program // Geneva Declaration on Armed Violence and Development.* Retrieved February 16, 2009, from http://www.humansecuritygateway.info/documents/UNDP_ArmedViolenceAsiaPacific_Overview.pdf.

Heidhues, M. S. (2000). *Southeast Asia: A Concise History*. London: Thames & Hudson.

Heller, D. (2005). The Relevance of the ASEAN Regional Forum (ARF) for Regional Security in the Asia-Pacific. *Contemporary Southeast Asia, 27*(1), 123-145.

Hew, D. (2008). The Malaysian Economy: Developments and Challenges. *Southeast Asian Affairs*, 207-222.

Hewinson, K. (2010). Rebellion, Repression and the Red Shirts. *East Asia Forum Quarterly, 2*(2), 14-17.

Hinton, A. (2006). Khmerness and the Thai 'Other': Violence, Discourse and Symbolism in the 2003 Anti-Thai Riots in Cambodia. *Journal of Southeast Asian Studies, 37*(3), 445-469.

Hook, G., Gilson, J., Hughes, C. W., & Dobson, H. (2005). *Japan's International Relations: Politics, economics and security* (2nd Edition ed.). London: Routledge.

Huntington, S. P. (2003). *The Clash of Civilizations and the Remaking of World Order* (Paperback Edition 2003 ed.). New York: Simon & Schuster Paperbacks.

Hwang, H.-d. (2006). APEC and emerging regionalism in North East Asia. *Asia Europe Journal, 4*(4), 499-510.

Ichihara, M. (2009). East Asia's Challenges to and Changes in the Peace Operations in East Timor. In S. Peou (Ed.), *Human Security in East Asia: Challenges for Collaborative Action* (pp. 94-107). New York: Routledge.

Ishii, Y. (1994). Thai Muslims and the Royal Patronage of Religion. *Law & Society Review, 28*(3), 453-460

Jackson, P. A. (1995). Thai Buddhist accounts of male homosexuality and AIDS in the 1980s. *The Australian Journal of Anthropology, 6*(3), 140-153.

Jackson, P. A. (1997). Thai Research on Male Homosexuality and Transgenderism and the Cultural Limits of Foucaultian Analysis. *Journal of the History of Sexuality, 8*(1), 52-85.

Jackson, P. A. (2003). Performative Genders, Perverse Desires: A Bio-History of Thailand's Same-Sex and Transgender Cultures. *Intersections*(9).

JICA. (2007). A Report from the Study Group on Assistance to the Southeast Asian Region
Regional Integration and Development Aid [Electronic Version]. *Institute for International Cooperation.* Retrieved December 17, 2008, from
http://www.jica.go.jp/english/publications/reports/study/country/souteastasia.html.

Jitpiromrisi, S., & McCargo, D. (2008). A Ministry for the South: New Governance Proposals for Thailand's Southern Region. *Contemporary Southeast Asia, 30*(3), 403-428.

John, R. B. S. (1994). Preah Vihear and the Cambodia-Thailand Borderland. *IBRU Boundary and Security Bulletin*(January), 64-68.

John, R. B. S. (2005). Democracy in Cambodia - One Decade, US$5 Billion Later: What Went Wrong? *Contemporary Southeast Asia, 27*(3), 406-428.

Joll, C. M. (2010). Religion and Conflict in Southern Thailand: Beyond Rounding Up the Usual Suspects. *Contemporary Southeast Asia, 32*(2), 258-280.

Jones, D. M., & Smith, M. L. R. (2007). Making Process, Not Progress ASEAN and the Evolving East Asian Regional Order. *International Security, 32*(1), 148-184.

Kamano, S., & Khor, D. (1996). Toward an understanding of cross-national differences in the naming of same-sex sexual/intimate relationships. *NWSA Journal, 8*(1), 124-132.

Katanyuu, R. (2006). Beyond Non-Interference in ASEAN: The Association's Role in Myanmar's National Reconciliation and Democratization. *Asian Survey, 46*(6), 825-845.

Keling, M. F., von Feigenblatt, Otto F. , Ajis, M. N. e., Shuib, M. S., & Nadzri, A. D. M. (2010). The Impact of East Asia's Nuclear

Energy Development Program on Southeast Asia Countries. *Journal of Politics and Law, 3*(2), 176- 183.

Keling, M. F., Saludin, M. N., Feigenblatt, O. F. v., Ajis, M. N. e., & Shuib, M. S. (2010). A Historical Approach to Myanmar's Democratic Process. *Journal of Asia Pacific Studies, 1*(2), 132-148.

Kershaw, R. (2001). *Monarchy in South-East Asia: The Faces of Tradition in Transition* (First ed.). London: Routledge.

Kershaw, R. (2003). Partners in Realism: Britain and Brunei Amid Recent Turbulence. *Asian Affairs (London), 34*(1), 46-53.

Kim, S. W., Fidler, D. P., & Ganguly, S. (2009). Eastphalia Rising? Asian Influence and the Fate of Human Security. *World Policy Journal, 26*(2), 53-64.

Kiong, T. C., & Bun, C. K. (Eds.). (2001). *Alternate Identities: The Chinese of Contemporary Thailand.* Singapore: Brill Times Academic Press.

Komori, Y. (2009). Asia's Institutional Creation and Evolution. *Asian Perspective, 33*(3), 151-182.

Kriesberg, L. (1997). The Development of the Conflict Resolution Field. In *Peacemaking, in International Conflict: Methods & Techniques* (pp. 51-77). Washington, D.C.: U.S. Institute of Pece Press.

Ku, S. C. Y. (2010). Brunei in 2009: Maturity in Doubt? *Asian Survey, 50*(1), 260-264.

Le-Coz, C. (2009). "His Untouchable Majesty" Thailand Censorship and Emprisonment: The Abuses in the Name of Lese Majeste [Electronic Version]. *Reporters Sans Frontiers*, 1-16. Retrieved September 20, from http://www.rsf.org/IMG/pdf/rapport_en_ok-2.pdf

Lee, K. Y. (2000). *From Third World to First: The Singapore Story: 1965-2000* (First ed.). New York: HarperCollins Publishers.

Lemert, C. (2004). *Social Theory: The Multicultural and Classic Readings*. Boulder: Westview Press.

Lim, A. C.-H. (2010). Breakfast with the Dictator: Memory, Atrocity, and Affect. *Theory & Event, 13*(4).

Limaye, S. P. (2007). United States-ASEAN Relations on ASEAN's Fortieth Anniversary: A Glass Half Full. *Contemporary Southeast Asia, 29*(3), 447-464.

Lin, H.-T. (2009). The Tributary System in China's Historical Imagination: China and Hunza, ca. 1760-1960. *Journal of the Royal Asiatic Society, 19*(4), 488-507.

Lintner, B. (2009). The Battle for Thailand: Can Democracy Survive? *Foreign Affairs, 88*(4), 108-118.

Liow, J. C. (2006a). International Jihad and Muslim Radicalism in Thailand? Toward an Alternative Interpretation. *Asia Policy*(2), 89–108.

Liow, J. C. (2006b). *Muslim Resistance in Southern Thailand and the Southern Philippines: Religion, Ideology, and Politics*. Washington, D.C.: East-West Center.

Lynch, C. (2008). Reflexivity in Research on Civil Society: Constructivist Perspectives. *International Studies Review, 10*(4), 708-721.

Macan-Markar, M. (2009). THAILAND: Lese Majeste Law Tests Mettle of Human Rights Groups [Electronic Version]. *Prachatai*. Retrieved September 23, from http://www.prachatai.com/english/node/1389.

Macdonald, S. (2007). British Social Anthropology. In P. Atkinson, A. Coffey, S. Delamont, J. Lofland & L. Lofland (Eds.), *Handbook of Ethnography* (Paperback ed., pp. 60-79). London: Sage Publications.

MacFarlane, S. N., & Khong, Y. F. (2006). *Human Security and the UN: A Critical History* (1st Edition ed.). Indianapolis: Indiana University Press.

Mandel, R. (1980). Roots of the Modern Interstate Border Dispute. *The Journal of Conflict Resolution, 24*(3), 427-454.

Manderson, L. (1992). Public Sex Performances in Patpong and Explorations of the Edges of Imagination. *The Journal of Sex Research, 29*(4), 451-475.

Mauthner, M., Birch, M., Jessop, J., & Miller, T. (Eds.). (2008). *Ethics in Qualitative Research*. London: Sage Publications.

McCargo, D. (2008). *Tearing Apart the Land: Islam and Legitimacy in Southern Thailand* (First ed.). Ithaca: Cornell University Press.

McCargo, D. (2009). The Politics of Buddhist identity in Thailand's deep south: The Demise of civil religion? *Journal of Southeast Asian Studies, 40*(1), 11-32.

Means, G. P. (2009). *Political Islam in Southeast Asia* (Paperback ed.). London: Lynne Rienner Publishers.

Millard, M. (2004). *Jihad in Paradise: Islam and Politics in Southeast Asia*. Armonk: East Gate Books.

Miller, J. (2009). Soft Power and State-Firm Diplomacy: Congress and IT Corporate Activity in China. *International Studies Perspectives, 10*(3), 285-302.

Montesano, M. J. (2009). Contextualizing the Pattaya Summit Debacle: Four April Days, Four Thai Pathologies1. *Contemporary Southeast Asia, 31*(2), 217-248.

Morgan, D. (2009). The Decline and Fall of the Mongol Empire. *Journal of the Royal Asiatic Society, 19*(4), 427-437.

Morris, R. C. (1997). Educating Desire: Thailand, Transnationalism, and Transgression. *Social Text, 52/53*(Autum - Winter), 53-79.

Morton, W. S., & Olenik, J. K. (2005). *Japan: Its History and Culture* (Fourth Edition ed.). New York: McGraw-Hill Inc.

Mulder, N. (1996). *Inside Southeast Asia: Religion, Everyday Life, and Cultural Change*. Chiang Mai: Silkworm Books.

Mulgan, A. G. (2008). Breaking the Mould: Japan's Subtle Shift from Exclusive Bilateralism to Modest Minilateralism. *Contemporary Southeast Asia, 30*(1), 52-72.

Murphy, C. (2009). Populism Erodes Thailand's Old Order. *Far Eastern Economic Review, 172*(5), 7-12.

Nair, D. (2008). Regionalism in the Asia Pacific/East Asia: A Frustrated Regionalism? *Contemporary Southeast Asia, 31*(1), 110–142.

Narine, S. (1997). ASEAN and the ARF: The Limits of the "ASEAN Way". *Asian Survey, 37*(10), 961-978.

Narine, S. (1998). ASEAN and the Management of Regional Security. *Pacific Affairs, 71*(2), 195-214.

Nisbett, R. E. (2003). *The Geography of Thought: How Asians and Westerners Thing Differently...and Why* (1st Paperback ed.). New York: Free Press.

Norsworthy, K. L., & Khuankaew, O. (2008). A New View from Women of Thailand about Gender, Sexuality, and HIV/AIDS. *Feminism & Psychology, 18*(4), 527-536.

Notar, B. E. (2008). Producing Cosmopolitanism at the Borderlands: Lonely Planeteers and "Local" Cosmopolitans in Southwest China. *Anthropological Quarterly, 81*(3), 615-650.

O'Toole, J. (2001). Army hasn't nixed talks: Thais *Phnom Penh Post*, from http://www.phnompenhpost.com/index.php/2011032448140/National-news/army-hasnt-nixed-talks-thais.html.

Ockey, J. (2007). Thailand in 2007: The Struggle to Control Democracy. *Asian Survey, 48*(1), 20-28.

Peng-Er, L. (2006). Japan's Human Security Role in Southeast Asia. *Contemporary Southeast Asia, 28*(1), 141-159.

Peou, S. (Ed.). (2009). *Human Security in East Asia: Challenges for Collaborative Action*. New York: Routledge.

Perkasa, K. (2008). *Patani: Behind the Accidental Border*. Los Angeles: KijangMas Perkasa.

Pieterse, J. N. (2007). *Ethnicities and Global Multiculture: Pants for an Octopus* (Hardcover ed.). Plymouth: Rowman & LIttlefield Publishers, Inc.

Pitiyanuwat, S., & Sujiva, S. (2005). *Civic Education in Thailand: Policies and Practices in Schools* (1st ed.). Bangkok: Chulalongkorn University Press.

Pitsuwan, S. (2010). ASEAN central to the region's future. *East Asia Forum Quarterly, 2*(2), 4-5.

Pongsudhirak, T. (2008). *Thailand's Transformation*. Paper presented at the ISEAS Regional Outlook. Retrieved February 25, 2009, from http://www.humansecuritygateway.info/documents/ISEAS_ThailandsTransformation.pdf.

Raszelenberg, P. (1999). The Khmers Rouges and the Final Solution. *History & Memory, 11*(2), 62-93.

Reporters-Without-Borders. (2009). Radio Host Forced to Resign Interviewing Exiled Former Primer Minister [Electronic Version]. *Reporters Sans Frontiers*. Retrieved September 20, 2009, from http://www.rsf.org/Radio-host-forced-to-resign-for.html.

Richards, G. (2010). Metropolitan Tourism: Competition, Collaboration and Creativity. *Asia Pacific World, 1*(1), 75-94.

Ritzer, G. (2008). *Sociological Theory*. New York: McGraw Hill Higher Education.

Robinson, F. (2009). Crisis of Authority: Crisis of Islam? *Journal of the Royal Asiatic Society, 19*(3), 339-354.

Rolfe, J. (2008). Regional Security for the Asia-Pacific: Ends and Means. *Contemporary Southeast Asia, 30*(1), 99-117.

Roux, P. L. (1998). To be or not to be: The Cultural Identity of the Jawi (Thailand). *Asian Folklore Studies, 57*(2), 223-255.

Ryang, S. (2010). To Be or Not To Be--in Japan and Beyond: Summing Up and Sizing Down Koreans in Japan. *Asia Pacific World, 1*(2), 7-31.

Saul, B. (2006). The Dangers of the United Nations' 'New Security Agenda': 'Human Security' in the Asia-Pacific Region *Asian Journal of Comparative Law, 1*(1), 1-35.

Saul, B. (2008). The Dangers of the United Nations' 'New Security Agenda': 'Human Security' in the Asia-Pacific Region. *Asian Journal of Comparative Law, 1*(1), 1-35.

Selth, A. (2009). Known Knowns and Known Unknowns: Measuring Myanmar's Military Capabilities. *Contemporary Southeast Asia, 31*(2), 272-296.

Severino, R. C. (2007). ASEAN Beyond Forty: Towards Political and Economic Integration. *Contemporary Southeast Asia, 23*(3), 406-423.

Shatkin, G. (2006). Colonial Capital, Modernist Capital, Global Capital: The Changing Political Symbolism of Urban Space in Metro Manila, the Philippines. *Pacific Affairs, 78*(4), 577-600.

Simon, S. (2008). ASEAN and Multilateralism: The Long, Bumpy Road to Community. *Contemporary Southeast Asia, 30*(2), 264-292.

Singh, D. (2008-2009). Southeast Asian Security: An Overview. In D. Nair & L. P. Onn (eds.), *Regional Outlook: Southeast Asia 2008-2009* (pp. 3-7). Singapore: Institute of Southeast Asian Studies.

Singh, L. P. (1962). The Thai-Cambodian Temple Dispute. *Asian Affairs, 2*(8), 23-26.

Skidelsky, R. (2010). *Keynes: The Return of the Master* (Paperback ed.). New York: PublicAffairs.

Stockwell, A. J. (2004). Britain and Brunei, 1945-1963: Imperial Retreat and Royal Ascendancy. *Modern Asian Studies, 38*(4), 785-819.

Storey, I. (2008). Securing Southeast Asia's Sea Lanes: A Work in Progress. *Asia Policy*(6), 95-127.

Suharto, E. (2009). Social Protection Systems in ASEAN: Social Policy in a Comparative Analysis. *Social Development Issues, 31*(1), 1.

Syukri, I. (1985). *History of the Malay Kingdom of Patani* (C. Bailey & J. N. Miksic, Trans.). Athens: Ohio University.

Szep, J. (2011). Thai, Cambodia troops clash for fourth day on border [Electronic Version]. *Reuters*. Retrieved March 24, 2011, from http://www.reuters.com/article/2011/02/07/uk-thailand-cambodia-idUSLNE71600G20110207?pageNumber=1.

Tagliacozzo, E. (2001). Border Permeability and the State in Southeast Asia: Contraband and Regional Security. *Contemporary Southeast Asia, 23*(2), 254-275.

Than, M., & Thein, M. (2007). Transitional Economy of Myanmar: Present Status, Developmental Divide and Future Prospects. *ASEAN Economic Bulletin, 24*(1), 98-118.

Thawnghmung, A. M. (2009). Responding to Strategies and Programmes of Myanmar's Military Regime: An Economic Viewpoint. *Southeast Asian Affairs, 2008*, 274-290.

Thayer, C. A. (2009). Cambodia: The Cambodian People's Party Consolidates Power. *Southeast Asian Affairs, 2009*, 85-101.

Thayer, C. A. (2010). US Rapprochement with Laos and Cambodia. *Contemporary Southeast Asia, 32*(3), 442-459.

TMOFA. (2011). Thai-Cambodian Situation. Retrieved March 26, 2011, from http://www.mfa.go.th/web/3034.php.

Togo, K. (2005). *Japan's Foreign Policy 1945-2003: The Quest for a Proactive Policy* (Second Edition). Leiden: Brill.

Tow, W. T., Thakur, R., & Hyun, I.-T. (Eds.). (2000). *Asia's emerging regional order: Reconciling traditional and human security*. Tokyo: United Nations University Press.

Trinidad, D. D. (2010). Domestic Actors, Market Reforms and Regional Integration in Southeast Asia. *Asia Pacific World, 1*(1), 95-115.

Tsygankov, A. P. (2008). Self and Other in International Relations Theory: Learning from Russian Civilizational Debates. *International Studies Perspectives, 10*(4), 762-775.

UNDP. (2009a). Human Development Report 2009: Brunei Darussalam. Retrieved October 28, 2010, from http://hdrstats.undp.org/en/countries/country_fact_sheets/cty_fs_BRN.html.

UNDP. (2009b). Human Development Report: Brunei Darussalam. Retrieved October 27, 2010, from http://hdrstats.undp.org/en/countries/country_fact_sheets/cty_fs_BRN.html.

UNDP. (2009c). Human Development Report: Singapore. Retrieved October 13, 2010, from http://hdrstats.undp.org/en/countries/country_fact_sheets/cty_fs_SGP.html.

UNDP. (2009d). Human Development Report: Thailand. Retrieved October 14, 2010, from http://hdrstats.undp.org/en/countries/country_fact_sheets/cty_fs_THA.html.

UNDP. (2009e). Human Development Report: The Philippines. Retrieved October 8, 2010, from http://hdrstats.undp.org/en/countries/country_fact_sheets/cty_fs_PHL.html.

UNDP. (2010). Country Profile of Human Development Indicators: Cambodia. Retrieved November 29, 2010, from http://hdrstats.undp.org/en/countries/profiles/KHM.html.

Ungpakorn, G. J. (2007). *A Coup for the Rich: Thailand's Political Crisis*. Bangkok: Workers Democracy Publishing.

Ungpakorn, G. J. (2010). *Thailand's Crisis & the Fight for Democracy*. London: WDPress.

Vu-Tung, N. (2007). Vietnam's Membership of ASEAN: A Constructivist Interpretation. *Contemporary Southeast Asia, 29*(3), 483-505.

Wang, Z. (2008). National Humiliation, History Education, and the Politics of Historical Memory: Patriotic Education Campaign in China. *International Studies Quarterly, 52*(4), 783-806.

Winfield, J. C. (2010). Buddhism and Insurrection in Burma, 1886-1890. *Journal of the Royal Asiatic Society, 20*(3), 345-367.

Wongboonsin, P., Pongsapich, A., Pongsapich, S., & Sookkhee, C. (Eds.). (2006). *Promoting Human Security in APEC Countries*. Bangkok: Chulalongkorn University Press.

WTO. (2007). Viet Nam joins WTO with Director-General's Tribute for true grit. Retrieved Jan 07, 2011, from http://www.wto.org/english/news_e/news07_e/acc_vietnam_11jan07_e.htm.

Wyatt, D. K. (2003). *Thailand: A Short History* (Thailand ed.). Chiang Mai: Silkworm Books.

Yegar, M. (2002). *Between Integration and Secession: The Muslim Communities of the Southern Philippines, Southern Thailand, and Western Burma/Myanmar*. New York: Lexington Books.

Yzawa, T. (2006). The Evolution of Preventive Diplomacy in the ASEAN Regional Forum: Problems and Prospects. *Asian Survey, 46*(5), 785-804.

Index

Index